THE ENVIRONMENTAL LAW LIBRARY
FROM WILEY LAW PUBLICATIONS

ENVIRONMENTAL REMEDIATION CONTRACTING

SUBSCRIPTION NOTICE

This Wiley product is updated on a periodic basis with supplements to reflect important changes in the subject matter. If you purchased this product directly from John Wiley & Sons, Inc., we have already recorded your subscription for this update service.

If, however, you purchased this product from a bookstore and wish to receive (1) the current update at no additional charge, and (2) future updates and revised or related volumes billed separately with a 30-day examination review, please send your name, company name (if applicable), address, and the title of the product to:

Supplement Department
John Wiley & Sons, Inc.
One Wiley Drive
Somerset, NJ 08875
1-800-225-5945

ENVIRONMENTAL REMEDIATION CONTRACTING

RANDALL L. ERICKSON

Crowell & Moring
Irvine, California

Wiley Law Publications
JOHN WILEY & SONS, INC.
New York • Chichester • Brisbane • Toronto • Singapore

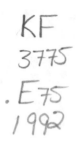
In recognition of the importance of preserving what has been
written, it is a policy of John Wiley & Sons, Inc., to have
books of enduring value published in the United States
printed on acid-free paper, and we exert our best efforts
to that end.

Copyright © 1992 by John Wiley & Sons, Inc.

This publication is designed to provide accurate and
authoritative information in regard to the subject
matter covered. It is sold with the understanding that
the publisher is not engaged in rendering legal, accounting,
or other professional services. If legal advice or other
expert assistance is required, the services of a competent
professional person should be sought. *From a Declaration
of Principles jointly adopted by a Committee of the
American Bar Association and a Committee of Publishers.*

Library of Congress Cataloging-in-Publication Data

ISBN 0-471-57325-6

Printed in the United States of America

10 9 8 7 6 5 4 3 2 1

To my wife, Kristy, who supports me in all things and tolerates the frequent and protracted absences entailed in their effort.

PREFACE

A dramatic expansion in the scope and intensity of environmental regulation occurred in the 1980s. A large number of excellent publications subsequently emerged to meet the needs of professionals faced with the problems of complying with environmental regulations or preparing a litigation defense. Unfortunately, much of the literature focused on just a single dimension of the environmental remediation field, either law or technology. Little has been done to attempt a meld of legal issues, technology, and contracting principles that would be addressed to those who are involved in environmental remediation work itself: owners of potentially contaminated property, remediation contractors, lenders involved in real property transactions, insurers faced with claims for remediation work or exposure costs, and environmental engineers. Yet each of these groups faces a particular set of problems for which counsel is required. The issues are analogous to problems in ordinary construction projects, but are uniquely defined by the regulatory environment and the technological uncertainty of remediation.

This book will serve the needs of those involved in the remediation process by dealing with such issues. It provides practical guidance and legal background to those who undertake, contemplate, or negotiate environmental remediation projects. The heart of the book lies in its contracting and project management approach. Its fundamental orientation is preventing unnecessary costs caused by conflict and mismanagement. By anticipating problems and applying feasible approaches at the contracting and contracts management stages, parties can avoid or minimize the extraordinary costs of delays and litigation that have plagued the industry.

The experiences of our clients have shown that many of the problems encountered result from a failure to anticipate and understand both the arcane requirements of the regulatory maze and the antagonistic relationships with regulating agencies. Thus, this book also pays serious attention to developing an approach to regulation. This approach includes assessing regulatory requirements, acquiring permits, and complying with health and safety regulations. Furthermore, problems encountered in common remediation projects and special regulations are discussed.

The book will prove interesting and understandable to a broad range of participants in this field, including owners, operators, contractors, lenders, insurers, engineers, consultants, and those who advise and represent each of these parties. Discussions of particular problems arising from ambiguous or ill-constructed rules and statutes should also interest persons drafting or promoting new legislation or regulations. Unlike many treatises in environmental law and remediation, this book demands no particular expertise from the reader. Although the book provides sufficient discussion of environmental statutes and case law to meet the needs of attorneys in the field, the book is written so as to be comprehensible to someone unfamiliar with legal precedence and jargon. Similarly, the book includes descriptions of both state-of-the-art and traditional remediation technologies as well as typical methods of remediation at a level that should familiarize rather than mystify the novice attorney or lender.

Irvine, California   RANDALL L. ERICKSON
August 1992

ACKNOWLEDGMENTS

I would like to express my appreciation to several people who have assisted immeasurably in the preparation of this book. Summer Associate, Diane Smith, assisted me in assembling background material to illustrate the need for such a text, as well as in the development of **Chapters 1** and **2**. Fredric Albert provided me with input into the permitting sections of **Chapters 3** and **5**. Laurie Wilson researched the permit requirements for **Chapter 5**. Harriet Alexson offered valuable insight into lender concerns about the remediation process. Thomas Quinn spent numerous hours developing the background information for the indemnity, insurance, and limitation of liability issues. Special thanks go to Barbara Mikalson who entered the project mid-stream and provided invaluable assistance in developing **Chapters 4, 6,** and **7** and in closing out the project. Her attention to detail and perseverance are greatly appreciated. Of course, none of it could have been accomplished without the dedicated work of our typists, Alicia Espinoza and Margaret Sullivan, who spent long hours correcting and proofing highly technical minutiae without complaint.

ABOUT THE AUTHOR

Randall L. Erickson is a partner in the Orange County, California, office of the law firm of Crowell & Moring, with offices in Washington, D.C., Irvine, California, and London, England. He is a graduate of the University of Wisconsin and Duke University School of Law, where he served as research editor of the *Duke Law Journal.* He has 20 years of experience in the construction industry, specializing in construction claims and arbitration, real estate development, and related environmental concerns. He has been actively involved in a variety of environmental remediation disputes. Mr. Erickson is a member of the Orange County Board of Directors of the Associated General Contractors of California and its legal advisory committee, and a member of the Legislative Committee of the Associated Builders and Contractors. He has written numerous articles on construction claims, contracting, and related environmental remediation issues, and has lectured extensively on these topics.

SUMMARY CONTENTS

DETAILED CONTENTS

SHORT REFERENCE LIST

Short Reference	Full Reference
A/E	architect/engineer
ARAR	applicable or relevant and appropriate standards, limitations, criteria, and requirements
ARB	Air Resources Board
CAA	Clean Air Act
CERCLA	Comprehensive Environmental Response, Compensation and Liability Act
CGL	commercial general liability
CGL	comprehensive general liability
CMA	Chemical Manufacturers Association
CPM	critical path method
CWA	Clean Water Act
DHS	Department of Health Services
DOE	Department of Energy
ECRA	Environmental Cleanup Responsibility Act
EIL	environmental impairment liability
EIR	environmental impact report
EIS	environmental impact statement
EPA	Environmental Protection Agency
ERCS	Emergency Response Cleanup Service

SHORT REFERENCE LIST

Reference	Full Reference
HAP	hazardous air pollutant
HWCA	Hazardous Waste Control Act
NCP	National Contingency Plan
NESHAPs	National Emissions Standards for Hazardous Air Pollutants
NIOSH	National Institute for Occupational Safety and Health
NPDES	National Pollutant Discharge Elimination System
O&M	operations and maintenance
OSHA	Occupational Safety and Health Administration
OSWER	Office of Solid Waste and Emergency Response
PCB	polychlorinated biphenyl
PEL	permissible exposure limit
PRP	potentially responsible party
RAQMD	Regional Air Quality Management District
RCRA	Resource Conservation and Recovery Act
RI/FS	remedial investigation and feasibility study
ROD	Record of Decision
SARA	Superfund Amendments and Reauthorization Act
SIP	State Implementation Plan
STEL	short-term exposure limit
TSCA	Toxic Substances Control Act
TSDF	treatment, storage, and disposal facility
UST	underground storage tank
VES	vapor extraction system

PART I

CONTRACTING OPPORTUNITIES

CHAPTER 1

IDENTIFYING, BIDDING, AND NEGOTIATING ENVIRONMENTAL REMEDIATION CONTRACTS UNDER FEDERAL LAW

§ 1.1   Introduction to Federal Contracting and Subcontracting Opportunities

Federal contracting and subcontracting opportunities are available for hazardous waste cleanup pursuant to the National Environmental Policy Act (NEPA)[1] and the Comprehensive Environmental Response, Compensation and Liability Act (CERCLA).[2] The preparation of an environmental impact statement (EIS) under NEPA presents contracting opportunities. The majority of the contracting or subcontracting opportunities available under federal law, however, are created pursuant to CERCLA.

NEPA, passed on New Year's Day 1970, was intended to put into law the belief that the nation should consider all direct, indirect, immediate, and cumulative effects on the environment as part of the decision-making process for all policies and programs. NEPA created the Council on Environmental Quality (CEQ), which promulgates NEPA regulations and standards.

More popularly known as Superfund, CERCLA was enacted in 1980 in response to the growing problem of hazardous waste disposal and its threat to human health and welfare. The Superfund Act was amended in 1986 via the

---

[1] 42 U.S.C. §§ 4321–4370 (1988).

[2] *Id.* §§ 9601–9675.

Superfund Amendments and Reauthorization Act (SARA).[3] SARA retained the federal regulatory scheme and renamed the Superfund as the Hazardous Substance Superfund (also known as Megafund). CERCLA makes the Environmental Protection Agency (EPA) responsible for identifying hazardous waste sites requiring cleanup.[4] Under CERCLA, the EPA can act:

> whenever (A) any hazardous substance is released or there is a substantial threat of such release into the environment, or (B) there is a release or substantial threat of release into the environment of any pollutant or contaminant that may present an imminent and substantial danger to the public health or welfare.[5]

§ 1.2   NEPA Process and Environmental Impact Statements

NEPA's EIS requirement creates contracting and subcontracting opportunities for persons schooled in the natural and social sciences, as well as in environmental design arts.[6] NEPA requires federal agencies recommending or reporting on a proposal for legislation, or planning a major action significantly affecting the quality of the human environment, to prepare a detailed EIS. In preparing the EIS, the federal agencies must consult with and obtain consents of agencies that have special expertise or jurisdiction by law over the environmental impact involved.[7] Moreover, the federal agency often calls upon the services of outside environmental consultants.

The first step for a federal agency involved with a proposal or action is to determine whether NEPA requires an EIS for the project. To make this assessment three questions must be addressed: (1) is it a federal action?; (2) is it a major action significantly affecting the environment?; and (3) is the action exempt from the EIS requirement? If a federal agency affirms the first two inquiries, and Congress has not created an exemption, an EIS is required. The next step is to ascertain the scope of the EIS.

If the federal agency decides that an EIS is not required, it files what CEQ calls a finding of no significant impact (FONSI), previously known as a negative declaration. The FONSI briefly presents the reasons an EIS is not necessary.[8] Usually, the agency also prepares an environmental assessment that sets forth the evidence and analysis supporting the decision to forgo an EIS.

---

[3] Pub. L. No. 99-499, 100 Stat. 1613.

[4] 42 U.S.C. §§ 9601–9675.

[5] *Id.* § 9604.

[6] 42 U.S.C. § 4332(A) (1988).

[7] *Id.* § 4332(C).

[8] 40 C.F.R. § 1508.13.

§ 1.3 —Deciding Whether an EIS Is Required

Determining whether an action is federal is sometimes simple; other times it is more complex. An action is clearly federal when a federal agency is directly involved with a project, for example, when a federal agency proposes building a facility. In less obvious situations, a careful analysis of all the facts and circumstances is necessary to determine whether the action is federal. Factors to be considered include the presence or absence of federal funding, employment of federal officials, or other federal government obligation or control.[9] Actions deemed federal have included federal agency approval of land leases to private parties through the issuance of licenses or permits.[10]

In deciding whether an action was major and would significantly affect the human environment, the court in *Hanly v. Kleindienst,*[11] the leading case on this issue, considered at least two relevant factors: (1) the extent to which the action will cause adverse environmental effects greater than those created by existing uses in the affected area, and (2) the absolute quantitative adverse environmental effects of the action, including the cumulative harm that would result from its contribution to existing adverse conditions or uses in the affected area.[12] The court in *Hanly* noted that when the action conforms to existing uses, its adverse consequences will be less significant. The court illustrated its point with the example that one more highway built in a neighborhood honeycombed with roads is less significant than a road constructed through a roadless public park.

Having answered affirmatively the first two inquiries for its proposal or action, an agency must address whether Congress created an exemption for the activity. To the extent that another statutory scheme is in clear and unavoidable conflict with NEPA, Congress has created an exclusion from the EIS requirement where the Secretary's duties under the Interstate Land Sales Full Disclosure Act conflicted with the EIS process.[13]

Congress has also created an exclusion in situations in which another statutory authority supports its policy behind NEPA, the promotion of which efforts will prevent or eliminate damage to the environment. For example, when Congress had already established a comprehensive scheme for the registration and regulation of pesticides, NEPA's EIS requirement was not also imposed on the registration process.[14] Similarly, the Resource Conservation and Recovery Act

---

[9] Almond Hill Sch. v. United States Dep't of Agric., 768 F.2d 1030, 1039 (9th Cir. 1985).

[10] Scientists' Inst. for Pub. Info., Inc. v. Atomic Energy Comm'n, 481 F.2d 1079, 1088–89 (D.C. Cir. 1973).

[11] 471 F.2d 823 (2d Cir. 1973).

[12] *Id.* at 830–31.

[13] Flint Ridge Dev. Co. v. Scenic Rivers Ass'n of Okla., 426 U.S. 776 (1976).

[14] Merrell v. Thomas, 608 F. Supp. 644 (D. Or. 1985), *aff'd,* 807 F.2d 776 (9th Cir. 1986), *cert. denied,* 108 S. Ct. 145 (1987).

(RCRA) is a later and more specific statute directly governing EPA's issuance of permits to hazardous waste management facilities.[15] As such, RCRA is an exception to NEPA's EIS requirement.[16]

§ 1.4   —Scope of an EIS

Once an agency concludes that it must prepare an EIS, the next step is to establish the scope of the statement. This process requires an agency to take into account a range of factors, including alternatives to the proposed action, economic, social, and psychological factors, and segmentation of large projects for impact statement purposes.

NEPA requires the agency preparing an EIS to "study, develop, and describe appropriate alternatives to recommended courses of action in any proposal which involves unresolved conflicts concerning alternative use of available resources."[17] The range of alternatives an agency might address is vast, beginning with the "no action" option: proposing that the agency abandon its project altogether. Other alternatives deal with modifications of the proposed action.

The scope of an EIS also depends upon the type of environmental impact it concerns. NEPA's EIS requirement obviously applies to the impact on the natural environment. More assertive proponents suggest that the EIS should also address an action's effects on the urban environment, as well as its social and economic effects.

The court in *Hanly* said that NEPA must be construed to include protection of the quality of life of urban dwellers. The court indicated that an action's effects on noise, traffic, the transportation system, crime, congestion, and even the availability of drugs, affect the urban environment.[18] The court, however, has not been as anxious to extend the scope of an EIS to include social, economic, and psychological effects. For example, the court in *Nucleus of Chicago Homeowners' Ass'n v. Lynn,* when considering a proposal to establish a job corps center in a building on a former college campus, rejected the extension of NEPA to social and economic effects.[19] Moreover, the Supreme Court in *Metro Edison Co. v. People Against Nuclear Energy* limited the extent to which determination of environmental impact should be based on the reactions of people affected by the agency's action.[20]

---

[15] *See generally* 42 U.S.C. §§ 6901–6992k.

[16] Alabama v. EPA, 911 F.2d 499 (11th Cir. 1990).

[17] 42 U.S.C. §§ 4332(C)(iii), (E) (1988).

[18] 471 F.2d 823, 847 (2d Cir. 1973).

[19] 524 F.2d 225 (7th Cir. 1975), *cert. denied,* 424 U.S. 967 (1976).

[20] 103 S. Ct. 1556 (1983).

When an agency considers beginning an EIS on a project, CEQ Guidelines, issued in the *Code of Federal Regulations,* mandate a "scoping" procedure.[21] First, these guidelines require that the agency give notice in the *Federal Register* of the agency's intent to work up an EIS. By this notice, the agency must invite any party involved with the project, such as other federal, state, or local agencies, to participate in the scoping process. Each group can then prepare a statement of its interests and concerns regarding the project. From these, the lead agency must determine the scope of the EIS.

Such a determination should eliminate any issues that are not significant or that have already been addressed in other reports. Any elimination, though, must be justified by a brief presentation reviewing the reasons for the elimination.[22] Once the issues have been defined, the lead agency can assign issues for review among the other agencies.

Finally, the lead agency has the right to set page and time limits for each issue addressed by other agencies. It can also call progress meetings and issue schedules regarding completion of the EIS. Through this scoping procedure, the CEQ aims to generate effective central control over the scoping of an EIS while maintaining channels for input and discussion.

§ 1.5   —Contents of an EIS

Section 102(C) of NEPA and the evolution of CEQ Guidelines, agency regulations, administrative determinations, and court interpretations set out the required contents of an EIS:

1. A description of the proposed action, its purpose, and the environment affected
2. The relationship of the proposed action to land use, plans, policies, and controls for the affected area
3. The probable environmental impact of the proposed action
4. Any unavoidable adverse environmental effects should the proposal be implemented
5. Alternatives to the proposed action
6. The relationship between local short-term uses of the environment and the maintenance and enhancement of long-term productivity
7. Any irreversible and irretrievable commitments of resources that would be involved, should the proposed action be implemented

---

[21] 40 C.F.R. § 1501.7 (1991).

[22] *Id.* § 1501.7(a)(3).

8. An indication of other interests and consideration of federal policies thought to offset the adverse environmental effects of the proposed action.

§ 1.6   CERCLA Process: Preremedial Work under Superfund

In determining whether or not to implement a cleanup action, the EPA performs an elaborate investigation of a site. First, the agency makes a preliminary assessment to determine if the site imminently threatens the public health or the environment. If further investigation is warranted, the next step is the site inspection. This inspection involves on-site sampling and laboratory analysis to determine the extent of contamination. On the basis of these two studies, the EPA determines either that the site is not hazardous enough to fall within the scope of the Superfund, that the site requires immediate attention and a removal action, or that the site, though hazardous, poses no immediate threat and should be ranked on the Hazardous Ranking System for subsequent cleanup in the form of a remedial action.[23]

§ 1.7   —Removal Actions

Removal actions are short-term, immediate measures that address a release or threatened release of a hazardous substance. A removal action includes the actual removal of the hazardous material, as well as any other additional measures considered necessary. The lead agency makes an initial determination of whether the contamination or hazardous waste problem is classified as a removal or remedial action pursuant to 40 C.F.R. § 300.415(b)5. The agency must consider both the potential exposure and harm to people, animals, wildlife, and the environment, and the time and expense required for the anticipated cleanup. For example, if the existing problem concerned several well-sealed drums of toxic material with no apparent leakage, which would require a few weeks for removal and disposal, the problem would probably be classified as a removal action. Removal actions are limited to those requiring a 12-month period and a $2 million budget.[24] In a removal action, the EPA seeks technical and management assistance, cleanup personnel, equipment, and materials.[25]

---

[23] *Superfund: What Every Manager Should Know,* Pub. Mgmt., Aug. 1990, at 11–15.

[24] Environmental Issues in Real Estate and Construction Projects in California, A Strategic Guide for the 1990's at 17-2 (June 20, 1991) (Cambridge Inst. seminar material) [hereinafter Environmental Issues].

[25] EPA, Superfund: Getting into the Act, Contracting and Subcontracting Opportunities in the Superfund Program (Apr. 1989) (distributed by National Technical Information Service, Pub. No. PB89-233431) [hereinafter Superfund: Getting into the Act].

§ 1.8   —Remedial Actions

If the EPA determines that a site does not require emergency action, but nonetheless is sufficiently hazardous to warrant cleanup under the Superfund, the site is scored on the Hazardous Ranking System (HRS). The HRS ranks the sites identified for cleanup in descending order of risk to the population from contaminated water, air, or other hazards. If the site is ranked high enough, the EPA may also place it on the National Priorities List (NPL) for Superfund cleanup.

Once placed on the HRS, several studies are made of the site, the most significant of which is the remedial investigation and feasibility study (RI/FS). This is a two-phased study. First, the extent of the contamination is defined, and second, alternative cleanup methods are evaluated. The public is then permitted to comment on the results of the RI/FS. After studying the RI/FS results and the public comments, the EPA issues its Record of Decision (ROD), explaining the cleanup method chosen and the reasons for its selection. Once the goals are defined in the ROD, a remedial design (RD) study is prepared, which provides the detailed engineering plan for a remedial action.

A remedial action provides for large-scale, permanent cleanup of a hazardous waste site and may require one to three years to complete. The remedial action also usually includes long-term monitoring of the site to ensure that remaining hazardous wastes do not pose a significant threat to the public. The EPA seeks contract work for technical assistance, as well as resources for cleanup activities, support of its enforcement actions, and community relations. Most work in a remedial action is done at the subcontractor level.[26]

§ 1.9   Background on Contracting
Opportunities under Superfund

The EPA published a document in April 1989, revised in September 1990, entitled *Superfund: Getting into the Act, Contracting and Subcontracting Opportunities in the Superfund Program.* The publication and its revisions provide descriptions of Superfund contract and subcontract opportunities. They also list some of the current contracts outstanding under Superfund, along with some contacts for contracting possibilities.[27]

The reader should be aware, however, that in August 1990, the Office of Emergency and Remedial Response (OERR) concluded a study that greatly affected the EPA's contracting method, as explained in *Getting into the Act.* The study included a broad analysis of the Superfund program's dependence on contractor support and recommended some changes, based on three principles:

---

[26] *Superfund: What Every Manager Should Know,* Pub. Mgmt., Aug. 1990, at 13.

[27] Superfund: Getting into the Act (Apr. 1989).

1. The need for an integrated, one-program approach to enforcement and site cleanup

2. The enhancement of competition through reduction of contract size and creation of greater opportunities for small businesses

3. A need for greater flexibility and oversight through decentralization of program responsibilities.

As a result of the study, the OERR recommended the Long-term Contracting Strategy for Superfund [hereinafter Long-term Contracting Strategy], which was approved by the EPA. The OERR intended the Strategy to be a road map for the next decade, but also planned to continually reevaluate the strategy in light of changes to Superfund. Following approval in September 1990, the EPA has been phasing in the new contracting structures as the original contracts expire.[28]

A myriad of contracting and subcontracting opportunities are available under Superfund, and descriptions of these opportunities follow in §§ **1.10** through **1.34**. Also included are an explanation of the contracts used during the transition to the Long-term Contracting Strategy, and a description of the methods to be used when the Strategy is fully in place.

Appendixes F, G, and **H** include contacts for Superfund contracting and subcontracting opportunities in all program areas for all contract types.

§ 1.10 Preremedial and Removal Contracts

Preremedial work under Superfund involves a preliminary assessment and, if necessary, site inspection. These two studies determine whether a removal action, a remedial action, or no action is needed. See §§ **1.7** and **1.8**. If the findings indicate that immediate action is necessary, the EPA will order a removal action. The EPA contracts out the preremedial and removal action work, and some contractors in turn employ subcontractors.

The Long-term Contracting Strategy seeks to combine some of the preremedial and removal work in some of its contracts. Thus, it is best to consider jointly the contracts and subcontracts available in the preremedial and removal areas.

§ 1.11 —Hazardous Site Field Investigation Team Contract

Originally, Field Investigation Team (FIT) contracts were the EPA's primary preremedial source for studying hazardous waste sites. The EPA contracted

---

[28] Off. of Solid Waste & Emergency Response, EPA, Long-Term Contracting Strategy for Superfund 2–5 (Aug. 31, 1990).

FITs for multidisciplinary professional technical assistance in conducting preliminary assessments and site inspections. One FIT was located in each region, and the size of the FIT staff varied depending upon the work load. FIT subcontracting opportunities included well drilling, geophysical investigative support, sample analyses, waste disposal, and other services.[29]

The EPA contracted with the FIT for two multiple-year, cost-plus-award fee prime contracts that came to term in October 1991. The Long-term Contracting Strategy, however, calls for merging FIT and Emergency Response Technical Assistance Team (TAT) (see § 1.12) work to provide subsequent preremedial and removal services. The merger was designed to meet two of the Long-term Contracting Strategy's goals: promotion of decentralization, and movement toward a one-program approach.

The combination of TAT and FIT functions may prove valuable for three reasons. First, it may lead to the integration of site discovery, inspection, and removal assessment activities. It may even lead to earlier action at Superfund sites, which will serve to mitigate immediate risks. Second, the integration may lead to the full cleanup of sites before they need to be ranked on the NPL. Third, the combination will enhance competition and will benefit small businesses by creating smaller regionally based contracts.

The Long-term Contracting Strategy mandates an interim approach before the merger of FIT and TAT activities. The OERR study determined that the EPA would use Alternative Remedial Contracting Strategy (ARCS) contracts (see § 1.17) for preremedial functions until an orderly transition to the merger with the TAT could occur. The OERR chose this transition method to fully utilize the existing capacity of the ARCS contracts, among other reasons. The OERR intends to develop procedures to ensure that the ARCS contracts provide the same capabilities (that is, rapid response) as the current FITs.

§ 1.12 —Emergency Response Technical Assistance Team Contract

Another type of contracting and subcontracting opportunity available in preremedial work and removal actions is the Emergency Response Technical Assistance Team (TAT) contract. The EPA originally created TAT contracts to provide their regional offices with technical assistance in removal actions. TAT contracts were also used in correction actions under the Underground Storage Tank (UST) Trust Fund and in the oil spill prevention program under the Clean Water Act (CWA).

The EPA originally established TAT offices for each of the EPA regional offices, for the Environmental Response Team in Edison, New Jersey, and for the EPA headquarters in Washington, D.C. Each TAT, consisting of 11 to 45 people,

---

[29] Superfund: Getting into the Act at 10–11.

was formed to monitor response activities, provide special services, collect samples, and coordinate the development and implementation of community relation plans. Furthermore, the TATs conducted compliance tests under the CWA and assisted the regional offices with planning activities. Specific examples of TAT subcontracts included aerial surveys, mapping support, analytical services, drilling of monitoring wells, and preparation of training materials.[30]

As discussed earlier, the Long-term Contracting Strategy requires TAT functions under the removal program to be combined with the preremedial work performed by FITs. See the discussion of the reasons for and effects of the merger in § 1.11.

§ 1.13   —Emergency Response Cleanup Service Contract

Another type of contracting or subcontracting opportunity available in a removal action is an Emergency Response Cleanup Service (ERCS) contract. An ERCS contract provides support for the removal programs and UST programs under Superfund. Originally, there were two types of ERCS contracts: the zone contract and the region-specific contract. Zone contracts required quicker response times and covered broader geographic areas than regional contracts.

ERCS contracts provide cleanup personnel, equipment, and materials as directed by an EPA On-Scene Coordinator (OSC). For example, the OSC may direct personnel to contain, recover, or dispose of hazardous substances. She may also require them to analyze samples or restore the site after the cleanup work is finished. Because of the short time frame involved in removal actions, zone and regional contractors frequently seek hazardous waste transportation, disposal, and analytical service subcontractors.[31]

The Long-term Contracting Strategy seeks to continue ERCS contracts. However, the strategy calls for integration of rapid remedial response capabilities into the ERCS contract structure, to promote a one-program approach for all time-critical activities and create more small, regionally based contracts with a single regional management.

§ 1.14   Remedial Contracts

If the preliminary assessment and site inspection indicate that cleanup work is not immediately necessary, the site will be ranked on the HRS. Several studies will be made of the site, including the RI/FS. Based on the RI/FS results and public comments, the EPA will issue a ROD and a remediation action will be

---

[30] Superfund: Getting into the Act at 6–7.

[31] Superfund: Getting into the Act at 7–8.

implemented. Contracting and subcontracting opportunities are available in the performance of the RI/FS and its related studies, and for the remediation action.

The Long-term Contracting Strategy combines all remedial activities, enforcement oversight, and non-time-critical removals into one regional contracting system with multiple remedial contracts in each region. The contract management will be performed by the existing management infrastructure used in ARCS contracts.

This approach is advantageous for several reasons. First, it serves the one-program principle, because it integrates remedial and enforcement oversight work. The integration gives the regions greater flexibility in pursuing enforcement options. Second, the multiple remedial contracts per region provide flexibility in responding to potential conflicts of interest and enhance post-award competition based on contractor performance. Third, even though the number of regional remedial contracts will be high the approach reduces the overall number of contracts because it eliminates the former oversight (Technical Enforcement Support) contracts. See § **1.27.**

§ 1.15 —United States Bureau of Reclamation Engineering and Construction Contracts

The Bureau of Reclamation assists the EPA in remedial planning, remedial design, and remedial action through the use of Interagency Agreements. Assistance is either provided in-house by Bureau of Reclamation personnel, or the Bureau contracts out the work.

The Bureau seeks contractors by advertising in the *Commerce Business Daily.* Any architect/engineering (A/E) firm may apply by completing the Architect Engineer and Related Services Questionnaire, standard forms 254 and 255. The Bureau makes its selection through a competitive bidding process, with the award going to the lowest responsive and responsible bidder. The Superfund work is handled through six regional offices: Boise, Sacramento, Boulder City, Salt Lake City, Billings, and Denver.[32]

§ 1.16 —Hazardous Site Remedial Engineering Management Contract

One type of remedial contract originally available under Superfund was the Remedial Engineering Management (REM) contract. REM contracts and

---

[32] Superfund: Getting into the Act, Addendum/Errata Sheets, OSWER Directive No. 9200.5-42, at 7 (Nov. 1990).

subcontracts were entered into for both remedial planning activities and the remediation work.

Contract work under an REM contract included RI/FSs, engineering design for remediation actions, construction of the design, community relations activities, and support of enforcement activities. Subcontract work included aerial photography, drum removal and remedial actions, waste disposal, geotechnical consulting services, monitoring wells and related geophysical services, enforcement support, analytical services, and preparation of RI/FSs.[33]

The EPA began phasing out the REM contracts and replacing them with ARCS contracts. See § 1.17. As discussed above, no further REM contracts will be written, because the Long-term Contracting Strategy uses a single, regional contracting system for all future remedial work.

§ 1.17   —Alternative Remedial Contracts Strategy Contract

The second type of remediation contract originally available under Superfund was the ARCS contract. ARCS contracts involved the same activities as REM contracts, and were the EPA's preferred choice for program management and technical services in remedial response activities.

The EPA awarded ARCS contracts in five discrete sizes, ranging from 25,000 to 70,000 hours in base awards and 145,000 to 780,000 hours in maximum contract capacity over a 10-year performance period. It awarded contracts based on a standard competitive process, and awarded as many as eight ARCS contracts in each region or multi-region zone. After evaluating standard factors, particularly contractor performance, the EPA allocated the work assignments among the various contractors in each region or multi-region zone.[34]

As noted in § 1.11, ARCS contracts will be utilized to perform preremedial work in the interim period before the FIT and TAT functions are combined. The Long-term Contracting Strategy also recommends the continuation of the ARCS contracts for RI/FS and related studies and for removal work; however, it recommends that the ARCS contracts be combined with all potentially responsible party (PRP) oversight work and all non-time-critical removal actions. The ARCS management infrastructure will be retained in this effort.

Because the Long-term Contracting Strategy anticipates the continued use of its ARCS contracts, subcontracting opportunities remain available under the outstanding ARCS contracts. The ARCS prime contractor, however, is restricted by the EPA in her manner of awarding subcontracts. First, the prime contractor must select subcontractors on a competitive basis, if possible. Second, the EPA has strict reporting requirements for subcontracting and requires strict oversight

---

[33] Superfund: Getting into the Act at 11–12.

[34] Superfund: Getting into the Act at 12–14; Environmental Issues at 17-3.

of the subcontracts by the prime contractor. The EPA can and has revoked some subcontract awards. Subcontracting opportunities available under ARCS contracts are similar to those that were performed under REM contracts.

§ 1.18   —Site-Specific Removal and Remedial Contracts

Under the original TAT, FIT, ERCS, REM, and ARCS contracts, the work was divided between contractors by regions or zones. If a contractor was under a zone or regional contract, she may have provided services for several removal or remedial actions within that region or zone.

Occasionally, however, the EPA has solicited bids from contractors for a specific removal. For a site-specific removal or remediation contract, the EPA will usually list the opportunity in the *Commerce Business Daily,* and all interested contractors will submit a proposal and bid. Because of the tediousness of this method, however, the EPA has moved toward a system of established bidding pools for site-specific contracts. Under this system, known as the Pre-Qualified Offerors Procurement Strategy (PQOPS), two to three times a year, contractors submit to the bidding pools their qualifications in using specific technologies. Then, when either a removal or remedial site-specific contract is under consideration, any contractor within the appropriate pool may submit a bid.[35]

§ 1.19   —United States Army Corps of Engineers Engineering Design and Construction Contracts

In large remedial actions valued at over $5 million where the EPA takes the lead, the United States Army Corps of Engineers manages the design and construction work. Although some of the work is performed in-house by Corps personnel, the majority of the work is contracted out to private firms under supervision of the Corps.

Originally, the Corps had two districts, Omaha and Kansas City, each responsible for the design and construction work in one-half of the EPA regions. These two districts hired and supervised professional A/E firms to perform all of the design work. In addition, each district advertised and awarded construction contracts. The districts then transferred the construction contracts to the district closest to the Corps for engineering and construction management. When the projects were completed, they were transferred back to the EPA regional office.[36]

---

[35] Superfund: Getting into the Act at 9.

[36] Superfund: Getting into the Act at 15–16; Environmental Issues at 17-4.

Subsequently, during 1990, the Corps shifted from its centralized control of design and construction to a more decentralized system. Instead of maintaining only two districts, the Corps formed 11 regional contracting offices. The decentralized system gives smaller firms a greater opportunity to obtain work. Engineering consultants view this change as encouraging because it will increase the level of participation.[37]

The Corps has a standard process for selecting A/E firms. It advertises synopses of its requirements in the *Commerce Business Daily,* requiring candidates to respond to the advertisement within 30 days. A response includes completion of the standard forms 254 and 255, the Architect Engineer and Related Services Questionnaires, available from the Contracting Office of the Corps in Baltimore, Maryland. Form 254 requests general information about the applying firm. A form 254 must also be completed for each independent consultant who will be used in the project. Form 255 requests information regarding the qualifications of the firm to handle the specific requirements of the project as advertised. The Corps usually conducts bidding to select its construction contractors. Awards are made to the lowest responsive and responsible bidder.

The Corps rigorously prescreens A/E firms for their technical qualifications. It bases selection, at a minimum, on the firm's specialized experience in the type of work required and its capacity to meet the designated schedule.[38]

§ 1.20   —State Procurement under Cooperative Agreements

The final contracting or subcontracting opportunity available involving remedial actions arises in states that choose to assume the lead in planning and implementing the cleanup of a site. The state assumes the responsibility for site cleanup by forming a Cooperative Agreement with the EPA. The state may perform the cleanup work either with its own resources or by contracting with private firms.

Superfund has given states strong incentives to assume cleanup responsibilities. For instance, Superfund will pay 90 percent of the cost of a private-site remediation and 50 percent of a state-site remediation. Superfund also permits the states to pay their share of the cleanup cost in cleanup and management services, if the state prefers.

The types of contracting and subcontracting work available vary by state. The major types of work include remedial investigation, feasibility study, remedial design, and remedial action. **Appendix I** includes a list of state agency

---

[37] Setzer, *DOD Reveals Cleanup Details,* Envtl. News Rep., Nov. 6, 1990, at 10.

[38] Superfund: Getting into the Act at 15.

contacts for procurement of opportunities under State Superfund Cooperative Agreements.[39]

§ 1.21   Remediation Actions Support Services

Remediation-type contracting work is not limited to removal and remedial actions under Superfund. The federal government has a demand for other support services related to the hazardous waste cleanup process. For example, the federal government needs support services for activities such as hazardous sample analysis, and for response and safety training of government officials in dealing with hazardous wastes.

§ 1.22   —Response Engineering and Analytical Contract

The Response Engineering and Analytical Contract (REAC) contractor provides techniques and technologies for the remediation of hazardous waste sites and spills. The REAC supports the EPA's Environmental Response Team (ERT) under the authority of CERCLA/SARA, RCRA, the Toxic Substances Control Act (TSCA), CWA, and other acts.

The REAC contractor conducts field investigations of various studies and issues reports on the results. These studies include multimedia extent of contamination, bioassessment, treatability, contaminant transport, engineering/feasibility, and risk assessment. The purpose of these studies is to assist the ERT in providing support to EPA regional OSCs in removal actions and Remedial Project Managers (RPMs) in remedial actions.

The REAC contractor also performs evaluation and engineering design studies of commercially available technologies. The REAC studies the technology with the objective of confirming and documenting the technology's feasibility. Again, the ERT utilizes this information to aid the regional OSCs and RPMs in choosing or proceeding with their chosen technologies for treating the contaminated site.

Finally, the REAC contractor provides analytical services to the regional OSCs and RPMs. Such services include on-site and mobile laboratory capabilities. For example, the REAC contractor conducts rapid analyses of complex waste mixtures and environmental samples. In addition, the REAC contractor develops analytical methods for on-site and field laboratory equipment.[40]

---

[39] Superfund: Getting into the Act at 16–17.

[40] Superfund: Getting into the Act at 18–19; Environmental Issues at 17-5.

§ 1.23 —Contract Laboratory Program

The EPA established the Contract Laboratory Program (CLP) as another method of providing analytical services to Superfund. Under the program, the EPA contracts out the evaluation of various chemical and physical factors of all environmental media, including air, soil, surface water, and groundwater. The contracts are awarded to the lowest responsible and responsive bidders on a fixed-price, indefinite-quantity basis.

The EPA requires that all data be of documented quality. To ensure that it is, the agency operates a comprehensive quality assurance program, involving analytical standards, performance evaluation samples, blind check samples, chain-of-custody procedures, and document control. The EPA audits the contract laboratories quarterly for technical competence and compliance with the terms and conditions of the contract.[41]

The Long-term Contracting Strategy did not reach any final conclusions on possible changes to the CLP. The study deferred a decision on decentralization of the CLP until further analysis is performed.

§ 1.24 —Quality Assurance Technical Support to the Contract Laboratory Program

The EPA created another contract opportunity to provide quality assurance technical support to the CLP for the Analytical Operations Branch (AOB).

The contract performs six different tasks:

1. Development and testing of performance evaluation materials, reference materials, and standards
2. Evaluation, creation, and standardization of existing and future analytical and quality assurance/control methods and equipment
3. Assistance in assessing laboratory performance
4. Creation and review of quality assurance and method guidelines and documents
5. Evaluation of statistical data and development of models of analytical performance
6. Other quality assurance related activities.[42]

---

[41] Superfund: Getting into the Act at 16–17.

[42] Superfund: Getting into the Act, Addendum/Errata, at 3 (Nov. 1990).

§ 1.25 —Environmental Services Assistance Teams Contract

The Environmental Services Assistance Teams (ESAT) contract is another vehicle for providing support to the Superfund sites. Although the EPA formed the ESATs primarily to support Superfund projects, ESATs also support the RCRA program and other non-Superfund analytical efforts.

The ESAT contractors mainly provide multidisciplinary technical assistance. The EPA directs each ESAT in specific work assignments to perform analytical and technical tasks for regions within a designated zone of responsibility. Task areas include hazardous waste chemical analysis, review and validation of CLP data, review of site-specific quality assurance, site investigation and sampling plans, support in developing new analytical methods, and logistical and administrative functions.[43]

The Long-term Contracting Strategy recommends maintaining the ESAT contracts; however, it calls for further decentralization of the ESAT functions. Therefore, the ESAT functions will be regionally-based. The EPA expects that decentralization will lead to greater competition and opportunities for small business participation, and flexibility in responding to specific regional needs. Both contracting and subcontracting opportunities thus remain available for ESAT contracts, although in some regions the teams consist only of subcontractors.

§ 1.26 —Hazardous Material Incident Response Training Contract

The EPA provides response and safety training for federal, state, and local government groups through its Hazardous Material Incident Response Training (HMIRT) contracts. The EPA, working through ERT and the efforts of HMIRT, provides a wide range of training to 5,000 students per year at 200 presentations of 15 different courses. The course material is adapted to the students' particular needs.[44]

§ 1.27 —Technical Enforcement Support Contracts

The EPA has entered into Technical Enforcement Support (TES) contracts to assist its regional offices in enforcing CERCLA and RCRA. The TES contractors provide a wide range of support services, such as providing expert

---

[43] Superfund: Getting into the Act at 18–19.
[44] Superfund: Getting into the Act at 19–20.

witnesses, searching for the responsible persons at a hazardous waste site, evaluating groundwater monitoring data, and inspecting RCRA facilities.[45]

The Long-term Contracting Strategy eliminates TES contracts. Under the strategy, oversight functions are combined with the remedial contracting work. See § 1.14.

§ 1.28   Policy, Program Management, and Administrative Support Contracts

In addition to the removal and remedial work done under Superfund and related support services, contracting opportunities involving the administration of the Superfund program are available. Without proper administrative and management controls, none of the cleanup work that Congress designed Superfund to accomplish would ever be completed. Thus, the EPA through the OERR has contracted to aid in the administrative aspects of Superfund.

§ 1.29   —OSWER Dedicated Training Support

The Office of Solid Waste and Emergency Response (OSWER) developed a strategy for providing to the EPA the planning, design, development, and delivery of technical and program training. The training support contract helps facilitate OSWER's strategy by assisting the office in analyzing, designing, developing, and providing support services for a national training program.

The training support contracts assist in all aspects of the training process. They begin by providing reports that analyze OSWER's training needs. They also design instructional courses, seminars and conferences, and provide and administer the delivery of the related training documents, such as course catalogues, calendars, and progress reports. Moreover, they maintain a catalogued repository for the training documents, video tapes, and technology transfer information. Finally, they give graphic support for management briefings that pertain to OSWER training programs.[46]

§ 1.30   —RCRA/Superfund Industrial Assistance Hotline Contract

The RCRA/Superfund Industrial Assistance Hotline contract provides the public with a telephone hotline that answers or directs questions related to the RCRA and CERCLA programs. The contractor maintains an automated documents list

---

[45] Superfund: Getting into the Act at 24.

[46] Superfund: Getting into the Act, Addendum/Errata, at 4 (Nov. 1990).

containing current RCRA and CERCLA documents and other related EPA library publications, to assist in accurately answering the inquiries. The contractor also performs other related services, such as preparing a caller-trend analysis, maintaining logbooks with information on the calls received, and preparing form letters for dissemination in response to written questions from the public and industry.[47]

§ 1.31 —Technical Support for Superfund Policy Formulation

The first type of contract opportunity available under the policy, program management, and administrative aspects of Superfund is the Technical Support for Superfund Policy Formulation. This type of contract provides assistance to the OERR in formulating, implementing, and assessing the effectiveness of Superfund programs.

The technical support contracts involve various aspects of the Superfund process, including engineering, public health, economics, and statistical concerns. The OERR requires the contractor to prepare a written analysis of technical issues involved in the aspect of Superfund addressed by the contract. In addition, the contractor must provide technical information and expertise in implementing the policies developed to deal with these technical issues.[48]

§ 1.32 —Support of Superfund Implementation and Evaluation

The second type of contract opportunity available under the policy, program management, and administrative aspects of Superfund is the Support of Superfund Implementation and Evaluation. This contract is similar to the technical support contract in that it provides support in planning, implementation, and evaluation of the Superfund program. Unlike the technical support contract, however, this contract provides a wide range of other support services unrelated to technical issues.

This support contract provides personnel, services, and materials to the OERR. The contract provides support in many areas, ranging from removal and remediation work to financial management. Examples of services are removal response, remedial response, training, community relations, financial management, development of ADP systems, and special studies for program management.[49]

---

[47] Superfund: Getting into the Act, Addendum/Errata, at 5 (Nov. 1990).

[48] Superfund: Getting into the Act at 28.

[49] Superfund: Getting into the Act at 28–29.

§ 1.33   —Policy/Analytic Support for Superfund Implementation Contract

The Policy/Analytic Support for Superfund Implementation contract provides support in planning, managing, implementing, and evaluating the Superfund policies and programs. This contract differs from the other administrative contracts because it focuses more on legislation and policy making.

The support services included under this contract are numerous. The work elements include the following:

1. Research and preparation of reports
2. Analysis of program, regulatory, and legislative issues
3. Analysis and development of regulatory and nonregulatory alternatives
4. Preparation of briefing materials
5. Drafting of alternative policy approaches and guidance in implementing the alternatives
6. Designing and proposing new approaches to addressing issues related to Superfund regulations, policy, and response activities
7. Development of training and workshop materials based on work the contractor has done in the other services provided under the contract
8. Assistance in drafting alternative regulatory approaches, or in preparation of technical and economic background materials for draft regulations
9. Assistance in analysis of and response to comments on notices published in the Federal Register.[50]

§ 1.34   —Analytical, Technical, and Management Services for OSWER

Another contract provides analytical, technical, and management services to a contractor conducting various programs for OSWER. The contract is not intended solely to provide support for Superfund, but many of its services have been oriented in that direction.

The work under this contract is divided into three major categories: (1) research and development, technology transfer, and training support; (2) general policy analysis and strategic planning; and (3) risk-benefit and risk assessment methodological studies. The contract includes short-term work consisting of analytical studies, and long-term analysis consisting of policy and implementation issues and development and implementation of training strategies.[51]

---

[50] Superfund: Getting into the Act at 29–30.

[51] Superfund: Getting into the Act at 30–31.

§ 1.35   Payment for Superfund Cleanup

After the EPA places a site on the NPL for cleanup, it must determine the financial backing for the work. The EPA proceeds with either an enforcement-lead or a fund-lead cleanup.

Enforcement-Lead Cleanup

In an enforcement-lead cleanup, the EPA looks to PRPs to clean up the site under its abatement authority pursuant to CERCLA § 106. In order to proceed with an enforcement-lead cleanup, the government must be able to identify a sufficient number of financially viable PRPs. Furthermore, the environmental conditions at the site must not require an immediate response, to allow time for negotiation or litigation.[52]

The EPA has identified four classes of PRPs:

1. The current owner or operator of the site
2. The owner or operator at the time of disposal of any hazardous substance
3. Any person who arranged to dispose of or treat hazardous substances at any vessel or facility owned by another person containing such hazardous substances
4. Any person who accepted any hazardous substances for transport to sites selected by such person.[53]

PRPs are responsible for all removal or remedial costs, including indirect, allocable costs, any other necessary response costs incurred by any other EPA-designated person, damages to or loss of natural resources including an assessment of the damage or loss, and the cost of any health assessment or health effects study carried out.[54]

If the PRPs recognize that they face significant exposure to liability, they may organize themselves in order to negotiate with the EPA. Resolution of the EPA claim against the PRPs entails the creation of a consent decree, which must be blessed by the court in which the action is pending. The consent decree is often the product of extensive negotiation between the EPA and the PRPs and is inextricably linked to the remediation contract. Because the EPA has recently put forth its proposed standard consent decree, it is reasonable to expect that the agency will become increasingly involved in remediation contractor selection and contract negotiations. This involvement is discussed in greater detail in **Chapter 3**.

---

[52] Environmental Issues at 14-2.

[53] 42 U.S.C. §§ 9607(a)(1)–(4).

[54] Environmental Issues at 14-3, 14-4, 10-11.

Fund-Lead Cleanup

In a fund-lead cleanup, the EPA cleans up the site itself with Superfund resources. The EPA usually decides to pay itself either because there are few, if
any, financially viable PRPs, or because the site requires an immediate response
to protect the public welfare or the environment. After the EPA completes the
work, it will sue any PRPs it can identify.[55]

In the fund-lead cleanup, the consent decree does not play a role, because the
EPA does all of the cleanup work itself.

---

[55] *Id.* at 14-2.

CHAPTER 2

IDENTIFYING, BIDDING, AND NEGOTIATING ENVIRONMENTAL REMEDIATION CONTRACTS UNDER STATE LAW AND UNDER OTHER PRIVATE CONTRACTS

§ 2.1 State Contracting and Subcontracting
Opportunities Generally

State contracting and subcontracting opportunities for hazardous waste cleanup arise pursuant to the enforcement of both federal and state laws. Under federal law, opportunities are available at the state level under cooperative agreements with the EPA, whereby the state administers a federal Superfund cleanup. See **Chapter 1**. The states also have their own statutes addressing environmental cleanups. In California, for example, contracting and subcontracting opportunities are available pursuant to the California Environmental Quality Act (CEQA) and under the Carpenter-Presley-Tanner Hazardous Substance Account Act, more commonly known as the California Superfund.[1]

CEQA was enacted in 1970 to impose environmental responsibility on California government agencies, including local, regional, and state agencies, boards, and commissions. It has also been interpreted to cover private actions that require permits, licenses, or order forms of state approval.[2] CEQA requires all entities under its authority to reduce or avoid significant environmental damage that could result from the entity's actions. The Act is administered on a project-by-project basis by a designated lead agency—normally, the state or local agency with the greatest responsibility for implementing or approving the particular project.

The Michigan Environmental Protection Act (MEPA) is Michigan's equivalent to CEQA. MEPA requires any major state action to be consistent with the promotion of public health, safety, and welfare in light of Michigan's concern for natural resource protection.[3] Few other states have enacted legislation as comprehensive as CEQA. Nonetheless, EISs are often required in other states pursuant to environmental regulations. For instance, New Jersey requires EISs for proposed coastal area developments, construction of highway turnpikes, and for specific legislative bills.[4] Moreover, in Texas, the *Policy for the Environment,* adopted by the Interagency Council on Natural Resources and the Environment, suggests that its participants prepare EISs for project proposals in order to appraise and lessen the environmental impact of their activities.[5]

---

[1] Cal. Pub. Res. Code §§ 21,000–21,005 (West 1986); Cal. Health & Safety Code §§ 25,350–25,358.6 (West 1986).

[2] Friends of Mammoth v. Board of Supervisors, 8 Cal. 3d 247, 502 P.2d 1049, 104 Cal. Rptr. 761 (1972).

[3] Thomas J. Anderson, Gordon Rockwell Environmental Protection Act of 1970, Mich. Comp. Laws § 691.1201 (1991).

[4] Conservation & Developments—State Parks & Reservations, N.J. Rev. Stat., tit. 13, § 19-7 (1990); Turnpikes, N.J. Rev. Stat., tit. 27 §§ 23–23.5 (1990); Economic & Environmental Impact Statements on Legislative Bills, N.J. Rev. Stat., tit. 52 § 52:13F-1 (1990).

[5] *Policy for the Environment, in* Environment for Tomorrow: The Texas Response (Division of Planning Coordination, Office of the Governor, Jan. 1, 1973).

The California Superfund was enacted in 1981 to provide a hazardous substance release response authority and to compensate persons injured from the release of hazardous substances. The California Superfund also provides the state's share of federal Superfund cleanup costs to the federal agency, and provides for the cleanup of additional environmentally hazardous sites that do not qualify for the federal Superfund program. The California Department of Health Services (DHS) administers the program in cooperation with the EPA, although local enforcement agencies in county or city governments usually lead the cleanup operations.[6]

Several states have versions of the California Superfund. Michigan's Environmental Response Act commands the governor to identify and evaluate the hazard of contaminated sites and to provide funding for appropriate response activity to eliminate the environmental contamination at those sites. Likewise, Illinois' Public Health and Safety Environmental Toxicology Act requires an initial assessment, and if necessary a comprehensive health study, for federal Superfund sites and sites placed on the state's Remedial Action Priority List.[7] Illinois' Public Health & Safety Code Emergency Planning and Community Right to Know Act permits cooperative agreements with the EPA to clean up contaminated sites.[8] Moreover, New Jersey's highly controversial Environmental Cleanup Responsibility Act (ECRA) requires either the approval of a cleanup plan or a negative declaration prior to the completion of a sale, transfer, or closing of certain industrial properties associated with hazardous wastes.[9]

The preceding discussion demonstrates that a number of states have been aggressive in implementing innovative environmental policy. California is in the forefront of this movement; therefore, a preponderance of the examples of state environmental statutes given in the following sections are taken from California law.

§ 2.2   CEQA Process

Generally, the lead agency in charge of a particular project on behalf of CEQA must: (1) decide whether CEQA applies; (2) prepare an initial study; (3) decide whether to prepare a negative declaration or an environmental impact report (EIR); (4) prepare draft negative declarations and EIRs for public review; and (5) prepare final negative declarations and EIRs for consideration and approval by the decision-making body.

---

[6] Environmental Issues in Real Estate and Construction Projects in California 2-6 (June 20, 1991) (Cambridge Inst. seminar material) [hereinafter Environmental Issues]; Hazardous Waste Education Program 7-8, -88, -138, -141 (1991) (Safety, Health, & Environment Committee, AGC training manual).

[7] Ill. Rev. Stat., ch. 3.5, para. 985 (1989).

[8] *Id.* para. 7706.

[9] N.J. Rev. Stat., tit. 13, § 1K-7 (1983).

The first step is to determine whether CEQA applies. Generally, CEQA applies to any project proposed to be completed, approved, or financed by a public agency. It does not apply, however, to certain types of projects the legislature has specifically exempted from CEQA, for example, feasibility and planning studies, discharge requirements, creation of timberland preserve zones, and adoption of coastal plans and programs.

§ 2.3 —Initial Study

Once the lead agency determines that CEQA does apply, the next step is to prepare an initial study of the project. The study thoroughly considers all phases of project planning, implementation, and operation, and is important because it allows the lead agency to make one of the most important decisions in the CEQA process: whether a negative declaration or an EIR is appropriate.

CEQA effectively requires an EIR whenever a proposed project may have a significant impact on the environment defined by CEQA as a "substantial, or potentially substantial, adverse change in any of the physical conditions within the area affected by the project."[10] However, CEQA also recognizes that the significance of the impact may vary according to the sites of the project.[11] California courts have held that an EIR is necessary whenever the project arguably will have an adverse environmental impact.[12]

§ 2.4 —Negative Declarations

If the initial study does not reveal any substantial evidence that the project may have a significant environmental impact, the lead agency may issue a negative declaration. If evidence of significant environmental impact is identified by the initial study, the agency may still issue a negative declaration if the project applicant agrees to implement revisions that would avoid or mitigate such effects. A negative declaration must be distributed for public review and include the project description and location. It must also include the proposed finding of no significant environmental impact, and any applicable mitigation measures.[13]

---

[10] 14 Cal. Code Reg. § 15,358.

[11] *Id.* § 15,064(b).

[12] *See, e.g.,* No Oil Inc. v. City of Los Angeles, 13 Cal. 3d 68, 85, 529 P.2d 66, 118 Cal. Rptr. 34 (1974); The California Environmental Law Handbook 271–72 (R. Denney, Jr. & M. Monahan eds., 5th ed. 1991) [hereinafter California Environmental Handbook].

[13] California Environmental Handbook 274–75.

§ 2.5   —Environmental Impact Report

The main purpose of an EIR is to inform the public. It has been called an "environmental alarm bell [alerting] the public to environmental changes before they have reached ecological points of no return."[14] The report develops information about the adverse environmental effects of a proposed project, involves the public in decision making, requires the agency to publicly disclose their environmental values, enables interagency communication, and develops alternative strategies. The lead agency is usually responsible for preparing the EIR, but the costs are funded by the project applicant.

An EIR goes through a draft and a final stage. The draft EIR is reviewed by the public, and the different agencies on the project use it for consultation. The final EIR is used by the agency to make decisions, and in addition to all the information in the draft version, it includes comments received in the review process by the public and other agencies, and the lead agency's response to those comments.

On the basis of the final EIR, the lead agency may decide not to approve or carry out the project under review, because of a significant potential adverse effect on the environment. The lead agency may also approve or carry out the project if the agency determines that the significant environmental effects have been eliminated or substantially lessened, and that any remaining unavoidable significant effects were acceptable because of overriding considerations.[15]

§ 2.6   California Superfund

The California Superfund, administered by DHS, is that state's version of the federal Superfund program. The program permits DHS to clean up hazardous sites not addressed under the federal Superfund, and it provides funds to pay California's share of California site cleanup costs that are covered by the federal program.

The California Superfund cleanup plan closely follows the federal investigation and cleanup process, beginning with the preliminary assessment and site inspection. DHS determines whether the presence of a hazardous substance poses a significant threat to the public health and welfare or the environment. If there is a significant and immediate danger, DHS will instigate a removal action. If the threat does not require an immediate response, DHS will conduct a remedial investigation to identify the type and extent of contamination. A remedial action plan (RAP) will be completed to identify the best approach to successful abatement. Finally, the remedial action will be conducted to clean up the waste, and long-term operation and maintenance will be performed to ensure

---

[14] County of Inyo v. Yorty, 32 Cal. App. 3d 795, 108 Cal. Rptr. 377 (1973).

[15] California Environmental Handbook 272, 275, 280.

that the extraction and decontamination or monitoring systems are in place and functioning properly.[16]

§ 2.7 —Contracts Available under California Superfund

All contracts are advertised in California's *Contract Register,* a bimonthly newspaper published by the state, which indicates all of the contracts for which the state is seeking bids. Potential contractors are invited to submit bids, and the most competitive, responsible bidder will likely be chosen. Once the state chooses these contractors, their names are public information, and subcontractors may contact them.

Several types of contracts are available under the California Superfund program. However, many are being rebid at present, and the final decision on the winning bidder will not be made for several months. **Sections 2.8** and **2.9** discuss the current contracts outstanding, along with a description of what each contract entails.

§ 2.8 —Preremedial and Cleanup Service Contracts

As in the federal Superfund, the California Superfund contracts out preremedial, removal, and remediation work. The preremedial work involves performing various samplings and borings to identify whether a removal action, a remediation action, or no action is necessary on a particular site. (The contractors often perform this work as a support service in a cleanup action. See **§ 2.9.**) The California program contracts out for the testing of a variety of hazardous wastes, including those contaminating soil and air.

When the preremedial investigation detects and identifies a significant amount of hazardous waste, the DHS will decide whether a remedial action or removal action is necessary. As under the federal Superfund, some contracts provide both remedial and removal services, some are only for one or the other, and some are site-specific (they provide a single removal or remediation action at a designated site). See **Chapter 1.** Examples of various contracts, including those for preremedial and the actual cleanup work, include the following.

Surface Geophysical Investigation. The contractor performs surface geophysical investigations using ground-penetrating radar, electromagnetic induction, gravimetric or magnetometric seismic refraction, and electrical resistivity tests.

---

[16] California Environmental Handbook 231, 239–40.

Downhole Geophysical Investigation. This contract involves acquiring geophysical data from boreholes, augerholes, or existing wells to depths of at least 500 feet.

Shallow Drilling. The contractor samples or cores waste, soil, and rock at depths of less than 100 feet.

Deep Drilling. This contract also involves sampling and coring of waste, soil, and rock; however, the contractor drills to depths in excess of 100 feet. The contract is also used for projects involving well drilling.

Air Sampling. This contract provides services including the collection of meteorological data to identify and measure airborne toxic contaminants.

Soil Gas Monitoring. This remediation contract involves the extraction of soil gases, and also identifies a broad range of volatile organic compounds (VOCs) and their concentration.[17]

§ 2.9 —Support Services and Policy Program Management Contracts

As in the federal Superfund program, contracting work under the California Superfund is not limited to preremedial, removal, and remediation contracting. The California Superfund program demands support services in performing its cleanup work. Examples of support services include control measures for hazardous substance releases, engineering consulting services, and laboratory testing services. In addition, the program requires program management work such as community relations programs.

One type of support services contract is the Small Project Implementation contract, providing services related to the preparation and implementation of controlled measures with respect to uncontrolled hazardous substances.

Another support services contract available is the Project Support contract, which provides engineering consulting services to aid in developing the remediation or removal technique. The contract also provides project management services for cleanup actions.

An increasingly important concern in the environmental cleanup industry is for health and safety. The Health and Safety contract provides health and safety plans that are designed primarily to protect workers on the site, as well as members of the general public who reside or work in or about the project. In

---

[17] Listing of Zone Contractors, Memorandum from the Toxic Substances Control Program, Sacramento, California (Nov. 3, 1989).

addition, this contract provides consultation for the state and its contractors regarding the implementation of their existing health and safety plans.

Laboratory services are crucial to the cleanup process. The Air and Industrial Hygiene Lab contract provides a complete range of analytical laboratory services including physical and chemical analysis. The Chem Laboratory contract also provides chemical analysis, of drinking water, groundwater, and industrial waste samples provided by the contractor.

The Community Relations contract involves a more administrative aspect of the California Superfund program. The contractor develops and implements Community Relations Programs that address the concerns and needs of communities affected by hazardous wastes, hazardous waste facility permits, or closure applications.[18]

§ 2.10   Private Contracting Opportunities

Because of the civil and criminal sanctions against violators of the federal, state, and local laws regulating hazardous wastes, various private entities demand environmental cleanup work to ensure their compliance. These opportunities are in addition to the federal and state lead environmental cleanups.

Opportunities are available in the private sector in

1. Superfund enforcement lead cleanups
2. Situations where jobsite construction uncovers hazardous wastes, including on previously undeveloped land
3. Real estate sales and loan refinancing transactions in which buyers, sellers, and lenders seek information about the presence of hazardous materials
4. Private audits when an entity wishes to ensure compliance with environmental laws
5. Prophylactic work in which an employer seeks an environmental study to prevent future claims of employers or labor unions.

§ 2.11   —Enforcement Lead Contracts

Under CERCLA, the PRPs in an enforcement lead cleanup coordinate the cleanup of the Superfund designated site. See **Chapter 1** for further discussion. Thus, the PRPs rather than the EPA seek contractors and subcontractors to perform the required work. It follows that an environmental contractor or

---

[18] Listing of Zone Contractors, Memorandum from the Toxic Substances Control Program, Sacramento, California (Nov. 3, 1989).

subcontractor seeking to sell services must place the bid with the PRPs rather than with the EPA.

§ 2.12 —Jobsite Discoveries of Hazardous Substances

Although an owner may not intend to build over contaminated areas, there is always a risk of encountering hazardous materials. For example, an excavation crew might unearth an abandoned underground storage tank (UST) that has leaked dangerous chemicals. In addition, while removing the tank, the crew might accidentally spill the hazardous contents onto the construction area. **Chapter 4** contains a more in-depth discussion of USTs and the law.

In situations in which a contractor unexpectedly encounters a hazardous waste problem, the contractor is required to report the incident and take appropriate response and corrective actions, pursuant to various federal and state laws. The environmental laws that apply in a given situation depend on the nature and location of the jobsite. Even so, it is inevitable that the contractor will need to perform or contract out the necessary response activity.[19] The cost issues involved in such efforts are discussed in **Chapters 3** and **4**.

§ 2.13 —Environmental Assessments in Real Estate Transactions and in Refinancing of Loans

Under CERCLA, the owner or operator of real property is a PRP, and may be held responsible, regardless of knowledge or participation for any activity that actually causes or creates the release or threatened release of hazardous substances.[20] The PRP may be jointly and severally liable, retroactively, on a strict liability theory, for removal or remedial costs incurred by the federal or state government or any other entity in cleaning up the hazardous waste.

As a result of this potential liability, parties to all real property transactions, including buyers, sellers, and lenders, will usually require that an environmental assessment be performed. An environmental assessment in this context has the very specific purpose of identifying and allocating liability for environmental concerns related to the site. The buyers, sellers, and lenders each have unique interests in the performance of the environmental assessment.

Some states mandate by statute that sellers disclose information concerning the property's environmental condition. For instance, the Illinois Responsible Property Transfer Act (IRPTA) requires sellers or mortgagors of certain types of real property to provide such information to the buyer and lender. IRPTA

---

[19] Environmental Issues at 19-1, 19-5 to 6.

[20] 42 U.S.C. § 9607a.

provides for pre-closing avoidance of any obligation to accept or finance a transfer if the disclosure document reveals any "environmental defects" previously unknown to the parties.[21] New Jersey's ECRA (see § **2.1**) goes even further than IRPTA and demands the expeditious cleanup of contaminated sites involved in a transfer. ECRA directs a seller either to detoxify the property or to obtain an approved negative declaration, as a precondition to the closure, sale, or transfer of certain properties associated with hazardous substances.[22]

A buyer's primary interest in an assessment is to avoid known or discoverable environmental problems and protect against any unknown risks. If the assessment identifies known environmental problems, the buyer can require, under the purchase agreement, that the seller assume such liabilities. Concerning unknown risks, the buyer can seek the innocent landowner defense and request indemnification from the seller.

The seller's first concern with the assessment is in identifying current environmental liability. If the assessment identifies problems, the seller and buyer can agree on the allocation of the cleanup cost. Alternatively, if the site complies with environmental law, the buyer can use that finding as a basis for environmental warranties and representations in the purchase agreement.

The seller's second concern is in limiting future liability for unknown environmentally hazardous conditions on the site. In this regard, the assessment report is an indicator of the environmental status of the property at the purchase date. The seller may claim that any contamination discovered subsequently is attributable to the buyer.

The lender involved in a purchase/sale agreement or in a refinance fears devaluation of the collateral or exposure to liability caused by the presence of any regulated substance stored, utilized, generated, treated, or disposed of at the property (such as asbestos or USTs). Likewise, he is apprehensive of potential liability from the contamination of the property from hazardous wastes.

Under present law, the lender is in a worse position than the buyer or seller regarding protection from future liability through the use of the environmental assessment. The lender may want to require an assessment in order to qualify for the innocent lender defense. However, a passive stance is necessary in regard to the property so as not to be deemed an operator or owner, and thus a PRP.[23] See **Chapter 3** for a more in-depth discussion of lender liability.

Based on the environmental concerns of the buyers, sellers, and lenders in real estate transactions and for lenders in refinances, the use of the environmental assessment in private transactions will continue to grow. This growth provides a ready market for the services of environmental contracting and subcontracting firms.

---

[21] Responsible Party Transfer Act of 1988, Ill. Rev. Stat. ch. 30, para. 904 (1989).

[22] N.J. Rev. Stat., tit. 13, § 1K-7 (1983).

[23] Environmental Issues at 15-1 to 5, 15-9 to 10.

§ 2.14   —Environmental Assessment

At present, no exact and agreed-upon definition exists for environmental assessments. When the parties to a real estate transaction speak of an environmental assessment, they usually refer to a project with up to four phases, followed by a continuing monitoring process. The following is a description of the general understanding of these phases.

First, the parties to the transaction (or someone with whom they contract) will perform a Phase I study of the project, sometimes known as an audit. This audit involves a visit to the property, an interview with appropriate personnel, a review of the title records for past owners and liens on the property, a review of the past users of the property, aerial photography, and other procedures considered necessary. The goal of the preliminary study is to determine whether further analysis should be performed. If, for example, the past records or aerial photographs indicate that potentially hazardous materials could be located on the property, the parties to the transaction may want to perform environmental testing.

Phase II involves environmental testing of the property, and usually requires some degree of technical expertise. Environmental consultants are generally hired for this reason. They are also hired because a well-documented report from a reputable consultant is good evidence of the buyer's due diligence. The property is examined by test borings and sample studies of the groundwater, the soil, and any underground tanks and pipelines. If Phase II tests determine that hazardous materials are present or that further studies may indicate their presence, Phase II will likely segue into Phase III.

Phase III involves similar procedures to Phase II, but is more extensive. The goal of Phase III is to identify the parameters of any contamination problem. If the problem is sufficient to violate environmental laws or to lead to their future violation, the environmental consultant will recommend Phase IV.

Phase IV involves the remediation work. Beyond the completion of the work, and depending on the nature of the remediation, the property may require future (possibly continual) monitoring for environmental compliance. The demand for environmental contracting and subcontracting capabilities occurs at every stage of the environmental assessment.[24] See **Chapters 3** and **4** for further discussion of the environmental assessment.

§ 2.15   —Audits to Ensure Compliance with Environmental Laws

Over the past 10 years, many corporations have established programs to audit their compliance with environmental laws. In the environmental sense, the term

---

[24] Environmental Issues at 13-3, 13-6.

"audit" implies a methodical examination involving analyses, tests, and confirmations of local procedures and practices, leading to a verification of compliance with legal and other requirements. Companies use various names to describe these examinations, such as review, surveillance, survey, appraisal, and assessment.

Many corporations have begun to view environmental auditing as a powerful management tool for monitoring their company's compliance with environmental laws. The corporations have also used audits for a variety of other purposes, including as a means of:

1. Improving environmental performance at the operating facilities
2. Assisting facility management
3. Increasing environmental awareness
4. Accelerating the development of environmental management control systems
5. Improving environmental risk management systems
6. Protecting the corporation from potential liabilities
7. Developing a basis for optimizing environmental resources.

Most corporations perform their audit process through an independent, internal staff frequently located in their internal audit department. Other companies audit through external auditors or a combination of internal and external auditors. Thus, the environmental firm seeking contracting opportunities may be able to sell its services as an external environmental auditor.[25]

§ 2.16 —Prophylactic Environmental Studies to Prevent Future Claims of Employees or Labor Unions

Many companies, fearing potential liability for suits brought by employees or labor unions claiming damages from environmental hazards at the worksite, have recently attempted to avoid liability by hiring environmental firms to perform studies. The purpose of the studies is to determine the presence, scope, or nonexistence of environmental hazards at the worksite, and the company's compliance with environmental laws. By performing these studies, companies hope to avoid future liability with a due diligence defense, similar to the innocent landowner/lender defense. Contracting and subcontracting opportunities may be available in this regard.

---

[25] EPA, Current Practices in Environmental Auditing 1-3 (Feb. 1984).

PART II
MANAGING THE CONTRACT

CHAPTER 3

DRAFTING CONTRACT TERMS UNIQUE TO A REMEDIATION CONTRACT

§ 3.1   Introduction

This chapter deals with contract terms unique to remediation contracting; however, the topics discussed below are typically found in any construction contract. Issues such as scope of work, responsibility for governmental compliance, permitting, bonding, insurance, change orders, delays, and payment are the bulwarks of construction practice. It is the unique way in which the remediation process affects these issues, and how the issues in turn affect the remediation contract, that is the focus of this chapter.

General contracting and remediation contracting experiences have formed the basis for the discussion which follows. Many of the suggestions in this chapter come as a result of the author's personal experience as a legal consultant in construction and remediation contracting. These experiences have generated the recommended remediation contracting terms offered and the unique considerations discussed in drafting such contract terms.

The relatively recent environmental movement has provided the impetus for creation of numerous laws and regulations designed to achieve certain environmental goals. As a result, environmental remediation contracting, while still in its infancy, has sprung almost overnight into a multibillion-dollar industry. Because of this quick growth, however, the field lacks the background of custom and usage and does not have the highly evolved contracts history of general contracting. Moreover, the manner in which many projects are approached is not systematic. All of these problems are compounded by the elimination, for the most part, of the traditional division between designer and contractor.

§ 3.2   Scope and Level of Remediation

The terms scope and level of remediation are often incompletely understood by the contracting parties because of inexperience in remediation contracting. Foresight in identifying potential problems is crucial in drafting the scope description; otherwise, the scope and level of remediation contract terms may prove to be insufficient to deal with future complications.

Several major concerns bear on the drafting of the scope and level of remediation terms in a remediation contract. First, while a remediation contract focuses on a specific site for cleanup, the project is often inextricably linked with contamination on adjacent sites. Furthermore, the technology used in remediation often has an impact on the environment. See § 3.3. These potential effects must be addressed when describing the scope of the project and work to be performed. Second, as remediation technologies improve and achievable remediation and detection levels change, the required level of remediation may also change. Therefore, the contract must carefully describe the exact level of remediation agreed upon, and whether contingencies will be made for changing the level to accommodate enhanced technology or changes in government standards. Third, the scope and level of remediation are affected by the technology available, and the feasible types of technology will vary as to cost, time for completion, and other factors. The parties should understand and contemplate these variations and agree upon the technology most in line with their needs.

Even the most voluminous of contract documents may be subject to criticism for failing to address certain elemental concerns. A recent United States Department of Energy (DOE) draft request for proposal (RFP),[1] for selection of an Environmental Restoration Management Contractor (ERMC) to manage cleanup of two DOE-owned contaminated nuclear weapons facilities in Ohio, has met with such criticism. Its length (340 pages) and inordinate detail notwithstanding, prospective bidders have stated that its scope and determination of liability remain unclear. Bidders have noted that it does not specify what the contract amount is intended to cover, or whether the ERMC is precluded from doing design or construction at the site.[2]

Problems in defining the scope and level of remediation are best addressed through examination of the remediation process in different contexts, as illustrated in following sections.

§ 3.3 —Remediation Scope Concerns in Soil and Groundwater Remediation Contracts

The identification of contamination in properties adjacent to the contracted site is of primary concern in soil and groundwater remediation contracts. When contracting for the remediation of one parcel, the parties need to anticipate the effects on or from surrounding parcels, as well as the effect that the remediation process may have on the environment in general. For example, if the contract

---

[1] 56 Fed. Reg. 34,057 (1991).

[2] *Huge Cleanup Contract Spelled Out by DOE,* Engineering News-Rec., Aug. 19, 1991, at 12–13.

focuses solely on the treatment of the contaminants on one site, without regard to the impact and possible contribution to contamination via the plume extension from or to adjacent properties, the contract may prove to be inadequate. By failing to address such potential effects, the contract will not adequately describe the scope of the work.

The remediation contract also needs to consider the potential impact of the chosen remediation technology on the air. In areas such as Southern California, where governmental authorities routinely require air permits in connection with almost any remediation process, this is a topic that must be included in the scope of the work. Air permitting concerns are particularly crucial when the parties agree to treat the contaminated soil via an air stripping technique. This type of technology is apt to have more impact on the air and trigger stiffer air permitting requirements than other types. Thus, when defining the scope and level of remediation, the parties must allocate the responsibility for dealing with air permitting and the potential adverse impact of a chosen technology on air quality.

In certain circumstances, a potentially responsible party (PRP) may be faced with an order to take corrective action beyond a property line. In both federal and state statutes, provisions exist to mandate corrective action beyond hazardous waste facility boundaries (as defined in those statutes) "where necessary to protect human health and the environment unless . . . it is demonstrated to the satisfaction of the Administrator that, despite [the PRP's] best efforts, [the PRP] was unable to obtain the necessary permission to undertake such action."[3]

The parties (especially the contractor) must have a feel for the mechanics of groundwater hydrology (movement of water beneath the ground surfaces). They must also be aware of the factors governing the migration of water and bulk contaminants within the soil.[4] Suffice it to say that no environmental cleanup takes place in a vacuum.

If a site lies in a large industrial complex or an area where many industrial and commercial activities have taken place on contiguous sites, the parties should attempt to determine whether the adjacent sites are contaminated. This determination can be made via the environmental assessment process. See **Chapter 2**. With the cooperation of the adjacent landowners, the contracting parties may perform environmental testing to determine if hazardous materials are present. If the property owners are not cooperative, the parties should at least perform a Phase I audit. This involves a review of title records for past

---

[3] Resource Conservation & Recovery Act § 3004(v), 42 U.S.C. § 6924(v) (Supp. III 1991); *see also* Cal. Health & Safety Code § 25,187(a) (West 1991).

[4] A simplified yet cogent discussion of these issues appears in Hazardous Waste Education Program Manual 115–20 (AGCC Safety, Health, and Environment Committee 1991) [hereinafter Cal AGC Manual]. For an example of how these migration issues became involved in environmental litigation, *see* United States v. Hooker Chems. & Plastics Corp., 540 F. Supp. 1067 (D.N.Y. 1982).

owners and lienholders and an observation of the property to determine the possibility and likelihood of contamination.

If testing confirms the contamination or likelihood of contamination of contiguous properties, the contract must address the potential contribution of that contamination to the specific property under contract. If owners of contiguous property will not contribute to the cost of cleanup, the owner could seek to force such contribution through legal action.[5] However, such action will only hamper completion of the work. To expedite matters, the owner could employ construction techniques. In one case, for example, the owners agreed to additional construction to seal off the treated site from the contaminated adjacent properties by use of a slurry wall.[6] In another case, gas chromatography was employed to distinguish the owner's contaminant from that of the adjacent property. When the vapor extraction system (VES) began to pull out the contiguous contaminant,[7] the amounts were recorded and used in the damage claim. In the meantime, the project went forward.

Regardless of how the parties agree to handle the potential contamination from contiguous parcels, they must recognize that they may incur added expense. Anticipating and contracting for this possible contamination may be a point of hot negotiation, but failure to deal with the issue could be disastrous, as in the following illustration.

In a recent California dispute, the remediation contractor used the VES technology to treat a property in a large industrial site near downtown Los Angeles. The site was surrounded by parcels containing an ancient blacksmith shop, a paint shop, and an auto body repair shop. Initial studies of the site led the contractor to conclude that approximately six months of pumping would be sufficient to adequately treat the volume of soils involved. The contracting parties, however, never investigated the contiguous sites for possible contamination. At the end of six months the contractor was still pumping at the same rate with no end in sight. Test wells of the perimeter of the site made it immediately clear that the contractor was treating the plume from adjacent properties.

In this situation, a Phase I review of the ownership histories and business records of those contiguous properties would have immediately revealed the possibility of contamination from the adjacent sites. The parties could then have contracted for an equitable method of dealing with the situation. Alternatively, the owner could have sought contributions from the contiguous property owners toward the cost of the remediation process. Perhaps the parties would have

---

[5] A host of common law theories are available to a landowner whose property has been contaminated by invasion of a plume from contiguous property, including nuisance, strict liability, fraud, negligence, and trespass. For an in-depth discussion, *see* Moskowitz, Environmental Liability and Real Property Transactions: Law and Practice 149 (John Wiley & Sons 1989) [hereinafter Moskowitz]. See also **Ch. 8.**

[6] *See also Methods of Site Remediation,* Pollution Engineering, Nov. 1990, at 58.

[7] See **Ch. 4** for further discussion of VES.

decided that, because of the contamination from the neighboring parcels, remediation to the desired level was impossible. In any event, the problem could have been addressed up front. Instead, the failure to address the issue led to a dispute between the owner and the contractor. The problem was further complicated by the fact that the owner had been given a lump sum price for the remediation, based on the contractor's initial estimate. The ramifications of pricing issues will be discussed further in § 3.7.

From the contractor's point of view, it may be desirable to obtain a warranty from the client concerning possible migration of contaminants. It could be written thus:

> Client is unaware that any previous owner of adjacent (contiguous) property has engaged in or permitted any operations upon that property in any way involving any hazardous materials, nor have any hazardous materials migrated or appeared likely to migrate from adjacent (contiguous) properties to the site of the Project.

This warranty could be modified by allowing the client to except out such items as are set forth in an attached exhibit. The warranty presupposes that the contract has carefully defined "hazardous materials" and "the site." For a suggested definition of hazardous materials, see § 3.12.

The impact of contiguous properties must also be considered in determining the scope. If work must be performed on those properties, whether or not they contribute to the contamination, the parties must consider the possibility and potential cost of acquiring such easements.

§ 3.4 —Remediation Level Concerns in Soil and Groundwater Remediation Contracts

Like the scope of remediation, the level of remediation must be carefully considered. As technology and expertise in the environmental remediation field improve, the attainable level of decontamination also improves. Thus, an acceptable level for a remediation contract in 1980 may not be satisfactory in 1991. This discrepancy is most graphically demonstrated in the action level of Trichloroethylene (TCE), now set at a level that was not even detectable a few years ago. Moreover, an acceptable level of remediation for an owner may not be acceptable for the permitting agencies with oversight control of the remediation process, or for the lender on the property who has liability concerns. Thus, the remediation contract is deficient if it fails to address the level of remediation desired by the owner as well as that required by the permitting agency and the lender.

The following illustration demonstrates the importance of determining the level of remediation as a contract term. The selling owner of a piece of property contracted with the purchaser to remediate TCEs and other contaminants in the ground to a level of nondetectability. The parties adopted this level to comply with what they understood to be the Water Quality Control Board's requirements, believing that the agency would accept nothing less. The seller was later able to persuade the agency to accept a higher concentration. Remediation proceeded along the lines of the newly approved level.

Subsequently, when the purchaser undertook his own testing of the property and found that the contract level of remediation, nondetectability, had not been achieved, he filed suit contending that the seller had breached their agreement. Technically, the seller was in breach because the contract's remediation level was not met; however, in terms of the underlying goal of the agreement and the parties' understanding in defining the level, the seller had achieved the contract goal of a level satisfactory to the local agency.

The dispute in this case could have been avoided if the parties had contracted to remediate "to the level of nondetectability (or, preferably, some more precise standard) or any other level deemed satisfactory to the Water Quality Control Board." This contractual language would have accurately memorialized the underlying agreement of the parties, while also allowing flexibility. Coincidentally, because of the difficulty in obtaining the only slightly lower concentrations at the level of nondetectability, the cost to achieve the added remediation was vastly increased. Furthermore, because the clause was arguably ambiguous, the owner elected to settle with the contractor for a portion of the extra costs, rather than pursue protracted and costly litigation.

Similar problems can occur when any amorphous concept is defined during the cleanup process. In one recent case, for example, a dispute arose when the cleanup goals of an EPA feasibility study for a consent decree turned into the cleanup levels to be mandated.[8]

§ 3.5 Drafting the Scope and Level of Remediation Contract Terms

The scope and level of remediation are, first of all, functions of the location of the properties involved in relation to other potentially contaminated properties, the nature of the contaminants involved, and the type of technology to be implemented. For a large-scale project located near potentially contaminated properties, greater specificity must obviously go into the writing of the terms. Similarly, where the technology selected may threaten groundwater and affect air quality, the scope must be extended. The parties should also consult with local, state, and federal authorities, as well as real property lenders, for their acceptable levels of remediation. Finally, site location must be considered. Remote properties often are amenable to more primitive treatment methods and require less pristine results than projects in populous areas. With these

---

[8] *See* Fairchild Semiconductor Corp. v. EPA, 769 F. Supp. 1553 (N.D. Ca. 1991).

guidelines in mind, the parties should agree on whether their goal is to meet the regulatory or lender level, or if they have some other goal in mind.

Before defining the scope of remediation, the owner and contractor must identify the presence and magnitude of potential contamination from or to adjacent properties. The owner and contractor would be advised to determine the scope of their work after an environmental assessment of such properties is performed. See § 3.3. Information gleaned from Phase I procedures is useful and may be adequate for the formation of the scope. However, it would be advisable, if possible, to proceed to Phases II and III by performing preliminary site work consisting of samples and test borings.[9] For further explanation of assessment phases see **Chapter 2**. Such procedures may quickly provide a profile of contamination sufficient to enable the parties to adequately determine how much work will be necessary.

In agreeing on the level of remediation, consultation with local, state, and federal authorities as well as lenders will quickly indicate what the contractually mandated minimum level must be. This consultation is important to avoid ambiguity in setting the level. The parties should also allow for changes in those standards. Sample language could read: "Remediation to level X or to the level acceptable to XYZ agency or lender as of (a set date)."

After performing the appropriate assessments of contiguous parcels, and investigating regulatory and lender standards for an acceptable remediation level, the parties will be in a better position to select the appropriate technology. They must weigh the benefits and drawbacks of the available technologies based on the scope and level of remediation and any peculiarities of the site. For instance, excavation means greater cost and liability exposure related to the transportation and storage of the extracted hazardous materials. If the parties use this technology, they must take into account the potential financial impact of hiring RCRA-permitted transporters (for a review of permitting under the Resource Conservation and Recovery Act, see **Chapter 5**) and storing the hazardous material at a RCRA-permitted site. See § 3.8. On the other hand, the basic pump-and-treat technology, although less complex than extraction, often proves inadequate in achieving the desired level of remediation. Similarly, VES is less disruptive than extraction, but may also be ineffective. Bioremediation, while cheaper, is often slower and less effective for certain contaminants. These variables are discussed in greater detail in **Chapter 4**. An excellent summary of some of these issues also appears in an article entitled "Science for Superfund Lawyers."[10]

---

[9] Failure to follow such protocols may be disastrous. *See, e.g., Cleaned up Sites Leaking,* Engineering News-Rec., May 20, 1991, at 17.

[10] Kopstein, *Science for Superfund Lawyers,* 19 Envtl. L. Rep. (Envtl. L. Inst.) 10,388 (Sept. 1989).

Several other factors are important in selecting a technology:

1. The location of the project, including accessibility and proximity to local freeways, transportation sites, and hazardous waste and storage sites.

2. Geography, climate, and other factors peculiar to the project area, such as potential seismic movement.

3. Time demands on the parties. If the owner has a particular time frame in mind for the completion of the work, certain technologies may be automatically ruled out.

4. If the selected technology is new, for example in-situ vitrification (see **Chapter 4**), the contract should reflect that and allow for uncertain results. Sample language could read:

    The parties recognize that the treatment method specified in paragraph [ ] is innovative and experimental. The parties will conduct [weekly] reviews of the progress of the project. Should they conclude that modifications are necessary, they shall institute necessary additions, deletions, and changes. Appropriate adjustments to the contract price and time may also be made.

5. Cost, always of the utmost concern. However, cheaper techniques may require more time, may not be approved by regulators, or may simply not work.

Ultimately, the parties must balance the benefits and drawbacks of the available technologies in light of the scope and level of remediation, the particular factors involved, and owner financial concerns, then choose the technology best suited to their needs.

§ 3.6 —Scope of the Work and Scope of the Project

Environmental commentators believe that scoping considerations are among the most important in the contract.[11] In a typical construction contract, the scope of the work and the scope of the project are differentiated. For example, American Institute of Architects (AIA) Document A201, *General Conditions of the Contract for Construction,* subparagraph 1.1.3, describes the work as the services required by the contract documents, including labor, materials, and equipment. The work may be all or part of the project. The project is defined by subparagraph 1.1.4 as the total construction and may include work performed by the owner and others. Similar distinctions may be made in design work.[12]

---

[11] Moskowitz at 13.

[12] O'Neal, *Risks Encountered in the Design Stage and How to Avoid Them, in* Risk Avoidance in Construction Contracts 41–42 (1991) [hereinafter O'Neal].

It is advisable to make the same distinction in a remediation contract. If, for example, a project may include work by parties other than the remediation contractor, that possibility should be spelled out. Furthermore, the scope of the work may well involve efforts that are not directed at achieving a level of remediation. For example, a contract that calls for attaining a level of remediation in accordance with a soluble threshold level of contaminant (STLC) may include the lining and capping of an impoundment area (the work) to comply with the terms of a consent decree or a closure plan (the project).

Determination of the scope of the work and project is tied to another critical issue: Does the remediation contract contemplate design work? In some cases, different entities will be hired for the design and construction phases, on the theory that having the same firm perform both functions invites a conflict of interest.[13] Such a bifurcated approach mirrors the arrangement more commonly found in the construction industry. Although contracting the design and construction to the same entity does not necessarily create a conflict, such action does expand the liability of the remediation contractor exponentially.[14] In that sense, it is more akin to the construction industry's design-build concept. Even where design work by the contractor is clearly called for, the scope of that effort should be carefully defined, and the parties should clearly understand the concepts set forth in that description.[15]

Finally, if the project is phased, the owner must decide whether one or more contractors will be used. Some owners prefer to use a number of contractors, believing they will get better prices. Others find that they achieve greater efficiency by limiting the number of contractors. Ultimately the best approach probably depends on what contractors are used and how clear their contracts are.

§ 3.7 —Contract Price and Time

Another crucial and particularly difficult term in the remediation contract is the contract price. It is in relation to the price that all other parts of the project must be considered.

While "[i]t may be nearly impossible to project total site remediation costs from the infancy of a project . . . ,"[16] a careful study of the site, clear delineation of alternatives (including attendant costs and viability), precise

---

[13] Moskowitz at 259.

[14] The government does not necessarily agree. For example, the EPA believes it is a conflict of interest for one firm to perform the TAT Scope of Work and the duties of the ERC simultaneously. *See, e.g.,* EPA Emergency Response Cleanup Services Users Manual, EPA Directive 9242.2-01B, II-28 (1987) [hereinafter ERCS Users Manual].

[15] O'Neal at 41.

[16] Fender, *A Guide to Controlling Site Remediation Costs,* Pollution Engineering, Nov. 1990, at 90.

identification of contaminants, and rigorous examination of the soils will increase the potential for economical and effective remediation. Cost cutting on the initial studies is unwise. First, a relatively small proportion of the cost is involved in Phase I and II assessment. Second, cost cutting at this level may doom the entire remediation to expensive failure. Further aspects of this project strategy will be discussed in **Chapter 7**.

Developing the contract price in remediation work is not entirely different from the typical construction scenario. As in any construction process, the estimation phase is of primary importance. The contractor must be extraordinarily careful in establishing the probable cost of various remediation systems. Unlike a typical construction project, however, the contractor often lacks a set of architectural plans and specifications from which she can do takeoffs on which to prepare her bid. Instead, the contractor is often faced with incomplete preparatory work consisting of some preliminary audits and perhaps some site work that may have been performed by another entity, and which may not be current or reliable. Depending on the sophistication of the supervising entity, there may or may not be an environmental assessment report on the site.

The second difference from the typical construction scenario is owner motivation. In a construction project, a few more dollars may improve the quality of aesthetics or functioning, translating into higher rental value or more economic operation of the project. An owner may be willing to incur unexpected costs to achieve these gains. In a remediation project, these types of inducements to spend more are generally not present. Thus, there is more pressure to maintain a low price.

Aside from the accuracy of the estimates and owner frugality, concern must also be focused on how the contract price is formulated and described in the contract. Certain risks are inherent in both the determination of the contract price and how it is couched in the contractual language. In this regard, consideration should be given as to whether or not the parties will utilize a fixed-price contract, a cost contract, or some derivative of a guaranteed maximum contract.

A fixed-price contract protects owners against spending more than was initially agreed to. However, any reduction of costs increases contractor profits, creating an incentive to sacrifice quality. Under a cost contract the owner pays all costs plus a fixed fee, offering no incentive to sacrifice quality. Unfortunately, there is also no motivation to economize. A guaranteed maximum contract (GMAX) occupies the middle ground. The owner pays all costs plus a fixed fee, subject to a cap on the total. When combined with a shared savings clause, the GMAX is an effective tool.[17]

---

[17] For a more detailed discussion, *see* Erickson, *Risks Associated with the Determination of the Contract Price, in* Risk Avoidance in Construction Contracts 50 (1991); Erickson & Albert, *Choosing a Contracting Format, in* Wiley Construction Law Update 3 (S. Goldblatt ed., John Wiley & Sons 1991).

In the remediation field, these concepts are little-known and underutilized. Most private contracts are time and materials (T&M) contracts that can be troublesome to an owner. Even when expressed as flat-rate contracts, they may, in effect, be T&M contracts if they are predicated on estimates.[18]

In the owner's view, the best way to control costs is to manage effectively, require frequent cost reports, and provide a "for convenience termination" clause in the contract.[19] Pay requests should be accompanied by a description of work accomplished, to prevent front-end loading (where a disproportionate share of the contract price is paid early in the contract, not commensurate with the volume of work performed). Frequent schedule updates should be required on a regular basis. The data that accompany these reports should be checked.[20] Thorough, timely, and comprehensive lab reports should be provided early in the project to insure the remediation technology is working.

From the contractor's point of view, the contract should include the right to receive assurances of sufficient committed funds to complete the work, at the start of and through the life of the contract. This right should be linked to a right to suspend and, ultimately, terminate the contract if such assurances are not provided. Failure of timely payment should also permit suspension and termination if the failure persists for more than 30 days. See § 3.29.

After carefully scoping the project, considering variables such as transportation, technology (speed and reliability), and the owner's particular needs, the parties should agree on a feasible time frame for completion of the work. If the owner has some particular needs in this regard, they should be spelled out. Provisions should be made for an original schedule using critical path method (CPM) techniques to monitor the progress of key items of work, and measure and project the impact of delay on other project activities (see § 3.25), and, for monthly updates (more frequent if possible). If there is a float period, it should be spelled out. If experimental or cutting-edge technologies are to be utilized, a more flexible schedule is desirable. Careful attention to the time issue in the contract may point out incompatible terms in other areas.

§ 3.8   Issues of Regulatory Compliance

The burden of regulatory compliance in the construction field has traditionally been contractually allocated. In the field of environmental remediation, this allocation is also a matter of contract; however, because of the labyrinthine body

---

[18] Moskowitz at 260.

[19] *See, e.g.,* AGCC Form No. 1, Standard Form Prime Contract Between Owner and Contractor, para. 19.3, at 10 (1988).

[20] Even when remediation has priority over costs, owners are questioning costs closely. *See, e.g.,* Rubin, *Contracts under Scrutiny,* Engineering News-Rec., July 1, 1991, at 10 (an article that examines EPA cost overruns in the ARC's program).

of laws and regulations concerning environmental remediation work, the contractor may have a direct obligation to certain government agencies, contractual provisions notwithstanding. In remediation work, satisfaction of government agencies is most often the goal of the contract, whereas in the construction field, such compliance is ancillary to the goal of completing the project. For this reason, these obligations warrant serious consideration.

The issue of compliance becomes even thornier if the contract is undertaken pursuant to a federal act, such as Emergency Response Cleanup Services (ERCS), or under the auspices of a Superfund cleanup. An ERCS contractor, for example, dealing directly with the federal government, faces a myriad of compliance requirements.[21] The typical ERCS contract runs 104 pages with an added 32 attachments, coming to approximately 400 pages.

In the context of Superfund, the new EPA Superfund model consent decree requires in part that the settling defendants must provide a copy of the consent decree to any persons (including contractors) who are representing any of the settling defendants with respect to the site or the work thereon. In addition, all contracts and subcontracts entered into for the cleanup will be conditioned upon the performance of the work in conformity with the consent decree, and a copy of the decree will be given to each contractor, thereby arguably binding the contractors to perform in accordance with its terms. At the same time, the settling defendants are primarily responsible for supervising the contractors and subcontractors to insure such compliance is achieved. The model consent decree also states that each contractor and subcontractor shall be deemed to be in a contractual relationship with the settling defendants within the meaning of CERCLA.[22]

In addition to these contractual safeguards in the model consent decree, the EPA retains the right to disapprove of the proposed supervising contractor without any showing of cause. Commentators have suggested that this right raises the specter of contractors involved in disputes with the EPA on jobsites being disapproved at other sites in retaliation, thereby harming the contractor's ability to represent the interest of her clients.[23]

In the context of private remediation, regulatory compliance issues are inextricably linked to the nature of the contaminant, the locus of the contamination (for example, contaminated soil versus affected groundwater), and the proposed method of treatment. Treatment of certain types of contaminants may produce byproducts or residue that are also contaminated to some degree and must be dealt with, for example, by removal and dumping in a storage site. This

---

[21] *See* ERCS Users Manual.

[22] 42 U.S.C. § 9607(b)(3); *see* Off. of Solid Waste & Emergency Response, EPA, Model CERCLA RD/RA Consent Decree, Directive NVM.9835.17 (1991) [hereinafter *EPA Consent Decree*].

[23] *See New EPA Superfund Model Consent Decree,* Thelen, Marrin, Johnson & Bridges Newsletter, July 11, 1991.

necessity, in turn, will generate more compliance issues, particularly if the substance qualifies as a RCRA solid waste. In such cases, the contractor must ascertain that both the transporter and the proposed dump site possess the necessary permits. To treat the material on site, the contractor may need an EPA TSDF (Treatment, Storage, and Disposal Facility) identification number. If groundwater is, or may be, affected by a soil remediation process, the contractor must consult the local water control authorities, who must consent to the proposed treatment. Similarly, if the treatment method generates regulated emissions, the contractor must consult the local air quality body.

The method of remediation also dictates which governmental agencies have to be sought out. Surface aeration of contaminated soil, for example, requires air permitting. In-situ bioremediation of contaminated soil must be performed so as to satisfy water quality officials that no leachate will migrate into the water supply. This technique may also require air permits.[24]

§ 3.9   —Permit Compliance

In private projects, the issue of regulatory compliance most often manifests itself in the context of obtaining permits and approvals for the work. The detailed requirements for each type of permit are discussed in **Chapter 5**. We deal here with the issue of responsibility for such compliance.

The flow chart in **Figure 3–1** has been developed for use in California, and is helpful when dealing with these issues.

Some commentators suggest that any permits that the owner is required to obtain be specifically identified, thereby indicating that the contractor is responsible for all other permits. The commentators believe this is a proper procedure, since the contractor, from experience, is usually more aware of which permits are necessary to perform the work and how to obtain them.[25] In the environmental remediation field, this argument is compelling, given the complicated regulations governing the performance of the work.

However, although environmental remediation contracting is in its infancy and lacks the rich variety of contracting forms and distinctions of the construction industry, it is safe to say that the approvals and permits required for a given project will depend on a variety of factors that are more byzantine than for any construction project. (When it is possible to determine that certain permits are

---

[24] *See* Cal AGC Manual at 151.

[25] Hummel, *Negotiating the Owner-Architect Agreement (Owner's Viewpoint): Supplemental Conditions to AIA Document B141 Standard Form of Agreement Between Owner and Architect 1987 Edition,* in Design and Construction Contracts 1, 22–23 (1989) [hereinafter Hummel]; *see also* Hart & Behrendt, *Modifications to AIA A201 1987 from Owner's Viewpoint,* in Wiley Construction Law Update 17 (S. Goldblatt ed., John Wiley & Sons 1991) [hereinafter Hart & Behrendt].

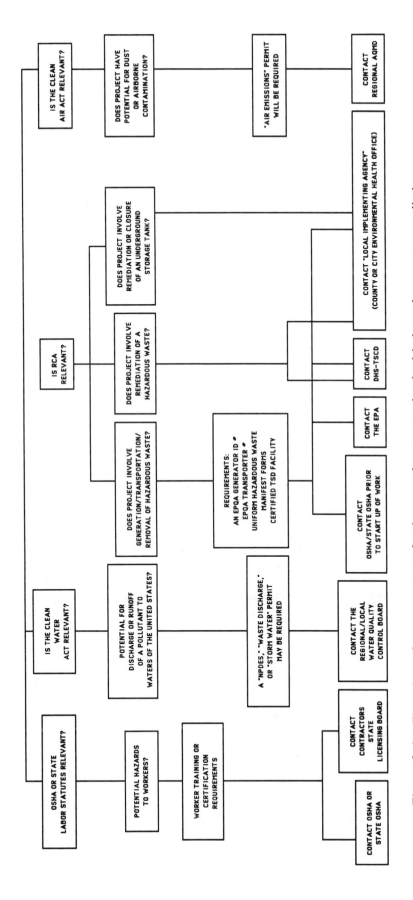

Figure 3–1. Flow chart of agency contacts for the general contractor involved in hazardous waste remediation.

clearly in the province of one party, that responsibility should be spelled out in the contract.) Furthermore, in remediation contracting, unlike the typical construction contract, the same party often designs the work plan, makes the necessary contacts with concerned agencies, and performs the work. (In this case, governmental compliance is properly the province of the remediation contractor. However, when the owner has designed the plan, or had it prepared by a third party, the owner should be responsible for compliance. In such a case, the contract should detail what precontract studies and plans were prepared by the owner or her agent. Furthermore, the contract should specify what assumptions the contractor is making based on that information.)

Consequently, a blanket provision laying responsibility for permits on one party or the other may be inadvisable. Instead, a detailed site assessment and outline of courses of action, coupled with a vigorous and thorough review of the potentially applicable regulations and meetings with the various regulatory agencies, should produce a logical allocation of permitting responsibilities between the owner and the contractor prior to execution of the remediation contract. See §§ **3.31** through **3.34** for a detailed discussion of the permit compliance issues.

§ 3.10   —Disclaimers

Determining proper allocation of responsibility for achieving the contractually and governmentally mandated remediation level and scope is further complicated by the inclusion of various disclaimers in the contract documents. Typically, these disclaimers are intended to exclude (or substantially limit) any responsibility for design. Often, the disclaimers attempt to avoid testing and sample maintenance responsibility. Many are attempts to avoid permitting obligations. Identification of these disclaimers is difficult because they are rarely, if ever, referred to as disclaimers. More often, they are inserted as options, or worse, become operative only as omissions from the description of the scope of the work. They may also be buried in other contract provisions limiting the contractor's obligations, or dealing with the design phase of the project.

The issue of disclaimers also highlights one of the more ambiguous areas of remediation work: the relationship between the RI/FS, design, and construction phases. In standard commercial construction, these vagaries have been disposed of through the evolution of contract language and judicial interpretations.

In commercial construction, the owner warrants the accuracy and adequacy of the plans and specifications to the contractor. The architect, who designs project, provides no such warranty. Rather, she commits to design the project in a non-negligent manner. Even here, however, at least one commentator has suggested that, to clearly define the architect's obligation to design in accordance with local law, an insert be added to subparagraph 2.4.1 of the AIA Document B141, *Agreement Between Owner and Architect,* as follows: "The Construction

Documents shall be accurate, complete and the design shall be in accordance with the requirements of federal, state and local laws, statutes, ordinances, building codes and rules and regulations."[26] Such a modification would be inherently reasonable, because subparagraph 3.7.3 of Document AIA A201, *General Conditions to the Contract Between the Owner and the General Contractor,* relieves the contractor from responsibility for assuring the contract documents comply with applicable laws, rules, and regulations. Similar language can be found in the AGC standard form of contract.[27]

The problems generated by this schism between designer and contractor obligations are exacerbated in remediation contracting, where the clear-cut dichotomy of designer (architect) and contractor has not yet developed. Indeed, as previously indicated, the designer and the contractor for remediation projects are often the same. The concern in this area is further heightened by the fact that in environmental cleanup projects, compliance with governmental requirements, and concomitant governmental acceptance of the cleanup, are often the primary goal of the construction process. In standard commercial construction, governmental compliance is incidental to the primary purpose of the project. In the remediation context, however, where the work is often motivated by a government mandate, the issue of compliance is of paramount importance. The entity that designs or contracts for remediation work should not be able to disclaim away the primary purpose of the project. Conversely, that entity should not be taxed with an obligation that was not within the scope of that contract.

For example, if the project is designed to achieve governmental acceptance of a closure plan, a contractual disclaimer that would frustrate that purpose should be ineffective. Often, however, the contract is unclear. In one recent project, the goal was to lower the pH level of a percolation pond to a level acceptable to the agency's STLC, which was at that time 12.5. Unfortunately, the contract only specified the level at "about 11.5." When the contractor achieved levels between 10.6 and 12.4, the owner claimed breach. In another case, the contract specified attainment of a series of STLC goals that were pegged to levels promulgated by the Local Water Quality Control Board. When the contractor subsequently convinced the Board that a slightly higher concentration would be adequate, the owner still attempted to hold him to the stricter standards of the contract. The entire problem could have been avoided by a simple contract clause obligating the contractor to achieve a specified goal, "or such level as the Regional Water Quality Control Board accepts." The number in the contract was not the goal; rather, the goal was to receive Board approval. The contract did not accurately describe the intent of the parties.

---

[26] Jaffe, *Contract Language Which Can Allocate Risk, in* Risk Avoidance in Construction Contracts 30 (1991) [hereinafter Jaffe].

[27] *See, e.g.,* AGCC Form No. 1, Standard Form Prime Contract Between Owner and Contractor, para. 11.2 (1988).

§ 3.11 —Owner Concerns in Regulatory Compliance

The owner should first decide whether to use one firm both to design the plan and to perform the work. If so, the owner would want the contract to contain many of the standard turnkey clauses, requiring the contractor to design a remediation program in compliance with all applicable regulations and meeting contract specifications, using language such as that suggested in § 3.3. The primary concern of the owner is to ensure that the contractor achieves the level and scope of remediation required under the contract, in accordance with the standards of the local governing body and within the contract time and price.

To achieve these goals, the contractor must be able to maintain a harmonious working relationship with the government agencies. To this end, the owner should attempt to identify which of the contractor's personnel will deal with local governing agencies. The owner should then ensure that these parties possess the necessary skills, and that they will be the only direct contact between the contractor and the agencies. These steps are particularly important when the government agencies involved must later certify that the remediation has been successfully accomplished in accordance with the work plan previously approved by that agency.

The owner should ensure that the contract clearly defines the contractor's specific responsibilities. Perhaps the best approach is to simply outline the owner's responsibility regarding government approvals, plans, surveys, and other information, and specify that the contractor is responsible for all design, approvals, and permits not specifically excepted. The owner might also suggest language that requires the contractor to inform the owner of any changes in relevant laws or ordinances, or in approval or permit requirements. The owner should also strike any language limiting the contractor's responsibility to ascertain that the work plan or remediation scope is in accordance with applicable law.[28] See § 3.10.

Failure to spell out responsibility for such compliance concerns can lead to litigation. For example, in *Straus Veal Feeds, Inc. v. Mead & Hunt, Inc.,*[29] an architecture/engineering firm (A/E) specializing in designs for the dairy industry designed a processing facility for a client who had developed a liquid veal feed production process. After the plant commenced operation, the owner was ordered to shut it down by the Indiana Stream Pollution Control Board because the industrial waste produced by the plant had an excessive biochemical oxygen demand level. The client then sued the A/E.

The evidence at trial indicated that the client did not specifically ask for consulting and design services from the A/E with respect to waste treatment or waste disposal. When the A/E questioned the client about meeting the

---

[28] *See, e.g.,* Hart & Behrendt at 25.

[29] 538 N.E.2d 299 (Ind. Ct. App. 1989).

requirements proposed by the Waste Water Treatment Regulations, the client indicated that there would be no problem because the system was clean. At trial the client successfully argued that the A/E had an independent duty to investigate the regulations and warn the client about potential waste disposal problems. The appellate court disagreed, holding that such a duty went beyond the scope of the parties' agreement. The court also noted that the client in this case occupied a significant position in the veal feed production industry and that the A/E's reliance on the client's experience was reasonable; therefore, the firm's performance fulfilled the standard of care for architects. If the contract had required the A/E to comply with governmental requirements on environmental issues, the result would have been different. While the owner probably would not have been able to hold the A/E to the charge of professional negligence, clearly it would have been a breach of contract not to have so complied.[30]

Any environmental remediation work must take into account all the relevant statutes and regulations governing performance of the work. The potential civil and criminal penalties for failure to do so are enormous. Accordingly, it is advisable that the attorney for the hiring party examine all documents, whether they be a rudimentary site analysis, an RI/FS, or a total remediation package.

§ 3.12   —Contractor Concerns in Regulatory Compliance

As previously discussed (see §§ **3.6, 3.8,** and **3.9**), contractor concerns will vary depending upon whether the remediation contractor designed and executed the work plan, or only performed work designed by another party. In either case, clear delineation of contractor responsibilities is of great help to both the owner and the contractor.

The contractor should also be aware that the owner of a contaminated site is faced with a situation that may have long-term effects, including extended monitoring requirements or obligations for future cleanup. If the contractor is not agreeing to provide such additional work, that should be clearly stated in the contract, perhaps by a limitation on the scope and duration of the warranty and on any provided indemnities. Such limiting contractual terms will not afford much protection, however, if the contractor claimed some particular expertise in the field,[31] and it can be shown that the owner relied upon that expertise.

If the contractor assumes the remediation plan deals only with a specific contaminant, the contract should spell out that limitation and warrant the absence of other hazardous materials. A hazardous material can be described as any substance:

---

[30] For an excellent discussion of the case, *see* Lynch, *Contract Liability, in* Wiley Construction Law Update 348 (S. Goldblatt ed., John Wiley & Sons 1991).

[31] *See* Hart & Behrendt at 24.

1. That is governed by any regulation or law, local, state, or federal
2. That is or becomes defined as "hazardous waste," hazardous substance, contaminant, or pollutant under any local, state, or federal law now extant or enacted in future with retroactive effect
3. That is covered by the Toxic Substances Control Act (TSCA)[32] or any similar state or local law or regulation
4. The presence of which on the site or adjacent properties could give rise to claims of nuisance, trespass, or other tort
5. That contains PCBs, asbestos, or petroleum hydrocarbons.[33]

§ 3.13 —Lender Concerns in Regulatory Compliance

The lender has an increasing obligation to accomplish environmental due diligence in the form of a Phase I environmental audit before entering into a borrowing relationship[34] during the term of the loan and before foreclosure. Typically, the Phase I contract includes certain information as contained in **Appendix A**. However, there are no statutory requirements as to the contents of a Phase I audit under CERCLA. The Phase I investigation should be part of a lender's environmental risk assessment policy.

In *United States v. Fleet Factors,*[35] the court created a new standard for environmental liability under CERCLA. A secured lender will be liable if its involvement with management of the facility is sufficiently broad to support the inference that the lender had the capacity to control hazardous waste operations.[36]

The *Fleet Factors* case was interpreted in *In re Bergsoe Metal*[37] by the Ninth Circuit Court, which held that when the secured lender has no involvement in the actual management of the lead plant, there is no liability.

Since each case is fact-specific as to the conduct of the lender, there is still no clear-cut rule as to what conduct a lender may safely undertake. The EPA, pursuant to its rule-making capability, has outlined some specific conduct that would not exempt the secured creditor from protection under the CERCLA "secured creditor exemption." Such activities include due diligence with regard to the environmental status of a prospective borrower's property, monitoring the

[32] 15 U.S.C. §§ 2601–2629.

[33] A more exhaustive definition is found in Cal. Civ. Code § 2782.6(2)(d) (West 1991).

[34] In United States v. Fleet Factors Corp., 901 F.2d 1550, 1558–59, n.12 (11th Cir. 1990), the court argued that "by narrowly construing the secured creditors exemption, lending institutions can require borrowers to submit periodic environmental reviews as a condition to receiving a loan."

[35] 901 F.2d 1550 (11th Cir. 1990).

[36] *Id.*

[37] 910 F.2d 668 (9th Cir. 1990).

credit, undertaking workouts, and foreclosing and liquidating the collateral within a six-month period. A complete and accurate Phase I audit may also help the lender qualify for the innocent landowner defense.

Although there is no standard lender environmental risk assessment policy, the Phase I audits are usually prepared by the prospective borrower's consultant for lender's review. The consultant is usually chosen from the lender's list of approved environmental consultants. Some lenders will not accept Phase I audits from consultants not on the list, while other lenders will accept such audits and scrutinize the results more carefully.[38] Certain large financial institutions have an in-house environmental risk management unit to evaluate the Phase I results; however, many lenders rely on the loan officer to evaluate the results of the Phase I audit. Most lenders are willing to rely on a Phase I audit prepared by the borrower's consultant because the lenders do not want to make representations about borrower's property, nor do they want to risk the possibility of having to report contamination to the borrower (or possibly to a regulatory agency).[39]

Additionally, depending on the lender's ultimate disposition of the loan (for example, sale of the loan in the secondary market), the particular federal agency, such as the Federal National Mortgage Association (Fannie Mae) or Federal Home Loan Mortgage Corporation (Freddie Mac) may have environmental risk assessment requirements.

Lenders typically draft provisions in the loan agreement with the borrower to protect themselves against environmental liability. Thus the loan agreement, the mortgage or deed of trust (if the loan is real property secured), the security agreement, and any other collateral documents govern the relationship between the borrower and the lender.

If the Phase I audit shows an environmental concern, the lender, if the loan is prospective, may not enter into the lending relationship. If the loan has been made, the lender will want to ensure that the borrower is in compliance with the loan documents and is responsible for all cleanup costs, environmental audit costs, and other potential costs.

In one case, the secured lender, before foreclosing on environmentally impaired real property of the borrower, negotiated and entered into a settlement agreement with the EPA as to the scope of the remediation and cleanup.[40] In this fashion, the lender was able to cap its exposure at a predetermined level. This

---

[38] Henry & Olshesky, Commercial Lending Policies: Facing the Environmental Liability Challenge 1 (Bank of Am. Envtl. Services, Orange, Cal. 1991).

[39] The "person in charge of the vessel or facility" is responsible to report the release . . . and the continuous release. The current owner/operator at the time of the disposal of hazardous waste, who accepted hazardous waste for transport and selected a hazardous waste facility without interim status or a permit, has the responsibility of notification. Thus, a lender does not have a reporting or notification obligation under CERCLA. 42 U.S.C. §§ 9602, 9603(a), (c), (f) (West 1983).

[40] *EPA Agrees to Limit Liability of Bank Set to Foreclose on Tainted Land,* 56 BNA Banking Rep. 20 (May 20, 1991).

illustration demonstrates the benefit of effective dealing with governmental agencies. The lender further benefited because it had an interest in ensuring that the scope of remediation also addressed a plan to avoid further contamination.[41]

Another mechanism that is being utilized is the environmental opinion letter. This opinion letter states the scope of investigation undertaken and its adequacy. The letter also summarizes the consultant's conclusions about potential liability.[42] The form of opinion may be attached to the remediation contract as an exhibit.

Generally, however, due to the uncertain state of the law, lenders are reluctant to dictate the scope of remediation or investigation (except in the context of a Phase I assessment for a prospective borrower).[43]

§ 3.14 Bonding

Payment and performance bonds have been an integral part of the construction process for years. Their obvious purpose is to assure the owner and the lender (and in the remediation field, concerned government agencies) that the project will be completed, notwithstanding breach by the contractor. Most often, this bonding requirement is passed on by the general contractor to subcontractors to protect against their default. The bonds are posted to insure that work is completed (the performance bond) and that subcontractors are paid (the payment bond).

In the field of hazardous waste remediation, bonding is a hot topic. For a discussion of bonding issues in greater detail see **Chapter 9**. Almost every contract will contain some kind of bonding requirement; however, sureties have been very cautious about issuing bonds in this field, because hazardous waste remediation work is regarded as being in its infancy, with a dearth of legal precedent, a very high risk, and with long tail liability for the surety.

The insurance industry has made an effort to approach the issue in an organized fashion, beginning by categorizing hazardous substance work. Categories include petrochemicals, asbestos, Superfund work, and nuclear materials. Petrochemical work is becoming better understood, and qualified contractors are increasingly able to provide performance bonds. Specialty contractors doing asbestos removal may receive bonding from specialty underwriters who have carefully analyzed each contractor and bond. Superfund bonds are perceived as

---

[41] Nation, *Minimizing Risk of Loss from Environmental Laws,* 4 Banking L.J., July–Aug. 1991.

[42] Del Duca, *The Environmental Consultant's Opinion Letter: A Step Beyond An Environmental Audit,* 20 Envtl. L. Rep. (Envtl. L. Inst.) 10,184 (May 1990).

[43] For example, in a recent transaction where environmentally impaired property was sold to a large multi-national purchaser, the lender relied on an indemnity with the purchaser/borrower's parent corporation (the real property was held in a single-asset subsidiary) and as of the close of the transaction had not approved a remediation plan.

extremely risky. Underwriters of such bonds are generally concerned with three major difficulties:

1. Extended delays in acceptance of the completed work by all regulatory agencies
2. Inheriting losses that would normally be claims against insurance policies when contractors are no longer in business
3. Lack of federal guarantees providing reimbursement to the surety in the event of a loss.[44]

§ 3.15   —Owner Concerns in Bonding

Private owners must satisfy lenders that the necessary environmental work can be accomplished on time and to the degree mandated by the lending documents and the remediation contract. Accordingly, performance bonds in the private sector are almost universally demanded. Owners obtaining such protection receive the financial guarantee of the bonding company plus the independent evaluation of the contractor's skills and abilities and analysis of their financial condition. Bonding is also an issue in hazardous waste and remediation project contracts issued by government agencies, which require performance bonds for their contractors. Superfund work, regarded by sureties as extremely risky, requires that the settling defendants under an EPA consent decree "establish and maintain financial security" in a form acceptable to the government. The surety bond is one of the five listed security devices and probably the one that the government would most likely accept.[45] Although the consent decree makes the settling defendants responsible for requiring such bonding, it is reasonable to anticipate that the defendants may try to pass the responsibility on to the contractor.

The difficulties in this area are further compounded by the varying bonding requirements of different government programs. The typical ERCS contract, for example, does not require a performance bond, and only demands payment bonds from subcontractors whose contract exceeds $50,000. The contract further provides for waiver of the requirement by the contracting officer.[46]

Problems in federal contracting are exacerbated by the acceptance of personal sureties for federal projects. Use of sureties of this type is fraught with peril for the owner and the contractor.

---

[44] Cal. AGC Manual at 175–76.

[45] *See* EPA Consent Decree, ch. 14, para. 45(a).

[46] *See, e.g.,* ERCS Contract No. 68-WI-0012, EPA Regions IX and X, Mar. 1, 1991.

§ 3.16 —Contractor Concerns in Bonding

The contractor's main concern is trying to find appropriate bonding that is acceptable to both the owner and to the regulators. The Army Corps of Engineers has released a study of these bonding difficulties, concluding that there was a reluctance by sureties to write bonds for such work for a variety of reasons.[47] The list of such difficulties reflects many of the anomalies that have been discussed elsewhere in this chapter in different contexts. For example, difficulties include:

1. Requirement of the surety to bond the project design under certain circumstances (not traditionally a surety bond activity, but reflective of the merger of the design-build functions in the remediation field)
2. Widespread litigation and the uncertain legal climate, leading to insurance company uneasiness about such bonding
3. Uncertain technology that may increase potential liability
4. Inadequacy of currently available insurance
5. Fear that a surety bond could be treated as a substitute for insurance if the insurance is inadequate
6. Lack of adequate EPA indemnification to protect sureties and contractors from these liabilities.

Although much has been said regarding proposals to alleviate these obstacles to bonding,[48] to date nothing of substance has occurred.

It may be possible to negotiate around a bonding requirement in certain contexts, such as by posting securities, a letter of credit, or a guarantee from a solvent, reliable third party. However, such mechanisms often generate their own difficulties.

Furthermore, an owner confronted with a request by a contractor for relief from a bonding requirement may obviously ask why such relief is necessary. Owners will often infer (perhaps justifiably) some financial inefficiency or poor claims history that may give rise to the request.

§ 3.17 —Lender Concerns in Bonding

The concern of a lender is that the cleanup be properly bonded (in accordance with all legal requirements), so that the work will be completed even if the

---

[47] Associated General Contractors of America, Hazardous Waste Bulletin No. 90-7, Aug. 28, 1990.

[48] Ichniowski, *Senate Panel Passes Superfund Liability Bill,* Engineering News-Rec., Oct. 11, 1990, at 7.

contractor becomes financially insolvent or otherwise unable to perform. In the context of a construction bond, lenders often require that they be named as dual obligee on the performance bond.[49]

Given the state of lender environmental liability, this requirement that the lender be named as dual obligee may not currently be part of a lender's environmental risk management policy, but should be reviewed on a case-by-case basis.

Because of surety reluctance to bond in the field of environmental clean-up,[50] the issue may be a point of negotiation for the borrower-owner and the contractor.

§ 3.18 Risk Allocation

There exist many uncertainties about the nature and extent of liability to which a contractor may be exposed under the environmental contract. Therefore, in addition to the particular technical aspects of the project, the contractor must address the allocation of possible tort or contractual liability. Clauses addressing insurance, indemnity, and limitations on liability should be considered at the contract formation stage. These clauses are common in the construction industry; however, issues peculiar to the environmental industry require that these clauses be specifically tailored to the particular environmental contract. In addition, the drafting of these clauses requires recognition of certain limitations on their availability and effectiveness in the construction contract. In combination however, these clauses can provide an effective means of allocating risk among the contracting parties so that both the owner and contractor derive the benefits to which they are entitled under the contract.

§ 3.19 —Insurance

Insurance is an important topic that must be addressed at the contract drafting phase. However, in other areas of the construction industry, insurance issues generally revolve around such specific concerns as who shall bear the responsibility for maintaining liability coverage and who shall be named an insured under the policy (as well as the limits of that policy). In the environmental remediation industry, insurance considerations may determine whether or not the contract should be entered into at all. In fact, commentators have suggested that the general unavailability of coverage for the environmental remediation contractor might be considered the most important factor in deciding whether to

---

[49] G. Hunt, Construction Surety and Bonding Handbook 12 (1990).

[50] Rubin, *Surety Bond Crunch Hiking Superfund Costs,* Engineering News-Rec., Aug. 23, 1990, at 8.

enter the hazardous waste cleanup business.[51] In light of these uncertainties, insurance (or the lack of available insurance) may significantly affect certain other clauses contained in the environmental cleanup contract, including those clauses relating to indemnity and risk allocation. See §§ **3.15** and **3.21** for a more detailed discussion. These issues may also affect the selection of technology by making the feasibility of radical cutting-edge systems dependent on whether or not coverage is available for them.

To understand these issues, it is important to grasp the role insurance generally plays in the construction contract. In that field, the type of insurance to be obtained is generally not a central issue in the contracting phase. Most contracts require the general contractor to carry comprehensive general liability (CGL) insurance, with the expectation that this type of insurance will protect the contractor against claims for bodily injury or property damage on any project. At the contract drafting stage, therefore, the owner will likely require that the general contractor obtain an endorsement to its policy making the owner an additional insured under the policy.[52] In addition, those parties for whom the owner might otherwise be held liable may also be named as additional insureds under the general contractor CGL policy. Contracts may also differ with respect to the limits of coverage required, which may be influenced by a number of factors, including the size of the project or the type of work being undertaken.

Construction contracts also generally require the contractor to carry the necessary workers' compensation insurance required by law, to protect the owner from any claims brought by the contractor's employees. The project may require such items as property and boiler and machinery insurance to be borne by the owner.[53] These requirements, however, are commonplace and should come as no surprise to the contractor.

The contractor on most construction projects can be relatively certain that these policies, including the CGL policy, will cover most claims for bodily injury and property damage. Likewise an owner, in requiring the contractor to maintain the above types of insurance to name the owner as an additional insured under the policies, can feel relatively certain of protection from claims arising out of the contractor's operations.

The types of insurance discussed above are no less important in the environmental contracting field. That is, the same types of property damage and bodily injury claims that occur in the construction industry generally, including employee claims, may occur in the performance of a cleanup contract. However, environmental cleanup projects raise certain critical new issues that must be addressed prior to executing a contract and commencing cleanup activity. These

---

[51] Miller & Murphy, *Insuring and Assessing Hazardous Waste Contracts, in* Hazardous Waste Disposal and Underground Construction Law 293 (R. Cushman & B. Ficken eds., John Wiley & Sons 1987) [hereinafter Miller & Murphy].

[52] AIA Doc. A201, General Conditions for the Contract for Construction, para. 11.1.1 (14th ed. 1987).

[53] *Id.* at 53, para. 11.2.1.

issues arise as a direct result of the presence of hazardous materials. In entering into a contract for the cleanup of hazardous waste or other contaminants, therefore, both the owner and the environmental contractor must recognize that the standard CGL policy and, indeed, any of the policies mentioned above may not protect either party from liability arising from the dispersal or discharge of pollutants. Further, both parties must realize that the standard CGL policy may not cover a claim by the owner against the contractor in the event the cleanup is not performed properly.

Coverage under CGL Policies

The reason for the CGL policy's insufficiency is found in how such policies have usually been written. Generally, CGL policies are written to cover bodily injuries or property damage arising from an occurrence.[54] In order to determine whether the particular loss was covered, the insured must first ascertain the date on which the loss occurred within the meaning of the policy. In the context of hazardous waste, CGL policies generally excluded losses arising from pollution unless the pollution was "sudden and accidental."[55] Because the release of hazardous waste into the environment is often gradual, such release was not likely to be a covered occurrence within the meaning of the policy. Courts addressing this policy language have uniformly interpreted it in favor of insurers, resulting in a denial of coverage for losses arising from the escape of hazardous waste under the CGL policy.[56] More recently, however, CGL policies have been written to include an exhaustive absolute pollution exclusion that excludes all discharge of pollutants, sudden or otherwise.[57]

A second and equally significant issue with respect to coverage under the CGL policy is the question of whether the loss amounts to either bodily injury or property damage. Although the term "bodily injury" is not the subject of significant dispute in the environmental cleanup context, the concept of "property damage" is. Generally the issue has arisen with respect to whether costs imposed under state and federal environmental regulations are insured under the CGL policy.[58] Courts are generally divided on this issue. However, the

---

[54] Environmental Issues in Real Estate and Construction Projects in California, ch. 7 (June 20, 1991) (Cambridge Inst. seminar material) [hereinafter Environmental Issues].

[55] *Id.* at 7-1.

[56] *See* Wall St. J., Aug. 28, 1991, at B8, col. 1. In three recent cases decided by the Michigan Supreme Court, the court ruled that the sudden and accidental pollution clause relieves the insurer from obligations to pay under the policy when pollution occurs as a result of standard company practices or over an extended period of time that can cover as little as two weeks.

[57] Miller & Murphy at 295.

[58] *See, e.g.,* Ascon Properties, Inc. v. Illinois Union Ins. Co., 908 F.2d 976 (9th Cir. 1990); New Castle County v. Hartford Accident & Indem. Co., 933 F.2d 1162 (3d Cir. 1991); AIU Ins. Co. v. Superior Court, 51 Cal. 3d 807, 799 P.2d 1253, 274 Cal. Rptr. 820 (1990). Most

California Supreme Court recently addressed the issue of whether EPA costs under CERCLA constituted property damage under the CGL policy. In *AIU Insurance Co. v. Superior Court,*[59] the California Supreme Court held that property damage, within the meaning of the CGL policy, embraced damages paid as reimbursement to the government for costs incurred by the government in cleaning up contaminated property, notwithstanding the lack of any ownership or proprietary interest held by the government in the property itself.[60]

Although the *AIU* decision may at first appear to be a significant victory for, among others, environmental cleanup contractors seeking to establish a firm basis for insurance under CGL policies, the decision's practical effect may be limited. In issuing its ruling, the court did not consider the effect of any policy exclusions as a potential bar to coverage.[61] Because most CGL policies either exclude all pollution other than that which is sudden and accidental, or absolutely exclude all pollution, the issue of whether or not the damages arising from pollution constitute property damage may not be very significant. In fact, the breadth of the current absolute pollution exclusions contained in most CGL policies render nearly moot the issue of pollution as property damage.

The issue of coverage under the CGL policy may also arise in connection with an owner's claim that the contractor failed to clean up the property in a manner consistent with the contractual obligations. In such a case, the issue of whether the loss constitutes property damage may be more significant. Because the claim brought by the owner is not likely to be based on an introduction of pollution into the environment by the contractor, but rather on the failure by the contractor to remove or clean up existing contamination, no property damage has occurred. The owner is only damaged to the extent that a second contractor may have to be hired to complete the work that the first contractor failed to complete. The claim, therefore, is in the nature of a contract claim, which is also specifically excluded under the CGL policy in most cases.[62]

Alternative Types of Coverage

At the time the contract is drafted, therefore, both the owner and the contractor must understand that although CGL coverage is valuable, and may well be a requirement in the environmental cleanup contract, it nonetheless may not provide coverage in connection with either the discharge of contamination or the performance of the contractor in cleaning up the contamination. As such, the owner and the contractor should, at the contract formation stage, consider

recently, however, CGL policies have been written to include an exhaustive absolute pollution exclusion which excludes all discharge of pollutants, sudden or otherwise.

[59] 51 Cal. 3d 807, 799 P.2d 1253, 274 Cal. Rptr. 820 (1990).

[60] 274 Cal. Rptr. at 825–26.

[61] Environmental Issues at 7-15.

[62] Giddings v. Industrial Indem. Co., 112 Cal. App. 3d 213, 169 Cal. Rptr. 278 (1980).

other kinds of insurance more specifically tailored to environmental issues. The parties may even wish to impose contractual requirements for the maintenance of this alternative type of insurance. In considering these possibilities, however, the contractor and owner must understand both the limitations of these policies and the effect that required maintenance of the policies may have on the final cost of the contract.

Pollution liability insurance exists as a significant alternative source of insurance for the environmental contractor. Often called Environmental Impairment Liability Insurance (EIL), these policies are also limited. First, only a few companies write EIL insurance policies.[63] Second, available policy limits have decreased for EIL policies in recent years.[64] Most importantly, the policies, as written, are of only limited utility because all EIL policies offered are claims-made in nature.[65] As such, the insured loss must be reported during the policy term. In addition, EIL policies are written for a 12-month period only, and are generally only written with respect to a particular project or piece of property.[66] Typically, claims arising from the discharge of pollutants into the environment are made long after the contamination occurs. Therefore these policies, unless maintained over a period of years, will not protect the contractor from claims made after the policy period. Many of these policies also contain specified retroactive dates for beginning of coverage. Thus, even if a loss is reported within the policy period, coverage does not exist unless the loss actually occurred after the retroactive date.[67]

Therefore, while an owner may want to require the contractor to maintain EIL coverage (in fact, the government entity under whose jurisdiction the cleanup is directed may impose such a requirement), said owner must realize that these policies may provide only limited coverage because of their claims-made nature as well as their short duration. Owners desiring extended coverage, or demanding extended coverage from the contractor, should be aware of the substantial cost of renewing the policy for a number of years. At the contract writing stage, one cannot determine with certainty when possible future discharge of pollutants may occur.

The EIL policies may also provide only limited coverage for claims brought by the owner against the contractor for failure to complete the cleanup properly. To the extent these claims are contractual in nature, wherein the owner claims that the contractor simply failed to perform its obligations under the contract, they are likely to be excluded under the EIL policy just as they are excluded under the CGL policy.

---

[63] Miller & Murphy at 297.

[64] Id.

[65] Id. at 298.

[66] Id.

[67] Environmental Issues at 7-27.

Another potential source of insurance to review prior to the execution of a cleanup contract is professional liability insurance. Generally, professional liability policies cover claims arising from the failure to use due care and the degree of skill expected of a professional in a particular field.[68] However, these policies generally at least contain an exclusion for claims arising from seepage pollution or contamination. Some commentators have noted that most professional liability policies issued recently contain endorsements excluding all coverage for claims connected in any way with hazardous waste work.[69] The general contractor's professional liability policy should therefore be reviewed prior to entering into the cleanup contract, to ascertain what, if any, coverage it may provide for the activities contemplated under the contract.

Obviously, the various types of insurance coverage available to the cleanup contractor may be of limited value with respect to claims arising from the treatment and handling of hazardous waste. Although certain of the policies may significantly protect the contractor from claims related to activities other than the actual handling of hazardous waste or potential discharge of hazardous waste, and may be required as a matter of course in an environmental cleanup contract, actual protection from liability arising from the treatment and handling of hazardous waste may be more usefully addressed by indemnity clauses or clauses limiting liability.

§ 3.20 —Indemnity

In light of the virtual absence of available insurance, environmental remediation contractors must consider risk allocations through other contract clauses. The inclusion of an indemnity clause that effectively apportions the prospective liabilities between the contracting parties may be most useful. In negotiating such a clause to be contained in the contract, the parties must first be aware of statutory limitations on the extent to which a contract can provide indemnity. A clause that is general enough to provide indemnity to the contractor for all liability, including that arising from the contractor's negligence, is not likely to be accepted by the other party to the contract, and will likely be voided by the courts if challenged. In California, for example, an indemnity clause purporting to indemnify a construction contractor for liability arising from the contractor's own negligence is void by operation of law.[70] The court will strike any such

---

[68] *Id.* at 7-34.

[69] Miller & Murphy at 301.

[70] Cal. Civ. Code § 2782 (West 1974) provides: "Except as provided . . . provisions, clauses, covenants, or agreements contained in . . . any construction contract and which purport to indemnify the promisee against liability for damages for death or bodily injury to persons, injury to property, or other loss, damage or expense arising from the sole negligent or willful misconduct of the promisee . . . are against public policy and are void and unenforceable; . . ."

clause contained in the construction contract, leaving the parties with no indemnity provisions whatsoever. An exception currently exists for the professional engineer or geologist hired to provide services with respect to hazardous materials identification, evaluation, preliminary assessment, design, or remediation services, as long as certain conditions are satisfied.[71] These conditions include the express limitation that indemnity may be provided only after the first $250,000 of liability.[72] Furthermore, the indemnity clause may not permit indemnification for the contractor's gross negligence.[73]

To arrive at an indemnity clause that provides a balance of liability between the parties and falls within the parameters of what the law permits, some commentators have suggested tying the indemnity provisions to the insurance provisions in the cleanup contract.[74] The EPA thus uses language in its contracts requiring contractors to maintain CGL and workers' compensation insurance, but provides government indemnity to the contractor for liability over $100,000 not covered by the insurance that the contractor either obtained or could have obtained at reasonable expense. The contractor is again not permitted indemnity for claims arising from the contractor's gross negligence.[75]

While this language has been used in some government contracts, in others this type of clause may be nonexistent or its application may be uncertain.[76] In

---

[71] Cal. Civ. Code § 2782.6 (West Supp. 1991) provides:

(a) Nothing contained in subdivision A of Section 2782 prevents an agreement to indemnify a professional engineer or geologist . . . from liability as described in Section 2782 in providing hazardous materials identification, evaluation, preliminary assessment, design, remediation services, or other services . . . , if the following criteria are satisfied: (1) The services in whole or in part address subterranean contamination or other concealed conditions caused by hazardous materials. (2) The promisor is responsible, or potentially responsible, for all or part of the contamination.

(b) The indemnification described in this section is valid only for damages arising from, or related to, subterranean contamination or concealed conditions, and is not applicable to the first $250,000 of liability or such greater amount as is agreed by the parties.

[72] *Id.*

[73] *Id.*

[74] Miller & Murphy at 302.

[75] *Id.* at 303.

[76] Most recently, the uncertainties of federal indemnification have been the subject of two articles in the *Engineering News-Record. See* Ichniowski & Bradford, *DOD Cleanup Liability Fears Raised,* Engineering News-Rec., May 6, 1991, at 7; *see also* Rubin, *News,* Engineering News-Rec., June 17, 1991, at 9; *Contractors Urge Restrictions on Liability, Tell Armed Services Panel Pool Could Dry Up,* Envtl. Rep., May 3, 1991, at 15, wherein the authors discuss the indemnity provisions provided in § 119 of CERCLA and their limited application. According to Thomas Dabrowski, president of Chem-Nuclear Remediation Inc., § 119 is interpreted to be applicable to Superfund sites only, thereby excluding other governmental projects, including Department of Defense Facilities.

dealing with the government, therefore, it is important for the contractor to recognize the potential for these limitations prior to entering into the contract.[77]

With certain alterations, this language might, however, be well-suited for contracts between the cleanup contractor and the private property owner. For instance, while the EPA contractual language, if used in a nongovernment contract, would provide the owner with certain protections by requiring the contractor to obtain insurance coverage and bear all liability up to a certain dollar limit, the owner may seek to further limit its indemnity obligations by demanding certain other protections.

For example, the owner might seek indemnification from claims arising from the contractor's failure to clean up the property as a result of the contractor's own conduct, whether mere negligence or gross negligence. Such terms may be used consistently and in conjunction with the above language by altering the language as follows:

> In the event a claim is brought against either the owner or the contractor, which claim arises out of the negligence of the contractor in performing its obligations hereunder, it shall be the obligation of the contractor to defend all such claims, and where brought against the owner, to defend and indemnify the owner from all liabilities arising out of such claims.

The contractor, however, should be concerned at the outset with specifically identifying its obligations with respect to the remediation. As discussed earlier, issues such as the level of remediation, existence of contamination on other properties, contamination to be remediated, and method of remediation should be addressed in the contract separately. In addition, however, these issues should be taken into account with respect to the indemnity clause contained in the contract. The contractor will likely want to tailor the indemnity language to limit its obligations to claims arising from the work it performed under the contract. In this case, language such as the following may be included:

> Contractor shall have no obligations either to defend or indemnify the owner from claims arising in any manner whatsoever from the existence of hazardous materials other than those previously identified by the parties hereto. In addition, the contractor shall not be obligated either to defend or indemnify owner for claims arising from the presence of contamination below the standard agreed upon herein.

Such clauses serve to limit the contractor's obligations to cleanup of only the contaminants described in the contract and attainment of only the remediation

---

[77] *See* 31 U.S.C.A. § 1341 (West 1983). *See also* Miller & Murphy at 297. Authors note that the Federal Anti-Deficiency Act, 31 U.S.C. § 1341, prohibits federal indemnification agreements unless a reserve of funds is established. According to a ruling by the General Accounting Office, the Anti-Deficiency Act applies to prevent the Environmental Protection Agency from indemnifying contractors under CERCLA for liabilities arising in connection with cleanup activity unless such a reserve fund is established.

level agreed upon. This line of thought is also reflected in certain suggested clauses concerning the owner's warranties. See § **3.3**.

The absence of effective insurance coverage heightens the importance of alternative clauses in the contract. Indemnity clauses, if appropriately tailored to address the specific scope of the contract, can provide an effective means of balancing the prospective liabilities of the parties.

§ 3.21   —Limitation of Liability

Another means of allocating prospective liability is through clauses limiting the liability of the contractor. Our review of a number of standard contract terms and conditions used by environmental contractors suggests that these clauses are in no way new to the environmental industry. However, the limitations on liability vary greatly. Clauses reviewed in connection with this book contained limitations ranging from $50,000 to $1,000,000.

The reasons for these variations are not clear. The liability limits in these cases may have been functions of the contractor's insurance policy limits. However, while in other areas of the construction industry use of policy limits in connection with clauses limiting contractor liability may be reasonable, such policy limits may be virtually meaningless in attempting to limit the liability of the environmental contractor. As discussed in § **3.19**, many uncertainties exist with respect to the application of insurance coverage for losses that are in any way connected with hazardous materials. See § **3.19**. An environmental contractor may have $1,000,000 each of CGL coverage and EIL coverage but still not ultimately have insurance coverage for any claim brought by the owner under a remediation contract for an alleged failure of the contractor to perform as obligated. Therefore, a limitation on liability clause that fixes liability at the limits of the contractor's insurance policy may not provide the contractor with the protection it expects against prospective liability.

If insurance coverage limits do not provide an adequate base on which to establish a limitation on liability clause, how should the liability limitation be established? An alternative recently upheld by the California courts in a construction contract is a clause limiting the liability of a contractor to the contract fee paid to the contractor. Thus, in *Markborough California, Inc. v. Superior Court,*[78] the court upheld a provision in a contract between a developer and a design engineer that limited the liability of the design engineer to $50,000 or the contract fee paid to the design engineer, whichever was higher. After the developer spent over $5,000,000 to remedy a defect in construction, the developer sued the design engineer to recover these monies.[79] As a result of the

---

[78] 227 Cal. App. 3d 705, 277 Cal. Rptr. 919 (1991).

[79] *Id.* at 921.

limitation on liability clause, however, the design engineer's liability was fixed at $67,640—the fee paid to the engineer under the contract.[80]

The *Markborough* case illustrates both the importance and effectiveness of a clause limiting liability in the contract. Although the clause discussed in *Markborough* arose in connection with a construction contract, its application is no less relevant to contracts used in the environmental remediation field. In fact, given the uncertainties about the prospective liability of the environmental contractor in all phases of the cleanup, from site assessment to ultimate remediation, clauses such as that discussed in *Markborough* may be a most valuable tool for the contractor seeking to limit liability.

The *Markborough* case demonstrates the importance of other issues with respect to drafting and negotiating clauses limiting liability. In *Markborough*, the clause ultimately upheld was challenged as being void under certain California state statutes.[81] Specifically, the developer contended that the California Civil Code required a clause to be negotiated and expressly agreed to by the parties for it to become effective.[82] According to the developer, the clause was void under the statute because it was not specifically negotiated. The court disagreed, ruling that as long as parties had the *opportunity* to negotiate the provision, it was effective. Of particular note to the court was a cover letter submitted to the developer with the proposed contract, giving the developer the opportunity to request changes in any provision of the contract.[83]

Depending on where the contract is executed, therefore, limitations may exist on the inclusion of a limitation of liability clause in the contract. The *Markborough* case suggests that in California, if the clause had been added on a take-it-or-leave-it basis, it might not have been valid. Other jurisdictions may similarly limit the effectiveness of clauses limiting liability. At the contract formation stage, the parties must respect the particular contracting limitations imposed on them by law.

Another means of limiting liability under the contract, similar to that discussed in connection with indemnity clauses (see § **3.20**), is to expressly address the scope of work to be performed as well as the standard of remediation to be used. See § **3.2**. While these concerns should also be addressed as separate terms in the contract, their inclusion in the limitation of liability clause is

---

[80] *Id.*

[81] *Id.* at 922.

[82] Cal. Civ. Code § 2782.5 (West 1974) provides:

Nothing contained in Section 2782 shall prevent a party to a construction contract and the owner or other party for whose account the construction contract is being performed from negotiating and expressly agreeing with respect to the allocation, release, liquidation, exclusion, or limitation as between the parties of any liability (a) for design defects, or (b) of the promisee to the promisor arising out of or relating to the construction contract.

[83] Markborough Cal., Inc. v. Superior Court, 227 Cal. App. 3d 705, 277 Cal. Rptr. 919, 926 (1991).

also prudent. In any case, an effective limitation of liability clause should include limitations both with respect to the dollar amount of prospective damages and to the subject matter of any future claim.

§ 3.22   —Lender Concerns in Risk Allocation

Issues of risk allocation are the most important issues negotiated between lenders and borrowers. These issues are usually addressed in the loan agreement between the borrower and lender, as well as through a separate indemnity agreement whereby the borrower indemnifies the lender for all costs, claims of remediation, or cleanup of any kind whatsoever.[84] The indemnity provisions may also be contained in the loan agreement.

In financing a remediation or cleanup, the lender may require the borrower to hold title in a subsidiary, and would not want to take a security interest in the property until after the cleanup. In this case, the lender may want access to information such as the periodic cleanup reports, to ensure that the cleanup has been properly completed. The lender should charge a higher interest rate to compensate for the risk.

In remediation contracts, contractors typically require the owner to indemnify and hold harmless the contractor. The lender would probably limit the amount that the borrower was liable to indemnify, as any contingent liability of the borrower would result in a decreasing ability of the borrower to repay the loan.

The contractor should contractually agree to use due care in performance of the services, and be able to provide $1,000,000 of professional errors and omissions insurance. In accordance with the owner concerns, the contractor, whether conducting remediation or investigative work, should also have acceptable coverage limits for workers' compensation and occupational disease, CGL coverage, and automobile liability insurance for bodily injury, death, or loss of or damage to property of third persons in an acceptable minimum amount per occurrence.[85]

Another issue is whether the lender should be named as an additional insured under the terms of the policy, whether it be general liability or specific insurance for environmental liability. In a strictly commercial loan setting, a lender is usually named as loss payee under the borrower's business insurance. This issue should be addressed as part of a lender's environmental risk management program; however, because of the uncertain nature of lender environmental liability law, a lender would not be an additional insured in an investigative

---

[84] The issue of whether these indemnities are secured or unsecured depends on the state. For example, in California the anti-deficiency statute may prohibit the recovery of the cleanup costs if secured by real property already foreclosed upon by lender.

[85] Moskowitz, app. Form C.

procedure, but should consider such coverage in a remediation situation with foreclosure imminent.

It is crucial to examine these risk allocation issues fully, and reflect them in the pricing of the credit. Fewer lenders will finance the smaller transactions as lenders seek to avoid risk of liability.[86]

§ 3.23 Unforeseen Circumstances, Hidden Conditions, and Differing Site Conditions

Unforeseen circumstances, or as they are often called, hidden conditions or differing site conditions, have formed the basis of construction disputes for years. Invariably, these disputes involve issues such as:

1. Superior knowledge (when, for example, the owner had reason to believe at the time that the contractor was mistaken as to the condition of the project site)

2. Contractor's superior skills and presumed ability to determine what site conditions were extant

3. Liability assumed and imposed by the contract terms, particularly in relation to the owner's representations

4. Standard of performance in the industry in that area

5. Actual and constructive knowledge of owner and contractor.

Presence of Unexpected Contaminants

In the typical environmental remediation context, these problems arise from the discovery of the presence of unexpected contaminants. Two cases illustrating this occurrence follow. The client began excavation on a project for an automobile dealer in West Los Angeles with whom the client had contracted to construct a new showroom and office complex on the site of a former gas station. During the excavation of the site, workers encountered leaky underground storage tanks (UST), with concomitant contamination from petroleum hydrocarbons that had seeped from the tanks. Because the contractor had received prior assurances from the owner that this particular problem had been disposed of, the contractor ceased work pending resolution of the issues concerning cost of cleanup and responsibility for the attendant delay. The dispute was concluded when the parties negotiated and agreed on a late start date and an assignment to the contractor of a portion of the proceeds from litigation, which the auto dealer had commenced against the oil company that had formerly utilized the site.

---

[86] O'Brien, *Thrift Briefs,* 55 Thrift News 3, at 102 (July 1990).

The second case resulted in an arbitration involving a similar yet much more complicated and potentially hazardous situation.[87] Although nominally discussed and analyzed as a right-to-stop-work case,[88] it is instructive from the environmental contracting standpoint as a highly unusual unforeseen circumstance that can arise. While excavating a project, the contractor encountered asbestos fibrils that were released during the excavation work. It later came to light that these fibrils came from a vein of asbestiform actinolite (asbestos in its natural rock form). Knowledgeable professionals in the area had never dealt with asbestos in this form. This was apparently the first construction project that had ever encountered such material. Neither the prebid soil and pouring information nor any of the contract documents contained any warning. There were no EPA or Occupational Safety and Health Administration (OSHA) regulations governing the removal of asbestos rock and neither the county nor the state had any prior dealings with this phenomenon. Moreover, it was not known whether existing approved asbestos abatement procedures covering asbestos removal in a closed area would be effective in coping with natural asbestos in the open air environment of the construction site. The problem was further compounded by the client's CGL policy excluding coverage for any damage arising from asbestos.

Paragraph 10 of the 1987 version of AIA Document A201 clearly states that the contractor cannot be forced to proceed when either asbestos or polychlorinated biphenyls (PCBs) are encountered on the jobsite (curiously, no such prohibition exists for other hazardous materials).[89] However, the contractor had contracted under the 1976 version, which contained no such clause. Notwithstanding this disparity, testimony revealed that, even prior to the enactment of the 1987 clauses, it was the practice of owners to deal directly with their own asbestos consultants to assume responsibility for removal of unanticipated asbestos.

Nature of Contaminant

A differing site condition claim may also arise where the nature of the contaminant is different from what was expected, as in the following illustration. A VES was employed to cleanse soil contaminated by petroleum hydrocarbons. During the initial phase of the remediation process, the decontamination curve was steady and upward. At some point, the curve flattened out and became asymptotic. Subsequent investigation revealed that the soil contained particulate matter composed primarily of asphaltenes that had been created when

---

[87] *See* McCarthy Fairoaks Phase II, American Arbitration Association Case No. 1611000349875, *in* Wiley Construction Law Update 381 (S. Goldblatt ed., John Wiley & Sons 1991).

[88] Schor & Walters, *The Right to Stop Work, in* Wiley Construction Law Update 381 (S. Goldblatt ed., John Wiley & Sons 1991).

[89] AIA Doc. A201, General Conditions of the Contract for Construction, para. 10.1.3 (1987).

the previous owner broke up a frontage road on the property. This material was not appropriate for VES treatment.

Absence of Contaminant

Finally, an unforeseen circumstance claim may arise from the absence of a contaminant that was presumed present. This case involves the cleanup and closure of a surface impoundment and percolation pond in a remote desert area. The chosen remediation process essentially involved two steps: First, fixating free metals, and second, lowering the pH of the material. The fixation process was to be silicate-based and was aimed at free copper and zinc. Based on the owner's prior site survey, the technicians had determined that there were sufficient sulfides present in the percolation pond to accomplish the task. Unfortunately, this determination proved to be wrong. The addition of supplemental sulfide evidently created hydrogen sulfide gas, necessitating the implementation of costly job safety programs. A dispute over the cost of these efforts was further complicated when it became clear that the contractor's assumption regarding the extent of sulfides present in the pond had not been documented in the contract. If the contract had been written to clearly reflect the contractor's reliance on this assumption in formulating a plan, the entire matter could have been easily resolved.

Dealing with Unforeseen Conditions

How are contracting parties to deal with disputes over these unforeseen complications? In some contexts, various statutes and rules shift the burden to the contractor. For example, the California Labor Code[90] provides that a contractor must make a good faith effort to determine if asbestos is present, when undertaking any work that could release such asbestos fibers into the air. While the statute is nominally designed to protect laborers, one can infer that failure to make such inspection could be used as a basis for denying a contractor an extension of time for an unanticipated asbestos-related delay.

Similarly, the federal government has proposed an amendment to the Federal Acquisition Regulation (FAR), including a new contract provision providing that bidders are "expected to inspect the site where the work will be performed and to satisfy themselves regarding all general and local conditions that may affect the cost of contract performance."[91]

In the absence of a statute or a contract provision, the contractor, under common law doctrine, assumes the risk and bears the costs associated with effects resulting from unforeseen conditions. Historically, contractors attempted to

---

[90] Cal. Labor Code § 6501.9 (West 1989).

[91] 56 Fed. Reg. 3954 (1991).

avoid or mitigate this risk by including a contingency fee in their contracts. This practice unfortunately resulted in contractors collecting the fee even when such unforeseen conditions were not encountered.

In an effort to lower bids and eliminate certain risk to the contractor, the concept of a changed conditions clause was implemented in federal construction contracts. These clauses have evolved into certain standard forms best represented by the FAR Standard Form 23A, which requires such a clause in all fixed-price federal construction contracts exceeding $25,000; by subparagraph 4.3.6 of the 1987 edition of AIA Document A201; and by subparts 7.1.4 and 7.2.1 of Associated General Contractors (AGC) Document 415. All of these clauses adopt the same basic concepts of the FAR Standard Form 23A. They require that notice be given before the differing conditions is disturbed, and further provide for recovery where the physical conditions encountered differ materially from what is indicated in the contract documents. Each clause would allow for recovery where the situation is unusual and differs materially from generally recognized conditions. This materiality standard is crucial to a hidden conditions claim. For example, the FAR recognizes a distinction between Type I claims (for conditions that "differ materially" from those indicated in their contract) and Type II (unknown physical conditions at the site, of an unusual nature which differ materially from those ordinarily encountered and generally recognized as inherent in work of the character provided for in the contract).[92] The standard DSC clause of the Federal Acquisition Regulation (FAR), Part 52, Differing Site Conditions (April 1984), which appears in FAR Standard Form 23A, states:

(a) The Contractor shall promptly, and before the conditions are disturbed, give a written notice to the Contracting Officer of (1) subsurface or latent physical conditions at the site which differ materially from those indicated in this contract [commonly referred to as a Type 1 DSC], or (2) unknown physical conditions at the site, of an unusual nature, which differ materially from those ordinarily encountered and generally recognized as inhering in work of the character provided for in the contract [commonly referred to as a Type II DSC].

(b) The Contracting Officer shall investigate the site conditions promptly after receiving the notice. If the conditions do materially so differ and cause an increase or decrease in the Contractor's cost of, or the time required for, performing any part of the work under this contract, whether or not changed as a result of the conditions, an equitable adjustment shall be made under this clause and the contract modified in writing accordingly.

(c) No request by the Contractor for an equitable adjustment to the contract under this clause shall be allowed, unless the Contractor has given the written notice required; provided, that the time prescribed in (a) above for giving written notice may be extended by the Contracting Officer.

---

[92] Federal Acquisition Regulation, 48 C.F.R. § 52.236-2 (1985).

(d) No request by the Contractor for an equitable adjustment to the contract for differing site conditions shall be allowed if made after final payment under this contract.

Commentators have noted that courts often grant relief under the Type II claim, and have surmised that a similarly expansive definition will be given to claims under AIA Document A201 subparagraph 4.3.6.[93] In any case, it seems clear that the presence of language such as that given above, in an environmental remediation contract, would give the contractor wide leeway to assert claims for such conditions.

Notwithstanding the presence of one of these clauses, recovery by the contractor will be dependent upon several factors, including:

1. The quality and quantity of the owner's representations and the degree to which represented conditions differ from the conditions actually encountered

2. The extent to which these unexpected conditions could have been anticipated

3. The actual and constructive knowledge of the owner and the contractor

4. The extent of the difference between reasonably expected conditions and those actually encountered.[94]

Application of these principles to the situations described earlier in this section would clearly call for contractor relief both in the case where USTs were encountered (because of the owner's assertion that there were no USTs) and where unanticipated natural asbestos was unearthed. Relief might not be as readily available when the contractor assumed the existence of a high level of sulfides but failed to specify her reliance on the owner's report in the contract.

§ 3.24   Change Orders

Construction commentators almost universally agree that a changes clause is an essential element of any commercial construction contract.[95] If this is true in the construction field generally, it is most assuredly so in the environmental remediation field. Remediation contractors constantly face new, different, and unexpected sources of contaminants. The contractors deal with fluctuating regulatory and governmental standards and constantly evolving effective

---

[93] T. Sweet, Sweet on Construction Industry Contracts 88 (John Wiley & Sons Supp. 1991) [hereinafter Sweet].

[94] For a thorough discussion of these issues, *see* Lane, *Differing Site Conditions: Part One— Contractual Remedies KC-News*, 8 Kellogg Corp. Newsl. 2, at 1 (June 1991).

[95] Sweet at 215.

technology. The effects of weather, topography, hydrology, seismic instability, the vicissitudes of chemical reaction, and the laws of physics on any remediation project can be dramatic.

Owners have traditionally viewed changes clauses as anathema, seeing such clauses primarily as a means to increase the price of the contract. However, the owner should recognize that the ability to direct changes in the work, with or without contractor acquiescence as to the impact on time and cost, is mandatory. The 1987 revisions to AIA Document A201 clearly reflect that opinion in the changes instituted by paragraph 7.3, which authorize the owner to direct changes in the work even without an agreement by the contractor as to the impact on cost and time. The AGC Standard Form of Prime Contract between owner and contractor contains similar provisions.[96] This change reflects the concept that in certain circumstances, the owner's need to get the work done must be given precedence over the contractor's need to insure a quantification of the impact on time and cost. I am not, however, urging that an environmental contract contain provisions similar to AIA Document A201, with its minute distinctions between changes, change orders, construction change directives, and minor changes in the work. Indeed, such distinctions are not feasible in the typical context of remediation contracting because the position of architect, which is so inextricably involved in the AIA Article 7 change process, is often nonexistent in the environmental contracting field. Even if a designer is present, it is often as part of the contracting team. Nonetheless, it is essential that some sort of change provision be incorporated into the remediation contract.

In this connection, owners should recognize that the changes clause serves functions beyond the authorization of design changes. The clause is also a mechanism to keep track of the accounts on the project, and operates in a book-keeping function to let the parties know what is due and what is owed on the project as it evolves.[97]

By providing a vehicle for addressing these issues, the change order also serves another valuable function; it prevents the parties from being expedient. The clause forces them to address the types of problems that should necessitate a change, as such problems arise. Even if there is no agreement as to time and money, the mere act of quantifying and contemporaneously documenting the claim prevents the revision that occurs when such claims are postponed until after completion of the contract.

The change system also provides a hierarchy to describe who can invoke changes, under what circumstances, how they are priced, and what happens if there is no agreement on price or time. All of these aspects of the change provision, if invoked properly and in a timely manner, facilitate the progress of the work by providing a harmonious and easily understood vehicle by which the

---

[96] *See* AGCC Form No. 1, Standard Form Prime Contract Between Owner and Contractor, para. 15.4, at 8 (1988).

[97] Sweet at 215.

course of the remediation project can be altered, redirected, expanded, contracted, or adjusted to.

In the environmental field, an additional hierarchy of local, state, and federal authorities may be involved. For example, the EPA model consent decree, Article VII, provides that any additional response actions must be reviewed by state authorities and then approved by the EPA. Thus, an additional tier of approval is mandated. Similarly, in the non-Superfund context, proposed changes in closure plans and the like are most likely subject to state and local scrutiny, just as though they were part of an original submission.

Whether the remediation contract borrows change order language from the FAR,[98] the AIA, the AGC, or is specially created, it must provide for prompt notice in order to qualify as a legitimate change. Furthermore, if the change relates to an unexpected situation as discussed in § 3.23, the clause should provide that the nonconforming condition remain undisturbed until the owner has an opportunity to investigate it. The contractor should document the condition to the furthest extent possible, with photos and videotape where appropriate.

§ 3.25 Delays

Delays in environmental remediation contracts can arise from many of the same factors encountered in standard commercial construction. These factors include:

1. Added work
2. Acts of God and force majeure
3. Unanticipated soil conditions
4. Acts of the State (in the remediation context, often via changed compliance standards)
5. Strikes or other labor disputes
6. Transportation difficulties
7. Unforeseeable weather conditions.

Delays may also occur because of the newness of the environmental contracting field. Technological failures, unanticipated chemical reactions, contamination from other sources (for example, an extended plume from contiguous properties) and other environmentally specific problems may create delays.

Generally speaking, in the absence of a contractual provision, the contractor is liable for delays or failure to perform. For that reason, most contracts contain some provision for relief. The delays are usually categorized based on whether they are excusable or inexcusable, compensable or noncompensable, supervening (or critical) or concurrent.

---

[98] 48 C.F.R. pts. 52.243-1 to 52.243-7.

Typically, excusable delays include unusual weather, acts of God, labor disputes, and acts beyond the contractor's control.

Inexcusable delays are, simply, all others. Whether the delay is excusable or inexcusable, it will not be compensable to the contractor unless the delay is unusual in nature and involves more or less egregious owner performance.

Even when the delay is both excusable and compensable, damages may be denied to the contractor, or substantially reduced, if they are concurrent with some delay caused by the contractor. In such cases, the finder of fact may allocate liability for the delays between the parties and apportion the damages, if there is a reasonable basis for doing so. Moreover, even such delays that are concurrent may be denied their concurrent status if, for example, they are delays on the float (the period between early and late start dates), as opposed to delays on the critical path.[99]

Finally, some owners will insist on the insertion of a no damages for delay clause. In California, such clauses are not valid on public works[100] but are upheld in the private context. The federal contract form does not contain such a clause, but they appear in many other state forms.[101] Even then, the court may find exception to the applicability of the no damages for delay clause. Among the exceptions are delays clearly beyond the contemplation of the parties, those caused by the owner's active interference with the progress of the work, unreasonable delays, and bad faith or fraud (usually where the owner has induced the contractor to enter into the contract with false statements). If the owner is adamant and insists on a no damages for delay clause in the contract, the contractor must be certain that the subcontracts contain identical language. In this context, I would not even rely upon the standard integration clauses (whereby the subcontractor is deemed bound to the general contractor as the general contractor is to the owner). The subcontract should clearly state that the subcontractor has no entitlement to delay the damages. The language should be identical to that contained in the general contract. That way, if one clause fails, both do. The general contractor thus avoids being in the unfortunate position in which the owner is immune to the contractor's delay claim, while at the same time the contractor is vulnerable to the delay claims of the subcontractors.

A delay claim cannot properly be analyzed without reference to some sort of benchmark. These analyses inevitably entail use of a network analysis technique, usually involving the CPM or one of its mutations, such as arrow-precedence diagramming or a bar chart. The federal government and most

---

[99] *See, e.g.,* Fishback & Moore Int'l Corp., ASBCA No. 18146, 77-1 B.C.A. (CCH) ¶ 112,300 (1977).

[100] Cal. Pub. Cont. Code § 7102 (West 1985).

[101] Ficken, *The Contract: Major Areas of Dispute, in* Hazardous Waste Disposal and Underground Construction Law 85 (R. Cushman & B. Ficken eds., John Wiley & Sons 1987).

private contracts now require the submission of schedules based on the CPM at the inception of the contract,[102] and also require frequent updates.

Many commentators espousing the owners' viewpoint have suggested that the no damages for delay clause be standard. The commentators would further provide that the contractor be narrowly restricted in obtaining even an extension of contract time, and would require that any float time be credited to the owner by deduction from any time extension.[103]

Finally, the parties must examine the facts to determine if they support a delay claim, regardless of the contract clauses and the presence or absence of a CPM. A pipe manufacturer had contracted to provide and install pipe for an underground connection between a reservoir and a dam. When the pipe delivery was delayed and then made out of sequence, the contractor withheld payment, contending that the delays in delivery had forced the pipe installation back into the rainy season, and that on many days torrential rains had floated the pipe from its foundations, requiring a reseating of the pipe with attendant delays. During arbitration on the matter, the contractor produced a field foreman who had a detailed diary describing each of the days on which the rain had affected the project. However, a check of the meteorological records for the area revealed that on many of the days described in the field diary as lost to rain, there had in fact been no rain for several days on either side of the date of entry. The field supervisor attempted to reconcile this apparent discrepancy by explaining that the meteorological service's catch basin was far removed from the site of the dam, and that there could be an abundance of rain at the project site with no measurable precipitation at the catch basin site. This testimony was substantially defused by a representative of the meteorological service, who testified that the catch basin was within three hundred yards of the project site, and that historically the project site received less precipitation than the catch basin area.

A compromise provision between the open-door policy favored by contractors and the no damages for delay approach asserted by owners is contained in the following suggested clause:

A time extension shall be the contractor's sole remedy and compensation for all such delays other than those resulting from the acts or negligence of the owner, the designer, or owner's separate contractors (collectively 'owner-caused delays'). For owner-caused delays, generally contractor shall be entitled to reimbursement for reasonable additional costs resulting from such delays but not for any additional profit or fee.[104]

---

[102] Wickwire et al., *Landmark CPM Decisions From 1980 to 1990, in* 1991 Wiley Construction Law Update, at 219–40 (S. Goldblatt ed., John Wiley & Sons 1991). This article contains an exhaustive and excellent treatment of the means and application of CPM techniques.

[103] Sweet at 343.

[104] *Id.* at 106 (Supp. 1990).

Along with the issues involved in the contractor's claim for delay, one must also consider the correlative owner's damages for delays. Typically, the damages include lost rent, extra interest, liquidated damages, and lost profit. In the remediation context, all but the liquidated damages are seemingly irrelevant because a remediation contract, unless it was tied to some commercial enterprise, would not involve any rent, interest, or lost profit. Furthermore, the liquidated damages must be tied to a reasonable standard. Therefore, determining the owner's damages for delay is more difficult in a remediation contract context.

The owner's ability to successfully assert a cause of action for recovery of damages often depends on how clear the connection is between the damages and the contractor's delay, and whether or not the contractor is made aware of the damages. In the surface impoundment and percolation pond case discussed in § 3.23, one of the damages claimed by the owner when the project was delayed was an additional permit fee required by the water quality board because of the failure to accomplish closure of the site within the period specified in the work plan. The contractor had not been told of this fee when the contract was signed, nor was the fee documented anywhere in the contract. Moreover, when the project was delayed, the owner did not notify the contractor of the possibility of this extra fee. Because the owner took no steps to mitigate the damage (such as ordering the contractor to speed the work), it is highly unlikely that the owner could have recovered for this damage.

For a successful claim, the damages from the delay must relate to the purpose of the contract. The time schedule must be clearly defined, and if the owner wishes to recover damages for any delay, it is best to specify foreseeable damages that might be caused by a delay, or to negotiate a liquidated damages clause that is reasonable in relation to the potential exposure of the owner.

§ 3.26 Licensing

It is necessary to distinguish between the permits for performance of a particular remediation or closure plan, and licensing of a particular contractor. Licensing requirements in the remediation field are a relatively new phenomenon. It was only in 1988 that New York State began requiring contractors who perform asbestos-related work to be licensed.[105] In California, similar legislation has existed since 1988, requiring any contractor who engages in removal or remedial action to have passed an approved hazardous substance removal certification examination. In addition, a contractor wishing to engage in this type of work in California usually must have an A contractor's license (general engineering) or C-12 (grading and paving) contractor's license. Certification for

---

[105] Sweet at 293 (Supp. 1990); N.Y. Labor Law § 901 (Consol. 1992).

hazardous substance removal and remedial action is available from the California State Contractors Licensing Board.[106]

The Court of Appeals for the Ninth Circuit recently held that an out-of-state contractor working on a federal project need not have a license.[107] Noting the similarity of the review given to candidates for licensure by the state contractors' license board to that of the federal government, the court found that California was effectively attempting to review the government's determination of responsibility, which was prohibited. The case is analogous to holdings on other state licensing systems.[108]

The contractor must also have permits to handle various kinds of hazardous waste (as opposed to permits necessary for the closure of a site). Involvement with UST may require an UST tester license, as well as UST installation closure, removal, and disposal permits and licensing. See **Chapter 5** for a detailed discussion of permitting requirements and procedures.

§ 3.27   Dispute Resolution Between Contracting Parties

Dispute resolution may take one of the following forms:

1. Litigation
2. Arbitration
3. Alternative dispute resolution (ADR).

There is a tendency in the remediation field to merely adopt the same solution for disputes as in construction projects: to provide for arbitration and leave it at that. Although dispute resolution in the environmental field may best be handled through arbitration or some form of ADR, one should not assume that these methods are a panacea for the multitude of disagreements among various factions that can arise in environmental cleanup. In some situations, arbitration may even be proscribed by statute or regulation. ADR typically involves mediation, with a mutually agreed-upon party serving as a facilitator to settlement discussions. In some cases, it may rise to the level of a non-binding mini-trial involving top executives.

Dispute resolution in this field is somewhat uncertain because of the often ambiguous relationship between the parties, the complexity of the problems, and the miasma of government regulations that affect the industry.

First, with so many different entities having an interest in the outcome of the project, one must carefully consider the definition of the term "parties."

---

[106] Cal AGC Manual at 153–55; Cal. Bus. & Prof. Code § 7058.5 (West 1992).

[107] Gartrell Constr. Inc. v. Autry, 91 D.A.R. 9006 (9th Cir. July 29, 1991) (not an officially reported case).

[108] Miller v. State of Arkansas, 352 U.S. 187 (1956).

Obviously the owner of the property is one party, as well as the contractor. However, if the remediation work will be conducted at a Superfund site, the contractor must be aware of the extent of the consent decree under which the work will be performed. In the context of Superfund, the contractor must also be acutely aware of possibly working for a number of PRPs, among whom intramural disagreements may arise as to the most efficacious manner of disposing of the contaminant. These problems are exacerbated by the need for EPA approval of the proposals.

To the extent that the remediation must comply with lender requirements, or in the event that the lender has pre-negotiated a cleanup agreement with the government prior to a foreclosure (see § **3.13**), the contractor's relationship with the lender must also be considered. If the design and construction aspects of the project are separate, the relationship of the contractor and the design team must also be considered.

Commentators have noted that "from the perspective of a consulting environmental engineer or a cleanup contractor, the Superfund program also presents novel concerns and issues that transcend prior experience."[109] That is an understatement. The remediation contractor may have exposure as a PRP under CERCLA, and may encounter numerous difficulties while trying to implement a remediation design scheme to accommodate the needs of both the PRPs and the government.[110]

The EPA model consent decree indicates the government's predisposition to negotiation or litigation. The decree states that disputes arising under the document will first be negotiated for a period not to exceed 20 days. Should the negotiations prove ineffective, the position advanced by the EPA is considered binding unless the settling defendants invoke the formal dispute resolution within 10 days after the conclusion of the negotiation period.

Disputes pertaining to the selection or adequacy of any response action, the adequacy or appropriateness of plans or procedures, and the adequacy of performance, are decided by the director of the Waste Management Division of whichever EPA region is involved. The director will issue the final administrative decision, which is binding on the settling defendants, subject only to subsequent judicial review. Any settling defendants seeking judicial review have the burden of demonstrating that the decision of the Waste Management Division director was arbitrary and capricious or otherwise not in accordance with law.[111]

---

[109] Bernstein, *Dispute Resolution Under CERCLA, in* Hazardous Waste Disposal and Underground Construction Law 245 (R. Cushman & B. Ficken eds., John Wiley & Sons 1987) [hereinafter Bernstein].

[110] *Id.* at 245.

[111] CEPA Model Consent Decree, ch. XX, at 50. *See also* Cohen, *Allocation of Superfund Cleanup Costs Among Potentially Responsible Parties: The Role of Binding Arbitration,* 18 Envtl. L. Rep. 10,158 (May 1988).

The binding administrative dispute resolution procedures established by Chapter XX will govern all remediation disputes once the consent decree is signed. This includes disputes among PRPs (settling defendants) and contractors regarding remediation techniques and adequacy of performance. Chapter III of the consent decree binds all settling defendants, as well as parties in privity with these defendants, to all terms of the decree, including Chapter XX dispute resolution. Chapter III achieves this broad jurisdiction by requiring all settling defendants to inform any entity involved with the cleanup of the terms of the consent decree. This requirement will complicate the contractor's job by channeling all remediation disputes through the EPA. The EPA may, however, be justified in requiring jurisdiction over the contractor, because the contractors have the right to claim Superfund money for unpaid work.[112]

Private Remediations

In private remediation not involving such issues or relationships to underlying federal agencies, dispute resolution can be dealt with in the context of the contract. In preparing an arbitration agreement for such a contract, the parties must first consider under whose auspices the arbitration will commence. Probably the most familiar and organized body for arbitration is the American Arbitration Association (AAA). Much has been written regarding the benefits of arbitration in terms of costs and time saving, availability of knowledgeable and expert arbitrators, final and prompt resolution, avoidance of punitive damages, and the privacy of the outcome.[113]

The parties also should consider whether or not they wish to have some sort of discovery provisions contained in their arbitration clause. Neither AIA Document A201 nor the AAA provide for such discovery.[114] Various state statutes do provide for the incorporation of liberal or limited discovery.[115]

The availability of pass-through clauses is another consideration in favor of arbitration as the method of dispute resolution. These clauses are typically used in construction contracts to provide for a consolidated arbitration among the owner, contractor, and subcontractors. The pass-through clause is normally handled as a contract clause whereby the subcontractor is deemed bound to the general contractor as the general contractor is bound to the owner, with the owner/general contractor agreement containing an arbitration clause. Before one assumes that such consolidation is easily available, one must consider case law

---

[112] Bernstein at 249 n.19.

[113] For an exhaustive treatment of these issues, *see* Wulfsberg & Lempres, *Advantage of Arbitrating Construction Disputes, in* Alternative Dispute Resolution in the Construction Industry 1 (Cushman et al. eds., John Wiley & Sons 1991).

[114] J. Murase & L. Marcowicz, Arbitration Advocacy for Attorneys 5 (Am. Arb. Ass'n, Mar. 1990) (a short document outlining AAA procedures).

[115] *See, e.g.,* Cal. Civ. Proc. Code § 1281.1 (West 1981).

holding that a party cannot be forced to arbitrate if the party does not have a representative on the panel.[116] In addition, the standard construction industry arbitration under AIA documents has historically precluded consolidation of the architect into any arbitration between the owner and the general contractor. This practice is probably more reflective of the AIA's desire to protect the architect than of an attempt to find a fair position on the issue.

Because of the construction industry's familiarity with and frequent resort to arbitration, the overlap between commonly-encountered environmental remediation contracting issues and typical construction issues, and the availability of an experienced panel of arbitrators, one would assume that arbitration would be the favored method of resolving disputes arising under a remediation contract.

Curiously, however, in recent disputes involving four different remediation contractors, no mention of arbitration provisions was made in the document. Accordingly, these highly technical, complex disputes were relegated to the mercy of the local court system.

When incorporating an arbitration provision into a contract, the parties should take steps to ensure that they do not end up with a situation not to their liking. Paragraph 4.3 of AIA Document A201 governing claims and disputes contains a highly technical, complicated, and time-driven set of guidelines on claims. The result of these provisions is that an arbitration may well be commenced during the life of the contract, thereby putting the parties in an adversarial position even before the project is completed. Experience with these 1987 revisions in construction disputes indicates that the revisions can create a situation that makes progress on the project difficult and often incompatible with simultaneous dispute resolution. An ongoing acrimonious arbitration during the life of a complex, highly technical, and constantly changing environmental remediation project would probably be even more destructive to the project.

Typical Contract Article

One particularly effective method of arbitration, which serves as an incentive to good-faith negotiation and settlement, is a procedure in which the costs of any litigation following final settlement offers are avoided by the prevailing party only if the award falls outside the scope of the final offers. The following contract article, drafted by Richard Burnham of the Perini Corporation and included here with permission, incorporates such a procedure.

DISPUTES

1. All disputes that arise between Owner and Contractor that cannot be settled through negotiation shall be resolved in the following manner:

---

[116] Tate v. Saratoga Sav. & Loan Ass'n, 216 Cal. App. 3d 843, 265 Cal. Rptr. 440 (1990).

First, through participation in a non-binding mini-trial, as more fully described in Section 2 below, and, if such mini-trial is unsuccessful in resolving the dispute; then

Second, by the mandatory, simultaneous exchange of written Final Offers followed by a final pre-litigation meeting of Principals, as more fully set forth in Section 3, below, and if such Final Offers and pre-litigation meeting are unsuccessful in resolving the dispute; then

Third, by litigation in any Court of competent jurisdiction, but pursuant to the stipulation that all legal costs, fees and expenses incurred by the Prevailing Party after the date of the Final Offer referred to above shall be borne by the losing party, as more fully set forth in Section 4, below.

2. Within thirty (30) days of a written demand by either Owner or Contractor, a mini-trial will be held at an agreed-upon site near the Project. While non-binding, the purpose of this mini-trial will be to inform the senior management of Owner and Contractor (referred to in this Article as Principals and more fully described in Section 5, below) of the positions of each of the parties and to require each party to present its "best case" regarding entitlement and quantum. In addition, a neutral advisor, agreed to in advance by the parties, may attend the mini-trial, not as an active participant, but solely for the purpose of commenting privately to the Principals regarding the relative strengths and weaknesses of each party's position. Failure to agree upon a neutral advisor shall not delay commencement of the mini-trial. Presentations at the mini-trial will be informal; rules of evidence will not apply. Lawyers may or may not participate, at each party's option. Principals may question witnesses. Unless otherwise agreed by the Principals, the mini-trial proceedings shall take no longer than two (2) days, held consecutively. At the conclusion of the proceedings the Principals shall meet and attempt to resolve the dispute. Each Principal may meet separately with the neutral advisor or the Principals may invite the neutral advisor to confer with them jointly. If the Principals cannot resolve the dispute within seven (7) days following conclusion of the proceedings, the mini-trial process shall be deemed terminated. No transcript or recording shall be made of the mini-trial proceedings, and all statements, materials and presentations in connection therewith shall be treated as confidential and inadmissible as evidence, even for purposes of impeachment, in any pending or future court action directly or indirectly involving these parties or this dispute, provided, however, that evidence which would otherwise be admissible in such court action shall not be rendered inadmissible as a result of its use at the mini-trial. The neutral advisor, if any, shall be disqualified as a witness, consultant or expert for either party in this or any other dispute arising out of or relating to this Agreement.

3. Within thirty (30) days of a written demand for a Final Offer by either Owner or Contractor, Owner and Contractor shall each present to an escrow agent a written Final Offer. Promptly after receipt of both Final Offers the escrow agent shall simultaneously deliver a copy of Owner's final Offer to Contractor and a copy of Contractor's Final Offer to Owner (the escrow agent will retain the original of each final offer), at which time the Principals will meet in an attempt to resolve the dispute. Unless the Principals agree otherwise, if the written Final Offers and all negotiations relating to them shall be treated as confidential, and except as

provided below, shall be inadmissible as evidence, even for the purpose of impeachment, in any pending or future court action directly or indirectly involving these parties or this dispute, provided, however, that evidence which would otherwise be admissible in such court action shall not be rendered inadmissible as a result of its use during negotiations.

4. At any time after termination of the Final Offer procedure, Owner or Contractor may commence an action in any Court of competent jurisdiction within the State where the Project is located, provided that it shall be, and hereby is, stipulated in such action that all reasonable legal costs, fees and expenses of the Prevailing Party relating to such action which are incurred after the termination of the Final Offer procedure shall be borne by the other party. It is further stipulated that if the Court awards an amount (exclusive of interest) which falls between the two Final Offers neither party will be considered, for purposes of this Article, the Prevailing Party, however, if:

(a) The amount of the award (exclusive of interest) is greater than the higher of the Final Offers, then the party making such higher Final Offer shall be the Prevailing Party; and

(b) The amount of the award is lower (exclusive of interest) than the lower of the Final Offers, then the party making such lower Final Offer shall be the Prevailing Party. If either party fails or refuses to make a Final Offer as set forth in Section 3, above, the party making the Final Offer shall be the Prevailing Party regardless of the amount of the award.

5. For the purposes of this Article the term "Principal" shall have the following meanings: (a) As to Contractor, "Principal" shall mean _____ or his or her successor (or anyone of senior rank within Contractor's organization), who shall be fully vested by Contractor with the authority to resolve the dispute in question, and (b) as to Owner, "Principal" shall mean _____ or his or her successor (or anyone of senior rank within Owner's organization), who shall be fully vested by Owner with the authority to resolve the dispute in question.

§ 3.28 Payment

For the remediation contractor, two contractual issues are of significant concern in regard to payment for work: the terms for payment (predicated on time and materials (T&M), monthly budget, an allocation based upon work performed, or some other criteria) and the source of payment.

The contractor must recognize that dealing with a single entity on a small contract involving one parcel is significantly different from contracting with a group of PRPs to perform work on a Superfund site. In the former circumstance the contractor normally deals with one owner or owner's representative. In the latter circumstance, the contractor deals with a trustee or agent for the PRPs who has limited or no ability to control payment issues. While it has been suggested that a remediation contractor on a Superfund site may make a claim against the fund itself, there is no statutory or case law authority to support this theory. Perhaps the contractor's best approach in that situation is to seek recovery against one or more of the PRPs, or more practically, against the financial security posted pursuant to Chapter 14, paragraph 45, of the EPA model consent decree.

Some private remediation contracts contain ambiguous payment terms not tied to any specific standard. Such cases often involve the rather primitive T&M-based terms, which in turn are based upon estimates of the work to be performed. As noted in § 3.7, these types of contracts may be exceedingly troublesome to an owner, and lack the precision customarily found in a construction contract.

The contract is often silent as well regarding the obligation of payment for ancillary costs or items that do not appear as part of the work per se, including:

1. Cost of permits
2. Cost of extraordinary handling
3. Cost of pre-mobilization and preliminary work (including health and safety, contingency, soil watering, air monitoring, ground watering, sampling and waste characterization, and waste treatment and disposal plans)
4. Cost of waste generated by operations
5. Cost for transportation of hazardous substances.[117]

These contracts also often fail to distinguish between those costs that are strictly design-related and those that involve the actual construction. The AIA Document B141, for example, suggests that architectural services be paid on the basis of percentage of completion.[118] The remediation contractor must also consider whether payment is by a progress payment for a normal course of the work or is related to the cost of the change to the work. The contract should clearly delineate the basis for the payment, what items are included within the owner's scope of obligation to pay, and what remedies are available to the contractor in the event of a nonpayment. For further discussion, see § 3.29. Finally, the contractor should consider the availability of lien and stop-notice remedies. For appropriate contract provisions, see **Appendix D**.

§ 3.29 Suspension and Termination

Standard construction practice is the best guide to issues of suspension and termination. Subparagraph 9.7.1 of AIA Document A201 provides for the contractor's right to suspend work in the event of nonpayment. The subparagraph

---

[117] D'Annunzio & Renda, *Bidding a Hazardous Waste Project, in* Hazardous Waste Disposal and Underground Construction Law 262 (R. Cushman & B. Ficken eds., John Wiley & Sons 1987).

[118] Sweet at 133.

provides for two seven-day waiting periods. If payment is not received within seven days after the architect's certificate is issued, the contractor can give an additional seven days' notice and suspend thereafter. Subparagraph 14.1.1 provides for "the contractor's right to terminate in the event of this and the work is stopped for a period of thirty (30) days through no fault of the contractor." Subparagraph 14.1.1 also presumably gives the contractor the right to terminate in the event that the owner fails, under subparagraph 2.2.1, to provide reasonable evidence that financial arrangements have been made to fulfill the owner's obligations under the contract.

The owner is given the right to terminate for cause under paragraph 14.2 for contractor breach, such as the contractor's failure to provide sufficient personnel and materials. Under paragraph 14.3, the owner is given the right to temporarily or permanently suspend the contract for convenience. In an environmental contract, the right to suspend for convenience is even more important, given the inherent uncertainties of the remediation process.

Two such clauses from an environmental remediation contract are set forth below.

Article 16. Suspension of Work

Client may, at any time, by ten (10) day written notice suspend further performance by Contractor. If payment of invoices by Client is not maintained on a current basis, Contractor may, by ten (10) day written notice to Client, suspend further performance until such payment is restored to a current basis. Suspension for any reason exceeding thirty (30) days shall, at the option of Contractor make the applicable Change Order subject to termination or to renegotiation. All suspensions shall extend the time schedule for performance in a mutually satisfactory manner and Contractor shall be paid for services performed and charges prior to the suspension date plus suspension charges. Suspension charges shall include, without limitation, the putting of documents and analyses in order, personnel and equipment rescheduling or reassignment adjustments, additional insurance/bonding coverage, and all other related costs and charges incurred and directly attributable to suspension.

Article 17. Termination

Client may terminate this Agreement or a Change Order for convenience, at its option, by sending a written Notice of Termination to Contractor. Contractor may similarly terminate for convenience in the event of delays or suspensions exceeding thirty (30) days as provided in the foregoing articles. The Notice of Termination shall specify when and which work will be discontinued and when termination shall be effective. Termination shall be effective ten (10) days from receipt of the Notice of Termination. Client shall pay Contractor no later than ten (10) days from receipt of final invoice for services performed and charges prior to termination, plus termination charges. Termination charges shall include, without limitation, the putting of project documents and analyses in order, personnel and equipment rescheduling or reassignment adjustments, additional insurance/

bonding coverage, and all other related costs and charges incurred and directly attributable to termination.

Either party can terminate this Agreement or a Change Order for cause if the other commits a material, incurred breach of this Agreement. Termination shall be effective ten (10) days after receipt of a Notice of Termination. The Notice of Termination shall contain specific reasons for termination and both parties shall cooperate in good faith to cure the causes for termination stated in the Notice. Termination shall not be effective if the breach has been remedied before expiration of the period specified in the Notice of Termination. In the event of termination for cause, Contractor shall be paid the same as in the case of termination for convenience and the parties shall have their remedies at law as to any other rights and obligations between them, subject to the other terms and conditions of this Agreement.

Client and Contractor recognize that professional standards and ethics govern Contractor's services under this Agreement. If circumstances arise which, in Contractor's opinion, preclude it for professional or ethical reasons from continuing performance, Contractor shall advise Client of that fact. The parties shall immediately attempt to arrive at a mutually satisfactory solution. If this cannot be done to both parties' satisfaction, either may terminate. If so, Client shall compensate Contractor in accordance with this Article.

We represented the contractor who utilized these clauses in a payment dispute with the owner of a fairly large contaminated parcel in an industrial area in Los Angeles. The dispute arose over the contract price (the price was an estimate, and when the T&M costs reached that estimated amount, the owner refused to pay more). Upon nonpayment, we promptly notified the owner of the contractor's intent to suspend. When the suspension without payment lasted 30 days, we terminated. The procedure was not challenged.

§ 3.30 Proprietary Information, Patents, and Confidentiality

Environmental remediation contracting is an exciting field where new technologies evolve almost daily. Avant-garde techniques such as cryo inserts, and in-situ vitrification help produce highly satisfactory results at a much lower cost, and often in shorter time than more primitive techniques such as slurry wall containment, excavation, and transportation. Designers or contractors who have designed or implemented these technologies may wish to keep the details of their operation highly confidential because of the uniqueness of the procedures. On the other hand, the owner who is paying a contractor proposing to use such unique technology has a vested interest in maintaining quality control to insure performance, and detecting potential defects or shortcomings in the technology to protect against unsatisfactory results. Thus, there is a dynamic tension between the contractor's desire to keep the technology secret and the owner's desire to thoroughly understand the workings and reliability of the processes.

The best way for the contract to resolve this tension is to provide some procedural safeguards within the documents. First, the owner's right to view tests and demonstrations and conduct an in-depth analysis of the proposed technology should be limited. That is, only a small number of owner's representatives should be allowed access to the details of the technology. Their investigation should only go so far as needed to assure the owner that the proposed technology will achieve the desired result. Finally, both the owner and representatives should individually sign agreements not to reveal any proprietary information subsequent to their examination of that technology.

The documents should also contain a reciprocal confidentiality agreement that any of the owner's trade secrets or confidential information gleaned by the remediation contractor would remain confidential. To the extent that the remediation contractor must acquire certain confidential information, the number of contractor's personnel involved would also be limited. This requirement might be coupled with a requirement that such information be routed through the owner's attorney, as are reports from the contractor. This latter requirement would be compatible with an assertion of attorney-client privilege and enhance the owner's ability to deny third parties access to this information. Such a restriction of access is highly desirable in light of the dramatic civil and criminal exposure of owners of contaminated properties.

§ 3.31   Permitting

As discussed in § 3.9, permitting issues play an important role in the contract formation stage. The contract should specifically indicate which party should obtain specific permits necessary to complete the project. In the remediation context, it is paramount to understand prior to contract formation what types of permits will be necessary.

A remediation contractor will usually ascertain what types of permits are needed prior to preparing its investigation and bidding for an environmental remediation contract. One major difference in the remediation field, compared to a typical construction project, is that remediation work performed at a site contaminated with hazardous waste is very strictly monitored and controlled under local, state, and federal laws and regulations. Conversely, the work may be exempt from many other apparently applicable laws, permit requirements, and fees.[119]

Environmental laws and regulations may differ for a particular job depending on the hazardous material involved and the location of the site, the type of work to be performed, and the situs of the property. More importantly, the permits required for performing each of these separate tasks will also differ.[120]

---

[119] Cal. AGC Manual at 151.

[120] *Id.*

As indicated, it is critical for a contractor to determine the types of hazardous materials present at a particular site prior to bidding and drafting of the environmental remediation contract. One of the reasons for doing so is to make certain that the contractor is appropriately licensed and is capable of obtaining the necessary permits.

In most states, including California, contractors may not engage in removal or remedial work unless they have passed an approved hazardous substance removal certification and are licensed and can obtain the appropriate permits for that specific project.[121] Typically, the onus is on the contractor to obtain all applicable permits unless contractual provisions provide otherwise. The contractor should contact each government agency directly for information on which permits are necessary and how to apply for them prior to commencement of the contract. The requirements for obtaining specific types of permits will be discussed in detail in **Chapter 5**.

However, there are many remaining issues with which a contractor must be concerned at the contract formation stage, including determining who will obtain permits for handling hazardous waste, discharging pollutants to water, excavation and grading, drilling, and any other activities necessary to complete the job.

One of the most important steps at the contract formation stage is determining which clauses are critical and how to draft those clauses. For a remediation contractor, permitting issues must be examined with great specificity. See **Chapter 5**. The contractor must fully investigate the source of the contamination problem prior to contracting to perform the remediation work. Such an investigation is needed to properly understand which permits will be required.

Another permitting issue that must be addressed at the contract formation stage is determination of when compliance with permits is necessary. The contractor should provide a complete and documented list of all required permits to the owner, so that the owner can decide who will bear the burden of obtaining such permits.

A contractor must also be concerned with renewing permits previously obtained by other contractors on the project. The replacement contractor does not want the responsibility of vouching for another contractor's performance, especially in procuring permits.

§ 3.32   —Owner Concerns in Permitting

One of the most common ways for an owner to allocate the risk of potential liability is to explicitly state in the contract that the contractor must comply with all applicable federal, state, and local laws and regulations. The owner will also attempt to shift liability by requiring the contractor to agree to comply with

---

[121] Cal. Bus. & Prof. Code § 7058.7 (West 1975 & Supp. 1991).

all requirements and permits issued by government agencies. The shifting of liability notwithstanding, the owner still has a greater stake than the contractor in making certain that the appropriate permits are obtained, since the owner cannot walk away from the property if the remediation work is unsuccessful.[122] Consequently, the owner has a vested interest in selecting and working with a contractor experienced in the remediation field.

Owners and contractors are more affected than other entities by compliance regulations that require permitting and approval procedures. Such compliance regulations appear like other rules, but complicate the contractor's bidding and scheduling. These tasks often require the best available technology, additional inspections or approval prior to the job completion, and lengthy testing procedures. In addition, the permitting agencies have the power to suspend work at a project indefinitely or impose substantial monetary penalties for noncompliance.[123] Owners must be concerned not only with the imposition of liability, but also with the allocation and limitation of such risk and liability. Consequently, owners may limit liability by requiring the contractor to obtain the appropriate bonds or indemnification agreements.

It may be prudent for the owner to share some of the permitting responsibilities, because the owner may be ultimately responsible to its lender to explain the status of the project and to provide environmental reports to any governmental agency.

Normal permitting obligations and issues of regulatory compliance have usually been the domain of the contractor. However, an astute owner will be concerned with assessing liability and understanding ways to avoid such liability at the contract stage when negotiating normal contractual permitting issues.

§ 3.33 —Contractor Concerns in Permitting

The contractor should bear in mind that the environmental laws and regulations applicable to a particular job may differ depending on the nature and location of the site, the hazardous waste involved, and the work to be performed. The permits required will also differ. The current permitting and licensing system makes possible the cradle-to-grave hazardous waste tracking system that follows the waste from its generation to transportation and eventual handling by TSDFs.[124]

A contractor who has either begun remediation or is about to enter into such a contract should secure the proper licenses, determine the potential for waste problems, adjust the bid documents accordingly, and strictly define the scope of

---

[122] Smith Landon Improvement Corp. v. Celotex Corp., 851 F.2d 86 (3d Cir. 1988), *cert. denied,* 109 U.S. 837 (1989).

[123] Environmental Issues at 16-1.

[124] Environmental Issues at 19-6.

the work. These precautions should help avoid liability for handling hazardous waste. During the construction process the contractor is normally responsible for obtaining all permits required to complete the remediation. Potential contractors in the remediation field are forewarned that penalties for liability in certain remedial and removal work are enormous. Contractors must develop a protection strategy involving practical, legal, statutory, and contractual protections. One of the areas in which a contractor must continually update the working knowledge of the expanding environmental regulation requirements is in the area of permitting. Such an update must not only include a review of regulations from each governmental level but also an understanding of the vast array of agencies enforcing these rules. The increase in governmental enforcement makes monitoring of new laws and regulations more difficult. This area of the law is still evolving, and it is possible that laws, regulations, and permitting requirements may overlap. Failure to investigate the relevant governing agencies can lead to devastating results for an unwary contractor.

Moreover, if a contractor is hindered in the ability to obtain a specific permit, and such hindrance causes significant and unjustified delays to the project, the contractor may face a significant delay claim, as well as liability for breach of contractual provisions. To avoid these potential pitfalls, a contractor should have specific contract provisions stating who will be responsible for any delays caused by the failure to obtain a requisite permit.

Drafting of these specific permitting clauses poses many potential problems for the unprepared or novice contractor. A contractor should approach these issues with trepidation and fully discuss and understand the magnitude of the project before assuming the accompanying responsibility.

§ 3.34 —Lender Concerns in Permitting

As previously discussed (see § 3.22), the lender's relationship with the borrower is governed by the loan documents. The loan agreement typically contains a representation and warranty as follows: "Borrower has obtained all permits and is in compliance with their terms." Additionally, the loan agreement usually contains a positive covenant that the borrower will comply with all laws.

Once the loan has been made and a remediation or cleanup is required, the lender would require that the consultant or remediation contractor acquire all permits needed for a complete remediation. Under current law, the lender does not have specific input into this provision because of the nature of environmental lender liability.

CHAPTER 4

CONDUCT OF THE REMEDIATION*

*John E. Altstadt of KPMG Peat Marwick and Barbara G. Mikalson of Crowell & Moring
contributed to this chapter.

§ 4.1   Developing a Comprehensive
Remediation Strategy

Remediation management, like other forms of construction management, must address three criteria: project goals, time, and cost. However, the unique nature of remediation work introduces more complex management problems.

Environmental cleanups are not motivated by altruistic intentions, but by legal mandate.[1] Thus, maintaining good relationships with regulating agencies and negotiating the web of regulations are fundamental parts of remediation conduct. Furthermore, since in remediation work the focus of the owner is on meeting legal requirements rather than creating a profitable enterprise, there is a greater emphasis on strict cost minimization. Unlike commercial construction, remediation does not usually offer an owner the potential for increased income to offset increased costs. The owner cannot recover expenditures through higher rents or more efficient operations. Thus a dynamic tension exists within the enterprise between the project goals and cost containment issues.[2]

Typical commercial construction is based on well-known techniques and therefore precise projections, whereas in remediation much of the technology is new and rapidly evolving, resulting in uncertainty regarding cost and performance. Certain new technologies hit the market and are touted as the ultimate answer to an environmental problem, only to fall just as quickly, burdened by their own press releases. In-situ vitrification[3] and the use of quicklime to treat polychlorinated biphenyls (PCBs) are cases in point.[4]

Sites often contain combinations of contaminants that are difficult to determine and present complex treatment problems.[5] The location of the contaminants can also create problems, for example, proximity to a drinking water source. The recent listing of a Westminster, California, residential area as a Superfund site has created inordinately complex remediation problems.[6] Media attention and the hysteria often associated with contamination concerns may create a climate of fear[7] and prompt officials to overreact.[8] Consider, for example, recent charges

---

[1] MacKerron, *Regulatory Muscle Drives the Market,* Chemical Week, Oct. 11, 1991, at 24 [hereinafter *Regulatory Muscle*].

[2] *Corporate Managers Profiled in Survey,* Engineering News-Rec., June 24, 1991, at 10.

[3] Shelley, *Turning up the Heat on Hazardous Waste,* 97 Chem. Engineering, Oct. 1990, at 47 [hereinafter Shelley]; Bradford, *Company Calls Foul Play on DOE Technology Rule,* Engineering News-Rec., July 22, 1991, at 7 [hereinafter Bradford].

[4] Ives, *PCB Remediation,* Oil & Gas J., Oct. 30, 1989, at 72.

[5] *See* Kopstein, *Science for Superfund Lawyers,* 19 Envtl. L. Rep. (Envtl. L. Inst.) 10,388, 10,389 (1989) [hereinafter Kopstein].

[6] Cone, *EPA Wants to Add O.C. Site to Superfund List,* L.A. Times, July 26, 1991, at A1.

[7] In *Potter v. Firestone Tire & Rubber Co.,* 274 Cal. Rptr. 885 (Ct. App. 1990), the court of appeals affirmed emotional distress damages caused by the fear of cancer from negligently dumped hazardous waste. This case is pending appeal in the Supreme Court of California.

[8] Easterbrook, *Perils of Pluralism,* Engineering News-Rec., June 3, 1991, at E-13, E-22.

that the evacuation of Times Beach, Virginia, instigated by government regulations regarding dioxin, may have been unnecessary.[9]

These characteristics of remediation work make it critical that the parties involved develop a comprehensive remediation strategy. Currently, only about 20 percent of the cost of a project is expended in the investigation and analysis phase.[10] The increasing occurrence of unanticipated site conditions calls for a broader scope in pre-contract investigation and a more flexible approach to contract management. Extensive and aggressive governmental regulation, as well as potential tort liability, requires firms to develop a strategy to reduce liability in a manner suited to their individual needs, while still ensuring compliance with applicable laws and regulations. While the primary responsibility remains with the owner, remediation contractors, consulting firms, lenders, and attorneys should all contribute to creating a strategy with sufficient adaptability, flexibility, and technological and financial foresight.

§ 4.2 Effective Cost-Conscious Approach to Regulation

An aggressive, cost-effective strategy is critically important in the current regulatory environment. Many owners and operators fail to remediate or even investigate hazardous wastes until forced to act by a regulatory body. While this strategy may produce short-term savings, in the long run it is counterproductive for a number of reasons.[11]

Delay increases the risk of incurring fines and penalties. Recent penalties have been substantial: In one extreme example, a plastics manufacturer in Florida has agreed to pay a $3.4 million fine, increase its pollution control efforts, and establish a $1 million fund for educational programs.[12] The EPA has announced that it is intensifying enforcement efforts, particularly regarding land dumping of hazardous wastes.[13] Finally, if regulators develop more stringent standards, remediation costs may increase drastically.[14]

Intentional postponement of hazardous waste cleanup for short-term gain may increase the penalties to be imposed. Failure to cooperate with an agency inquiry may result in an administrative order to do so. If no response is made to

---

[9] Gorman, *The Double Take on Dioxin*, Time, Aug. 26, 1991, at 52; *Eight Paper Mills Facing Tougher Dioxin Limits*, Engineering News-Rec., Apr. 22, 1991, at 21.

[10] *Regulatory Muscle* at 24.

[11] *Liability Aspects of Engineering: Risks and Avoidance*, 5 Focus 1 (Jan. 1990) [hereinafter *Liability Aspects*].

[12] *EPA Levies Largest RCRA Fine*, Engineering News-Rec., Mar. 11, 1991, at 5.

[13] *EPA, Justice Crack Down on Land Dumping Ban*, Engineering News-Rec., Mar. 4, 1991, at 7.

[14] Fender, *A Guide to Controlling Site Remediation Costs*, Pollution Engineering, Nov. 1990, at 86 [hereinafter Fender].

the order, the violator can incur fines up to $250,000 and criminal penalties.[15] Moreover, civil penalties under RCRA are based on deviation from requirements and the violation's potential for harm, and may be adjusted according to the violator's good faith efforts to comply and the profitability of the violation.[16] Corporate officers[17] or controlling shareholders[18] may be personally liable when they exercise authority[19] or have responsibility for hazardous waste disposal.

Delay also increases and extends the exposure of the owner to tort liability. Contaminants can migrate, harming nearby residents, workers, and wildlife, as well as property values. In *Woodrow Sterling v. Velsicol Chemical Corp.*, more than $5 million was awarded to individuals for injuries from migrating chemical waste.[20]

The primary drawback of the ostrich approach, however, is that it effectively shifts much of the control over the remediation process to regulators. Although they do have some level of expertise, regulatory agencies have little or no incentive to consider the goals, cost, and time factors from the firm's viewpoint. EPA criteria stress the technical possibility of remedial actions, rather than practicality or cost effectiveness.[21] As of 1990, EPA standards require hazardous waste to be treated by the best demonstrated available technology (BDAT) regardless of the cost.[22] EPA feasibility studies have been open to criticism along these lines.[23] See § **4.3**. Observers have noted that decisions under the recent National Contingency Plan (NCP) guidelines reflect an increasing emphasis on permanent remedies and more complex and costlier cleanups.[24] The EPA has no mandate to base a decision on cost-effectiveness, nor to consider how the treatment decision might affect the financial position of an owner, except to the extent that the company may be unable to accomplish the remediation.[25]

---

[15] *See, e.g.,* Cal. Health & Safety Code § 25,189.5(b), (e) (West 1984); Bois, *How to Survive an Administrative Environmental Investigation,* Orange County Law., June 1991, at 16 [hereinafter Bois].

[16] S. Owens & J. Mollenkamp, Hazardous Waste Cleanup 1991: Civil Penalties and Criminal Enforcement 27-28 (Feb. 1991) (paper presented to CLE International, Denver, Colo.).

[17] United States v. Ward, 618 F. Supp. 884 (E.D.N.C. 1985).

[18] State of N.Y. v. Shore Realty Corp., 759 F.2d 1032 (2d Cir. 1985).

[19] For a review of the issues, *see* Salus, *CERCLA: The EPA Cleans Up With Individual Liability,* Orange County Law., June 1991, at 10 [hereinafter Salus].

[20] Rubin & Setzer, *The Superfund Decade: Triumphs and Troubles,* Engineering News-Rec., Nov. 26, 1990, at 38, 40 [hereinafter *Superfund Decade*].

[21] Fender at 86–87. For critiques of RCRA regulations, *see* Williams & Cannon, *Rethinking RCRA for the 1990's,* 21 Envtl. L. Rep. (Envtl. L. Inst.) 10,063 (1991) [hereinafter Williams & Cannon]; Sarno, *Improving Superfund Remedy Selection,* 22 Env't Rep. (BNA) 26 (1989) [hereinafter Sarno].

[22] *See* 42 C.F.R. 260 (1991); Williams & Cannon at 10,066.

[23] *Superfund Decade* at 38–40.

[24] Fender at 86.

[25] Fender at 88–89.

The EPA has also been criticized for failing to set clearly defined cleanup standards and evaluation criteria for remediation selection.[26] This failure creates significant difficulties for owners, contractors, and environmental consultants in evaluating and proposing remediation plans or challenging the EPA's orders.[27] State agencies have created similar difficulties. When the Florida Department of Environmental Regulation recently rejected waste treatment permits for a $100 million facility, officials of the applicant company were surprised, and noted, "We're kind of confused as to the reasons for the denial."[28] In *Avon Products, Inc. v. New Jersey Department of Environmental Protection,* the court held that the department's failure to promulgate standards for acceptable levels of hazardous waste rendered enforcement of a cleanup order arbitrary and capricious.[29]

An additional disadvantage of a regulation-driven response is the tendency of the regulating body to rely on enforcement of established routines (such as BDATs) or techniques of remediation rather than consideration of site-specific factors, including the tradeoff between cost and the risk reduction from decreased contamination.[30] The owner may lose control over the goal of the remediation, as well as the selection of treatment method, with potentially severe effects on the cost and timing of the remedial process.[31] In some cases, owners have charged that the EPA is requiring them to use an unproven and overly costly technology rather than a more viable alternative preferable to the owner.[32]

This insensitivity to cost-effective remediation strategies is particularly problematic because the cost of reducing contaminants may increase rapidly at higher levels of remediation.[33] Consequently, small increments of additional remediation will be obtained only at exorbitant cost.[34] A recent study suggests that this problem is widespread in the Superfund program.[35] The researchers found that the EPA enforcement programs at both simple and complex sites caused unnecessary costs by failing to tailor remedial efforts to the specific sites.[36]

---

[26] Sarno at 26; *Superfund Decade* at 38.

[27] Sarno at 26; *Unproven Technology, Liability Hamper Site Cleanups, Waste Coalition Says in Report,* 22 Envtl. Rep. 309 (June 7, 1991) (full report, *entitled* The Hazardous Waste Practice, Technical and Legal Environment 1991, *available from* H.W.A.C., 1015 15th St. NW, Washington, D.C. 20005, (202) 347-7474).

[28] *First Treatment Plant Rejected in Florida,* Engineering News-Rec., Sept. 27, 1990, at 23.

[29] 243 N.J. Super. 375, 378, 380, 579 A.2d 831 (1990).

[30] Fender at 86–88; Williams & Cannon at 10,066–68.

[31] *Costly Nitrogen Fix Looms,* Engineering News-Rec., June 24, 1991, at 9 [hereinafter *Costly Fix*].

[32] *See, e.g.,* Bradford at 7.

[33] Bradford at 7–9. For problems of meeting higher clean water standards, see *Costly Fix* at 9.

[34] Rubin et al., *Clean Water Act Debate Swirls On,* Engineering News-Rec., Oct. 7, 1991, at 28; Fender at 87.

[35] Sarno at 26; *Cleanup Approaches Studied,* Engineering News-Rec., Sept. 23, 1991, at 16.

[36] Superfund Decade at 40; *Cleanup Approaches Studied,* Engineering News-Rec., Sept. 23, 1991, at 16.

There are additional reasons to take an aggressive approach to remediation in an attempt to avoid the imposition of regulatory control. Regulatory processes involve bureaucratic delays.[37] Conflicts in philosophy between the official positions of regulatory agencies and the actions of agency personnel can lead to ambiguities in what actions are required.[38] In many cases, the responsible authority may not have complied with its responsibility to publish acceptable standards.[39] Governmental pollution charges can damage a firm's relations with customers or clients, and can increase the firm's exposure to the influence of community groups on remedial efforts or even potential litigation, such as toxic tort suits.[40] Finally, as discussed in § **4.21**, a carefully orchestrated cleanup will facilitate efforts to recover cleanup costs from third parties.

An owner who tries to resist regulatory control by challenging an agency action may still incur the same costs, along with the potential costs of litigation.[41] For publicly traded companies, a stonewall approach may expose them to securities problems and a reporting obligation.[42]

Most owners facing problems of hazardous waste contamination will eventually come under regulatory scrutiny. Developing a comprehensive remediation strategy can facilitate relations with regulators in several ways. Most important, such preparation improves the owner's negotiating position.[43] Regulators are interested in encouraging private potentially responsible parties (PRPs) to cover as much of the cost of cleanup as possible. An owner who has voluntarily and responsibly addressed remediation is more likely to be viewed as cooperative and treated favorably. In addition, by preparing a site investigation and evaluation (especially if an environmental consultant familiar with regulatory procedures and officials was involved), there is a much greater chance of facilitating and influencing the regulatory process and having the preferred work plan approved.

---

[37] Krickenberger & Rekar, *Superfund Settlements: Breaking the Log Jam,* 19 Env't Rep. (BNA) 2384 (Mar. 10, 1989) [hereinafter Krickenberger].

[38] *Id.* at 2384.

[39] Avon Prods. v. New Jersey Dep't of Environmental Protection, 243 N.J. Super. 375, 579 A.2d 831 (1990).

[40] For a discussion of who seeks out the government's environmental records and for what purposes, *see* Miller, *The Value of Government Records,* Orange County Bus. J., 1991 Environmental Guide, at 20.

[41] For a discussion of the costs of litigation, *see* Krickenberger at 2384.

[42] *In re* United States Steel Corp. Exchange Act Release No. 16,223 [1979–1980 Transfer Binder], Fed. Sec. L. Rep. (CCH) ¶ 82, 319 (Sept. 27, 1979).

[43] Bois at 7, 16.

§ 4.3   Formulation of Remediation Goals

Formulation of remediation goals is a process involving owners, operators, environmental consultants, attorneys, and regulators. There are four areas of analysis or investigation that contribute to goal assessment:

1. Site investigation
2. Assessment of regulatory requirements and legal liability
3. Remedial investigation and feasibility study (RI/FS)
4. Analysis of the alternative remediation proposal's impact on the owner's and contractor's financial, legal, and business situations.

As discussed in **Chapter 3**, it is critical to invest a sufficient amount of money and time in precontract investigation. An incomplete site investigation can lead to the use of ineffective or even hazardous treatment methods.[44] Furthermore, comprehensive information obtained on site conditions and available technology will improve the cost and time projections. For example, a $30 million waterfront cleanup and construction project in South Carolina was delayed when soil tests performed during the construction phase found benzopyrene levels at 10 times the EPA's limit.[45] Such accuracy will not only minimize unnecessary delays in the project, but reduce the potential for negotiations over change orders and cost increases, and potential litigation between the parties.

§ 4.4   Remedial Investigation

The investigation into site conditions and feasible remediation methods will, in most cases, involve hydrologists, soil engineers, biochemists, and design engineers. An environmental consulting firm can help integrate various types of expert information and communicate and negotiate with the technical personnel of regulatory agencies.[46] Owners should be careful, however, to consider the issue of confidentiality regarding information obtained by the consultant, and potential conflicts of interest with other clients.[47] Suggested contract clauses on confidentiality and conflicts of interest are given in **Appendixes B, C,** and **D** (sample phase I and II proposals and remediation contract).

---

[44] EPA, Pub. No. PB84-158-807, Design and Development of Hazardous Waste Reactivity Testing Protocol 1 (1984). For a discussion with specific treatment methods, *see* Kopstein at 18; McVeigh, *Sampling and Monitoring of Remedial-Action Sites, in* Standard Handbook of Hazardous Waste Treatment and Disposal 12.9 (H. Freeman ed., 1989) [hereinafter McVeigh].

[45] *Toxic Soil May Delay Waterfront Projects,* Engineering News-Rec., Sept. 30, 1991, at 22.

[46] Andrews, *Hiring Environmental Expertise,* Cal. Law., Oct. 1991, at 55–56.

[47] *Id.* at 56.

The site assessment has two stages. First, information is assembled regarding past owners and uses of the site, and of adjacent sites from which pollutants may have migrated, to identify potential contaminants, pollutant pathways, and hazards.[48] Any existing business records of materials disposal, water or soil testing, and health and safety reports of public agencies are examined. Finally, employees and neighbors should be interviewed for any evidence of contamination. A site inspection should be conducted to verify this information, if possible.

The second stage of the remedial investigation involves on-site sampling of soil and water, and identification of the properties of any contaminants found at the site. Several new concerns emerge at this stage. First, any handling of hazardous waste may be governed by a number of regulations. Those parties performing the sampling may be required to obtain permits and licenses from local, state, or federal authorities. Disposal of even small amounts of high-hazard samples is strictly controlled under RCRA.[49]

It is also critical, when conducting material analysis, to protect sample integrity and maintain a clear record of testing data. Because sampling typically continues throughout the site remediation project, and even during the post-closure period, a coherent system of data management, analysis, and reporting should be created.[50] This system should anticipate all applicable reporting requirements of regulatory agencies. If a contractor is involved in the project at this stage, or the use of a particular type of remediation is anticipated, the scope of the site assessment should include information relevant to the construction project.

An attorney should be involved in creating the recordkeeping system. The manifold opportunities for regulatory agencies and third parties to institute litigation over environmental cleanup issues make it wise to approach most projects as though litigation were imminent. Detailed information regarding the time and location of samples taken, provisions for spills, and preservation of a proper chain of custody for evidentiary purposes are all important. Sensitive reports should be funneled through outside counsel, to maintain the reports' confidentiality under the attorney-client and attorney work product privileges.

The following is a sample data management program and recordkeeping system protocol:

1. Suspected contaminant
2. Soil samples
   —Boring location
   —Date
   —Custody of sample

---

[48] McVeigh at 12.2–12.4.

[49] Wetzel, *Site Remediation, in* Standard Handbook of Hazardous Waste Treatment and Disposal 12.31 (H. Freeman ed., 1989) [hereinafter Wetzel]; *see, e.g.,* 42 U.S.C. § 6924(d).

[50] Wetzel at 12.30; AGC of Cal., Safety, Health, and Environment Committee, Hazardous Waste Education Program Training Manual 124–25 (1991) [hereinafter Cal AGC Manual].

3. Groundwater samples
   —Date
   —Sample location
   —Custody of sample
4. Lab test
   —Date
   —Results
   —Custody of sample
5. Reporting requirements
   —Agencies
   —Information requirements
   —Time to report
6. Environmental agencies
   —Date of contact
   —Person contacted
   —Comments
      —Current violation?
      —Permitting implication
7. Contemplated remediation methods
   —Consulting firm
   —Methods recommended
   —Methods used in analysis
8. Further recommended tests
9. Comments.

§ 4.5 Opinion Letter

An environmental consultant often prepares an opinion letter following a site assessment. When the site assessment was conducted as an environmental audit, the opinion letter may serve as a basis for negotiating a property transaction. In other situations, the letter offers guidance for proceeding with remediation.[51]

The opinion letter contains a brief summary of the nature, scope, and results of the site investigation. The cost of a single groundwater remediation order under RCRA and CERCLA could be many times the entire value of the property or business, and involve considerable disruption and delay.[52] Therefore, the consultant should also evaluate the reliability of the information obtained.

---

[51] Del Duca, *The Environmental Consultant's Opinion Letter: A Step Beyond an Environmental Audit,* 20 Envtl. L. Rep. (Envtl. L. Inst.) 10,184, 10,185 (1990).

[52] DeMeester, *Practical Guide for Due Diligence Environmental Auditing,* 18 Envtl. L. Rep. (Envtl. L. Inst.) 10,210, 10,227 (June 1988) [hereinafter DeMeester].

Reported conclusions, which may include projections of the extent of legal liabilities and cost of remediation, should be specific. Projections should include the bounds on both liability and costs, as well as the likelihood of incurring potential levels of cost and liability, and any controlling factors. Other issues that consultants may address include the extent of contamination, potential health and safety concerns, and potential costs of waste control devices and practices.

An opinion letter may have a variety of purposes. It may be a means of presenting the results of an environmental audit to the community or to employees and unions to gain their confidence, or to regulatory agencies to show good faith and establish credibility.[53] The consultant's conclusions must be well-substantiated, to avoid exposure to increased liability.

As with assessment reports, it may be best to have the letter routed through the owner's outside lawyer, to maintain confidentiality of the information contained therein.

§ 4.6 Evaluation of Regulatory Requirements, Nature of Contaminants, and Other Sources of Liability

In the preliminary stages of the remedial investigation, it is important to determine the regulatory requirements and potential civil or criminal liability relevant to the presence of contaminants on the site. This determination is integral to the site investigation process because it is necessary to know which tests are required to prevent liability and what substances or effects are prohibited. In addition, all aspects of the remediation process, including testing, recordkeeping, and selection of treatment, should be conducted so as to prepare the best possible defense against eventual litigation claims.[54]

For example, a client who suspects that other parties contributed to the contamination should attempt to quantify the scope of such probable contribution. Such findings would be helpful both in resisting government claims and in seeking financial or other assistance from the suspected contributors for the cleanup. The client who wishes to be established as a de minimis contributor to a problem site would want an objective basis for distinguishing and isolating contaminants for which the client is responsible from other contamination at the site.

The guidelines determining what constitutes a hazardous substance and what invokes liability can be broad and ambiguous. For example, RCRA defines as hazardous

a solid waste or combination of solid wastes which, because of its quantity, concentration, or physical, chemical, or infectious characteristics, may either: (a) cause,

---

[53] DeMeester at 10,214.

[54] *Superfund Decade* at 41.

or significantly contribute to, an increase in mortality or an increase in serious irreversible, or incapacitating reversible, illness; or (b) pose a substantial present or potential hazard to human health or environment when improperly treated, stored, transported, or disposed of, or otherwise managed.[55]

The regulations enacted pursuant to RCRA and CERCLA have established lists of specific hazardous substances[56] as well as characteristic criteria to determine whether a substance is hazardous for the purpose of either of the Acts. Any substance is defined as hazardous under RCRA if it meets specified levels of any of the following characteristics: (1) flammability; (2) corrosivity; (3) reactivity; (4) toxicity; and (5) environmental persistence.[57]

The court system is constantly at work hastening the evolution of definitions and regulations. For instance, in *Shell Oil Co. v. EPA,*[58] the Court of Appeals for the District of Columbia Circuit summarily invalidated the EPA mixture, derived-from-rules, and leachate monitoring requirements (see **Chapter 8**) because of the Agency's failure to provide adequate notice and opportunity for public comment prior to the requirements' enforcement. Although the uncertainties of this ruling have been partially ameliorated by the enactment of interim measures, the ruling is representative of the general uncertainty regarding regulatory requirements in the remediation field.

Environmental consultants, contractors, owners, and operators should also be aware of this early stage of actions that may create liability, because the definition of such actions may be extraordinarily broad. Simply moving contaminated soil to a new location at the site may be sufficient to make the contractor liable as a generator of hazardous waste under CERCLA.[59] Numerous disparate cases whose outcomes depend on extremely fine factual distinctions add to the uncertainty of what actions can create liability. In a recent case, the sale of a building without the disclosure that it contained asbestos products, where both parties contemplated demolition of the building, was held to constitute disposal of hazardous substances for the purposes of CERCLA.[60] On the other hand, the use of asbestos in the construction of a building, by itself, has been held not to be disposal of hazardous waste for the purpose of establishing cleanup liability of a former owner.[61]

A clear understanding of which regulations are applicable, which agencies are involved, and who may be liable is necessary to insure that the parties can negotiate the liability issue in the contracting phase. For example, regulations under

---

[55] 42 U.S.C. § 6903(5) (Supp. III 1991).

[56] *See, e.g.,* 54 Fed. Reg. 33,418 (1989).

[57] 42 U.S.C. § 6921(a) (Supp. III 1991).

[58] 950 F.2d 741 (D.C. Cir. 1991).

[59] *See* 42 U.S.C. § 9607(2)-(4) (Supp. III 1991); Salus at 10.

[60] C.P. Holdings, Inc. v. Goldberg-Zoino & Assocs., 769 F. Supp. 432 (D.N.H. 1991).

[61] 3550 Stevens Creek Assoc. v. Barclays Bank of Cal., 915 F.2d 1355 (9th Cir. 1990).

the Clean Air Act apply if remediation work involves any contaminant with a potential for becoming airborne or emitting toxic fumes.[62]

The issue of tort liability should also be examined prior to the election of a remediation technique and the formation of contracts. Common law and other theories of liability are discussed in **Chapter 8**. Response cost recovery actions are dealt with in § **4.21**. Environmental consultants, design engineers, and contractors, as well as owners, need to be aware of their long-term liability for toxic torts and future cleanup costs. Environmental consultants and design engineers in particular may have significant exposure, and often have no indemnification from the owner.[63] Finally, these parties need to be aware of any limitations in their insurance coverage with regard to hazardous wastes. See **Chapter 3** for discussion regarding indemnity and insurance.

An essential part of the remedial investigation is to determine the level of contamination that the remedial effort must achieve under law. In recent amendments to the Superfund program, Congress mandated that the level or standard of control must meet applicable or relevant and appropriate requirements (ARARs) under federal environmental laws, or state environmental laws if those are more stringent.[64] Applicable requirements have been defined by the EPA as "cleanup standards, standards of control, and other substantive environmental protection requirements, criteria, or limitations promulgated under federal or state law that specifically address a hazardous substance, pollutant, contaminant, remedial action, location, or other circumstance at a CERCLA site."[65] Relevant and appropriate requirements are standards or criteria that, although not directly applicable to the particular hazardous substance or remedial action, "address problems or situations sufficiently similar to those encountered at the CERCLA site that their use is well suited to the particular site."[66]

Because of the enormously complex and overlapping system of environmental regulations, the determination of ARARs is necessarily subjective. It is thus essential to try to influence this determination process by attempting to establish the nature of the remediation and the appropriate level of abatement.

There are three types of ARARs:

1. Chemical-specific—limits of concentration for specific substances in various environmental media
2. Action-specific—controls or restrictions on specific remedial actions
3. Location-specific—restrictions on remedial actions because of site location or characteristics.

---

[62] Cal. AGC Manual at 152; *see generally* 42 U.S.C. § 7412(a)-(c) (Supp. III 1991).

[63] Korman & Setzer, *Sticking It to the Other Guy,* Engineering News-Rec., May 20, 1991, at 39.

[64] CERCLA, § 121(d)(2), 42 U.S.C. § 9261(a)-(b) (Supp. III 1991).

[65] OSWER, Pub. No. EPA/540/G-89/006, CERCLA Compliance with Other Laws Manual: Interim Final 1–10 (1988).

[66] *Id.* at 1–10.

A remedial action may be excepted from meeting the ARARs on the following grounds:

1.   When the action is only part of a comprehensive remedial action that will satisfy the ARARs
2.   When the noncomplying action achieves lower environmental risk than would compliance
3.   When compliance is technically impractical
4.   When the standard that will be achieved is equivalent to that required
5.   When the state standard at issue has not been consistently applied within the state
6.   For government remedial actions under Superfund, when the increased protection of public health and the environment is not justified by the expenditure of monies from the fund.[67]

The importance of effectively determining ARARs, or influencing whether and how an exception is made, should be obvious. The determination of environmental and health risks, technical impracticability, and standards of performance all rely not only on scientific investigation, but the balancing and evaluation of various factors in those investigations. To the extent that an owner, contractor, or environmental consultant can intercede early in the process, he may be able to influence how these factors are considered, and thus the final evaluation. As discussed in **Chapter 5**, the development of constructive relationships with regulatory agencies in the permitting process can favorably influence the agency toward the project and the parties involved, thus affecting the established requirements.

§ 4.7   Feasibility Study

The feasibility study uses the data regarding contamination and the physical and social environment collected in the site investigation, and evaluates the possible application of various technologies. As mentioned in **§ 4.4**, the feasibility study should be performed concurrently with site assessment so that the relevant data can be collected. Remedial methods are evaluated in terms of technological feasibility, cost, and impact on the environment and public health.[68] For example, use of land treatment methods necessitates evaluation of the porosity and clay

---

[67] CERCLA § 121(d)(4), 42 U.S.C. § 9621(d)(4) (Supp. III 1991).

[68] Patel et al., *Methods of Site Remediation,* Pollution Engineering, Nov. 1990, at 60 [hereinafter Patel].

content of the soil, as well as wind currents that could carry organic degradation byproducts (offensive odors) to residential areas.[69]

The feasibility study addresses three related considerations. First, the study must evaluate the various technologies from a technical standpoint, including: effectiveness of the technology in reducing the contaminant levels; risks involving leaks, spills, leaching, or airborne particulates; and requirements of construction and treatment materials, energy, equipment costs, and operation management and monitoring costs. For parts of this analysis, the parameters are sufficiently understood so that information obtained from the remedial investigation can be loaded into a computer program to obtain estimates of results. However, since each site presents a unique combination of physical properties and environmental characteristics, laboratory or on-site treatment testing is almost always performed. For example, in bioremediation (see § 4.12) the effectiveness of a microorganism can be seriously impaired by predators. Since the impact of predators is difficult to estimate theoretically, and may be both significant and out of the control of the remediation management, it is important to perform on-site testing.[70] Such testing may be required by regulation, as for land treatment units.[71]

The feasibility study is required under CERCLA § 104 for every Superfund site targeted for remediation.[72] Feasibility studies may be prepared either by the EPA or by private owners or operators. Feasibility studies prepared by the EPA, however, have been criticized for failing to evaluate important alternatives, failing to support recommendations with sufficient data and rationale, and delays in preparation.[73] As noted in § 4.2, by conducting its own feasibility study, the owner could avoid these problems.

The second consideration addressed by the feasibility study is an evaluation of the applicable regulations. Each of the possible technologies involves a different combination of contaminants that may be released, migrate, or be created as byproducts of the remediation process itself. Even at the testing stage, both owners and those parties conducting the tests should anticipate that, to the extent the testing process may produce or pose a risk of air or water contamination, there may be an associated liability risk and need for permits. Furthermore, special techniques or disposal problems will involve various special regulatory or permit requirements. For example, special regulatory

---

[69] See, e.g., EPA, Pub. No. BP89-179-014, Hazardous Waste Land Treatment (1983) [hereinafter Land Treatment].

[70] Patel at 66.

[71] Land Treatment.

[72] 42 U.S.C. § 9604 (Supp. III 1991); 40 C.F.R. § 300.430(a)(1)-(2) (1991).

[73] Bixler et al., Selecting Superfund Remedial Actions 493–96 (Nov. 1984) (presented at 5th National Conference on Management of Uncontrolled Hazardous Waste Sites, Hazardous Materials Control Research Inst.).

programs have been established for underground storage tanks (USTs)[74] and land treatment units.[75]

Since the EPA has been attempting to shift the burden of regulatory responsibility from the federal to state and local governments, the number of regulatory agencies with which owners, contractors, and environmental consultants and engineers must contend may be extremely large. In one case, a temporary conditional use permit for a portable rock crushing machine was delayed six months while the local agency contemplated the effect of 75 cubic yards of grading on surface water runoff, to determine whether a National Pollution Discharge Elimination System Permit (NPDES) was required. (The decision was not even theirs to make, as the Clean Water Act does not permit the EPA to delegate the NPDES permit program to local agencies.) The regulatory coverage is also extraordinarily broad. For example, waters covered under federal regulations have been defined to include wetlands, sewers, and rain runoff systems. In addition, review by federal, state, and local environmental agencies generally requires comment by the community. Therefore, technologies must be evaluated with respect to public relations.[76] If off-site treatment or disposal is considered, regulations under RCRA and state and local laws regarding the transportation, storage, and disposal of hazardous materials apply.

Finally, the feasibility study must consider the questions of cost and time. Since a remediation project can be extremely costly, and since these costs are difficult to estimate up front, it is important to evaluate both risks and costs with respect to the owner's insurance and cash flow. The owner may be facing a tradeoff between time and cost, or cost and risk, such that the specific corporate needs are important in selecting the optional remediation approach. For example, an owner in a tight cash-flow position may prefer lower expenditures over a longer period of time. On the other hand, a higher level of immediate expenditure to reduce potential libility may be preferable, if the owner is attempting to raise capital or has relatively large assets that may be exposed to liability.

The option of no remediation should always be considered, and in fact is required under NCP guidelines.[77]

---

[74] See Ammon & Cochran, *Underground Storage Tanks, in* Standard Handbook of Hazardous Waste Treatment and Disposal 1.47 (H. Freeman ed., 1989). For federal regulations, *see* 40 C.F.R. §§ 280.10–.112 (1991). Many states also have special UST programs, which may be approved by the EPA pursuant to 40 C.F.R. § 281.50 (1991).

[75] 40 C.F.R. §§ 264.300–.317 (1991); Reinhardt, *Summary of Resource Conservation and Recovery Act Legislation and Regulation, in* Standard Handbook of Hazardous Waste Treatment and Disposal 1.9 (H. Freeman ed., 1989); EPA, RCRA Orientation Manual (1986).

[76] Sarno at 26.

[77] 40 C.F.R. § 300.420 (1991).

§ 4.8 Choice of Remediation Technologies

Remediation not only involves a large variety of treatment technologies: A single project may often use more than one kind of treatment. For example, slurry walls may be constructed to prevent waterborne migration in a water treatment project.[78] In bioremediation, soil or water is often treated with chemicals to affect the pH balance or the oxygen or sulfate content, to increase the degradation rate.[79]

New technologies for hazardous cleanup are rapidly emerging, because of the rapid expansion of the remediation industry and the recognition that conventional technologies were often not sufficiently effective to meet required standards, or required huge amounts of money or time. Government programs have also led to new technology. The EPA has developed the Superfund innovative technology evaluation (SITE) program to aid the development, testing, evaluation, and reporting of new cleanup methods.[80] Publications under this program provide a wealth of information regarding the feasibility of applying technologies to sites with various kinds of contaminants and hydrological and environmental characteristics.[81] EPA publications also provide guidelines to environmental consultants and contractors for evaluating technologies for particular types of remediation or types of waste, evaluating procedures to test for and classify wastes, making permit applications, and provide information on the best developed available technologies (BDATs).[82] These documents, as well as other information on treatment technology and applications, costs, and case studies are available on EPA's database, available at its 17 regional libraries.[83]

The following sections briefly describe the various kinds of remediation technologies and some of their advantages and disadvantages. The discussion is intended for laypersons, and demonstrates the EPA's movement toward permanent remedies and away from disposal methods, with attendant high risks associated with transporting hazardous wastes. This movement has led to a shift toward on-site remediation techniques. There has also been much development

---

[78] Wetzel at 12.58.

[79] *See* EPA, Pub. No. 540/2-84-001, Slurry Trench Construction for Pollution Migration Control (1984). For a description of such a system in Nashua, New Hampshire, *see* Barvenik et al., *Quality Control of Hydrologic Connectivity and Bentonite Content During Soil/Bentonite Cut-Off Wall Construction* 66–79 (1985) (presented at 11th Ann. Res. Symp. on Land Disposal of Hazardous Wastes, EPA).

[80] *Toxics R&D: A Brave New World,* Engineering News-Rec., Aug. 3, 1989, at 30; Stanford & Yang, *Summary of CERCLA Legislation and Regulations and the ERA Superfund Program, in* Standard Handbook of Hazardous Waste Treatment and Disposal 1.42 (H. Freeman ed., 1989).

[81] *See, e.g.,* EPA, Guide to the Disposal of Chemically Stabilized and Solidified Waste (1982).

[82] For a set of abstracts of such documents, *see* EPA, Compendium of ORD and OSWER Documents Relevant to RCRA Corrective Action (1988).

[83] Dorris, *Data on Cleanup Technology is in the ATTIC,* Engineering News-Rec., Aug. 3, 1989, at 37.

in technologies that separate out compounds that either cannot be treated with other wastes, or cannot be treated by conventional technologies.

§ 4.9   —Land Treatment

The term "land treatment" simply describes the method of treating hazardous wastes in a soil medium and can be achieved through a variety of technologies. Generally, hazardous waste is added to soil with or without chemical or biological additives, and the contaminants in the waste are degraded, transformed, or immobilized in the soil. This method is highly effective in treating solvents, pesticides, and waste oils.[84] Its primary advantages are low cost and serving as a means of both treatment and permanent disposal.

However, land treatment must be carefully managed and monitored: there can be problems of leaching to groundwater or of contaminants or odors becoming airborne. On-site land treatment can also be a lengthy process, and thus inappropriate if delays in land use are undesirable.

§ 4.10   —Immobilization

Liquid or semisolid waste can be transformed structurally, into a solid block with high structural integrity, or chemically, when materials mixed with the wastes interact to reduce the toxicity and mobility of the waste. Portland cement, lime fly ash, and asphalt are commonly used to mix with waste materials. Recovery of substances such as mercury, which volatilizes during the process, may be a profitable byproduct.[85] These treatments, known collectively as microencapsulation, are usually well-tested, and inexpensive because they can be done in-situ.

Immobilization is usually effective in treating metals, asbestos, and inorganic corrosives and cyanides.[86] Thermal microencapsulation has also been used effectively in treating radioactive waste.[87] Since this technology depends upon transforming waste into a product that does not interact with its environment, waste compatibility is important. It is necessary to do extensive testing on the transformation process and the substance produced.

In-situ vitrification, a molten glass process, is a new method of immobilizing contaminants in soils and sludge by using electricity to heat the soil to a molten mass. After several months of cooling, the result is a glassy solid, similar to

---

[84] EPA, Hazardous Waste Land Treatment 3–5 (1983).

[85] Shelley at 48.

[86] Kopstein at 22.

[87] Patel at 61.

obsidian, that meets the EPA's most stringent leachability tests.[88] This treatment breaks down organic materials and macroencapsulates heavy metals and radioactive isotopes, leaving them inert. Therefore, the treatment may be well-suited for otherwise hard-to-treat combinations of contaminants. However, the process requires the removal of adjacent groundwater, and there is some concern regarding the production of off-gases. Recent articles have also suggested there are limits to the effectiveness of this technology.[89]

§ 4.11   —Thermal Treatment

In thermal treatment, contaminated soils or other hazardous waste are heated in incinerators or other heating devices, until the hazardous chemicals are either converted to nontoxic forms or stripped out of the soil and treated separately, either thermally or chemically. Although thermal treatment is widely used, it has two major disadvantages. First, it requires a significant amount of soil preparation (crushing, grinding, and screening). In addition, control of gases, ash, and unanticipated toxic byproducts may be difficult and costly.[90]

The potential for hazardous effluents, and frequent use of the thermal process to handle highly toxic materials, has led to widespread opposition to such methods.[91] Therefore, it is important to expressly consider the public health risks inherent in the handling, transportation, and treatment of wastes, and seek community input regarding such risks. Concerns about public opposition may put additional importance on implementation of a program to recover hazardous substances produced by the thermal process as well, because the public may be more inclined to favor such alternatives.[92]

Thermal treatment is primarily used for small amounts of highly contaminated soil, where low levels of contaminants must be achieved. Cement kilns,[93] wet air oxidation, and various types of incinerators have been effective in treating PCBs, pharmaceutical wastes, and non-halogenated organics.[94] For example, mobile circulating bed combustor units were successfully used to clean up a PCB spill in the Swanson River field in Alaska under extremely cold

---

[88] Shelley at 47–48.

[89] Bradford at 7.

[90] Kopstein at 18.

[91] For example, Greenpeace led a campaign against the permitting of waste-burning kiln, in Xenia, Ohio. *Toxics in cement kilns fuel industry disputes,* Engineering News-Rec., Sept. 27, 1990, at 80.

[92] Chadbourne, *Cement Kiln, in* Standard Handbook of Hazardous Waste Treatment and Disposal 8.62 (H. Freeman ed., 1989).

[93] *Id.*

[94] Copa & Gitchel, *Deep-Shaft Wet Air Oxidation, in* Standard Handbook of Hazardous Waste Treatment and Disposal 8.77 (H. Freeman ed., 1989).

conditions.[95] However, thermal treatment is inappropriate for wastes with a high inorganic salt or metal content. This exclusion is particularly important to consider in the site assessment phase, since undetected metals remaining in the soil can often leach into the groundwater.[96]

§ 4.12   —Bioremediation

Biological treatment, or bioremediation, is the use of microorganisms to convert hazardous waste into nontoxic forms. Bioremediation is well-suited for treatment of organic wastes, because such wastes contain carbon and an energy source, which are primary requirements for bacterial growth.[97] If the right kind of organisms are present in the soil or water, nutrients are added to stimulate their growth and the subsequent degradation process. Soil may also be aerated by soil mixing or shaft drilling, to encourage the growth of aerobic bacteria. If the microbes present are inadequate, the application of new microorganisms (bioaugmentation) may be used.

The commercial application of bioremediation, used in some forms for centuries, is rapidly expanding.[98] Perhaps the largest and most successful application has been in the Exxon Valdez oil spill, where bacteria and nutrients were applied to decompose the oil into carbon dioxide and water.[99] Bioremediation is particularly effective in the treatment of PCBs and hydrocarbons, but cannot be used to treat heavy metals.[100] General Electric Company is currently conducting field tests of a technique using aerobic bacteria to augment the natural anaerobic bacteria in the Hudson and Housatonic Rivers.[101] Caisson reactors will be used to stir oxygen into river sediments.[102] Although there is concern that adding new organisms may disrupt the ecology in some cases, biological treatment may offer ecological improvement for restoring wetlands,[103] or converting hazardous substances that would simply be transferred to the air with other treatment methods.[104]

---

[95] Ives, *PCB Remediation,* Oil & Gas J., Oct. 30, 1989, at 72.

[96] Fender at 62–63.

[97] Irvine & Wilderer, *Aerobic Processes, in* Standard Handbook of Hazardous Waste Treatment and Disposal 9.3 (H. Freeman ed., 1989) [hereinafter Irvine & Wilderer].

[98] Henley, *Microbes Finding Their Way to More Cleanups,* Waste-Tech News, Mar. 25, 1991, at 1 [hereinafter *Microbes/Finding Cleanups*].

[99] Lawson, *Alaska Spill Creates Giant Laboratory,* Engineering News-Rec., Aug. 3, 1991, at 33.

[100] Irvine & Wilderer at 9.4–9.5.

[101] *GE brings PCB fix to life in first test,* Engineering News-Rec., July 22, 1991, at 25.

[102] *Id.*

[103] *See, e.g., Marsh Treats Effluent,* Engineering News-Rec., July 22, 1991, at 23.

[104] *Microbes Will Recycle Toxic Wood Utility Poles,* Engineering News-Rec., Sept. 16, 1991, at 12 [hereinafter *Microbes/Toxic Wood*].

Much of the technique's popularity, however, is attributable to the cost advantage. For example, the cleanup of Biocraft Laboratories in New Jersey, involving contaminated soil and groundwater, cost an estimated 25 percent of what the more traditional form of treatment (pumping and off-site disposal) would have cost.[105] Similar cost savings were achieved in a recent cleanup in Torrance, California.[106] Bioremediation is also considerably more cost-effective than incineration when cleaning soils contaminated by leaking diesel and oil tanks.[107]

One of the primary reasons for the lower cost is that bioremediation is typically done in-situ, avoiding the costs of excavating and transporting waste. However, the method also requires considerable space for treatment units.[108] Bioremediation has also been criticized for requiring too much time.[109] The EPA, for example, was elliptically critical of the duration of the Torrance cleanup[110] even though the desired levels were achieved at considerable cost savings. This criticism illustrates the differing points of view of owners and regulators as to the efficacy of a cleanup, for reasons unrelated to the goal of the remediation. Because of the complex effects of environmental conditions such as nutrient levels, temperature, and predators, rates of waste degradation may be very difficult to predict.[111] Thus, selection of this technology may pose a substantial risk if the use value of the land is high.

§ 4.13 —Physical and Chemical Treatment

Hazards posed by unstable waste mixtures, and combinations of hazardous substances that require different and often incompatible treatments, are common obstacles to remediation. Certain decontamination techniques are also difficult to apply when the hazardous substance remains in the soil, a slurry, or a liquid solution such as groundwater. These problems are often resolved by applying physical treatments to segregate the different constituents in waste mixtures into separate waste streams.

Air and steam stripping techniques have been successfully used to remove volatile organic contaminants (VOCs), including solvents such as benzene and toluene, from groundwater or other aqueous solutions.[112] Steam stripping can

---

[105] Kaufman, *Applied Bioremedial Technology,* Hazmacon, Apr. 1991, at 2.

[106] *Industrial toxic cleanup is largest of its kind,* Engineering News-Rec., Aug. 5, 1991, at 16 [hereinafter *Industrial Cleanup*].

[107] One such estimate is 10–15%. *See Microbes/Toxic Wood* at 12.

[108] *See, e.g., Industrial Toxic Cleanup Is Largest of Its Kind,* Pollution Engineering, Oct. 1989, at 44.

[109] *Microbes/Finding Cleanups* at 1.

[110] *Industrial Cleanup* at 16.

[111] Patel at 66.

[112] Boegel, *Air Stripping and Steam Stripping, in* Standard Handbook of Hazardous Waste Treatment and Disposal 6.108–6.114 (H. Freeman ed., 1989).

have technical advantages over air stripping in application to a challenging remediation problem such as spent solvents and higher concentrations of VOCs, but is generally inappropriate for groundwater decontamination, because of higher capital and operating costs relative to air stripping.[113] Vacuum pumps and extractors, and soil mixing aeration devices such as rototillers, are commonly used in air stripping treatments. Heating devices may also be used to facilitate the extraction of VOCs from soil.[114]

Adsorption processes, such as activated-carbon adsorption, are a common variant of physical remediation treatment. These processes can be used to filter waste water or remove contaminants from groundwater, gaseous mixtures, or slurry mixtures.[115] The process is reversible, which means that substances can be removed to be recycled or destroyed and the activated carbon filters can be reused.[116] While carbon adsorption processes and filtration systems have been widely used in mobile units, the process is complex and requires thorough testing and monitoring of operations.[117]

Soil washing, flushing, and filtration techniques have been successfully developed for mobile remediation units. Soil flushing is commonly used to remove contaminants such as VOCs, arsenic, selenium, and soluble organic contaminants, that are leaching from permeable soils.[118] Water is typically extracted through wells drilled into groundwater. The water is then decontaminated and reinjected into additional wells drilled at an upgrade from the site.

Chemical remediation treatments convert hazardous or unstable chemical compounds into nonhazardous substances by the application of chemical compounds such as reduction-oxidation agents. Because chemical treatment may involve hazardous chemical additives and unstable chemical reactions, thorough analysis of substances present at the site, as well as testing of the chemical treatment under on-site conditions, must be performed.[119] This process has been widely used for manufacturing waste, and is effective for heavy metals and organic compounds that are otherwise difficult to treat.[120] Because many of the chemical agents used, and the byproducts produced, are highly toxic, special protective equipment must be used and the site must be carefully monitored.[121]

---

[113] *Id.* at 6.114.

[114] Kopstein, at 10,392.

[115] T. Voice, *Activated-carbon Adsorption, in* Standard Handbook of Hazardous Waste Treatment and Disposal 6.3–6.4 (H. Freeman ed., 1989).

[116] *Id.* at 6.3.

[117] Kopstein at 10,391.

[118] *Id.* at 10,392.

[119] *Id.* at 10,393.

[120] Fochtman, *Chemical Oxidation and Reduction, in* Standard Handbook of Hazardous Waste Treatment and Disposal 7.41–7.49 (H. Freeman ed., 1989).

[121] *Id.* at 7.43–7.47.

A wide variety of other chemical processes have been applied to the remediation field. These include chemical precipitation, in which dissolved heavy metals can be precipitated out of groundwater or other aqueous solutions,[122] and photolysis, in which pesticides, including dioxins, have been successfully treated by photodegradation techniques.[123]

§ 4.14   Remedy Selection: The *Hardage* Case

United States v. Hardage[124] is perhaps the prime example of remedy selection litigation and the cost of recovery litigation. The case's significance in that context is discussed further in § **4.21**. The discussion here focuses on the aspects of the case concerning remedy selection.

The Oklahoma site was opened in 1972 as a hazardous waste land disposal facility owned and operated by Mr. Hardage. During the eight-year period of the facility's operation, over 20 million gallons of waste were transported there for storage and disposal. When finally closed in 1980, the site consisted of chemical impoundments including a large unlined, unsealed main pit with a series of small ancillary temporary pits, and two large mounds known as barrel or sludge mounds. The type of wastes deposited were primarily oil recycling wastes, acids, caustics, lead, cyanide, arsenic, pesticides, PCBs, and other substances.[125]

The State of Oklahoma originally filed complaints in 1978, and began proceedings to revoke the permit for the facility in 1979. Concurrently in 1979, the EPA conducted preliminary investigations that reported poor waste management practices posing a significant threat to public health and welfare. In September 1980, the U.S. Department of Justice filed suit against Hardage, who ultimately filed for bankruptcy in 1985, was discharged, and ceased to be a significant player in the subsequent litigation. The court designated the original action as *Hardage* I.

Hardage II

From 1982 through 1984, the EPA conducted studies of the site and, in December 1984, notified numerous companies that they had been found to be PRPs. In 1986, the government filed an action against 32 waste generators and 3 waste transporters. These defendants, in what was designated the *Hardage* II case,

---

[122] Chung, *Chemical Precipitation, in* Standard Handbook of Hazardous Waste Treatment and Disposal 7.21–7.26 (H. Freeman ed., 1989).

[123] Kerney & Mazzocchi, *Photolysis, in* Standard Handbook of Hazardous Waste Treatment and Disposal 7.33–7.38 (H. Freeman ed., 1989).

[124] 750 F. Supp. 1460 (W.D. Okla. 1990).

[125] *Id.* at 1467–68.

organized themselves into a group known as the HSC defendants. This group brought third-party complaints against approximately 180 additional parties (including the federal government) for contribution, and to obtain reimbursement of the HSC defendants' costs for response and remedial action.[126]

The court divided the litigation into four phases:

1. Remedy selection
2. Liability
3. Third-party claims
4. Cost allocation.

The government's proposed remedy involved a two-step process of substantial excavation followed by use of a vapor extraction system (VES) to remove volatile organic compounds from the soil. The defendants proposed a containment strategy designed to pump large quantities of waste from the site, while at the same time erecting certain barriers, which in combination with the natural bedrock features would create a bathtub effect wherein the bedrock acts as a liner to hold contaminants as a bathtub holds water, and keeps the contaminants out of the groundwater. The government estimated that its two-step remedy would cost approximately $70 million (the HSC defendants contended that the cost would actually be $150 million). Both sides agreed that the HSC defendants' remedy would be about $54 million.

The government essentially attacked the HSC containment proposal on the grounds that all containment remedies eventually fail. The defendants attacked the government's proposal on the grounds that the approach was intended mainly to buttress unsound litigation strategies, and because it was also a moving target that changed often and dramatically. There were 45 trial witnesses, 8000 pages of affidavits and deposition transcripts, 200 pages of stipulations, and more than 470 exhibits, totaling more than 150,000 pages of record.

In pursuing site cleanup, the EPA did not elect to clean the site itself, but rather sought injunctive relief to compel the cleanup. The court concluded that this action expanded the scope of the remedy trial. After dealing with government contentions asserting restrictions on the court's ability to review the scope of the remedy, the court decided to conduct a de novo judicial review of the proposed remedies. The court also noted that, because of the patent defects in the government's approach, the court's decision to reject the government proposal would have been the same under any standard of review.

The clerk appointed a special master who was involved for over three years in formal hearings and dialogues, and provided periodic reports to the court. With this informed background and evidence elicited at trial, the court rejected the government's proposed remedy. In support of this finding, the court authored, as

---

[126] *Id.* at 1469.

part of its opinion, a 10-page review entitled *Flaws in the Government's Proposed Remedy.*[127]

Court's Analysis

The review noted that the primary reason for the rejection of the government's remedy was that the proposal was primarily for excavation. The court was not impressed by the witnesses who testified in favor of excavation, and was also troubled by the fact that the State of Oklahoma's opposition to excavation had not been considered. The court was struck by the ambiguity and unreliability of the government's proposals and estimates.

The opinion detailed the "vacillating nature of the government's remedy,"[128] noting that the EPA's final proposal, coming after years of preparation, was only formally announced the month before trial was to begin, and that the record of decision (ROD) was filed only two days before trial and executed by the EPA director two hours before his deposition. The court also noted that there was inconsistency between the ROD suggestion for vertical extraction wells and the trial lancing remedy proposed by the government. Also of concern was the fact that the VES extraction proposal was developed in connection with the lancing remedy, but was not changed when the EPA's excavation remedy displaced the lancing remedy.

While noting that at first the "Court was logically and conceptually attracted to the government's excavation remedy,"[129] it found that the three chief government excavation witnesses were not experts in this field, and that "[i]t was in the practical aspects of excavation at the Hardage site that the government's case fell apart."[130] Evidently, each of the three expert witnesses described a different method of excavation, and there was no detailed, consistent proposal for drum excavation. This inconsistency, coupled with an inaccurate estimate of the number, location, condition, and contents of the drums, caused the court further concern about the ability to properly excavate the material. Also of concern was the testimony of the review team leader for the EPA's draft feasibility study that the study was fatally flawed because not one containment program, such as that proposed by the HSC defendants, was evaluated in detail by the government. There was also a variety of testimony, some of which came from the EPA's own experts, that contrary to the government's position, the condition of the drums was such that most of them were probably empty or nearly empty.

It was further pointed out that excavation would expose the remediation workers to health threats that would require wearing heavy protective clothing during the hot summer months, thereby adversely affecting the completion of the work. There were substantial discrepancies in the estimated amount of exposed

---

[127] *Id.* at 1474.

[128] *Id.* at 1475.

[129] *Id.* at 1476.

[130] 750 F. Supp. 1460, 1476.

surface area to be excavated, and some indication that excavation-based remediation at other EPA sites had been delayed because of unacceptable vapor emissions. The court also found that implementation of the excavation plan would result in significant risks to local residents, and the EPA had failed to adequately assess the risks and costs of handling, testing, storage, transporting, and incineration of drums, liquid, sludge, and other materials. The opinion also noted that, even after the excavation, approximately 500,000 gallons of waste would remain at the *Hardage* site.

Moving to a discussion of the VES proposal, the court found that, while the VES phase of the remediation was not subject to the same criticism as extraction, the technology was nonetheless inappropriate for the site.

The court then adopted the main part of the remedy favored by the HSC defendants, consisting of an imaginative use of the existing underground strata, placement of a few court-ordered liquid recovery wells in certain strategic locations, and pumping from the main pit area. This proposal was found to achieve the necessary level of remediation, prevent further migration of contaminants from the site, and reduce the already low risk to public health and the environment.

It is readily apparent that the government's proposed remedy was developed from a series of ill-considered, often inconsistent, and totally insupportable premises. Inconsistency of the ROD with the proposed trial remedy, the grafting of the VES technology (originally contemplated for the lancing proposal) onto the excavation technique without any significant analysis, the failure to consider the need for level A and B protective clothing and the impact of the heavy clothing on the ability of workers to perform during an Oklahoma summer, and the fact that this proposal was only pulled together at the last minute following years of study, all indicate a totally uncoordinated approach to the remediation of this site. Even the government's own employees characterized the feasibility study as hopelessly flawed.

The HSC defendants, on the other hand, submitted a proposal that was consistent with the health and safety of the local residents, utilized the natural terrain and strata to maximum effect, sealed off contiguous areas from migration of contaminants, contemplated pumping and treating local groundwater, and was highly practical.

Although the court's review of the proposed government solution was undertaken to determine consistency with the NCP and with the dictates of CERCLA, under any standard, whether judicial review under CERCLA, or a commonsense contracting approach, the approach used to support the government's remedy selection process in this case was totally insupportable.

The case further supports the idea that parties faced with governmental cleanup edicts or investigations are better served by active participation than by remaining passive. By vigorously opposing the government's remedy and pursuing a solid, viable, and supportable alternative, the HSC defendants saved millions of dollars, and avoided becoming involved in performing an inappropriate remediation that could have greatly increased their exposure to liability.

§ 4.15   Management Tools

The four management tools that will best assure a cost effective, timely, and efficacious treatment are:

1. Cost projections
2. Scheduling projections
3. Notices, particularly as they relate to changed conditions
4. Dispute resolution.

All too often, these tools are viewed as solely for use in litigation over project disputes. In fact, rigorous, timely, and proper utilization of these tools (even dispute resolution) will often assist in achieving the desired results. However, proper utilization requires that the parties clearly understand what the tools are designed to accomplish. They must be seen as complementary. Cost and scheduling projections, for example, are merely projections. The assumptions underlying the projections should be clearly spelled out. If one or more of the assumptions fails, then notice of such failure must be given in a timely and proper manner. Finally, assuming there is no quick resolution of any attendant delay and cost issues, the dispute resolution procedures must also be invoked in a timely and proper manner. Such action will ensure that the parties' respective positions are crystallized early, while facts are fresh, and that each party's rights have been properly preserved, so that they may get on with the remediation's essential purpose of completing the cleanup. Such an early and clear delineation of positions may also promote early resolution via settlement.

§ 4.16   —Cost Projections

As previously observed, it is very difficult to accurately project the cost of a hazardous waste cleanup. At the same time, contractors must prepare bids, consultants must project costs, and owners must evaluate alternatives and choose contractors on the basis of those estimates. To help in accurate cost estimating, the EPA publishes bidding guidelines for certain types of remediation work. Computer programs can also help estimate materials costs, based on the data collected in laboratory tests performed during the site investigation. Perhaps more important, awareness of potential problems can help the parties allocate risks and prepare strategies for dealing with additional costs.

There are three types of cost factors that are more important to consider in a remediation project than in other types of construction:

1. Unanticipated conditions
2. Scope of the contract
3. Liability and indemnity.

While these factors have been previously discussed (see **Chapter 3**) in terms of the formation of the contract, some additional points should be raised in the context of project assessment and conduct of the remediation.

Unanticipated conditions are very often encountered in remediation projects, and will likely generate disputes between the parties over who should bear the incurred additional costs. As noted in **§§ 4.4** and **4.8**, the compatibility between the existing contaminants and site conditions and the optimal treatment method is critical, and difficult to assess. Therefore, the treatment(s) being applied may not be as effective as anticipated, or may result in generation of hazardous byproducts.

Several kinds of problems may arise from these results. Additional sampling, analysis, and testing may be required. Furthermore, to the extent that a hazardous byproduct or a newly selected treatment method poses different environmental risks, new regulations and permit requirements may be applicable. For example, undetected heavy metals could result in unanticipated contaminant migration to a sewer system, and ineffective incineration could necessitate transporting waste to an off-site facility.[131] Complying with new regulations could, in turn, mean costly delays to both owners and contractors.

For the owner (and contractor, if one is involved at this stage), the best defense against these risks is adequate investment in a RI/FS performed by a reputable environmental engineering firm. Both the owner and contractor should also create an explicit agreement about what constitutes unanticipated conditions, to what degree the parties are relying upon pre-contract investigations, and who bears the risk of unanticipated results and the cost of extra work.

These issues overlap with other issues covered under the scope of the contract, for example, who has responsibility for monitoring, additional testing, and post-closure costs of the project. It is particularly important to ascertain who will have responsibility for which tasks or portions of the remediation process in projects utilizing impoundment, stabilization, or biological treatment, for which post-closure monitoring is generally required under permitting and other regulations. The unwary contractor may find that, by agreeing to obtain permits, its liability has increased for long-term expensive monitoring and potential leakage or migration.[132]

§ 4.17   —Scheduling Projections

Project schedules are used to sequence and schedule project tasks, thereby serving as a basis for scheduling subcontractors, ordering materials, and setting interim and final completion dates. The most common scheduling techniques for construction projects are Gantt charts (a type of bar chart) and critical path

---

[131] Patel at 66.

[132] *See, e.g.,* EPA, Guidance Manual: Cost Estimates for Closure and Post Closure Plans (1986).

method (CPM).[133] A third method, program evaluation review technique (PERT) charts, are more often used in research and development, but may offer advantages in remediation work.

Gantt charts depict the estimated start date and duration of the major tasks of the project in bar form, possibly broken down by areas of construction. The advantage of bar charts is that they are very easily understood. However, because they do not indicate the interdependencies of various tasks, or whether a task is actually being performed at a particular time, bar charts are generally not adequate for scheduling complex projects where scheduling adjustments need to be made.

CPM, on the other hand, is a network diagram technique that outlines a set of activity sequences.[134] A CPM schedule can use arrow diagramming, which illustrates the flow between different activities.[135] Precedence diagramming, on the other hand, allows more flexibility, showing which tasks may be performed concurrently or only upon completion of other tasks.[136] The primary advantage of CPM is the information it provides contractors in responding to delays, by indicating alternative paths and changes in material, equipment, and labor required.[137] CPM is also an important tool in managing the float—the extra scheduled time that may be allocated to each activity or to the project as a whole. When delays occur, their potential effect on completion time can be assessed.

This degree of flexibility in scheduling, and of detailed information in responding to delays or changes, may be critical in large projects involving multiple subcontractors. The fact that regulatory agencies and permitting requirements may also be involved, and unanticipated conditions more likely to arise, make this flexibility even more important in remediation work.

Computer systems have been developed to integrate the design data into the construction scheduling, as well as into operations and maintenance planning. For example, a computer-designed standardization program has been credited with putting the $6.1 billion Boston Harbor cleanup project on schedule.[138] The Water Resources Authority spent over $10 billion on the computer system, put all top management through a two-week training course, and required all firms involved in project design to use the system.[139] The limitation of using CPM in remediation work is that the float is fixed, and thus does not reflect the degree of uncertainty in the schedule.

---

[133] Callahan, *The Law Behind Construction Schedules, in* Deskbook of Construction Contract Law 49 (1981) [hereinafter Callahan].

[134] Clough, Construction Project Management 58 (1st ed. 1972).

[135] *Contract Schedule Preparation and Updating Provisions,* K-C News, June 1991, at 6.

[136] *Id.* at 6.

[137] Callahan at 54–56.

[138] Kosowatz, *Harbor Cleanup Builds Momentum,* Engineering News-Rec., Oct. 21, 1991, at 29.

[139] *Id.* at 29.

PERT charts, which were developed for scheduling the building of newly designed ships, are intended for projects where the parties are not sufficiently experienced to know the time needed for various activities.[140] The time scheduled for each activity is based on optimistic, pessimistic, and expected time estimates. This approach may be more realistic for scheduling remediation work in which the treatment technique, site conditions, or regulatory processes create a high degree of uncertainty.

§ 4.18   —Notices and Changed Conditions

The contract drafting issues relating to notices and changed conditions have been discussed in **Chapter 3**. It is important to note that a notice provision is only as good as the person who wields it. Such person must know when notice is required and be aware of time limits in the contract, and must know what the contents of the notices should be under the terms of the contract. An example would be a notice requirement obligating the contractor to provide written notice to the client within 20 days of encountering a geological obstacle to excavation. The notice would have to describe the nature of the obstacle, its impact on immediate progress of the work, and the estimated time and cost effects on the project. In this regard, there is no room for expedient measures. The contracts manager should have a précis or extract of the contract notice provisions at hand throughout the life of the contract, for ready reference as to who gets notice, how, in what time frame, what the contents of the notice should be, and any response time allocated to recipients of the notice. When in doubt about whether a notice is required, the manager should give the notice. An unnecessary notice is merely superfluous. Failure to give a required notice could be fatal, as claims arising from the event could be time-determined or time-barred, or the client could contend that lack of timely notice prevented a quick response, thereby compounding damages.

§ 4.19   —Dispute Resolution

The uncertain nature of hazardous waste cleanup and related complex liability issues often create disputes. The court system is cumbersome, time-consuming, and generally ill-adapted to handling disputes where delays may be critical. Thus, it is important that the parties involved address the problem of dispute resolution in advance.

Arbitration is a common alternative (see **Chapter 3**), but it has several drawbacks.[141] Arbitration is only binding on parties that have agreed to it.

---

[140] Callahan at 57.

[141] *See* Alternative Dispute Resolution in the Construction Industry 213 17 (R. Cushman et al. eds., John Wiley & Sons, 2d ed. 1990).

Thus, if arbitration is required under an owner/contractor contract, the liability of environmental engineers, suppliers, and other parties may not be resolved in the same proceeding, depending upon the ability of the parties to bring in other parties via joinder or consolidation. In California, such joinder is liberally granted. Without a contractual provision, discovery is not customarily required in arbitration, so that parties without access to information may be at a severe disadvantage. For example, if the liability for a hazardous waste leakage is at issue, the owner may have a difficult time establishing a defense without access to the contractor's waste tracking records. Furthermore, since appeal allowed from arbitration awards is limited to seldom-found circumstances, an uninformed or ill-reasoned judgment is still binding. Arbitration is generally not favored by the EPA and is not provided for in the model consent decree.

A more reasoned approach may be to select a method designed to resolve issues promptly and fairly. Such methods, called alternative dispute resolution (ADR) techniques, rely on a process of formal mediation, which becomes binding arbitration only if no mediated settlement is reached.[142] See **Chapter 3** for further discussion of ADR.

Another alternative is to try to separate the process of dispute resolution from the remediation work. For example, the issue of who is a PRP for a contaminated site can be a long, drawn-out battle, because the potential costs or damages may be very large. If this dispute delays the remedial investigation, or the remediation itself, the increased costs could be significant. Therefore, it is prudent for the parties to agree to support the remediation work, limiting the total costs and exposure to liability; and to have the issue of the extent of each party's liability decided separately.

As to management of disputes, the contracts manager must be alert to problems and situations that may give rise to a dispute. The manager should promptly give all appropriate notices and be prepared to proceed with the chosen method of resolution. The expedient action of overlooking such situations is not appropriate.

§ 4.20   Cost Mitigation Factors

The parties involved in a remediation project, having carefully assessed and surveyed the nature of the contamination on the property, evaluated all available technologies, and integrated the results into a comprehensive contract document, may reasonably assume that the cost of the actual remediation will approximate their estimates. The only remaining question is whether there are any collateral techniques available to help offset the cost of this time-consuming and expensive project. At least three identifiable areas of recovery are extant:

---

[142] *Id.*

1. Recovery from others
2. Possible tax benefits from avant-garde high technology research and development (R&D) remediation systems
3. Salvage.

If a party plans to seek recovery of cleanup costs from others, that plan should be included in the initial assessment of the project, the contract, and execution of the remediation program. If tax benefits are to be sought through use of R&D technology, implementation of that type of technology must be adequately assessed at the beginning. If the owner hopes to recoup some of the cost through salvage of byproducts, that plan must be considered when selecting the remediation technique and must be reflected in the contract for the remediation. These factors must be addressed at the outset, before the contract is entered into and certainly before the work is started.

§ 4.21   —Designing the Remediation to Facilitate Recovery from Third Parties

One of the best methods to mitigate the impact of remediation costs is to seek contribution or recovery from third parties who may have contributed to the problem. In order to facilitate this effort, the remediating party must develop a strategy and remediation plan that is consistent with the eventual goal of seeking such recovery or contribution.

A review of CERCLA Superfund recovery standards is instructive. The provisions of CERCLA provide different standards of recovery when costs are being sought by government entities and when they are being sought by individuals. CERCLA permits both state and federal recovery of "all costs of removal or remedial action incurred . . . [not inconsistent with the National Contingency Plan (NCP)]." Conversely, the Act provides that responsible parties are essentially liable for all necessary costs of response consistent with the NCP that are incurred by private parties.[143] In practice, the subtle distinction between the language of these two sections has given rise to a clear dichotomy in the standards applied to recovery of such remedial action costs by government agencies and by private citizens.

Cost Recovery by Government

While the NCP has differing standards for evaluating the propriety of removal actions versus remedial actions,[144] the courts have gone to great lengths to justify

---

[143] CERCLA § 107(a)(4)(A), (B), 42 U.S.C. § 9607(a)(4)(A), (B) (Supp. III 1991).
[144] See 40 C.F.R. §§ 300.415(B)(2), 300.420 (1991).

the recovery of government response costs from private parties. Some courts have even gone to the point of recognizing a rebuttable presumption that the government actions are consistent with the NCP.[145] The courts have reached this conclusion notwithstanding various criticisms of EPA for failing to properly manage Superfund contractors. See § **4.2**. Furthermore, the courts have found that in governmental recovery, all costs incurred are recoverable, rather than only those that are reasonable or necessary (which is closer to the standard of private recovery actions). To this extent, the courts have applied a cost recovery standard that the end justifies the means in actions in which the government seeks recovery from third parties. The practical result of this standard has been that government cost recovery actions have a lower burden of proof in showing that the treatment utilized was both reasonable and necessary. The pending appeal in the *Hardage*[146] case (see § **4.14**) may articulate further limitations on this approach.

Some limitations have already been articulated. For example, in a recent California case that will have broad implications, the trial court in a cost recovery action held that certain portions of a municipality's claims were time-barred.[147] The Torrance Redevelopment Agency brought the action for recovery of certain cleanup costs under provisions of the California Health and Safety Code[148] that were enacted effective January 1, 1991. Pointing out that neither the legislative history nor the statute itself mentioned retroactivity, the court found no basis for retroactive application of the statute. The opinion is somewhat incongruous, given the judicial and statutory penchant for retroactive application of liability under CERCLA, and the frequent references to CERCLA in the bill that evolved into the statute.

Cost Recovery by Private Party

The preceding discussion of the statutory and case law distinctions between governmental claims and private claims actions for recovery of costs is highly relevant to a private party's selection of a remediation method. First, the 1990 NCP provides special rules for private parties conducting cleanup activities.[149] Under this articulation, private parties can only recover their costs by showing that they have acted "in substantial compliance" with the NCP and have achieved a "CERCLA-quality cleanup."[150] Significantly, the 1985 version of the

---

[145] *See* United States v. Northeastern Pharmaceutical & Chem. Co., 810 F.2d 726 (8th Cir. 1986).

[146] United States v. Hardage, 733 F. Supp. 1424 (W.D. Okla. 1989), (*appeal pending*, No. 90-6325 (10th Cir.)).

[147] Torrance Redev. Agency v. Solvent Coating Co., 763 F. Supp. 1060 (C.D. Cal. 1991).

[148] Cal. Health & Safety Code § 33,459 (West 1991).

[149] *See* 40 C.F.R. subpt. H (1990).

[150] *See* Preamble to the 1990 NCP, 55 Fed. Reg. 8793 (1990).

NCP had been interpreted to require strict compliance with a list of requirements. The 1990 amended NCP requires only substantial compliance. In one
instance, it was held that the substantial compliance standard applied even to a
pre-1990 cleanup, to the extent that the new standard did not create even more
onerous requirements.[151]

To achieve this CERCLA-quality cleanup, a response action must satisfy at
least three remedy selection factors of CERCLA § 121:[152]

1. Be protective of human health and the environment, utilize permanent so-
    lutions and alternative treatment technologies or recourse recovery tech-
    nologies to the maximum extent practicable, and be cost effective

2. Attain applicable or relevant and appropriate standards, limitations, crite-
    ria, and requirements (ARARs)

3. Provide for meaningful participation by interested parties.[153]

Case law has approved the concept that private parties may bring such cost
recovery actions against other PRPs,[154] and that they may do so even in the
absence of any governmental involvement or governmental approval of the private parties' cleanup activities.[155]

In the seminal case of *Dedham Water Co. v. Cumberland Farms Dairy,
Inc.,*[156] the court listed four factors that must be present to establish a prima
facie private cost recovery case:

1. The site in question must be a facility.

2. The defendant must be a covered person under CERCLA § 107(a).

3. The release or threatened release of a hazardous substance must have
    occurred.

4. The release (or threatened release) must have caused the plaintiff to incur
    response costs.

Contrary to the rebuttable presumption adopted in situations where the government is attempting the recovery of cleanup costs, courts in a private cost
recovery claim situation have imposed on the party seeking to recover such costs
the added burden of proof that its costs were both necessary and consistent with

---

[151] Con-Tech. Sales Defined Benefit Trust v. Cockerham, Civ. No. 87-5137, 1991 U.S. Dist.
LEXIS 14624 (E.D. Pa. Oct. 9, 1991).

[152] 42 U.S.C. § 6922 (Supp. III 1991).

[153] *See* 53 Fed. Reg. 8793 (1988).

[154] Piccolini v. Simon's Wrecking, 686 F. Supp. 1063 (M.D. Pa. 1988).

[155] Pinole Point Properties v. Bethlehem Steel, 596 F. Supp. 283, 288, 289 (N.D. Cal. 1984).

[156] 889 F.2d 1146, 1150 (1st Cir. 1989).

the NCP.[157] In a case that preceded the adoption of the substantial compliance standard, it was held that remedial costs incurred by such a private party would be found to be consistent with the NCP if the private party could show that it:

1. Provided for appropriate site investigations and analysis of alternatives
2. Complied with the NCP format
3. Selected the cost-effective response
4. Provided an opportunity for public comment concerning the selection of the action.[158]

Thus, assuming the party seeking to recover such costs has successfully demonstrated achievement of requirements of a CERCLA-quality cleanup and has been found to be in substantial compliance with the NCP, the party is then faced with the additional hurdle of demonstrating that the actual costs incurred were necessary. The *Hardage* court, in reviewing the legal issues, noted that CERCLA does not define necessary response costs.[159] A series of lower court cases have reached a differing conclusion. One court noted that necessary meant "logically unavoidable."[160] Another held that to define an action as necessary entailed an inquiry into a number of factual issues, including what alternative measures were available.[161] Another court held that, unless it could be shown that the private party went beyond the ARARs, the response action could be considered necessary.[162]

These decisions suggest that, for their costs to be found as necessary, the claiming party must establish that:

1. Alternatives were considered
2. The costs are logical
3. The actions did not exceed ARARs.

In *Hardage*, the trial court disallowed several claimed response costs as too inextricably intertwined with litigation strategy. In some instances, costs that would seem to be recoverable appear to have been rejected simply because of

---

[157] United States v. Northeastern Pharmaceutical & Chem. Co., 579 F. Supp. 823 (W.D. Mo. 1984), *aff'd in part, rev'd in part on other grounds*, 810 F.2d 726 (8th Cir. 1986), *cert. denied*, 108 S. Ct. 146 (1987); City of N.Y. v. Exxon Corp., 633 F. Supp. 609 (S.D.N.Y. 1986).

[158] Versatile Metals v. Union Corp., 693 F. Supp. 1563 (E.D. Pa. 1988).

[159] 750 F. Supp. 1460, 1509 (W.D. Okla. 1990).

[160] Allied Corp. v. Acme Solvents Reclaiming, 691 F. Supp. 1100, 1107 (N.D. Ill. 1988).

[161] Hopkins v. Elano Corp., 30 Env't Rep. Cas. (BNA) 1782 (S.D. Ohio 1989).

[162] General Elec. Co. v. Litton Indus. Automation Sys., 920 F.2d 1415 (8th Cir. 1990).

the involvement of litigation counsel. Costly bedrock studies, barrel mound studies, and a $50,000 chain-of-custody system were all denied because they appeared to be strictly litigation-oriented.[163]

This reasoning presents the potential claimant with a dilemma. To maximize potential recovery, the claimant must consult with counsel to tailor the remedy for compliance with complex and ambiguous standards. If counsel is consulted, however, the claimant risks having the costs disallowed. Perhaps the safest solution is to carefully separate the litigation related costs from the response costs. The *Hardage* court noted, for example, that the HSC defendants "presented no evidence demonstrating it had attempted to separate litigation related activities from non-litigation related activities."[164]

Finally, if the first three tests are met and passed, the possibility of exclusions must also be addressed. In *Mid Valley Bank v. North Valley Bank,*[165] the defendants in a CERCLA cost recovery action alleged the petroleum exclusion[166] prevented recovery. The facts supported the application of the exclusion because the contamination arose from a leaking UST that had contained petroleum products. After reviewing the elements necessary to establish a § 107 cost recovery claim, the court found that the exclusion did not apply because the waste oil was alleged to be adulterated by the addition of other substances, which removed it from the exclusion.[167]

The *Mid Valley* decision is also noteworthy for a number of other reasons. First, it contains a highly critical (but accurate and detailed) evaluation of the grammatical and other shortcomings of the statute. Second, the decision has a comprehensive survey of the case law in this area. Third, the decision points out that, to be liable, the defendant must not only have committed the release or threatened release, but also must have caused the incurring of response costs. The opinion is in general a scholarly and complete review on the law in this area.

Scope of Recoverable Costs

If the cleanup has been found to be of CERCLA quality and substantially consistent with the NCP, and if the costs have been determined to be necessary, and no exclusions apply, the scope of those costs that are recoverable can be very broad. They can include such mundane items as security and fencing costs,[168]

---

[163] 750 F. Supp. 1460, 1517.

[164] *Id.*

[165] 764 F. Supp. 1377 (E.D. Cal. 1991).

[166] 42 U.S.C.A. § 9601(14) (West 1983).

[167] Mid Valley Bank v. North Valley Bank, 764 F. Supp. at 1382. *See* 50 Fed. Reg. 13,460 (1985).

[168] Cadillac Fairview/Cal. v. Dow Chem. Co., 840 F.2d 691, 695 (9th Cir. 1988).

prejudgment interest,[169] costs of monitoring and investigation,[170] time spent by corporate officials on the cleanup,[171] site closure costs under RCRA,[172] and the cost of providing an alternative water supply.[173]

The decisions are inconsistent as to whether or not attorneys' fees are recoverable.[174] The court in *Bolin v. Cessna Aircraft Co.,*[175] reviewed the case law in this area and noted that the statute is subject to criticism for failing to provide a satisfactory definition of response costs. The court felt, therefore, that the more reasonable interpretation of the statute would allow for recovery of legal fees as response costs.

The Supreme Court has held, in *Exxon Corp. v. Hunt,*[176] that CERCLA does not provide relief for economic harms, but does for property diminution, economic loss, and personal injury expenses.

Practice Notes for Private Party Cost Recovery Actions

As noted above, prior government action or authorization is not a prerequisite to a private party cost recovery action, but the *Hardage* court has suggested that, if a government agency is already involved at a site, independent action without government approval may not be deemed consistent with the NCP. Therefore, the remediating party's decision on how to proceed with a program will be dictated, at the outset, by the question of whether or not the government is involved.

The private party must also demonstrate the actual incurring of response costs before it can maintain a recovery action.[177] This necessity has been interpreted as requiring the plaintiff to cite at least one incurred response cost in the pleadings and the complaint.[178] The mere allegation of response cost incurred only gets the claimant past the pleading stage. It is advisable to maintain diligent cost accounting records to document those costs.

A preliminary investigation and ARAR selection process must be completed to support the claim that the response cost was taken in substantial compliance, because the responding party must be able to identify the ARARs for any site

---

[169] *See* CERCLA § 107(a), 42 U.S.C. § 9607(a)(4) (Supp. III 1991) as amended by SARA, which provides that amounts recoverable in such an action will include interest.

[170] Tanglewood E. Homeowners v. Charles-Thomas Co., 849 F.2d 1568 (5th Cir. 1988).

[171] T & E Indus., Inc. v. Safety Light Co., 680 F. Supp. 696 (D.N.J. 1988).

[172] *See* Chemical Waste Management v. Armstrong World Indus., 669 F. Supp. 1285 (E.D. Pa. 1987); Mardan Corp. v. C.G.C. Music, 600 F. Supp. 1049 (D. Ariz. 1984), *aff'd,* 804 F.2d 1454 (9th Cir. 1986).

[173] Lutz v. Chromatex, 718 F. Supp. 413 (M.D. Pa. 1989).

[174] *Compare* General Elec. Co. v. Litton Indus. Automation Sys., 920 F.2d 1415 (8th Cir. 1990), *with* State of New York v. SCA Servs., 754 F. Supp. 995 (S.D.N.Y. 1991).

[175] 759 F. Supp. 692 (D. Kan. 1991).

[176] 475 U.S. 355 (1986).

[177] 42 U.S.C. § 9613(g)(2) (Supp. III 1991).

[178] Ascon Properties, Inc. v. Mobil Oil Co., 866 F.2d 1149 (9th Cir. 1989).

cleanup.[179] The party seeking to recover such costs should be able to demonstrate the evaluation of an array of remedies, and must have performed an analysis of alternatives prior to selection of a remedy. Finally, even if all the foregoing steps have been properly taken, failure to provide for meaningful public comment may preclude recovery.[180] The *Tinney* case is further instructive because it demonstrates what happens when an attempt to recover cleanup costs is not properly documented.

The party seeking contribution from other parties must also evaluate the nature of the acts of the party from which contribution is sought. For example, in *Danella Southwest, Inc. v. Southwestern Bell Telephone Co.,*[181] the court held that a contractor who performed an excavation, transport, and disposal of soil in a professional and workmanlike manner consistent with the contract, could not be held liable for contribution to response costs when it was later revealed that the soil was contaminated by dioxin. Even though the court found that the contractor was a responsible party under CERCLA § 107(a)(4) as a transporter, that finding did not automatically create liability. Rather, the question then became how much the contractor was responsible for under CERCLA § 113,[182] which permits the court to allocate liability on equitable grounds. This permission is not to be confused with holdings stating that equitable defenses not enumerated in the statute (for example, laches and unclean hands) are not available to avoid liability.[183]

While the standards for establishing a prima facie case for recovery (CERCLA-quality cleanup, action consistent with the NCP, the necessity of the cleanup, and actual incurring of costs) have largely developed in the context of Superfund, case law has also indicated that such costs may be recoverable in a RCRA-based action.[184] It is at least arguable that any state court attempting to make a determination about the recoverability of such claims would look to this case law for support or guidance.

Thus, any party faced with a costly and time-consuming remediation project should, at the outset, endeavor to determine whether or not there is potential for recovery against third parties. If so, the party should evaluate whether the cleanup would be a CERCLA cleanup, RCRA cleanup, or some other form of government-mandated cleanup. In any case, the party seeking to assert such recovery against third parties should take care that the remediation program is

---

[179] 40 C.F.R. § 300.700(C)(5)(iii) (1991).

[180] *E.g.,* County Line Inv. Co. v. Tinney, 30 Env't Rep. Cas. (BNA) 1062 (N.D. Okla. 1989), *aff'd,* 933 F.2d 1508 (10th Cir. 1991) [hereinafter *Tinney*].

[181] 775 F. Supp. 1227 (E.D. Mo. 1991).

[182] 42 U.S.C. § 9613(f)(1) (Supp. III 1991).

[183] United States v. Monsanto Co., 858 F.2d 160 (4th Cir. 1988), *cert. denied,* 490 U.S. 1106 (1989) (withdrawn by publisher, reported at 28 Env't Rep. Cas. (BNA) 1177 (4th Cir. 1988)).

[184] *See* Chemical Waste Management v. Armstrong World Indus., 669 F. Supp. 1285 (E.D. Pa. 1987); Mardan Corp. v. C.G.C. Music, 600 F. Supp. 1049 (D. Ariz. 1984).

developed against a strategic background such as that discussed above. The party should consider notifying the potential contributor(s) prior to implementing the plan, and providing them with an opportunity for comment. The party should also maintain vigorous and detailed accounts of charges incurred and, moreover, the reason why the particular charges were incurred.

§ 4.22 —Tax Credits for Research and Development Expenditures

In addition to seeking cost recovery from third parties, there is another avenue open for recovering remediation costs. The Internal Revenue Code allows for certain accelerated deductions and tax credits designed to reduce a firm's overall tax liability. The two primary areas that we will address in this section are (1) credits for R&D expenditures, and (2) accelerated deductions related to the amortization of pollution control facilities (see **§ 4.23**).

As of December 31, 1991, taxpayers can take a federal tax credit[185] for certain qualified research expenses paid or incurred before June 30, 1992, in carrying on their trade or business.[186] The annual credit is equal to the excess of qualified research expenses incurred by the taxpayer over the base amount, plus 20 percent of basic research payments made to another party for research conducted on behalf of the taxpayer.[187] This aspect of the credit is particularly noteworthy in the remediation context, as it ostensibly would allow an owner to claim such a credit for R&D work performed by a remediation contractor in connection with developing a remedy. This aspect may also allow such a credit to a contractor who employs a consultant to develop such technology. In general, the base amount is determined by first computing the taxpayer's qualified research expenses as a percentage of its gross receipts, during a base period consisting of tax years beginning after December 31, 1983, and before January 1, 1989. This percentage cannot exceed 16 percent. The base amount is the above percentage multiplied by the taxpayer's average annual gross receipts for the four years preceding the current tax year. But the base amount cannot be less than 50 percent of qualified research expenses for the current year. For tax years beginning before 1990, the base period research expenses are the average of qualified research expenses for each of the three tax years immediately preceding the current tax year, but not less than 50 percent of qualified research expenses for the current year.

---

[185] I.R.C. § 41 (1990).

[186] H.R. Res. 3909. The Revenue Reconciliation Act of 1990 had originally extended the credit to amounts paid or incurred before January 1, 1992.

[187] Tax Reform Act of 1986, Pub. L. No. 99-514, 100 Stat. 2085 (codified as amended in scattered sections of 26 U.S.C.).

Qualifying for the Credit

To qualify for the credit, research expenses must qualify for expensing or amortization under Internal Revenue Code § 174, the research must be conducted in the United States, and be paid by the taxpayer (not funded by government grant). The research must also be R&D in the experimental or laboratory sense[188] and pass a three-part test:

1. The research must be undertaken to discover information that is technological in nature. It must rely on the principles of the physical, biological, engineering, or computer sciences.

2. The research activities must involve elements of a process of experimentation relating to new or improved function, performance, reliability, or quality. Research involves a process of experimentation only if the design of the item as a whole is uncertain at the outset (for example, developing a new drug, designing a new computer system, or developing a new process for filtering pollutants).

3. The intended application of the research must be for use in the development of a new or improved business component. This component is a product, process, software, technique, formula, or invention to be sold, leased, licensed, or used by the taxpayer in a trade or business.

These three requirements are first applied to the whole product level, and then to smaller groups of the product's components. If the product as a whole does not qualify for the credit, a portion of the total cost may qualify. For example, research on an entire new computer system may not satisfy all the requirements, but the development of a specific new chip or circuit may qualify.

Computer software developed primarily for the taxpayer's internal use qualifies for the credit only if it is used in qualified research (other than the development of the software itself) or in a production process that involves a credit-eligible component. As an example, a company might develop new software to use in analyzing chemical contaminants as part of the process of designing new testing equipment.

Expenses That Do Not Qualify for the Credit

Research expenses related to the following items do not qualify for the credit[189]:

1. Style, taste, cosmetic, or seasonal design elements
2. The social sciences, arts, or humanities

---

[188] Treas. Reg. § 1.174-2(a)(1) (1987).

[189] Prop. Treas. Reg. § 1.174-2(a)(3) (1989).

3. Efficiency surveys, management studies, market research (including advertising and promotion), routine data collection, and routine quality control testing or inspection

4. Expenses incurred after commercial production has begun

5. The costs of ascertaining the existence, location, extent, or quality of any ore or mineral deposit (including oil and gas)

6. The development of internal computer software for general or administrative functions (such as payroll or accounting)

7. Development of any plant process, machinery, or technique for the commercial production of a business component, unless the process is technologically new or improved

8. Adaptation of a business component to suit a particular customer's needs

9. Partial or complete reproduction of an existing business component from plans, specifications, a physical examination, or publicly available information.

As an example in the environmental field, § 174 research expenditure credit has been denied for analysis of the environmental impact of power plant construction, to determine the utility of the site and to provide a basis for comparison of alternative designs and sites. By contrast, § 174 credit has been permitted for pilot energy conservation programs and research into alternative energy sources.

Interpreting "Research or Experimental"

Whether costs related to specific environmental cleanup projects would qualify for the credit depends on the earlier definitions. If costs are incurred to discover new technological information, for example, an argument could be made that the credit could be claimed. Additionally, as described in § 4.8, new treatments and equipment are being continually introduced to battle environmental problems. Companies that pay for these new advancements have a strong argument for the research and experimental nature of these expenses.

The phrase "research or experimental" is a term of art for tax purposes. It is not clear that the term differs in any important respect from the term "research and development" as used for financial accounting purposes. As a matter of practice, most corporate taxpayers use their financial accounting system's determination of R&D costs as the starting point in determining their research or experimental expenditures for tax purposes. Moreover, upon audit, the IRS generally requires that taxpayers provide a more complete justification of the classification of costs as research or experimental expenditures for tax purposes if the costs are not also classified as such for financial reporting purposes. Care must be taken in the interpretation of these statutes, and early involvement by a company's tax advisors is strongly recommended. In addition, practical considerations demand that an assessment and determination be made as to whether the work performed is truly research and experimental, or merely a reworking of conventional remediation methods.

Tax Credit for Years after 1986

For tax years beginning with 1986, there is tax credit equal to 20 percent of all basic research expenses in excess of a special base amount.[190] The credit is available to any corporation other than a service organization, an S corporation, or a personal holding company. Basic research consists of any original investigation for the advancement of scientific knowledge not having a specific commercial objective. The research does not have to be in the same field as the taxpayer's trade or business. The expenses are not deductible until actually paid in cash under a written agreement between the taxpayer and the qualifying organization. Qualifying organizations include most colleges, universities, tax-exempt scientific research organizations, and certain tax-exempt conduit or grant organizations (other than private foundations).

The base amount of expenses consists of the minimum basic research amount, plus the maintenance-of-effort amount. The minimum basic research amount is the greater of either the amount of credit-eligible basic research expenses during the base period, or 1 percent of the average of in-house research expenses, contract research expenses, and credit-eligible basic research expenses during the base period. The base period is generally the three-tax-year period ending with the tax year that immediately precedes the first tax year beginning after 1983. The maintenance-of-effort amount is the average of all nondesignated university contributions made during the base period, adjusted by cost-of-living factors, less nondesignated university contributions made during the current tax year.[191]

Basic research expenses eligible for the basic research credit are not eligible for, and are not figured into, computing the qualified research expenses 20 percent credit. That is, the expenses are not included in base-period research expenses. However, basic research expenses that are ineligible for the basic-research 20 percent credit because of the special base amount do count as expenses eligible for the qualified research expenses 20 percent credit.

Tax Credit for Years before 1986

For pre-1986 tax years, the credit covers only qualified research expenses comprising in-house expenses and contract expenses. The credit is measured against a three-year base period (found as with post-1985 years). Qualified research is for the development or improvement of a pilot or experimental model, process, product, formula, or invention, performed within the United States. The

---

[190] I.R.C. § 41(e); U.S. Income Tax Rep. (RIA), para. 410 (1990).

[191] *Id.* § 41(b).

search cannot involve the social sciences or humanities, or be funded by a private or government grant. The rules for § 174 generally apply.

In-house expenses include:

1. Wages, except those used for targeted jobs credit of personnel in qualified research or for supervising such personnel
2. Supplies used in qualified research other than real or depreciable property
3. Payments to others for the use of personal property (for example, computers) in qualified research.[192]

Contract expenses are: (1) 65 percent of amounts paid to or incurred by any person (other than the taxpayer's employee) for qualified research (prepaid amounts qualify only in year research is done); and (2) 65 percent of amounts paid by a corporation to a college, university, or certain tax-exempt organizations for certain basic research.[193]

Limitations on Amount of Credit Utilized

The research credit is combined with other business-related credits for the tax liability limitations and the carryover rules of the general business credit.[194] The amounts of research credits for tax years beginning after 1988 (50 percent of the amount of research credits for tax years beginning before 1990) that are unused at the end of the carryover period can be deducted in the following year.[195]

When an S corporation, partnership, estate, or trust earns a research tax credit, the party passes the credit through to its shareholders, partners, or beneficiaries. Individuals are restricted to a maximum credit no greater than the amount of their tax liability attributable to the entity passing through the credit. The law allows individuals unable to use their research credits fully because of the pass-through rules to carry their unused credits back three years or forward 15 years.[196]

Expenses by members of a controlled group of corporations are aggregated. The credit is then allocated among the members according to the amount of research expenditures made by each. The term *controlled group* generally has the same meaning as for surtax allocation purposes,[197] except "more than 50

---

[192] *Id.* § 41(b)(2), para. 410.

[193] *Id.* § 41(b)(3), para 410.

[194] *Id.* § 38; U.S. Income Tax Rep. (RIA), para. 380 (1990).

[195] *Id.* § 196; U.S. Income Tax Rep. (RIA), para. 1960 (1990).

[196] *Id.* § 49(g); U.S. Income Tax Rep. (RIA), para. 490 (1990).

[197] I.R.C. § 1563(a); Treas. Reg. § 1.1563-1(a) (1984).

percent is substituted for "at least 80 percent." Similar rules apply to partnerships, proprietorships, and other businesses under common control.

Generally, for tax years beginning after 1989, the § 174 deduction for qualified research expenses or basic research expenses is reduced by the research credit for the tax year (by 50 percent of the credit for tax years beginning in 1989). For capitalized research expenses, the amount chargeable to a capital account for the tax year is reduced by the excess of credit for qualified research expenses for the year (50 percent of the credit for tax years beginning in 1989), over the amount of qualified and basic research expenses allowable as a deduction for the year (determined without regard to the § 174 reduction rule).[198]

To avoid the above reductions, the taxpayer can elect to take a reduced research credit. For tax years beginning after 1989, the credit is reduced by the product of the top corporate income tax rate (currently 34 percent) and the full credit. For tax years beginning in 1989, the credit reduction was half of this amount. This irrevocable election must be made on a timely income tax return for the year in question.[199]

Given the unique situations and various combinations of contaminants encountered at contaminated sites, it requires little imagination to hypothesize situations in which the R&D credit may be sought. The evolution of increasingly site-specific remedies will require increasingly innovative approaches to evaluating tax credits. The willingness of courts to consider alternative remedies to those structured by the government (as in *Hardage*), the need for flexible and safety-sensitive remediations, and a host of other factors will make such R&D work even more prevalent. Parties employing cutting-edge technology will want to do so in a manner that optimizes potential cost savings.

§ 4.23   —Special Amortization for Pollution Control Facilities

A taxpayer can elect to amortize a certified pollution control facility over a 60-month period regardless of the facility's useful life.[200] This special amortization deduction was introduced into the tax law as a part of the Tax Reform Act (TRA) of 1969. The general purpose of the provision was to encourage private enterprise to cooperate in the nation's efforts to cope with the increasing problems of industrial pollution.

A *certified pollution control facility* is defined as a "new identifiable treatment facility which is used in connection with a plant or other property in operation before January 1, 1976 to abate or control water or atmospheric pollution or contamination by removing, alternating, disposing, storing or preventing the

---

[198] I.R.C. § 280C(c); U.S. Income Tax Rep. (RIA), para. 28,060 (1990).

[199] *Id.* § 280C(c)(3); U.S. Income Tax Rep. (RIA), para. 28,060 (1990).

[200] I.R.C. § 169; U.S. Income Tax Rep. (RIA), para. 1690 (1990).

creation or emission of pollutants, contaminants, wastes, or heat"; and that has been certified by the state and federal pollution control authorities as being in conformity with applicable regulations.[201] The concepts involved in this definition are discussed below.

The Economic Recovery Tax Act of 1981 replaced the system of depreciation under I.R.C. § 167 for most property placed in service after 1980 with the Accelerated Cost Recovery System (ACRS) of § 168. Depending on the type of property, ACRS permits recovery of capital expenditures using accelerated recovery periods, without regard to the asset's useful life. It may be advantageous to many taxpayers to use ACRS where the facility has a short recovery period, rather than elect five-year amortization under § 169.

The 1986 TRA revised the ACRS, effective with respect to property placed in service after 1986. The revised ACRS introduced two categories into which property may be classified, a seven-year class and a 20-year class, and extended the depreciation period for most real property to 31.5 years (27.5 years in the case of residential rental property).

Much property that was included in the three- or five-year categories before the 1986 TRA, was reclassified into the five- or seven-year classes as a result of the classification rules applied under the revised ACRS. However, a more favorable depreciation rate based upon the 200 percent declining balance method is employed in determining the depreciation deductions under the revised ACRS for three-, five-, seven-, and 10-year property. Consequently, for pollution control facilities that remain in the five-year class (such facilities will not fall within the three-year class), post-1986 TRA ACRS depreciation is generally more favorable, but for property in the other categories, a § 169 amortization election may prove more beneficial.

Another significant change wrought by the 1986 TRA was the revision of the alternative minimum tax (AMT) and its extension to corporate as well as non-corporate taxpayers, effective generally for taxable years beginning after 1986. Under the revised AMT, the amortization deduction of § 169 on a pollution control facility placed in service after 1986 is treated as an adjustment that is eliminated from the minimum tax base, and replaced by a depreciation deduction determined under the alternative depreciation system of § 68(g). The alternative depreciation system generally uses the asset depreciation range (ADR) class life and straight-line method.[202] Consequently, for AMT purposes, the required adjustment for the § 169 deduction after the 1986 TRA generally results in a substantially reduced deduction.

---

[201] I.R.C. § 169(e)(1); U.S. Income Tax Rep. (RIA), para. 1670 (1990).

[202] I.R.C. § 168(g); U.S. Income Tax Rep. (RIA), para. 1680 (1990).

Qualifying for Special Amortization

The first step in qualifying a facility for rapid amortization under I.R.C. § 169 is to have both the state and federal authorities certify that the facility satisfies the pollution control standards of each jurisdiction. The federal certifying authority is also given the responsibility for policing various restrictions contained in § 169. The federal certifying authority is the regional administrator of the EPA. The certification procedure is quite long and requires an extensive presentation by the taxpayer. If a taxpayer objects to any decision of the EPA regional administrator, the taxpayer may appeal.[203]

After filing an application with EPA for certification of the pollution control facility, the taxpayer is in a position to elect the 60-month amortization deduction with respect to that facility. This election is normally made by attaching a statement of election to the tax return for the first taxable year in which the deduction will be taken.[204] This election may be made either before or after certification has been received from EPA, so long as the application has been filed. In special circumstances, the election may be made by filing an amended return.

To limit the availability of the special deduction under § 169, Congress specified that qualifying facilities are only those that can be acquired or completed after January 1, 1969, and are used in connection with old plants; that is, plants in operation before January 1, 1976.[205] This limit is based on the supposition that the cost of modifying an existing plant substantially exceeds the cost of incorporating pollution control facilities into a new plant.

To qualify as a plant or other property in operation before 1976, the plant or other property must be actually performing the function for which it was constructed or acquired before January 1, 1976. Property will not be disqualified simply because it is being used at partial capacity or as a standby facility. The regulations also state that the property must be performing the function for which it was acquired or constructed before January 1, 1969; however, the Code has been changed to read January 1, 1976.

Treasury regulation § 1.169-2(a)(4) defines the *plant or other property* as "any tangible property whether or not such property is used in the trade or business or held for the production of income." The regulations state that the term includes a papermill, a motor vehicle, or a furnace in an apartment.

Presumably, a papermill would be a plant, and a motor vehicle or a furnace would be other property. For the majority of situations there is no question whether the plant or other property was in operation prior to January 1, 1976; therefore, it is not necessary at this point to refine the definition of plant or other property.

---

[203] The process is described in detail in EPA Regs. § 20.3(h), Treas. Reg. §1.169-4.

[204] Treas. Reg. § 1.169-4(a)(1) (1971).

[205] I.R.C. § 169(d)(1); U.S. Income Tax Rep. (RIA), para. 1690 (1990).

A pollution control facility must have been completed or acquired after December 31, 1968, to be considered a *new* facility under § 169. Property acquired after December 31, 1968, will qualify only if the original use of the property commences with the taxpayer and such use commences after the above date. For a facility completed after December 31, 1968, but begun prior to that date, amortization can be taken under § 169 for that portion of the taxpayer's basis attributable to post-1968 construction, reconstruction, or erection. In the case of any treatment facility used in connection with any plant or other property not in operation before January 1, 1969, amortization can be taken under § 169 for that portion of the taxpayer's basis attributable to post-1975 construction, reconstruction, or erection.

The original use of the facility means the first use to which the property is put, whether or not this use is the same as that of the taxpayer. Thus, a rebuilt machine acquired by the taxpayer for pollution control will not be considered put to original use by the taxpayer, whether or not the former owner used the machine for purposes other than pollution control.

In determining whether a facility has been acquired after December 31, 1968, the principles set forth in Treasury regulation § 1.167(c)-1(a)(2) and the examples under Treasury regulation § 1.167(c)-1(b) apply. Likewise the principles and examples under § 1.48-2 apply, in determining whether a facility has been completed after December 31, 1968. Thus, for example:

1. Property is considered as constructed, reconstructed, or erected by the taxpayer if the work is done in accordance with the taxpayer's specifications.
2. It is not necessary that the construction material be new, in use, or acquired after 1968. If construction began after December 31, 1968, the entire cost may be taken into account in determining the facility's adjusted basis, regardless of the time of purchase of the materials. Construction begins when physical work on the facility is started.
3. Property is deemed to be acquired when reduced to physical possession or control.

Example. The M Corporation began construction of a pollution control facility on March 1, 1968. All of the materials for the construction were purchased before March 1, 1968, at a cost of $100,000. By December 1, 1968, $80,000 worth of the materials had been utilized and $50,000 had been expended on labor and other costs. The facility was completed on March 1, 1969, after the expenditure of another $30,000 for labor. No other costs were incurred. The adjusted basis for purposes of computing the amortization deduction as of January 1, 1969, is $50,000, computed as follows: $30,000 (portion of labor expenses attributable to post-1968 construction), plus $20,000 (portion of materials cost attributable to post-1968 construction), is equal to $50,000 (total costs attributable to post-1968 construction).

Eligible Facilities

The regulations under § 169 define two concepts, a *treatment facility* and a *new identifiable facility*. Property that has been acquired after December 31, 1968, will qualify as a new identifiable facility only if the the original use of the property commences with the taxpayer, after December 31, 1968. A *treatment facility* is defined as a facility that: (1) is used to abate or control water, atmospheric pollution, or contamination by removing, altering, disposing, or storing of pollutants, contaminants, wastes, or heat; and (2) is used in connection with a plant or other property in operation before January 1, 1976. The latter requirement has been discussed in detail above. The first requirement is met when the facility has been certified by the EPA.[206]

The determination of whether a facility is used to abate or control air or water pollution is made by the EPA, although the EPA relies on the state certifying authority for determining compliance with the various state standards. In making its determination, the regional administrator of the EPA will consider whether the applicant is in compliance with:

1. All the regulations of federal agencies applicable to the use of the facility, including conditions specified in any permit issued to the applicant by the Army Corps of Engineers under § 13 of the Rivers and Harbors Act of 1899, as amended

2. All applicable water quality standards, including water quality criteria and plans of implementation and enforcement established pursuant to § 10(c) of the Federal Water Pollution Control Act or state laws or regulations

3. Plans for the implementation, maintenance, and enforcement of ambient air quality standards adopted or promulgated pursuant to § 110 of the Clean Air Act

4. Recommendations issued pursuant to § 10(e) and (f) of the Federal Water Pollution Control Act or §§ 103(e) and 155 of the Clean Air Act

5. Water pollution control programs established pursuant to §§ 3 or 7 of the Federal Water Pollution Control Act

6. Local government requirements for control of air pollution, including emission standards

7. Standards promulgated by the Administrator of the EPA pursuant to the Clean Air Act.[207]

Under the Treasury regulations, facilities used in part for functions other than pollution control are treated as two facilities, only one of which is a

---

[206] I.R.C. § 169(d)(4)(a), (a)(ii); U.S. Income Tax Rep. (RIA), para. 1690 (1990).

[207] EPA Regs. § 20.8(a), (b), (c), Treas. Reg. § 1.169-2.

qualifying treatment facility. This treatment is reflected in the EPA's certification procedure.

The EPA has published guidelines for its regional offices and for taxpayers, which give some concrete examples of pollution control facilities. Of course, such facilities will not be certified unless they meet the conditions discussed above. The following devices may constitute pollution control facilities:

1. Inertial separators (such as cyclones)
2. Wet collection devices (scrubbers)
3. Electrostatic precipitators
4. Cloth-filter collectors (baghouses)
5. Direct-fired afterburners
6. Catalytic afterburners
7. Gas absorption equipment
8. Vapor condensers
9. Vapor recovery systems
10. Floating roofs for storage tanks
11. Afterburners, secondary combustion chambers, or particle collectors used in connection with incinerators
12. A contact sulfuric acid plant in a flash copper smelting furnace.[208]

The following types of equipment may constitute water pollution control facilities:

1. Pretreatment or treatment facilities that neutralize or stabilize industrial or sanitary waste for disposal in a municipal waste treatment facility
2. Skimmers or similar devices for removal of greases, oils, and fat-like materials from an effluent stream
3. Facilities that concentrate and recover vaporous byproducts from a process stream for reuse as raw feedstock
4. A facility to concentrate and recover tars or polymerized tar-like materials from the waste effluent previously discharged in the plant effluents
5. A device used to extract or remove a soluble constituent from a solid or liquid by use of a selective solvent.[209]

Any large-scale remediation plan could entail the use of any one of these devices. In fact, to the extent that a plan contemplates removal and treatment

---

[208] EPA Guidelines § 2(a), Treas. Reg. § 1.169-2.
[209] Id. § 3.

at a facility, some modifications to that facility could qualify for the accelerated depreciation described above, to the extent that the IRS regulations can be followed.

The § 169 election is available for preventive facilities installed at a plant in existence before January 1, 1976. As with other certified pollution control facilities, preventive facilities cannot significantly increase the output or capacity, extend the useful life, or reduce the total operating costs of the plant to which they are attached, nor can they alter the nature of the manufacturing or production process or facility.

The legislative history indicates that significant change means a change of more than 5 percent. Furthermore, the legislative history states that, in determining how significant the effect is on output, capacity, costs, or useful life, the relevant area of examination is to be the operating unit most directly associated with the pollution control facility.

According to the legislative history, the broadened definition of an eligible facility includes a facility at a plant site that prevents pollution by removing sulfur from fuel before it is burned at the plant, and a recovery boiler that removes pollutants from material at some point in the otherwise unchanged production process. On the other hand, if a plant that has employed heat to process material converts to an electrolytic process, the latter is not a qualified pollution control facility because it is a new process, even though it may prevent the creation or emission of pollutants.

Under pre-1976 TRA law, a facility that simply removed elements or compounds from fuels, which otherwise would be released as pollutants when the fuel was burned, would not have been certified.

The statute itself does not explicitly deny amortization to facilities that treat fuel prior to combustion. The EPA guidelines contain additional examples of devices that do not qualify as treatment facilities, including:

1. Modification of boilers to accommodate cleaner fuels, such as the removal of stokers from a coal-fired boiler and the addition of gas or oil burners

2. Replacement of a heavily polluting iron cupola furnace with a minimally polluting electric induction furnace in a cast iron plant

3. Any device that is a part of a disposal system for subsurface injection of inadequately treated industrial or sanitary wastes or other contaminants

4. In-plant process changes that may prevent the production of pollutants but do not, by themselves, remove or dispose of wastes

5. Devices that simply disperse the pollutants, such as a high-stack chimney (except for devices such as cooling towers, which dissipate heat and prevent increase in the temperature of the receiving stream).[210]

---

[210] *Id.* § 7.

The argument has been made that § 169, by giving rapid amortization for various kinds of hardware, discourages the use of sounder methods of reducing pollution, such as changes to prevent the production of pollutants. There is no doubt that a positive incentive, such as a substantial tax credit, would have this effect, but it is unlikely that the cash flow advantages of § 169 are sufficient to cause major changes in pollution control techniques. Of course, by reducing the relative cost of hardware, there will be some misallocation.

§ 4.24 —Benefits from Waste Minimization and Material Recovery

Another means of mitigating the cost in a remediation project, as in any construction project, is to implement a waste minimization program. Such a program may include the recovery of materials and recycling of hazardous waste, as well as reducing the amount or cost burden of hazardous wastes created in the project.

In addition to its cost-effectiveness, such a policy may benefit the company's relationship with regulatory agencies, because these measures promote these agencies' view of environmental management as prophylactic. For example, the EPA has established a hierarchy of methods of waste management, prioritizing them in the following order: (1) source reduction; (2) recycling; (3) treatment; and (4) land disposal.[211]

Environmentally sound policies and practices may also improve a company's public image, which may in turn be important in creating a constructive dialogue with community groups when obtaining permits and approvals for remediation projects.

Source reduction, recovery, and recycling have become more important options to consider because of the rising costs of waste disposal. In the case of land disposal, more stringent regulations regarding landfills and increased land prices have driven the cost of waste disposal from a modest figure of around $10 per ton to a current cost of at least $240 per ton.[212] The difficulties in complying with transportation, storage, and handling regulations are significant as well. For a review of these requirements, such as those regarding land disposal under the 1984 RCRA amendments, see **Chapter 5**.

A waste minimization program should be established in the planning stage of a remediation project. The costs of doing so are likely to be paid back even in a small project. Furthermore, the knowledge gained from one project can apply to future projects, and formal plans can be modified according to each project's needs.

---

[211] EPA, Pub. Nos. 530-SW-86-033, 530-SW-86-034, I & II Report to Congress: Waste Minimization (1986) [hereinafter Waste Minimization].

[212] Waste Minimization at 3.

The waste minimization plan has three essential components:

1. Materials management
2. Modification of equipment and production processes
3. Waste handling procedures

Materials management involves the minimization of the loss or spillage of hazardous substances through the creation of an inventory and tracking system, and by adequate training of employees. An inventory and tracking system can reduce loss, by making workers who handle such materials accountable and by monitoring procedures and activities to prevent possible spills, leakages, or inappropriate use or disposal of such materials. Proper employee training and management procedures can reduce misuse and consequent loss or spillage of hazardous substances, as well as insure the proper use and maintenance of pollution abatement equipment.

The modification of equipment and production processes can be an important method of waste minimization in remediation work. The waste minimization plan should reflect consideration of potential contamination (such as air pollution) generated by such equipment, and the hazardous substances involved in the equipment's maintenance (such as spent solvents or oil). Alternative types of equipment or pollution abatement devices for use in the production process should also be explored.

For example, spent solvents have been a considerable hazardous waste problem in construction, generated by painting, cleaning, and degreasing equipment.[213] Alternative techniques of paint stripping that avoid the use of solvents have been developed, such as bead blasting (an abrasion process) and cryogenic techniques.[214] Simply shifting from oil-based to water-based paints avoids generation of spent solvents. Proper maintenance of equipment can eliminate leaks of hazardous substances and reduce air pollution emissions. This maintenance is not only environmentally sound, but can help to avoid costly permit violations.

A plan for waste handling has two primary components. First, the plan must include procedures to segregate different types of hazardous substances and wastes. Not only is the total volume of hazardous waste reduced (by leaving nonhazardous waste uncontaminated), but the potential for recovery or recycling is increased, thus simplifying the problem of treatment considerably. For a discussion of the problems that emerge when certain types of hazardous substances are combined, see §§ 4.9 through 4.13.

The potential for recycling or recovery should also be considered in a waste-handling plan. It may be possible to recycle materials on the project itself, or to sell or give material away for use, recycling, or recovery through a hazardous

---

[213] EPA, Pub. No. 530-SW-90-027j, Construction (1987).

[214] EPA, Pub. No. 530-SW-90-044, Waste Minimization: Environmental Quality with Economic Benefits 15 (1990).

waste exchange. Such exchanges are generally information networks, run by government or profit-making organizations, to put generators and users of specific substances or types of waste in contact with each other. For a list of such exchanges, see **Appendix J**.

The potential use of waste from landfills is related to recycling. Solid waste may be used to generate electricity or heat, and the treatment of hazardous wastes, including incineration, generates energy that can be captured and used on-site.[215] Treated solid waste from landfills may be sold for use as cover dirt.[216] Officials of a county landfill in Florida have estimated a return of $5.5 million through the sale of cover dirt and humus from degraded organic material.[217]

Finally, recovery of valuable waste materials, such as heavy metals, may be a viable additional or alternative treatment. For example, heavy metals such as mercury have been recovered from off-gases emitted by vitrification, and are a profitable part of remediation projects.[218] This recovery may be particularly beneficial, because heavy metals can be difficult to treat, especially in combination with other contaminants. For a discussion of this difficulty see § **4.15**.

Mud contaminated from off-shore oil drilling has been incinerated to produce materials used as road aggregate.[219]

---

[215] Waste Minimization at 4.

[216] *Waste Makes Haste,* Engineering News-Rec., July 18, 1991, at 22.

[217] *Id.* at 22.

[218] Shelley at 47.

[219] Kemeziz, *Marine Shell Technology Is Hot Issue,* Engineering News-Rec., Aug. 3, 1989, at 35.

CHAPTER 5

ENVIRONMENTAL PERMIT REQUIREMENTS FOR REMEDIATION WORK

MANAGEMENT OF THE PERMITTING PROCESS

§ 5.1   Overview: Management of the Permitting Process

Effective management of the permitting process is critical to any remediation project. Successfully negotiating the quagmire of federal, state, and local agencies and regulations can be a confounding task; however, failure to correctly anticipate and meet permitting requirements can be extremely costly. If a remediation contractor submits an application that inadequately addresses both the formal procedural and informational requirements, and the unwritten requirements, the regulatory agency may demand that sampling, testing, design work, or other aspects of the remedial investigation be revised or redone.

In more serious cases, defects in permit applications may lead to the denial of a permit or extended negotiation with the permitting agency, leading to greater costs from delays in the project, and litigation. Since a remediation is usually not elective, the option to forego the project is seldom available. Permitting errors will lead to greater costs, delays, and sometimes a failed effort. At a deeper level, the failure to establish clear communications and good working relationships with personnel, and to approach the application process in an active and comprehensive manner, can lead to problems in compliance with permit requirements, increased problems with inspections (see **Chapter 7**), and subsequent fines and penalties.

Poor management of the permitting process typically results in one or more of three errors:

1. Inadequate applications
2. Failure to anticipate the need for a permit
3. Failure to anticipate the time needed to obtain permits.

In some cases, such as for permits issued under the Clean Air Act (CAA) (described in § **5.9**), the application itself acts as a shield against citations for not having such CAA permits. However, this protection is only available if the permit was sought in a timely fashion.[1]

In one illustrative case, the contractor brought a mobile rock-crushing unit into a remediation project, unaware that a conditional use permit was required for its operation. Considerable delays and expense resulted from the six months required to obtain such a permit. It turned out that the party who had notified the regulatory authorities operated a competing permitted plant. It was arguable that no permit was actually needed, because of the location and short term of the project. The authorities were really more interested in appeasing the competitor, who operated a permitted facility within the city, than in seeking regulatory compliance. The entire controversy could have been avoided by either working out a deal with the competing operator, or by forcing the regulatory authorities to concede that no permit was needed before the contractor commenced operations and became at risk. Ultimately, six months of regulatory reviews were needed to obtain a six-month permit.

---

[1] 42 U.S.C. § 7661b(d) (Supp. III 1991).

There are four primary stages to the permitting process:

1.   Determination of permit and application requirements
2.   Investigation (audits, surveys, Phase I, or II) and preparation of applications and related documents
3.   Submission of the application
4.   Responses to agency reviews, requests for information, and intent-to-deny letters.

The permit assessment should be accomplished during the initial planning phase of the project. In addition to the pure cost of delays, evolving permit standards and changing requirements for information and documentation for permit applications can radically alter a plan in the later stages. Such requirements must be considered, and permits sought, during the remedial investigation phase, when the sampling and testing of the site is planned and performed, and other studies (such as hydrological or geological studies) and survey work are done. Delays in seeking these permits could render the entire work plan meaningless. To the extent that time and costs related to the permitting process are significant for the project as a whole, or that such expenditures vary with different remediation methods, permitting information should be considered in the feasibility study. See **Chapter 4**.

§ 5.2   —Assessment of Permit Requirements

The initial step in acquiring permits is to contact all potentially implicated regulatory agencies, and find out if any contemplated activities, equipment, or materials and substances planned for use require any type of permit, license, certificate, or letter of approval, or invoke any type of regulation through which authority could be denied or revoked. It cannot be overemphasized that environmental regulations include a large number of local ordinances, all of which must be investigated. An experienced renovation contractor in California, who had applied for all the usual environmental permits and approvals, was cited during a project by the city fire department for failing to obtain a permit for work potentially involving asbestos-containing materials. The situation arose from a bureaucratic anomaly in California. Permitting of certain types of remediation projects was delegated to the cities in certain areas. Lacking funds to create agencies for supervision of such work, several cities (including Los Angeles) assigned the task to their fire departments. This fact is not widely known.

In some states, clearinghouse agencies exist to provide information necessary to determine which permits are required for a particular project. Other states have what are called *lead agency systems:* One agency (generally determined by the overall classification of the project) functions as a permit administrator, by coordinating the preparation of applications, reviewing for completeness, and holding hearings for other agencies.[2]

The need for simplification of the information gathering and application process is recognized. In California, for example, along with the reorganization of the state EPA, a centralized system for environmental permitting has been slated for development.[3] In addition, permitting agencies are realizing that educational outreach programs and improved processing facilitate compliance.[4] To this end, agencies may give seminars on permitting requirements for certain types of operations, allow permit-completeness review by certified environmental engineers, and permit equipment in response to manufacturers' applications. The agencies may also create computerized permitting systems, and consolidate the process for projects by reviewing the project as a whole rather than by piece of equipment, type of activity, or part of site.[5]

More commonly, environmental consultants or specialized remediation contractors provide the necessary knowledge and experience regarding the permitting process to project management.

Some crucial steps in the process of permit assessment include the following:

_____ 1.   The parties must exercise diligence in assessing which permits will be required. It is better to contact four agencies in order to find the one that requires a permit than to find out later that vital information has been overlooked. If a regulatory agency that should require a permit or license says that no such permit is required, that position should be confirmed in writing to the person representing the agency. While such action may not prevent liability, it does demonstrate good faith and may purchase some leniency.

_____ 2.   Once the relevant agencies have been identified, it is advisable to arrange an initial meeting with the lead or primary agency or agencies. In this way, the applicant can receive guidance on specific aspects of the permitting, provide information to the agency about the project, and begin to establish a good relationship with the agency. The applicant should prepare for the meeting by obtaining beforehand application forms and basic printed information about permit requirements from the agency. If environmental consultants, engineers, or subcontractors experienced with remediation work are involved in the project, they should be consulted regarding their past experience and particular concerns.

---

[2] D. Rona, Environmental Permits 19 (1988) [hereinafter Rona].

[3] Ronan, *CAL-EPA: New Era of Environmental Regulation,* Cal. Manufacturer, Nov.–Dec. 1991, at 23.

[4] *See, e.g., AQMD launches major reforms for business,* Advisor, SCAQMD, Winter 1991–1992, at 1; *New Name Means New Emphasis, id.* at 3.

[5] *AQMD's 12-point program,* Advisor, SCAQMD, Winter 1991–1992, at 1.

_____ 3. When possible, the names and particular idiosyncrasies of relevant agency personnel (temperment, jurisdictional mandate, emphasis on substance or procedure) should be learned in advance. A subjective as well as an objective approach should be taken, by remaining alert for issues peculiar to the permitting personnel, as opposed to issues peculiar to the application, permit, or treatment involved. A particular person at the agency, as well as a backup, should be designated as the primary contact. If personnel are changed, the contractor should seek an immediate coordinating meeting with the successors.

_____ 4. The applicant should review all materials and commentary that will be presented to the agency, and draw up a list of questions or potential problems. This review should include the hazardous or other substances present, the type of treatment anticipated (including potential kinds of equipment), existing project plans, and any information available about the site.

_____ 5. The applicant should keep in mind the goals of the agency involved. For example, it is preferable to try to meet with the highest possible official, because any early negotiation over definitions and modifications to procedures or requirements must involve someone with requisite authority. Such a meeting will also help the applicant understand that individual's views regarding agency goals and priorities. The attitude of individual agency officials is also important. To facilitate obtaining a permit, the agency officials should perceive the applicant as cooperative, desirous of achieving an environmentally sound project oriented toward compliance with agency goals, and appreciative of the time and effort expended by the agency on the project.

_____ 6. At the pre-application meeting, the applicant should learn as much as possible about that agency's permit process, including the expected timetable, specifications of documents required, post-permit requirements, and whether there are any special support services such as help for small businesses or permit seminars. There may be some room for negotiation in this process, so the applicant should attempt to work out both a timetable and procedural strategy with the agency. If appropriate, the applicant should also inquire as to whether permits will be required for sampling and testing. Finally, the agency can provide the applicant with the checklist it uses for permit review.

§ 5.3   —Preparing and Submitting Permit Applications

The next step in the permitting process is to conduct a remedial investigation, and prepare the application and support documents. In doing so, it is important to coordinate the investigatory and permit processes so that all supporting information is consistent, and presented in a form familiar to the agency. One common mistake is for applicants to submit drawings to one agency and later submit updated and modified drawings to another agency. The dissimilarities between the drawings may result in permit delays, denials, or an inspection leading to a work stoppage. Accuracy (both substantive and perceived) is essential in all aspects of the application, since permits may be denied or revoked for misrepresentation.[6] For more information regarding revocation, see § **5.4**.

Once the application and supporting documents are completed, they may be submitted all together or in stages. Submitting segmentally may allow the applicant to get feedback from the agency prior to completing the entire application; however, some agencies will not begin the review process, or at least the review time clock, until all materials are submitted. Submitting complete applications can also make the company appear both cooperative and competent.

Recordkeeping is important during the entire permitting process, but becomes critical at the application submission stage. The applicant should send a confirmation letter to the agency after each meeting or contact, to confirm any agreements made and information obtained. (This letter also offers a good opportunity to thank officials.) Records should be kept of all documents submitted to the agency, and all agency comments regarding requested changes or revisions to those documents.

§ 5.4 —Responding to Information Requests or Intent-to-Deny Letter

The agency will review the application for completeness and compliance with legal requirements, and may request clarification or further information. The agency may also indicate that the plans are not in compliance, request specific changes, or issue an intent-to-deny letter.

It is important to maintain a constructive relationship with the agency while dealing with problems arising during or after the review process. If the agency asks for additional information, such information should be provided quickly, but with serious consideration of the potential problems such requests may indicate. If the requests seem to contradict the initial agency-established requirements, the applicant should review those agreements with the agency, and then proceed as necessary to either make the required changes or clarifications, or protest the modification if compliance is intolerable. A carefully documented history of the agency agreement is helpful.

A more serious situation exists when the agency responds with an intent-to-deny letter. Although such a letter means the agency has decided to deny the permit, this position is not final. The permit applicant can appeal the decision

---

[6] *See, e.g.,* Cal. Health & Safety Code §§ 25,186(c), (d) (West 1992).

by requesting a technical hearing, in which the applicant will attempt to convince the judge that the denial was unjustified or that an exception to the agency's requirement should be made.[7] To make such an argument, the applicant usually must hire an expert to make reports or provide testimony based on the letter of intent, which must include the reasons for the agency's denial.[8]

In addition to (or in lieu of) the appeals process, the applicant can attempt to negotiate an agreement with the agency following an intent-to-deny letter. Since the costs already spent at this stage (from investigation, sampling, testing, and environmental studies) may be a large portion of the project's budget, there may be a significant temptation to proceed at any cost. However, the applicant should be careful to avoid agreeing to infeasible solutions under the pressure of a pending denial. If the applicant is eventually unable to comply with the new requirements, the result could be revocation or potentially costly litigation.

An example of Title V permit regulation illustrates the appellate process. Following revocation of the permit, an applicant is allowed 60 days to file a petition with the agency. The administrator is then required to either grant or deny the petition within 60 days of its filing; however, if the permit has already been issued, its effectiveness will not be postponed while the administrator arrives at a conclusion.[9]

Furthermore, if the administrator finds cause to terminate, modify, or revoke and reissue a permit, such action must be reported to the applicant and the issuing agency. The issuing agency then has 90 days to respond to the administrator's findings; after that time, the administrator may proceed with the proposed changes.[10] Again, it is in the applicant's best interest to maintain accurate records of all communication in this process, and to submit all requested information within the required period of time.

If agency officials do not understand the costs of technical compliance, there may be a stalemate between the applicant and the agency regarding the feasibility of certain requirements. The best strategy for the applicant is to work with the highest official possible at the agency and to offer economically feasible alternatives, in order to continue the negotiations and pressure agency officials into a compromise.

§ 5.5 Programs for Banking and Trading Permits

On December 4, 1986, the EPA implemented its emissions trading program, known as the environmental bubble policy.[11] The program allows permit holders

---

[7] Rona at 81.

[8] *Id.*

[9] 42 U.S.C. § 7661d(b)(2) (Supp. III 1991).

[10] *Id.* § 7661d(e).

[11] 51 Fed. Reg. 43,818 (1986).

with one or more plants (stationary sources) to increase emissions at one or more emission units, in exchange for compensating decreases in emissions at other units. Within each bubble (an imaginary cover that defines emissions in a particular geographic area), emissions must meet baseline emission levels (BLEs), calculated according to the formula:

$$BLE = \text{source emission rate} \times \text{operating hours} \times \text{capacity utilization}$$

BLEs are expressed in either tons of emissions per year or pounds per day.

Whether an emissions offset (permitting certain emissions by reduction of emissions in other areas) will be available may depend on whether the source is in a nonattainment or an attainment area. An attainment area is an area in which relevant emission target levels have been achieved; in nonattainment areas, such levels are still exceeded. In nonattainment areas, bubbles must achieve a 20 percent net reduction in emissions after the BLEs have been applied, and cannot rely on reductions that occurred before the application of pollution credits.[12]

The owner of a source may store qualified emissions reduction credits (ERCs) in EPA-approved banks for later use in bubbles or offsets. ERCs may be sold or transferred to other firms with the bank's approval. States are allowed to establish emissions banking and generic trading rules as part of their State Implementation Plans (SIPs). For further information on SIPs, see § **5.8**.[13]

To create, use, or bank ERCs, the following requirements must be met:

1. The ERCs must not be currently required by law, must be approved by the state, and be enforceable, permanent, and quantifiable.

2. ERCs trades must involve the same criteria pollutant, and all use of ERCs must satisfy applicable ambient air quality tests.

3. Trades may not be used to meet National Emissions Standards for Hazardous Air Pollutants (NESHAPS) (for application to asbestos remediation, see **Chapter 6**) or to increase emissions beyond NESHAPS-prescribed levels, or to meet technology-based requirements (such as the new source performance standards (NSPS), the best available control technology (BACT) under the prevention of significant deterioration (PSD) program, or the lowest achievable emission rate (LAER) under the nonattainment program).[14]

As an example, California regulations allow local air districts to develop banking programs for stationary sources that reduce air emissions below

---

[12] *Id.*

[13] 40 C.F.R. pt. 51, app. S (1991).

[14] Environmental Issues in Real Estate and Construction Projects in California 3-23 (June 20, 1991) (Cambridge Inst. seminar material) [hereinafter Environmental Issues].

applicable standards. Such sources receive pollution credits for their reduction efforts. The state Air Resources Board (ARB) must approve banking systems developed by air districts.[15] Reductions not otherwise required by federal, state, or local air district laws, rules, orders, permits, or regulations, may be banked and used to offset future increases in emissions. Such reductions must be approved for banking by the applicable air district.[16]

One example of such an emissions banking program is that of the Bay Area Air Quality Management District (BAAQMD), the stated purpose of which is to promote development of new technologies and provide incentive for emission reductions.[17] The BAAQMD requires that, to qualify for emissions banking, the emissions reduction must exceed the levels achievable using "reasonably available control technology," and must be permanent, quantifiable, and enforceable.[18] The BAAQMD issues a preliminary decision within 60 days following acceptance of a complete application.[19] The application is then open to public comment and a final decision made within 30 days of the close of the comment period.[20] The air district will then issue certificates of ownership of emissions credits, and maintain a registry of approved emissions reductions.[21] Refusal to certify a source for emissions banking may be appealed by the applicant within 30 days of the notice of refusal.[22]

REGULATIONS INVOLVING ENVIRONMENTAL PERMITS

§ 5.6 RCRA Permits

The Resource Conservation and Recovery Act (RCRA) regulates the generation, transportation, and management (treatment, storage, and disposal) of hazardous waste.[23] It is the most commonly encountered permitting statute in environmental remediation work. However, permits are only required under RCRA for hazardous waste treatment, storage, and disposal facilities (TSDFs). See **§ 5.7.**

---

[15] Cal. Health & Safety Code § 40,709 (West 1992).

[16] *Id.*

[17] BAAQMD R. & Regs. 2-4-101.

[18] *Id.* 2-4-201.

[19] *Id.* 2-4-403.

[20] *Id.* 2-4-405.

[21] Cal. Health & Safety Code § 40,711(a) (West 1992); BAAQMD R. & Regs. 2-4-406.

[22] Cal. Health & Safety Code § 40,713 (West 1992).

[23] 42 U.S.C. §§ 6901–6992k (Supp. III 1991); *see also* 40 C.F.R. §§ 240-281 (1989).

Generally, waste generators and waste transporters do not need a RCRA permit unless they also own or operate a TSDF, as defined under the regulations.

RCRA defines *hazardous waste* as

> a solid waste, or combination of solid wastes, which because of its quantity, concentration, or physical, chemical, or infectious characteristics may:
>
> (i) cause, or significantly contribute to an increase in mortality or an increase in serious irreversible, or incapacitating reversible, illness; or
>
> (ii) pose a substantial present or potential hazard to human health or the environment when improperly treated, stored, transported, or disposed of, or otherwise managed.[24]

If a high-quantity generator retains wastes for more than 90 days, in which case it is considered a storage facility, a TSDF permit will be required.[25] Normally, transporters and generators of hazardous waste will only be required to register with the Department of Transportation (DOT) and obtain state or local permits and approvals. Activity may be classified as waste generation if it includes excavation of contaminated soil or removal of hazardous building materials such as asbestos.[26]

Previously, the EPA only regulated establishments generating more than 1000 kilograms of hazardous waste per month. The EPA has recently increased the number of establishments that will be considered generators for the purposes of RCRA requirements, by including establishments that generate from 100 to 1000 kilograms per month, called small quantity generators (SQGs). At minimum, EPA requires SQGs to treat, store, or dispose of their waste at an approved hazardous waste facility, and to obtain a storage permit if waste is kept on the premises for more than 180 days (or 270 days if the waste will be transported more than 200 miles).[27]

Generators of over 1000 kilograms of waste per month must comply with the following requirements:

_____ 1. Obtain an EPA identification number

_____ 2. Use only transporters and TSDFs having EPA identification numbers

_____ 3. Prepare a manifest for each shipment

_____ 4. Certify on each manifest that (a) it is implementing an on-site hazardous waste reduction program and (b) it has selected the safest available treatment, storage, and disposal methods for its waste

---

[24] 42 U.S.C. § 6903(5) (1982).

[25] 40 C.F.R. § 262.34(b) (1991).

[26] Hazardous Waste Education Program 152 (1991) (AGCC Training Manual) [hereinafter Waste Education].

[27] 40 C.F.R. § 262.34(f) (1991); EPA, The New RCRA, A Fact Book 2 (1985) [hereinafter *The New RCRA*].

____ 5. Comply with EPA regulations regarding packaging, labeling, marking, and placarding

____ 6. Meet certain recordkeeping and reporting requirements

____ 7. Obtain a TSDF permit if waste is stored on-site for more than 90 days at a time.[28]

A threshold inquiry in determining what permits are going to be required is whether the project is a removal action or a remediation. Wastes designated as hazardous under RCRA Subtitle C[29] must be disposed of at facilities permitted under that Subtitle.[30] Generally, removal is not the favored vehicle for cleanup of a contaminated site; however, removal is still a viable alternative. Under certain situations, such as when there is limited available on-site space for treatment or storage, removal may be the only viable solution.

Hazardous wastes may not be disposed of on-site without a valid TSDF disposal permit.[31] Thus, many on-site remediations may call for such a permit. Conversely, if the contaminant is to be removed, different requirements apply. Transporters are regulated under DOT and RCRA for all transportation of hazardous waste off the site where it was generated. Such off-site transport requires registration and an EPA identification number, which can be applied for with EPA Form 8700-12. Transporters must also comply with the uniform hazardous waste manifest system,[32] which includes a description of the nature and quantity of wastes shipped, the name and address of the facility designated to receive the waste, the number and types of containers used, special handling instructions, and any significant discrepancies between the waste as described on the manifest and the waste actually shipped. Sections of the manifest form must be completed by each participant in the hazardous waste handling process.[33] Finally, transporters are required to take certain actions in response to hazardous waste discharges during transport.[34] Hazardous waste may only be transported to facilities that have been permitted under Subtitle C.[35]

---

[28] 40 C.F.R. §§ 262.10–262.70 (1991). *See also* Cal. District Attorneys Assoc., the Complete Guide to Hazardous Materials Enforcement and Liability, at VI-13 to VI-14 (1991) [hereinafter Cal. D.A. Assoc.].

[29] RCRA § 1004(5), 42 U.S.C. § 6903(5) (Supp. III 1991) (definition of hazardous waste).

[30] EPA, Decision-Maker's Guide to Solid Waste Management 18-19 (1989).

[31] 40 C.F.R. 270.1(c) (1991); Waste Education at 130.

[32] 40 C.F.R. §§ 262.20–.23 (1991).

[33] Cal. D.A. Assoc. at VI-12 to VI-13.

[34] *Id.* at VIII-3 to VIII-4.

[35] 42 U.S.C. § 6923 (Supp. III 1991). *See* Waste Education at 59.

§ 5.7 —Treatment, Storage, and Disposal Facility Permits

A RCRA permit is required before construction and operation of a TSDF unless the facility is exempt.[36] The application for a RCRA permit consists of a part A and a part B. Rules on issuance of permits require a facility to file part A of the application to seek interim status if the facility was in existence or under construction on November 19, 1980. Such facilities will be treated as having a permit to operate until such time as the EPA or an authorized state agency requests the filing of part B of the permit application.[37]

Part A of the application includes a description of processes used to treat the wastes, the design of the facility, and the wastes to be treated. Part B is more in-depth, and requires submission of detailed information on how the facility will meet technical standards promulgated under RCRA, including contingency plans for emergencies, waste analysis procedures, inspection schedules, operating procedures to prevent environmental contamination at the site, facility design and layout, engineering, groundwater protection, closure and post-closure plans, and detailed information on containers, tanks, and incinerators used at the site.[38]

When submitting an application to the EPA, the applicant should use a binder that will allow revisions or additions during the subsequent review by the EPA. Part A of the application is to be presented on Forms 3510-1 (Form 1) and 3510-3 (Form 3). There are no EPA forms for a part B permit application because the detailed information required is site-specific and may be presented in several different ways. However, the EPA will evaluate the application according to the following checklist based on the RCRA regulations promulgated under 40 C.F.R. § 122.25:

General information requirements.

_____ 1. Part A of the permit application if not previously submitted or if information has changed since submitted

_____ 2. General description of the facility

_____ 3. Process code or codes (from the part A permit application) that identify the types of units for which permits are requested, such as containers (40 C.F.R. §§ 122.25(b)(1) and 264.171 to 264.176), tanks (40 C.F.R. §§ 122.25(b)(2), 264.191, and 264.192), waste piles (40 C.F.R. §§ 122.25(b)(4) and 264.250 to 264.253), surface

---

[36] RCRA § 3005, 42 U.S.C. § 6922 (Supp. III 1991); 40 C.F.R. §§ 264.1, 270 (1991).

[37] Id.

[38] M. Worobec & G. Ordway, Toxic Substances Controls Guide 180–81 (1989) [hereinafter Worobec & Ordway].

impoundments (40 C.F.R. §§ 264.220, 264.221, and 264.226 to 264.231), or incinerators (40 C.F.R. §§ 264.340 to 264.345, 264.347, and 264.351).

____ 4. Chemical and physical analyses of hazardous wastes to be handled

____ 5. Waste analysis plan

____ 6. Security description for the active portion of the facility

____ 7. General inspection schedule and description of procedures (including specific requirements for particular unit types)

____ 8. Preparedness and prevention documentation, or justification of waiver request

____ 9. Contingency plan documentation (including specific requirements for particular unit types)

____ 10. Documentation of preventive procedures, structures, and equipment for control of unloading hazards, waste runoff, water supply contamination, effects of equipment failure and power outages, and undue personnel exposure to wastes

____ 11. Documentation of procedures for prevention of accidental ignition or reaction (including specific requirements for particular unit types)

____ 12. Traffic documentation

____ 13. Facility location documentation

____ 14. Personnel training program documentation

____ 15. Closure plan documentation (including specific requirements for particular unit types)

____ 16. Documentation of deed notice (applicable to existing facilities only)

____ 17. Closure cost estimate and documentation of financial assurance mechanism

____ 18. Post-closure cost estimate and documentation of financial assurance mechanism

____ 19. Documentation of insurance

____ 20. Documentation of coverage by a state financial mechanism (if applicable)

____ 21. Topographic map showing contours at 0.5 to 2.0 meter (2 to 6 foot) intervals, map scale and date, 100-year flood plain area, surface waters (including intermittent streams), surrounding land uses, wind rose, north orientation, legal boundaries of facility, access control, infection and withdrawal walls, buildings and other structures, utility areas, barriers for drainage or flood control, and location of operating units including equipment cleaning area. Each hazardous waste management unit should be shown on the map with a unique identifier (such as a number) and the associated process code from the part A application.

Specific information requirements.

_____ 1. Unit-specific information will be required for each permit sought (see part A).

Water-specific information requirements.

_____ 1. Summary of groundwater monitoring data obtained during the interim status period
_____ 2. Identification of aquifers beneath the facility
_____ 3. Delineation of waste management area and point of compliance for groundwater monitoring on topographic map
_____ 4. Description of any existing plume of contamination in groundwater
_____ 5. Detailed groundwater monitoring program description (combined with items 6, 7, or 8 as appropriate)
_____ 6. Detection monitoring program description, if applicable
_____ 7. Compliance monitoring program description, if applicable
_____ 8. Corrective action program description, if applicable
_____ 9. Justification for any proposed waiver to the 40 C.F.R. part 264, subpart F, Ground-Water Protection Standards.[39]

Land disposal permit applications are subject to a particularly high level of scrutiny. The EPA maintains that, although such information and demonstration requirements are burdensome, they are justified by the potential long-term hazard of land disposal of hazardous wastes. The EPA has concluded that increased difficulty in preparation and review of permit applications must be accepted "in order to provide for full consideration of the serious implications that the facility might have for the public's health and welfare for decades to come."[40] EPA also believes land disposal should be used only if there is no other feasible alternative.

Practice Points

The permit application should be prepared and presented in two distinct sections: a basic or general application, and a series of specific attachments. A

[39] EPA, Permit Applicants' Guidance Manual for Hazardous Waste Land Treatment, Storage, and Disposal Facilities 4–2 to 4–5 (1984) [hereinafter Guidance Manual]; EPA, A Guide for Preparing RCRA Permit Applications for Existing Storage Facilities 14-20 (1982) [hereinafter RCRA Permit Applications).

[40] EPA, Pub. No. PB 81-246431, Hazardous Waste Management System: General Standards Applicable to Owners and Operators of Hazardous Waste Treatment, Storage, and Disposal Facilities; and Hazardous Waste Permit Program 13-17 (1981).

separate attachment is suggested for each major technical aspect of the permit application.[41] (Examples of attachments are given in **Appendix C**.) Thus, if some of the attachments require revision, they can be returned to the applicant without returning the entire permit application.

As of August 8, 1985, each application for interim-status operation must be accompanied by certain exposure information addressing potential hazardous waste releases in the course of transportation to or from the waste disposal unit, potential accidents during normal operations, and potential pathways, magnitude, and nature of human exposure to such releases.[42] Owners or operators must submit a completed Endangerment Information report (EIR) to the EPA regional office for review. Such a health assessment will be conducted whenever the unit poses a substantial risk to public health. The EPA may also use RCRA §§ 3004(u), 3008(h), 3013, and 7003 to obtain more definitive indications of releases and exposures.[43]

The part B permit application will be the source of much of the information required in the EIR. Such information can simply be cross-referenced. However, the EIR will require data beyond the scope of the part B application concerning the wastes handled, the area around the facility, inspection and compliance records, and insurance information.[44] It is important to identify the potential pathways of human exposure to hazardous waste or waste constituent releases from the facility. Detailed information is required on pathways such as groundwater, surface water, air, subsurface gas, and soil. Information concerning transport of wastes on-site and in the immediate vicinity is also required, although this information may have been previously submitted in part B. Furthermore, the applicant is asked to supply information regarding management practices and known releases.[45] Owners or operators must also prepare a narrative discussion on the potential for public exposure to hazardous wastes or hazardous constituents through releases related to the unit.[46]

Permit Review

The EPA reviews all permit applications upon submission, and the public is informed that a request for a hazardous waste facility permit is pending. If the application is deemed incomplete, the EPA requests the missing information through a notice of deficiency (NOD), which specifies the information needed

---

[41] Guidance Manual at 4–2 to 4–5.

[42] The New RCRA at 5.

[43] *See* 42 U.S.C. §§ 6924, 6928, 6934, 6973; EPA, Permit Applicants' Guidance Manual for Exposure Information Requirements under RCRA Section 3019, at 1–6 (1985).

[44] *Id.* at 2–2.

[45] *Id.* at 2–6 to 2–13.

[46] 42 U.S.C. § 6939a(a) (Supp. III 1991); RCRA Permit Applications at 10–11.

to complete the application. Once the EPA has decided to grant the permit, the Agency announces this fact and schedules time for public notice, public comment, and public hearings. Public notice provides a minimum of 45 days for interested persons to comment on the draft permit.[47] The permit will be issued for a period of 10 years, but may be reviewed, modified, or revoked by the EPA if deemed necessary.[48] The RCRA amendments of 1984 require that, beginning 12 months after the date of enactment, and no less than every two years thereafter, the EPA or authorized state agencies must inspect all TSDFs for which a permit is required. The EPA or the state agencies must also annually inspect all TSDFs owned or operated by a federal agency, starting 12 months from the date of enactment. No waivers or variances are permitted.[49]

Regulation of Underground Storage Tanks

In 1985, Subtitle C of RCRA was amended to include detailed requirements for the regulation of *underground storage tanks* (USTs), defined as any tank with 10 percent or more of its volume underground (including the volume of pipes).[50] EPA has promulgated regulations under the statute, including requirements for maintaining a leak detection system, an inventory control system, a tank testing system, and comparable systems designed to identify releases.[51] The regulations also include requirements for maintaining records of these systems, for reporting releases and corrective action taken in response to releases, for closure of tanks to prevent future releases, and for financial responsibility.[52]

Enforcement

Enforcement of the permitting process is conducted by both EPA and the states. As an example, for violations of RCRA requirements, the EPA may issue a compliance order, suspend or revoke the permit, impose a $25,000 per day penalty for noncompliance with RCRA, and impose a $25,000 per day penalty for each day of noncompliance with the compliance order.[53] For violations of UST provisions, the EPA may issue a compliance order and collect $25,000 per day for noncompliance.[54] Other violations, such as submitting false information to the local authority about the status of a tank, may result in penalties of $10,000 per tank. The EPA may also seek to restrain activities that present an imminent and

---

[47] Worobec & Ordway at 181.

[49] 42 U.S.C. § 6925; The New RCRA at 6.

[50] 42 U.S.C. § 6991 (Supp. III 1991); 40 C.F.R. § 280.12 (1991).

[51] 40 C.F.R. § 280 subpts. C, D, E (1991).

[52] 42 U.S.C. § 6991b(c) (Supp. III 1991); 40 C.F.R. 280 (1991).

[53] 42 U.S.C. §§ 6928(a)(1), (a)(3), (c).

[54] *Id.* § 6991e(a).

substantial danger to health or the environment.[55] For a knowing violation of RCRA, a $50,000 penalty for each day of violation and two to five years' imprisonment may be imposed.[56] The states have similar penalties, making noncompliance a costly endeavor.

§ 5.8   Federal Air Regulations

Enacted in its present form in 1970, after 15 years of investigation, the CAA[57] provides the basic framework for federal and state air pollution control. CAA regulates both mobile and stationary sources of air pollution,[58] and comprises the National Ambient Air Quality Standards Program (NAAQS) and the NESHAPS. The Act is implemented through the states by mandatory SIPs. Each plan must be evaluated by the EPA,[59] which has four months to approve or disapprove a SIP.[60] Furthermore, the EPA can make its own requirements enforceable at the local level.[61] See § 5.11.

Until amendment of CAA in 1977, no permits were required by the federal statute for any air pollution source. The 1977 amendments brought with them the PSD and nonattainment programs, requiring permits for the construction of major emitting facilities in attainment areas, and for the construction and operation of major new or modified stationary sources in nonattainment areas (areas that are not in compliance with NAAQS).[62] When EPA designates a nonattainment area, the corresponding SIP must require permits for the construction and operation of new or modified major stationary sources anywhere in the area. This source will be eligible for a permit only if the source obtains offsetting reductions in emissions of relevant air pollutants.[63] See § 5.5.

CAA was again amended in 1990, introducing a more tightly regulated operating permit scheme. However, the 1990 amendments do not directly affect construction or modification activities. Such activities continue to be governed by the federal NSPS and their state-enacted counterparts. The standards set maximum emission levels for several pollutants, and are applicable to facilities constructed, modified, or reconstructed after a standard is proposed. These

---

[55] *Id.* § 6973(a).

[56] *Id.* § 6928(d); Waste Education at 64.

[57] 42 U.S.C. §§ 7401–7671 (Supp. III 1991).

[58] Environmental Issues at 1-7.

[59] 42 U.S.C. § 7410 (Supp. III 1991).

[60] Environmental Issues at 3-9.

[61] Waste Education at 13.

[62] J. Stensvaag, Clean Air Act 1990 Amendments: Law and Practice 14-2 (John Wiley & Sons 1991) [hereinafter CAA Amendments].

[63] 42 U.S.C. § 7503(a), (c) (Supp. III 1991); *see* Calif. D.A. Assoc. at X-1d.

federal standards are designed to discourage plants from moving to states with less stringent air pollution regulations, by requiring compliance regardless of location.[64]

Federal permitting standards for construction and modification can be divided into the areas of construction permits for new and modified sources of either attainment or nonattainment areas. Within the attainment source area there are five issue-specific considerations:

1. The PSD program requires comprehensive preconstruction review and application of BACT for all facilities.

2. No new construction may be started on a major source or modification in attainment areas without preconstruction review of air quality effects, and the issuance of a construction permit setting forth emission limitations that will protect the PSD increment. The permit application must be accompanied by an air quality impact analysis.[65] Major stationary sources are specified sources that emit or have potential to emit 100 tons or more per year of any air pollutant regulated under the Act, and any other sources that emit or have the potential to emit 250 tons per year.[66]

3. The source must demonstrate, by modeling, that it will not cause or contribute to a violation of NAAQS or of any allowable increment over the baseline concentration.

4. The application must contain an analysis of ambient air quality (monitoring) for each pollutant emitted in a significant amount, regardless whether the source is major for that pollutant. (Normally, 4 to 12 months of data are required.)

5. Sources must apply BACT on a unit-by-unit basis for each regulated pollutant.

All new or modified sources that seek to locate in nonattainment areas must obtain a permit from the EPA or state agency before construction begins.[67] The primary requirements are:

1. Preparing an air quality impact analysis to determine whether the proposed new source or modification will cause or contribute to emission levels that exceed the allowance permitted by the nonattainment plan. If the analysis shows the source or modification will exceed the allowance, or if the EPA has not approved a growth allowance for the area, the source must obtain emission offsets, on a one-for-one basis, of emissions from the existing source sufficient to represent reasonable further progress toward attainment.

---

[64] Worobec & Ordway at 14-6.

[65] CAA § 165(a), 42 U.S.C. § 7475 (Supp. III 1991).

[66] 40 C.F.R. § 52.21(b)(1)(i) (1991).

[67] 42 U.S.C. § 7503 (Supp. III 1991).

2. Meeting the LAER for sources of pollutants for which the increased allowable emissions exceed 50 tons per year.

3. Certifying that all of the applicant's major sources in the state comply with all applicable SIP and CAA requirements, and providing supporting evidence.[68]

Title V of CAA 1990 amendments requires the establishment of air emissions operation permit programs nationwide.[69] The program is modeled on the National Pollutant Discharge Elimination System (NPDES) permit program already established under the federal Clean Water Act. Title V requires that states develop and implement permit programs along federal guidelines.[70] However, Title V imposes operating permit requirements only, and does not affect construction or modification activities as discussed above.[71] Operating permits are required for facilities that have been targeted for control under other portions of CAA, plus any Title V sources designated by the EPA.[72]

An operating permit will be issued for a fixed term of not more than five years.[73] Each permit must specify the following:

1. Emission limitations and standards
2. A compliance schedule
3. A requirement that the permit holder submit, at least every six months, the results of any required monitoring to the permitting agency
4. Inspection, entry, monitoring, compliance certification, and reporting requirements to ensure compliance with permit terms
5. Any other conditions necessary to ensure compliance with CAA.[74]

The 1990 amendments specifically allow states to establish additional permitting requirements so long as they are not inconsistent with CAA.[75] Within 18 months of receipt of a completed application, the permitting authority must approve or disapprove the application and issue or deny the permit. Copies of the application, the compliance plan, the monitoring report, certification, and Title V permit must be available to the public.[76]

Except for construction and modification permits under the nonattainment program and PSD program, which must be obtained before engaging in those

---

[68] Environmental Issues at 3-9 to 3-16.

[69] 42 U.S.C. § 7611(a).

[70] *Id.* Cal. D.A. Assoc. at X-1i.

[71] CAA Amendments at 14-6.

[72] *Id.* at 14-7.

[73] 42 U.S.C. § 7661a(b)(5)(B) (Supp. III 1991).

[74] *Id.* § 7661c(a), (b).

[75] *Id.* § 7661e(a); Cal. D.A. Assoc. at X-1j to X-1k.

[76] CAA § 503(e), 42 U.S.C. § 7661b(e).

activities, timely submission of a complete Title V permit application shields the applicant from the violation that would normally result from failure to have a permit.[77] Finally, a permit can be terminated within 90 days after notice to the permitting authority and the permittee if the administrator, in accordance with fair and reasonable procedures, finds that cause exists.[78]

The EPA has broad powers of enforcement, including requiring a source owner or operator to monitor emissions, maintain records, and submit reports. The agency may also conduct its own inspections.[79] For violations of CAA, including any SIP, NSPS, or NESHAP standard, the EPA may issue administrative compliance orders specifying a reasonable time for compliance.[80] Penalties may also be imposed based on the economic value to the owner of the delay in compliance.[81] The EPA can also bring a civil action for injunctive relief or $25,000 per day of violation, or both.[82] The agency may also enjoin construction of a new facility that will not meet emission standards. Finally, knowing violations of SIPs may result in fines of $25,000 plus imprisonment for five years, and a false statement connected with any document filed with the EPA may result in fines or imprisonment or both.[83]

§ 5.9   Federal Water Regulations

The discharge of pollutants into the nation's waters is regulated under the Federal Water Pollution Control Act (FWPCA), enacted in 1948.[84] The Act's important amendments in 1972 and 1977 constitute what is now referred to as the Clean Water Act (CWA).[85] The objective of CWA is "to restore and maintain the chemical, physical, and biological integrity of the nation's waters,"[86] using the NPDES permits.

A national pollutant discharge elimination system (NPDES) permit must be obtained before discharging pollutants into waters of the United States.[87] The terms "pollutant" and "discharge" are broadly defined. A *pollutant* is defined as "dredged spoil, solid waste, incinerator residue, sewage, garbage, sewage

---

[77] 42 U.S.C. § 7661b(d).

[78] *Id.* § 7661d(e).

[79] *Id.* § 7414 (Supp. III 1991).

[80] *Id.* §§ 7413(a)(1), (3), (4) (Supp. III 1991).

[81] *Id.* § 7413(d), (e).

[82] *Id.*

[83] 42 U.S.C. § 7413(c).

[84] 33 U.S.C. §§ 1251–1387 (Supp. III 1991).

[85] *Id.*

[86] *Id.* § 1251(a).

[87] *Id.* § 1342(a)(1).

sludge, munitions, chemical wastes, biological materials, radioactive materials, heat, wrecked or discarded equipment, rock, sand, cellar dirt, and industrial, municipal, and agricultural waste discharged into water."[88] Under this broad definition, almost any material, including vegetation itself, could be considered a pollutant for the purposes of CWA.[89] Further, *discharge of a pollutant* is defined as the "addition of any pollutant to navigable waters."[90]

Under CWA, the EPA is required to set uniform national guidelines, called effluent limitations, capping discharge of particular pollutants from industrial point sources.[91] A *point source* is defined as a "discernible, confined and discrete conveyance" into water.[92] The means through which these mandatory federal standards are achieved are NPDES permits. NPDES permits are generally administered by the states consistent with federal guidelines or, in the absence of a state program, by the EPA itself.[93]

NPDES permits may be obtained by application to the EPA or to a state having a certified CWA program.[94] There must be an opportunity for public hearing, and the EPA must hold a hearing if it finds, on the basis of one or more written requests, a significant degree of public interest in a draft permit.[95] NPDES permits are effective for a maximum of five years.[96]

In addition to enforcing national standards, the permitting agency may, on a case-by-case basis, impose further conditions it believes necessary to achieve the purpose of CWA. Precise conditions of the permit are subject to negotiation between the issuing agency and the applicant, and are then subject to judicial review. In addition to the defined effluent limitations, a permit may also include monitoring and reporting requirements, and a schedule for compliance.[97] Additionally, a best management practice(s) (BMP) plan may be required and incorporated into the NPDES permit.[98]

Until October 1, 1992, permits are not required for point source discharges composed only of storm water, unless they are one of the following:

1. Storm water discharges that have been permitted under CWA prior to February 4, 1987

---

[88] *Id.* § 1362(6).

[89] *See* Waste Education at 151.

[90] 33 U.S.C. § 1362(12).

[91] Cal. D.A. Assoc. at XI-6; Worobec & Ordway at 132–33; 42 U.S.C. § 1311(b)(1)(A).

[92] 33 U.S.C. § 1362(14).

[93] Worobec & Ordway at 137; 42 U.S.C. § 1342.

[94] 33 U.S.C. § 1342(a)(1).

[95] 40 C.F.R. § 124.12(a) (1991).

[96] *Id.* § 122.46(a).

[97] 33 U.S.C. § 1342(a)(2).

[98] 40 C.F.R. § 125.103 (1991).

2. Storm water discharges associated with industrial activity, including hazardous waste TSDFs and construction activities such as clearing, grading, and excavation activities of areas over five acres

3. Storm water discharges from municipal separate storm sewer systems serving a population of 250,000 or more, and from municipal separate storm sewer systems serving a population of between 100,000 and 250,000

4. Storm water discharges that the EPA or the state determines contribute to a violation of a water quality standard or are a significant contributor of pollutants to waters of the United States.[99]

A permit application should be submitted at least 180 days before a new waste discharge, or a new discharge of storm water associated with industrial activity, is to commence. An application for renewal must be submitted at least 180 days before the existing permit expires.[100] After the permitting authority is satisfied that an application is complete, a preliminary determination is made to issue or deny the NPDES permit. The applicant must provide detailed information, including the name and location of the facility and its operator, the nature of any existing permits or construction approvals received or applied for under RCRA, CWA, or CAA, among others, maps of the facility including its intake and discharge structures, and treatment of the discharge. Such information must be listed on the form provided by the authority.[101] Existing manufacturing, commercial, mining, and silvicultural waste dischargers must supply information on the outfall location, a line drawing of the facility, average flows and treatment, maximum production, and improvements.[102]

The goal of the NPDES permit system is to establish specific effluent limitations for the source in question in terms of amount and concentration.[103] If the authority decides to issue the permit, a tentative permit will be prepared containing the proposed effluent limitations, a proposed schedule of compliance for meeting those limitations, and a description of any other restrictions or conditions deemed necessary by the authority to meet the goals of CWA.[104] Similar to the requirements for RCRA permits, proposed NPDES permits will be subject to public notice, a period of public comment, and a public hearing if requested by the applicant or an interested party.[105] NPDES permits are issued for a maximum period of five years, and the facility's effluent will be subject to regular testing by the permitting authority. If the authority finds that the

---

[99] 33 U.S.C. § 1342(p)(2).

[100] 40 C.F.R. § 122.21(c), (d) (1991).

[101] *Id.* § 122.21(f).

[102] *Id.* § 122.21(g).

[103] Cal. D.A. Assoc. at XI-5.

[104] Environmental Issues at 3-3.

[105] *Id.* at 3-3; 40 C.F.R. §§ 124.57, 124.74 (1991).

effluent limitations, or the allowed variances thereon, have been exceeded, the permit may be revoked by the state or the EPA.[106]

Violations of permits typically result in administrative compliance orders issued by the EPA, which require the facility to comply with its permit and to report to the agency about the cause of the violation and subsequent actions to comply.[107] After such a compliance order has been issued, the permittee may be found to have knowingly or willfully violated permit conditions, and may be subject to criminal sanctions.[108]

For negligent permit violations, the EPA may impose fines of up to $25,000 per day and one year of imprisonment. A knowing violation may be subject to fines of $50,000 per day and three years' imprisonment. Knowingly placing another person in imminent danger of death or serious bodily injury may result in a fine of $250,000 and 15 years' imprisonment.[109]

The EPA may also impose civil penalties in both the administrative and judicial forums.[110] Factors in setting a fine include the nature and extent of the violation, the discharger's culpability, the capability of payment, and any economic benefit gained from the violation.[111]

CWA is due for a renewal because funding under its authorized programs is running low. The upcoming legislative bill is S. 1081, a massive rewrite of the 1987 law,[112] and has the potential to substantially affect the NPDES program and permitting. Reauthorization under S. 1081 will emphasize reducing industrial use of toxic chemicals through process change or materials substitution.[113] This emphasis will give the government direct control over the operation and development of industry,[114] and will also expand NPDES control to include indirect dischargers.[115] It must be noted that these proposed changes to the 1987 law may affect permitting processes already under way. Therefore, special attention must be paid to the results of the implemented changes.

§ 5.10   State Hazardous Substance Regulations

As discussed in § 5.6, states are authorized under RCRA to establish their own regulatory schemes with respect to hazardous waste. This section highlights the

---

[106] Worobec & Ordway at 136–38; 33 U.S.C. § 1341(a)(5).

[107] 33 U.S.C. § 1319.

[108] *Id.* § 1319(c).

[109] *Id.* § 1319(c)(3)(A).

[110] *Id.* § 1319(g).

[111] *Id.* § 1319(g)(3).

[112] L.R. Ember, *Clean Water Act is Sailing a Choppy Course to Renewal,* Chem. & Engineering News, Feb. 17, 1992, at 18 [hereinafter Ember].

[113] *Id.* at 19.

[114] *Id.* at 20.

[115] *Id.*

resulting programs in various key states, programs that are often more stringent than the federal regulations.

Management of Waste in California

The management of hazardous waste in California is regulated principally by the Hazardous Waste Control Act (HWCA),[116] which closely parallels the federal RCRA. HWCA is enforced primarily by the Department of Health Services (DHS) through a substantial body of regulations.[117] If there will be a discharge of a hazardous waste into waters of the United States, the contractor must also contact the Regional Water Quality Control Board for permits. This requirement will be discussed further in **§ 5.13**.

Management under HWCA refers to the transportation, transfer, recycling, recovery, disposal, handling, storing, processing, or treating of hazardous waste.[118] Thus, like RCRA, HWCA regulates hazardous waste from generation to final disposition. RCRA provides that states may obtain authorization or interim authorization from the EPA to operate their programs in lieu of the federal program.[119] Until the state obtains RCRA authorization, EPA regulations adopted under RCRA are deemed to be regulations of the DHS, except that any state statute or regulation that is more stringent or more extensive than a federal regulation shall supersede the federal regulation.[120] For example, HWCA and its corresponding regulations are more stringent and extensive than RCRA regulations with respect to small quantity generators, for which there is no exemption.[121]

Under § 25,117 of California Health & Safety Code, *hazardous waste* is defined as a waste that causes or significantly contributes to an "increase in mortality or an increase in serious irreversible, or incapacitating reversible, illness," or which poses "a substantial present or potential hazard to human health or environment when improperly treated, stored, transported, or disposed of, or otherwise managed." If a waste falls into this category, it must be managed in accordance with the provisions of HWCA, unless the material is subject to an existing exception or exemption from HWCA. For example, certain hazardous recyclable materials may be excluded from such classification, and hence regulation under the HWCA, if they are recycled in accordance with certain standards.[122] Also exempt are emptied and drained household hazardous materials and pesticide containers of one gallon or less, hazardous

---

[116] Cal. Health & Safety Code §§ 25,100–25,249.100 (West 1992).

[117] Cal. Code Regs. tit. 22, §§ 66,001–67,786 (1991).

[118] Cal. Health & Safety Code § 25,117.2 (West 1992).

[119] 42 U.S.C. § 6926(b), (c).

[120] *See* 42 U.S.C. § 6929 (Supp. III 1991).

[121] Baker & Hostetler, California Environmental Law Handbook 9 (5th ed. 1991).

[122] Cal. Health & Safety Code § 25,143.2 (West 1992).

waste produced incidental to owning and maintaining a place of residence, storage and transport of certain batteries, short-term storage prior to shipment and transport, and actions "to immediately contain or treat a spill" of hazardous material.[123]

California Manifest System

As under RCRA, HWCA requires that all shipments of hazardous waste be accompanied by manifests. Under DHS regulation, each manifest must contain:

1. Manifest document number
2. Generator's name, mailing address, telephone number, and EPA identification number
3. Each transporter's name and EPA identification number
4. Name, address, and EPA identification number of the facility designated by the generator to handle the waste, and an alternate facility, if any
5. Description of the waste as required by U.S. Department of Transportation regulations[124]
6. Total quantity of each hazardous waste by units of weight or volume, and the type and number of containers shipped.[125]

Portions of the manifest are completed by the generator, the transporter, and the hazardous waste facility, which must note any significant discrepancies between the waste as received and the waste as described in the manifest.

Regulation of Generators

All generators, regardless of quantity of output, are strictly regulated; however, as a practical matter small generators often escape regulation.[126] A *generator* is defined as an entity producing hazardous waste or first causing a hazardous waste to become subject to regulation.[127]

A generator must first determine whether the waste it generates is regulated under HWCA.[128] If so, the generator is subject to the following requirements:

---

[123] Cal. Code Regs. tit. 22, § 66,262.10(h) (1991).

[124] 49 C.F.R. §§ 172.101, 172.202–172.203 (1991).

[125] Cal. Code Regs. tit. 22, § 66,264.71; Cal. D.A. Assoc. at VI-30. (A copy of the DHS manifest form 8022(a) is included in app. 6-C of that book).

[126] Cal. D.A. Assoc. at VI-31.

[127] Cal. Code Regs. tit. 22, § 66,260.10.

[128] *Id.* § 66,262.11.

1. Before generating any hazardous waste, a generator must file a hazardous waste notification statement with the DHS, containing the name and address of the generator, the address and location of the generation site, the name and number of a contact person in the event of an emergency at the site, the quantities of hazardous waste handled annually, a description of the generation activity, and a general description of the hazardous waste being handled.[129] A generator will be exempt from this notification requirement if it has filed a preliminary notification of hazardous waste activity with the EPA, and with owners of sites where remedial action is taking place.[130]

2. Each generator must have an EPA identification number, and entrust its waste only to transporters and hazardous waste facilities having EPA identification numbers.[131]

3. Generators must comply with the manifest requirements discussed above.

4. Any generator shipping hazardous waste off-site must submit a biannual report to the DHS by March 1 of each even-numbered year.[132]

5. Before offering hazardous waste for transportation off-site, generators must package the waste and label, placard, and mark the packages in accordance with the applicable federal regulations.[133]

HWCA also contains regulations similar to RCRA regarding accumulations of hazardous waste. Under California Code of Regulations title 22, § 66262.34(c), a generator must secure a hazardous waste facility permit if hazardous wastes are accumulated on-site for more than 90 days at a time, unless the DHS grants an extension. Extensions may be granted for up to 30 days if the DHS determines that the hazardous wastes must remain on-site for more than 90 days "due to unforeseen, temporary, and uncontrollable circumstances."[134] Accumulations of small amounts of waste may qualify for an exception.[135]

Regulation of Waste Facilities in California

Permit requirements for hazardous waste facilities under HWCA closely parallel requirements under RCRA. Each owner or operator of a hazardous waste facility must obtain an EPA identification number.[136] Facility owners and

---

[129] Cal. Health & Safety Code §§ 25,158(a), (b).

[130] *Id.* § 25,158(f).

[131] Cal. Code Regs. tit. 22, § 66,262.12.

[132] *Id.* § 66,262.41.

[133] *Id.* §§ 66,262.30–.34.

[134] *Id.* § 66,262.34(c).

[135] Cal. Health & Safety Code § 25,123.3(d).

[136] Cal. Code Regs. tit. 22, § 66,264.11.

operators must also comply with the manifest procedures and keep a copy of each manifest for at least three years from the date of delivery of the respective shipment.[137] A hazardous waste facility permit is required for the treatment, storage, or disposal of hazardous waste.[138] The owner or operator of the TSDF must file an application for a permit with the DHS.[139] The HWCA application, like the RCRA application, consists of an introductory part A and a more detailed part B. Both parts must be submitted at least 180 days prior to construction of a new hazardous waste facility.[140] Each permit application must be accompanied by a disclosure statement containing information about the permit applicant, its principals, its operations, other permits held or applied for, and administrative or legal actions taken against the applicant.[141]

After submission of the application, the DHS decides whether to deny the application or prepare a draft permit.[142] Denial may be proper if the applicant misrepresented or failed to fully disclose all relevant facts, and the DHS determines that denial of the application is necessary to protect human health or the environment, or if the applicant is in noncompliance with any condition on an interim status document.[143] If the DHS decides to prepare a draft permit, it must give public notice of the draft permit's preparation and allow at least 45 days for public comment, during which any interested person may submit written comments on the draft permit and make a written request for a public hearing.[144]

If the DHS receives a written notice of opposition to a draft permit and a request for a hearing, or if it finds, on the basis of a hearing request, a significant degree of public interest on the draft permit, the Department is required to hold a public hearing.[145] A final permit issued by the DHS is typically effective for five years, and under HWCA may not exceed 10 years.[146]

Subsequent to receipt of a final hazardous waste facility permit, all permittees are required to:

1. Report any noncompliance that may endanger health or the environment
2. Properly operate and maintain the facility

---

[137] *Id.* §§ 66,264.70–.77.

[138] *Id.* § 66,270.1(c).

[139] *Id.* § 66,270.1(c)(1)(B).

[140] *Id.* § 66,270.10(f)(2).

[141] Cal. Health & Safety Code §§ 25,200.4(a), 25,112.5(a).

[142] Cal. Code Regs. tit. 22, § 66,271.5(a).

[143] *Id.* § 66,270.43.

[144] *Id.* §§ 66,271.9–.11.

[45] *Id.* § 66,271.11.

[46] Cal. Health & Safety Code § 25,200(c); Cal. Code Regs. tit. 22, § 66,270.50(a).

3. Give advanced notice to the DHS of any plan changes in the facility that may result in noncompliance

4. Disclose any relevant information requested by the DHS to determine whether cause exists to modify, revoke, reissue, or terminate the permit

5. Allow inspection of records, equipment, and operations of facilities

6. Apply for and obtain a new permit if the permittee continues an activity addressed by the permit beyond the permit's expiration date.[147]

The DHS may also establish other permit conditions on a case-by-case basis.[148] The permit may subsequently be terminated or renewal denied for any of the following reasons:

1. Noncompliance with any permit condition

2. Failure of the permittee in the application or during the permit issuance process to fully disclose all relevant facts

3. Misrepresentation of any relevant facts by the permittee at any time

4. A DHS determination that the permitted activity endangers human health or the environment and can only be regulated to acceptable levels by permit modification or termination.[149]

In addition to permitting requirements, DHS regulations require the following of hazardous waste facility owners and operators:

1. Inspection of their facilities for malfunctions, deterioration, operator errors, and hazardous discharges

2. A detailed chemical and physical analysis of a represented sample of the waste

3. Personnel training for emergency procedures

4. Annual reports submitted to the DHS and the local Regional Water Quality Control Board (RWQCB) by March 1 of each year

5. A compliance monitoring program detailing the vertical and horizontal extent of hazardous waste constituent migration from the facility, operation records, closure and post-closure plans, liability coverage, and financial assurance for operation, closure, and post-closure.[150]

An intentional or negligent violation of a regulation or provision of HWCA may lead to a fine up to $25,000 per day.[151] Disposal of hazardous waste at an

---

[147] Cal. Code Regs. tit. 22, § 66,270.30.

[148] *Id.* § 66,270.32.

[149] *Id.* § 66,270.43.

[150] *Id.* §§ 66,264.10–.148.

[151] Cal. Health & Safety Code § 25,189(b).

unauthorized site, whether intentional or negligent, may result in a $25,000 per day fine.[152] Criminal penalties, including imprisonment of up to three years, plus a $100,000 per day fine, may be imposed on anyone who knows or should know that they are disposing, transporting, or storing hazardous waste at an unauthorized facility.[153] In addition, if the violation results in great bodily injury, criminal fines of $250,000 per day plus six years' imprisonment may be imposed.[154] Finally, a reward of up to $5,000 is authorized for information resulting in the imposition of a criminal fine.[155]

California recently attempted to simplify the tortuous network of permitting requirements, and dispel the state's resulting antibusiness reputation, by creating the Permit Streamlining Act (PSA).[156] Enactment of PSA was prompted when Dow Chemical, after spending $4.5 million in an attempt to obtain 65 required permits, withdrew its applications to build a $500 million chemical plant in northern California. The Act considerably shortens the time frame during which the responsible and lead agencies must act in issuing an application.

Critics have charged, however, that the Act has been rendered almost completely ineffective.[157] Problems include the need to await legislative action before an approval can be granted, the lack of penalties imposed on agencies that fail to make determinations within the statutory time allotment, and the potential denial of due process because of deemed approval in cases concerning permits that would otherwise require public notice and an opportunity for a hearing.[158]

Management of Waste in Pennsylvania

The Pennsylvania analogy to RCRA is the Solid Waste Management Act (SWMA),[159] which is enforced by the state Department of Environmental Resources (DER). SWMA provides for a permitting program very similar to that of California. The Act states that no one may store, transport, process, or dispose of residual waste unless it is in conformity with DER regulations and the party has first obtained a valid permit.[160] Furthermore, under SWMA it is unlawful to fail to take precautions necessary to protect the environment from emissions or leaching from a site, or for a transporter to fail to use such methods

---

[152] *Id.* §§ 25,189(c), (d).

[153] *Id.* §§ 25,189.5(b), (c), (d), (e).

[154] *Id.* § 25,189.5(e).

[155] *Id.* § 25,191.7(a).

[156] Cal. Gov't Code §§ 65,920–65,963.1.

[157] R. Merritt, *The Permit Streamlining Act, The Dream and the Reality,* 1 CEB, Land Use Forum, No. 1, Fall 1991, at 31.

[158] *Id.* at 34–35.

[159] 35 Pa. Cong. Stat. §§ 6018.101–.1003 (1991).

[160] *Id.* § 6018.301.

and equipment that will protect the environment and public health. Notably, a party may be subject to liability for harm to the public or the environment even if after exercising the utmost care to prevent such harm.[161] The Act also establishes that a person dealing with hazardous waste is presumed liable, without proof of fault, negligence, or causation, for all damages and pollution within 25,000 feet of the perimeter of the area where the activities are taking place.[162] This presumption may be rebutted only by clear and convincing evidence that the presumed responsible party did not contribute to the damage or pollution. However, because this provision does not provide a private right of action for citizens, there is less worry of opening a floodgate of litigation.

Criminal penalties in Pennsylvania are quite severe, with fines of $100,000 per day and prison terms of 10 years for operation without a proper permit.[163] A reckless violation of the Act may constitute a first degree felony punishable by a $5,000 per day fine and 20 years in prison.[164] Knowing transportation of hazardous waste to an unlicensed facility is punishable by a $25,000 per day fine, with steeper penalties for repeat offenders.[165]

Management of Waste in New Jersey

As discussed in **Chapter 2**, the controversial New Jersey Environmental Cleanup Responsibility Act (ECRA) provides for widespread self-investigation of industrial establishments within the state.[166] An *industrial establishment* is defined under ECRA as any business engaged in operations involving the generation, manufacture, refining, transportation, storage, handling, or disposal of hazardous substances.[167] Under the Act, almost any transaction involving such an establishment, including sale, transfer, dissolution, or closure, triggers the cleanup plan or negative declaration requirement. Penalties for violation include the purchaser's right to void the sale and seek damages from the seller, and civil penalties of $250,000 for each day of continuing violation.[168] Significantly, under ECRA a management official who knowingly directs or authorizes a violation of the Act may be personally liable for the above civil penalty. Furthermore, any current owner of an industrial establishment who becomes aware of information that a discharge may have occurred on the property must inspect within 10 days, or face penalties of $50,000 per day.

---

[161] *Id.* § 6018.401(b).

[162] *Id.* § 6018.611.

[163] *Id.* § 6018.606(f).

[164] *Id.* § 6018.606(g).

[165] *Id.* §§ 6018.606(d)(1), (e).

[166] N.J. Stat. Ann. §§ 13:1K-6 to 13:1K-35 (West 1991).

[167] *Id.* § 13:1K-8(f).

[168] *Id.* § 13:1K-13.

§ 5.11   State Air Regulations

Federal, state, and local air regulations will apply whenever any contaminant or toxic fumes may become airborne during the course of remediation. As discussed in § 5.7, the federal CAA specifies that the primary responsibility for maintaining air quality rests with the states.[169]

California has one of the most progressive state clean air acts, which has served as the model for much of the federal Act. California's regulatory program is implemented by the state Air Resources Board (ARB), Local Air Pollution Control Districts (APCDs) and Regional Air Quality Management Districts (RAQMDs). For each basin in the state, the ARB defines ambient air quality standards that may vary from basin to basin.[170] Air districts are authorized to establish a permit system to build, erect, alter, replace, operate, or use a source.[171] Therefore, permitting standards may vary greatly from district to district.

CAA requires each state to prepare a SIP.[172] Each SIP must contain specific requirements for non-mobile air pollution sources in individual air basins, and must comply with NAAQS. Generally, local agencies pass implementing requirements, which are then approved by state agencies and the EPA. The EPA can also make its own requirements enforceable at the local level. Under the California Clean Air Act of 1988, a permit system shall require, upon annual renewal, that each permit be reviewed to determine that permit conditions are adequate to ensure compliance with, and the enforceability of, district rules and regulations under Health and Safety Code § 42,301(c).

Each district is authorized to impose fees for processing permit applications and for annual permit renewal under Health and Safety Code §§ 40,506(b) and 42,311. These fees are often the source of financing for the programs, and may be substantial.

A permit may be suspended, revoked, or denied for the following reasons:

1. Refusal to provide information, analyses, plans, or specifications requested[173]

2. Violations of orders, rules, or regulations[174]

3. Failure to correct any condition as required by an air district[175]

4. Fraud or deceit in obtaining a permit.[176]

---

[169] 42 U.S.C. § 7401(a)(3) (Supp. III 1991).

[170] Cal. Health & Safety Code § 39,606(b).

[171] *Id.* § 42,300.

[172] 42 U.S.C. § 7410.

[173] Cal. Health & Safety Code § 42,304; 42 U.S.C. § 7410.

[174] Cal. Health & Safety Code § 42,307.

[175] *Id.* § 42,309(e)(1).

[176] *Id.* § 42,303.5.

A permit applicant whose application has been denied may request a hearing before the relevant hearing board within 10 days of receiving a notice of denial or suspension of a permit.[177] Any aggrieved person who participated in an action before an air district that led to the issuance of a permit may request a public hearing to determine whether the permit was properly issued.[178]

Anyone who negligently violates a rule or regulation pertaining to emissions limitations may be fined up to $10,000 and serve nine months in jail.[179] A violation with knowledge and failure to take corrective action within a reasonable time may lead to a $25,000 fine and a one-year prison term.[180] These penalties may be imposed for each day of continuing violation. Furthermore, civil penalties of up to $25,000 may be imposed for intentional or negligent violation of an abatement order. Reasonable care will be a defense to such penalties.[181]

Variances may be allowed for certain permits, excluding permits to build, erect, alter, or replace an air contaminant source regulated by a district permit program, if the following conditions exist:

1. The petition will be in violation of a standard.
2. The cause of the noncompliance is a condition beyond the reasonable control of the petitioner.
3. Forced compliance would result in either arbitrary or unreasonable taking of property or the closing of a lawful business.
4. The closing or taking of property would be without a corresponding benefit in reducing air contaminants.
5. The application has considered curtailing operations of the source in lieu of obtaining a variance.
6. During the period the variance is in effect, the applicant will reduce excess admissions to the maximum extent feasible.
7. The applicant will monitor emission levels from the source, if requested to do so by the district, and report these emission levels to the district.[182]

Hearing boards have wide discretion in this area, and may require a bond as a condition for granting a variance.[183]

California also allows air districts to develop a banking program for stationary emissions sources. Such a program allows sources to have received credits

---

Id. §§ 42,302, 42,306.

[178] Id. § 42,302.1.

[179] Id. § 42,400.1(a).

[180] Cal. Health & Safety Code § 42,400.2(a).

[181] Id. §§ 42,401, 42,402.

[182] Id. § 42,352(f).

[183] Id. § 42,355(a).

for certain reductions in air emissions, and use the credits to offset future increases in emissions. This scheme is discussed further in § **5.5**.

Permitting schemes similar to that of California have been enacted in Pennsylvania and New Jersey. In New Jersey, permits may be denied on the grounds that the equipment fails to incorporate the latest advances in pollution control.[184] The state Department of Health is empowered to completely ban operations of a source in violation, and the Act further provides for severe civil and criminal penalties.[185] If the party responsible for such a violation fails to notify the Department immediately, the party may be subject to the above penalties. In addition, New Jersey has recently allowed the imposition of criminal sanctions like those of California for violation of the air quality codes.[186]

The Pennsylvania Air Pollution Control Act[187] requires a permit for the operation of an *air contamination source,* defined as any facility from which air contamination is emitted.[188] Pennsylvania's system of permitting is based on maximum permissible quantities of contaminants,[189] which parallel the ambient air quality standards of California. Pennsylvania law also contains penal provisions, imposing fines in addition to costs of prosecution.[190] Subsequent offenses yield higher fines and possible imprisonment.[191] A notable provision of the Pennsylvania Act allows imprisonment of the responsible officer or employee of a corporation or firm for a violation.[192] This provision represents a trend in environmental law to attribute liability to the responsible party within a corporation.

§ 5.12 State Implementation Plans

As discussed in § **5.9**, states are entitled under CWA to seek authorization of their own regulatory programs in lieu of federal requirements. If a state's program is unauthorized under CWA, both federal and state regulations will apply. As usual, states are free to enact more stringent programs than those promulgated under CWA.

---

[184] State Dep't of Envtl. Protection v. Midland Glass Co., 145 N.J. Super. 108, 366 A.2d 1343 (1976).

[185] N.J. Stat. Ann. §§ 26:2(C)–19(a).

[186] *Id.*

[187] 35 Pa. Cons. Stat. Ann. §§ 4001–4106 (1991).

[188] *Id.* §§ 4006.1(b), 4003.7.

[189] *Id.* § 4005(2).

[190] *Id.* § 4009(a).

[191] *Id.* § 4009(b).

[192] *Id.* § 4009(d).

California

In California, water quality and water pollution are regulated primarily under the Porter-Cologne Water Quality Act.[193] Regulations promulgated under the Porter-Cologne Act are enforced by the State Water Resources Control Board (SWRCB), the nine Regional Water Quality Control Boards (RWQCBs), and local governments. All CWA powers delegated to the state by the EPA are enforced through the SWRCB.[194] The SWRCB also has special responsibilities in the regulation and management of hazardous wastes in California, and in this regard works in close coordination and cooperation with the Department of Health Services Toxic Substances Control Division (DHS/TSCD). The SWRCB is mandated to ensure adequate protection of water quality and statewide uniformity in siting, operation, and closure of waste disposal sites (generally hazardous as well as solid waste), with the exception of sewage treatment plans or sites containing fertilizer or radioactive material.[195]

CWA requires all dischargers of pollutants from point sources to have NPDES wastewater discharge permits.[196] California has been delegated permitting responsibility under Water Code § 13,374, and the state's equivalent of an NPDES permit is known as a Waste Discharge Requirement (WDR). Unlike CWA, the Porter-Cologne Act applies to groundwater. Thus, permits are required for discharges of waste into groundwater as well as to surface water bodies. The definition of a *waste*

> includes sewage and any and all other waste substances, liquid, solid, gaseous, or radioactive, associated with human habitation, or of human or animal origin, or from any producing, manufacturing, or processing operation of whatever nature, including wastes placed within containers of whatever nature prior to, and for purposes, of disposal.[197]

The Porter-Cologne Act applies to all *waters of the state,* which are defined as "any water, surface or underground, including saline waters, within the boundaries of the state."[198]

Any party discharging or proposing to discharge waste (except into a community sewer system) that could affect the quality of the "waters of the state" is required to file a report of waste discharge with the appropriate RWQCB.[199] This report is essentially a permit application and must contain sworn information required by the regional board, accompanied by a fee set under a state

[193] Cal. Water Code §§ 13,000–13,999.19 (West 1992).
[194] *Id.* § 13,160.
[195] *Id.* § 13,172.
[196] 33 U.S.C. §§ 1341, 1342.
[197] Cal. Water Code § 13,050(d).
[198] *Id.* § 13,050(e).
[199] *Id.* § 13,260(a).

board fee schedule.[200] After receipt of a discharge report, the regional board will issue WDRs, which are analogous to a permit with conditions prescribing the nature of the permitted discharge.[201] The discharge requirements must implement applicable RWQCB plans and must take into consideration the beneficial uses of the waters involved, other waste discharges, the need to prevent nuisance, and water quality objectives set by the regional board.[202] The board may waive WDRs for a specific discharge or specific type of discharge where such waiver is not contrary to the public interest.[203]

Because the California statute explicitly covers groundwater, WDRs are required for discharges of waste to land as well as to surface water bodies. As a result, all hazardous waste land disposal activities in the state fall under both RWQCB and DHS regulatory authority. A party must file for a WDR at least 120 days prior to initiating a new waste discharge or making a material change in an existing discharge (unless an RWQCB waiver has been issued).[204] The established requirements may be reviewed and adjusted on the RWQCB's own initiative, or upon petition by an interested party.[205] WDRs must be reviewed at least every five years,[206] and may be terminated for a violation of the Porter-Cologne Act or a change in conditions.[207] Adoption of WDRs does not require the filing of an environmental impact report (EIR) under the California Environmental Quality Act (CEQA).[208]

The Porter-Cologne Act also contains reporting requirements for discharge of a hazardous substance into waters of the state.[209] The DHS and SWRCB have established reportable quantities of hazardous waste, based on the quantity of the material that would pose a risk to public health or the environment.[210] These requirements will be discussed further in § 5.15.

The Porter-Cologne Act states that any discharger in violation of a WDR shall clean up or abate the effects of such waste.[211] Parties permitting or causing a hazardous substance to be discharged into water, creating a condition of pollution or nuisance, will be held strictly liable.[212] Civil penalties for parties

---

[200] *Id.* § 13,260.

[201] *Id.* § 13,263.

[202] *Id.*

[203] Cal. Water Code § 13,269.

[204] *Id.* §§ 13,264(a), 13,269.

[205] *Id.* § 13,263(c), (e).

[206] *Id.* § 13,380.

[207] *Id.* § 13,381.

[208] *Id.* § 13,389; Pacific Water Conditioning Ass'n v. City of Riverside, 73 Cal. App. 3d 546, 555–56, 140 Cal. Rptr. 812 (1977).

[209] Cal. Water Code § 13,271(a)(c). See § 5.15.

[210] Cal. Water Code § 13,271(f).

[211] *Id.* § 13,304(a).

[212] *Id.* § 13,350(b).

who intentionally or negligently violate a cleanup or abatement order, or who are in violation of a discharge permit may be fined by the board up to $5,000 or by a court up to $15,000, for each day of the violation.[213] Defenses include an act of war or natural occurrence, governmental negligence, an intentional act of a third party not preventable by due care or foresight, and any other circumstances that cause the discharge despite the exercise of every reasonable precaution to prevent it.[214] Civil penalties will be determined by a court in light of the nature, circumstances, extent, and gravity of the violation, the violator's ability to pay, the effect on the violator's ability to continue in business, cleanup efforts, prior history of violations, degree of culpability, and any economic advantage to the violator resulting from the discharge.[215]

Heavy criminal penalties may also be imposed in a number of situations, including intentional or negligent violation of a reporting requirement, permit, cease and desist order, order prohibiting discharge in a certain area, or violations of CWA. Such penalties range from $25,000 per day and a one-year prison term for negligent violations, up to $50,000 per day and a three-year prison term for knowing or intentional violations.[216] Subsequent convictions may yield much higher fines. Fines are even higher if a violator knowingly places one in risk of serious bodily injury, with fines reaching $1 million for a first offense.[217] Significantly, the standard is subjective, depending on actual awareness of both present and potential violations.[218]

New Jersey and Pennsylvania

New Jersey and Pennsylvania have also developed permit programs acceptable to the EPA, leaving those states with exclusive authority over state waters. The New Jersey Water Pollution Control Act issues five-year permits that set effluent limitations, compliance deadlines, and set up a self-monitoring process.[219] The New Jersey Act is enforced by the Department of Environmental Protection (DEP), which may conduct reasonable searches and impose a wide range of civil and criminal penalties for violations. When faced with a violation of a water quality standard, effluent limitation, or other provision or regulation, the DEP may issue an order to comply, commence a lawsuit for an injunction and damages, impose a civil fine, immediately commence a lawsuit for such penalty, or ask the appropriate authority to institute criminal proceedings.[220] Civil and

---

[213] *Id.* § 13,350(a).

[214] *Id.* § 13,350(c).

[215] *Id.* § 13,351.

[216] Cal. Water Code §§ 13,387(a), (b), (c).

[217] *Id.* § 13,387(c).

[218] *Id.* § 13,387(d)(2).

[219] N.J. Stat. Ann. §§ 58:10(a)–6(f).

[220] *Id.* § 58:10(a)-10.

criminal fines may reach $50,000 per day for a first offense. Furthermore, anyone knowingly making a false statement in any document required under the Act is subject to fines and imprisonment.[221] The New Jersey statute notably provides for the imposition of criminal penalties against the corporate individual officially responsible.[222] New Jersey utilizes the economic benefit of noncompliance for the violator in arriving at a damages amount. In addition, a gravity component is considered, which takes into account the actual or possible environmental harm, the significance of the violation, the number of violations, and the duration of noncompliance. Other factors in arriving at civil penalties include the degree of willfulness or negligence, "the degree of cooperation, noncooperation, history of recalcitrance, and the ability to pay."[223]

Unlike California statutes, the Pennsylvania clean streams law (CSL) does not create a private right of action for citizens.[224] Liability for water pollution will be imposed on the owner or occupier of the source, regardless of fault.[225] Further, *owner* or *occupier* has been broadly defined to include the owner of an easement.[226] It is unclear whether knowledge of the polluting activity is required.[227]

The Pennsylvania statute includes, in its broad definition of water pollution contamination, substances that alter "the physical, chemical or biological properties" of water, or change "the temperature, taste, color or odor thereof."[228] Liabilities under the Pennsylvania law reach $10,000 per day in civil penalties and $25,000 per day in criminal penalties for initial violations.[229]

§ 5.13   Local Hazardous Substance Regulations

The contractor who embarks on a remediation project should first contact the local enforcement agencies for the planned work area. These local agencies, often called lead agencies, coordinate, monitor, and enforce hazardous waste remediation under the direction of state and federal agencies.[230] In California, the county and city Offices of Environmental Health will typically enforce federal and state regulations concerning hazardous waste. Specifically, the

---

[221] *Id.* § 58:10(a)-(f).

[222] *Id.* § 58:10(a)-3(1).

[223] Environmental Dispute Handbook 106 (D. Carpenter et al. eds., John Wiley & Sons 1991).

[224] *See* Lutz v. Chromatex, Inc., 718 F. Supp. 413 (M.D. Pa. 1989); Fluck v. Timmons, 374 Pa. Super. 417, 543 A.2d 148 (1988).

[225] 35 Pa. Cons. Stat. Ann. § 691.316 (1991); *see* Western Pa. Water Co. v. Commonwealth Dep't of Envtl. Resources, 127 Pa. Commw. 26, 560 A.2d 905 (1989).

[226] *See id.*

[227] *See id.;* Western Pa. Water Co. & Luckenbaugh v. Shearer, 37 Pa. D. & C.3d 588 (1984).

[228] 35 Pa. Cons. Stat. Ann. § 691.1.

[229] *Id.* § 691.602(a)(b).

[230] Waste Education at 138.

regional offices conduct inspection of hazardous waste facilities and small quantity generators, and review reports for UST requirements.

Regional offices of the Toxic Substances Control Division are also responsible for the inspection of hazardous waste facilities, as well as the inspection of hazardous waste transporters. The offices also ensure compliance with hazardous waste control laws by prosecuting violators and assessing civil and criminal penalties, encouraging mutual settlement letters, holding district attorney hearings, issuing administrative orders, and referring violators for federal administrative penalties.[231]

California has also adopted a statutory scheme to coordinate the processing of permits with local land use decision applications for new and modified hazardous waste facilities. The scheme provides for state review of land use decisions by local agencies concerning citing and construction,[232] and seeks to provide an appeals process for local agency decisions on land use.[233] Under this scheme, applications for land use and for hazardous waste facility permits may be simultaneously submitted to and considered by the appropriate state and local agencies.

The statute also establishes procedures for consideration of new or modified specified hazardous waste facilities, which are off-site hazardous waste facilities serving more than one generator. First, the operator of the facility must file an advance notice of intent to apply for a land use decision relating to the project at least 90 days, but not more than one year, before so applying. The advance notice of intent will describe the project and its location. The notified agencies then are required to provide specified notices to other agencies, adjacent property owners, and the public.[234] Advance notice serves to inform the public of the proposed project and the procedures for approving applications for the project.[235] Second, the statute provides for the appointment of a local assessment committee, which is appointed by the local agency within 30 days after the application for land use is deemed complete by the local agency. The seven-member committee is composed of three community representatives, two environmental or public interest representatives, and two business representatives.[236] The committee serves as an advisor to the local agency on the terms and conditions under which the proposal may be acceptable to the community. In carrying out this function, the committee may:

1. Seek to reach an understanding with the project applicant about health, safety, and environmental measures to be observed in the project's

---

[231] *Id.* at 141–49.
[232] Cal. Health & Safety Code §§ 25,199–25,199.14.
[233] *Id.* § 25,199(a)(4).
[234] *Id.* § 25,199.7(a).
[235] *Id.* § 25,199.7(c).
[236] *Id.* § 25,199.7(d)(1).

operations, and compensation to be provided to either the city or county for local costs

2. Represent the interest of local residents in meetings with the proponent
3. Receive and expend technical assistance grants to hire a consultant for assistance in reviewing the project and in reaching an agreement with the applicant
4. Participate in specified public and other meetings with the project applicant, with specified assistance to be provided by the Office of Permit Assistance.[237]

§ 5.14   Local Air Regulations

California implements its permit system for stationary sources through coordinated state regional and local efforts. Each air district may establish distinct requirements regarding limitations, permits, and other programs. The ARB is responsible for developing ambient air quality standards and making an inventory of air pollution sources (including natural sources) for each air basin in California.[238] In addition, the Board is required by the California Clean Air Act of 1988 to identify districts in which air pollutants transported by wind from areas outside the district cause or contribute to a violation of state ambient air quality standards for the ozone.[239]

California contains three legislatively designated air quality management districts: The BAAQMD (discussed in § 5.5), the South Coast Air Quality Management District (SCAQMD), and the Sacramento Metropolitan Air Quality Management District (SMAQMD).[240] The state is also divided into county and regional air pollution control districts.[241] Air districts may enact rules for regulating stationary sources, after 30 days' notice to the ARB and the public, and subject to public hearing.[242] Air districts must also adopt and enforce rules necessary to meet both state and federal ambient air quality standards.[243] Each air district must have a five-member hearing board, consisting of an attorney, a professional engineer, a qualified medical professional or toxicologist, and two members of the public.[244]

---

[237] *Id.* §§ 25,199.7(f), (g), (h).
[238] Cal. Health & Safety Code § 39,607(b).
[239] *Id.* §§ 39,610(a), (d).
[240] *Id.* §§ 40,200–40,201, 40,400–40,408, 40,950.
[241] *See id.* §§ 40,100–40,104, 40,300–40,304.
[242] *Id.* §§ 40,702, 40,725.
[243] *Id.* § 40,001.
[244] Cal. Health & Safety Code §§ 40,800, 40,801.

Air districts are authorized to establish a permit system to build, erect, alter, replace, operate, or use a site as a source.[245] In addition, a permit may soon be required for any building that can be classified as an indirect source under the new SCAQMD program. The Indirect Source Program (ISP) is aimed at buildings that attract a substantial amount of traffic, which is at the root of the district's severe pollution problems. For example, a study by the ARB "estimates that auto emissions associated with the single large regional shopping center (one million square feet) can reach 3,200 pounds per day of reactive organic gases, 23,700 pounds a day of carbon monoxide, and 4,500 pounds per day of nitrogen oxides."[246]

The 1990 amendments to CAA introduce a program to reduce hazardous air pollutant (HAP) emissions from area sources, and public health risks associated with these sources.[247] The amendments encourage states to develop programs to implement and enforce emission standards and other requirements of the air toxics program.[248] However, because California already has an extensive program to regulate HAPs, the effects of these amendments are not yet clear. The ARB provides for a special statewide program to evaluate the risks associated with toxic air contaminants and develop control methods.[249] *Toxic air contaminants* are defined as any "air pollutant which may cause or contribute to an increase in mortality or an increase in serious illness, or which may pose a present or potential hazard to human health."[250]

The SCAQMD has recently removed the dry-cleaning chemical perchloroethylene from an EPA list of air emissions, the carcinogenic effects of which require notification of residents within a quarter mile of the emissions source. The rationale behind the district's action was the perchloroethylene was not yet on the ARB list of toxic pollutants. The board also voted to remove three other toxics—lead, diesel exhaust, and styrene—from the list of air toxics, despite protests over the public's right to know.[251] This right to know arises under District Rule 212, which requires generally that a company installing new equipment or expanding its business must let members of the public know that they will be exposed to a known carcinogen, or to a chemical whose malign effects are undergoing review. However, although Rule 12 requires notification, District Rule 1401, the rule that governs granting a permit to install

---

[245] *Id.* § 42,300.

[246] R. Visser, *Sometimes All You Need Is The Air That You Breathe,* 33 Orange County Law. 20 (1991).

[247] 42 U.S.C. § 7412(k).

[248] *Id.* § 7412(k)(1).

[249] Cal. Health & Safety Code §§ 39,650–39,675.

[250] *Id.* § 39,655.

[251] J. Pasternak, *Dry Cleaners Get Reprieve on Warnings,* L.A. Times, Sept. 7, 1991, at 3.

new cancer-preventing equipment, does not list perchloroethylene as a carcinogenic air contaminant.[252]

§ 5.15 Reporting Requirements

This section addresses provisions for release reporting, including emergency response and cleanup, of discharges into land, water, and air.

Under CWA, any party in charge of a vessel or facility, whether onshore or offshore, who has knowledge of an unauthorized release of oil or other hazardous substance from that vessel or facility, must immediately report the release in a manner consistent with the National Contingency Plan (NCP).[253] Once the appropriate federal agency is notified of a release, that agency must immediately notify the appropriate agency of any state that is, or may reasonably expect to be, affected by the release.[254]

In California, under the Porter-Cologne Act, a party causing a discharge must immediately notify the Office of Emergency Services, and either the SWRCB or the appropriate RWQCB.[255] Notification must be given as soon as the person has knowledge of the discharge, notification becomes possible, and can be given without substantially impeding cleanup or other emergency measures.[256] Notification to the appropriate federal agency will substitute for notice to the above state agencies. Appropriate federal agencies include the National Response Center, the EPA, the Coast Guard, or a federally designated on-scene coordinator.[257] Failure to give such notice constitutes a misdemeanor and can result in fines and imprisonment.[258]

CERCLA expands on release reporting requirements under CWA, by requiring all owners and operators of facilities or vessels who know of an unauthorized release of hazardous substances to immediately report to the National Response Center all such releases that equal or exceed specified reportable quantities (RQ) established by the EPA.[259] Under CERCLA, hazardous substances include all toxic pollutants and hazardous substances listed under CWA, hazardous wastes regulated under RCRA, any hazardous air pollutant under CAA, and chemicals designated as eminently hazardous under the Toxic Substances Control Act (TSCA). In addition, CERCLA allows the EPA to designate additional substances, if they present a substantial danger to the public health,

---

[252] R. Greg Goldin, *Cancer In The Air,* L.A. Weekly, Sept. 6–Sept. 13, 1991, at 16.

[253] 33 U.S.C. § 1321(b)(5) (Supp. III 1991); 40 C.F.R. pt. 300.125 (1991).

[254] 33 U.S.C. § 1321(b)(5).

[255] Cal. Water Code § 13,271(a).

[256] *Id.*

[257] *Id.* § 13,271(e).

[258] *Id.* § 13,271(c).

[259] 42 U.S.C. § 9603(a) (Supp. III 1991); 40 C.F.R. § 302.4 (1991).

welfare, or environment when released.[260] Failure to notify the National Response Center in the event of a release, or knowing submission of false or misleading information, is punishable by fine or imprisonment for not more than three years, or five years for a second or subsequent conviction.[261] Notification of release may not be used in a criminal case against the person reporting the information, except in prosecutions for perjury or giving a false statement.[262]

The EPA under RCRA imposes a number of reporting requirements on hazardous waste transporters and TSDFs. If a discharge of hazardous waste occurs during transport, the transporter must take "appropriate immediate action" to protect human health and the environment.[263] If an air, rail, highway, or water transporter discharges hazardous waste, the transporter must first file an incident report (DOT Form F 58,000.1) with the U.S. Department of Transportation (DOT) within 30 days after discovery of the discharge.[264] Second, the transporter must notify the National Response Center by telephone if, as a direct result of the discharge, any of the following occur:

_____ 1. A person is killed.

_____ 2. A person receives injuries requiring hospitalization.

_____ 3. Property damage is estimated to exceed $50,000.

_____ 4. Fire, breakage, spillage, or suspected radioactive contamination occurs in connection with the shipment of radioactive waste.

_____ 5. A situation results that is "of such nature that, in the judgment of the carrier, it should be reported."[265]

Federal rules require each TSDF to have at least one emergency coordinator, who is available either in person or on call at all times, and who must be familiar with all aspects of the facility's operation, layout, and contingency plan.[266] In the event of an imminent or actual emergency at the site, the emergency coordinator must activate all alarms or communication systems to warn all facility personnel, and notify the appropriate state or local agencies if their assistance is needed.[267] If the emergency involves a release, fire, or explosion, the emergency coordinator must also identify the character, source, amount, and extent of any released materials, as well as assess possible hazards to human

---

[260] 42 U.S.C. § 9602 (Supp. III 1991).

[261] *Id.* § 9603(b)(3).

[262] *Id.*

[263] 40 C.F.R. § 263.30(a) (1991).

[264] *Id.* § 263.30(c)(2) (1991); 49 C.F.R. § 171.16(a) (1990).

[265] 40 C.F.R. § 263.30(c)(1) (1991); 49 C.F.R. § 171.15(a) (1990).

[266] 40 C.F.R. § 264.55 (1991).

[267] *Id.*

health or the environment.[268] If human health or the environment are threatened, the coordinator must immediately contact by telephone either the National Response Center or the government official designated in a regional contingency plan as the on-scene coordinator for the locality.[269]

Within 15 days after an emergency, the facility owner or operator must submit to the EPA a written report containing the owner's name and address, the facility's name and address, the date, time, and nature of the incident, the name and quantity of materials involved, the extent of injuries, assessment of hazards to health or the environment, a disposition as to the present whereabouts of recovered materials and actions involved in recovery, and the estimated quantity of recovered materials.[270]

Regulations adopted by the California DHS under HWCA require essentially the same emergency response and reporting procedures given in the EPA regulations promulgated under RCRA.[271] A transporter filing an incident report with the state DOT pursuant to the regulations discussed above must send a copy of the report to the California Highway Patrol within 30 days after discovery of the incident.[272]

In the event of leakage from a UST, an owner or operator must conform to a corrective action schedule, including notification of the regulatory agency within 24 hours of the leakage. The agency will then investigate, and may require additional action.[273] Operators must also submit a written report to the local agency within five working days.[274] Unauthorized releases require a review of the UST permit by the local agency.

The 1985 California Hazardous Materials Release Response Plans and Inventory Act[275] requires that any actual or threatened release of any hazardous material be reported immediately by "the handler, or any employee, authorized representative, agent, or designee of a handler" to its administering agency and the state Office of Emergency Services.[276] However, no notice is required if there is a reasonable belief that the release or threatened release poses no significant present or potential hazard to human health and safety, property, or the environment.[277] All releases should probably be reported, because the standards are not clearly defined.

---

[268] *Id.* § 264.56(b).

[269] *Id.* § 264.56(d)(2).

[270] *Id.* § 264.56(j).

[271] Cal. Code Regs. tit. 22, §§ 66,264.50–.54.

[272] Cal. Code Regs. tit. 13, § 1166(b) (1990).

[273] 40 C.F.R. §§ 280.61–.67.

[274] Cal. Health & Safety Code § 25,295(a); Cal. Code Regs. tit. 23, § 2650.

[275] Cal. Health & Safety Code § 25,500–25,542.20.

[276] *Id.* § 25,507(a); Cal. Code Regs. tit. 19, §§ 2701–2705 (1990).

[277] Cal. Code Regs. tit. 19, § 2703(c).

The federal Superfund Amendments and Reauthorization Act of 1986 (SARA) requires facilities handling hazardous materials to provide additional information to agencies and the public, and requires planning for releases of extremely hazardous substances. Section 304 of SARA requires reports to the local planning district's emergency coordinator, containing the identity of the substance, whether the substance is listed as an extremely hazardous substance (EHS), the quantity released, the time and duration of the release, the media into which the release occurred, any known or anticipated acute or chronic health risks associated with the emergency, proper precautions, and names and telephone numbers of persons to be contacted for further information.[278]

---

[278] 33 U.S.C. § 11,004(p)(2) (Supp. III 1991); 40 C.F.R. § 355.40(b) (1991).

TYPICAL REMEDIATION PROJECTS*

*Barbara G. Mikalson of Crowell & Moring contributed to this chapter.

ASBESTOS REMOVAL

§ 6.1 Asbestos Remediation

The extreme toxicity of asbestos, and the widespread existence of asbestos-containing material (ACM) in buildings, makes asbestos-related regulation an important issue in remediation. Some evidence suggests that exposure to even microscopic amounts of asbestos fibers can cause asbestosis (white lung) or a form of cancer called mesothelioma, both of which are debilitating and often fatal diseases. It has been estimated that half of all buildings constructed between 1940 and 1970 contain some form of ACM[1] and over 500,000 existing commercial or public buildings contain friable (decaying, easily crumbled by hand) asbestos.[2] The EPA has projected the total cost of conducting remediation of commercial buildings alone at nearly $1 trillion.[3]

In response to the dimensions of the problem, a vast array of laws and regulations have been enacted, affecting requirements for inspection, disclosure, abatement, and disposal. These obligations and regulations arise from a number of sources, including federal regulation under the Clean Air Act (CAA) (see § 6.2), court decisions regarding liability for asbestos remediation under CERCLA, worker health and safety regulations under both federal and state Occupational Safety and Health Administration (OSHA) programs and state labor or health and safety codes (see §§ 6.4 through 6.7), and special requirements for inspection and abatement for schools, hospitals, and other special facilities.

The stringent requirements imposed by statute and by regulatory agencies have been challenged, and to some extent eased, on the grounds that the dangers of asbestos have been exaggerated. The scientific evidence is inconclusive regarding the degree of health risk at various levels of asbestos exposure,[4] and some studies suggest that no hazard is posed by very low levels of airborne asbestos fibers.[5] The EPA's recent attempts to ban all manufacturing and use of ACMs, pursuant to the unreasonable risk provisions of the Toxic Substances Control Act (TSCA)[6] were invalidated and remanded to the EPA by the Fifth

---

[1] Brown, *What Lawyers Must Know About Asbestos,* 73 A.B.A. J. 74 (Nov. 1987).

[2] 18 Env. Rep. (BNA) 2257 (Mar. 4, 1988); EPA, Study of Asbestos-Containing Materials in Public Buildings, A Report to Congress 8 (Feb. 1988).

[3] A.B.A. Sec. Nat. Resources L., Nat'l Energy L. & Pol'y Inst., Natural Resources Law 197 n.1 (1988), *cited in* J. Moskowitz, Environmental Liability and Real Property Transactions: Law and Practice 14 (John Wiley & Sons 1989) [hereinafter Moskowitz]; American Law., July/Aug. 1988, at 6, *cited in* Moskowitz at 14.

[4] *Asbestos study leaves questions in its wake,* Engineering News-Rec., Oct. 7, 1991, at 11.

[5] Mossman, *Asbestos: Scientific Developments and Implications for Public Policy,* 247 Science 294 (1990).

[6] *See* 54 Fed. Reg. 29,460 (1989), *codified at* 40 C.F.R. §§ 763.160–.178 (1990).

Circuit.[7] The court based its decision primarily on the finding that the EPA had failed to produce sufficient evidence of the extreme hazards of asbestos, and the resulting net social benefit of such a ban.[8]

OSHA has also encountered stiff resistance to its intensified efforts to reduce the exposure of workers to asbestos. When the agency amended its rules to reduce the allowable exposure limits from 2.0 to 0.2 asbestos fibers per cubic centimeter, it faced multiple challenges from the construction industry.[9] While the result has been a general easing of regulations by granting exemptions or lowering standards in certain situations, OSHA is considering even stricter standards for its 1992 rules.

The EPA's overall policy has also shifted from an emphasis on asbestos removal to a reasoned evaluation of whether other remedial techniques, such as sealants, will sufficiently lower the overall release rate of airborne fibers.[10] This is not to suggest that removal is necessarily disfavored. Consultants believe that the removal of asbestos may often be in a building owner's best interests, because on-site management of ACM may be just as expensive in the long run.[11]

ACMs that are typically subject to remediation work (or demolition concerns) are found in the following forms:

1. Insulation of structural steel, heating ducts, and water pipes
2. Surfacing material on acoustical ceilings and walls
3. Insulation material in furnaces and air conditioners
4. Mixed into building materials such as tile adhesives, wallboards, wall insulation, and roofing materials.

Asbestos remediation is very expensive, costing approximately $10 to $20 per square foot for removal and replacement.[12] This cost is due both to the location of ACMs and to the licensing, worker safety, handling, and disposal requirements. For these same reasons, the remediation is also time-consuming. According to one expert, discovery of unanticipated asbestos in a remediation, renovation, or demolition project renders the existing construction schedules and budgets almost meaningless.[13]

---

[7] Corrosion Proof Fittings v. EPA, 947 F.2d 1201 (5th Cir. 1991).

[8] *Id.* at 1229.

[9] Fine, *Asbestos Update,* Orange County Bus. J., Apr. 29, 1991, at 22 [hereinafter Fine].

[10] EPA, Managing Asbestos in Place 2-3 (July 1990).

[11] Fine at 21.

[12] Moskowitz at 14.

[13] Hummel, *Dealing with Asbestos-Containing Materials in the Construction Industry,* 4 Prac. Real Est. L. 9, 11 (1988).

§ 6.2   Asbestos Remediation Methods

As discussed in § **6.1**, treating asbestos contamination is a costly and time-consuming process. Therefore, even though asbestos remediation itself is not usually complicated, the complexities of unknown or difficult combinations of hazardous substances, along with migration problems such as leachate to groundwater, mean the choice of treatment may be critical to achieving the desired remediation in a cost- and time-effective manner. Furthermore, the choice of treatment often involves a decision by the owner regarding whether, and when, to invest in a permanent remediation solution. There are four primary methods for the abatement of asbestos contamination in buildings:

1. Removal
2. Encapsulation
3. Enclosure
4. Maintenance with monitoring.

Asbestos removal requires a significant amount of preparation (which may amount to as much as one-third of the total cost of abatement), necessitates expensive enclosure structures, and filtration and respirator equipment (for details, see § **6.6**). If complex surfaces such as pipes, ducts, or gaskets are involved, removal can be particularly time-consuming. Damage to the building may result from the wetting procedures or the construction and removal of partitions. Although removal completely eliminates the source of asbestos fibers, and therefore reduces the need for future monitoring and remediation, the high short-term costs make this treatment cost-effective only if the ACM is damaged, deteriorating, or threatened with damage or exposure.[14]

Preparation of the work area involves completely isolating the area by setting up temporary partitions and covering all exposed surfaces with plastic sheeting. All air passages, including vents and ducts, must be sealed or filtered. High-efficiency filtration systems must be set up to control fiber levels in air circulating within and to the outside of the work area. All ACM that will be affected is then wetted down with amended water (water to which a chemical wetting agent or surfactant has been added). During physical removal, the asbestos must remain wet at all times. When removed, the asbestos-containing waste must be sealed in impermeable bags or other approved containers, and labeled according to RCRA and OSHA regulations.[15] These wastes can be disposed of only in approved landfills pursuant to RCRA and various regulations.[16]

---

[14] M. Esposito, Decontamination Techniques for Buildings, Structures and Equipment 20 (1987) [hereinafter Esposito].

[15] 29 C.F.R. § 1910.1001 (1991).

[16] 40 C.F.R. § 61.154 (1991).

Once the waste is totally contained, all surfaces, including fixtures and other equipment in the sealed-off area, must be wiped and cleaned with vacuums that filter their exhaust through high-efficiency filters. Facilities for decontamination of workers, including a portable shower with special drain filters and a changing area for storing contaminated clothing, may be required. Finally, air monitoring equipment personnel are necessary during most of the project.

In spite of these extensive precautions, a number of health and safety problems exist. In addition to lung damage from the inhalation of asbestos fibers, workers can suffer heat stress from increased temperatures and humidity in sealed areas, failure of the ventilation system, or the protective clothing. The use of sprayers to wet down asbestos poses the risk of electric shock where electric equipment is used.

Encapsulation involves the treatment of ACM with a chemical penetrant or special sealant that binds the asbestos fibers and prevents further decay. The primary advantage of this method is the lower initial cost. The sealant itself is sprayed on quickly. Furthermore, the asbestos continues to perform its insulating function.

Encapsulation is, however, only a temporary abatement solution. Such treatment merely creates a barrier between the environment and the asbestos, which is still toxic. This barrier is vulnerable to erosion or destruction, thereby allowing asbestos emission. Moreover, the sealants used may themselves create significant problems, such as destroying the fire retardant properties of the ACM, and making the material more difficult to eventually remove. In addition, this method is only appropriate if the ACM is in good condition and not exposed to water.

The safety requirements described above (and in §§ 6.6 through 6.8) for removal, including the preparation of an enclosed workspace and decontamination procedures, apply as well to encapsulation, but will be required for considerably shorter periods of time. Although materials used to contain the workspace must be disposed of as ACMs, the total amount of contaminated waste is minimal, and the problem of disposing of contaminated water is absent (no wetting down is required).

Asbestos enclosure is really a method of containment, rather than treatment. Enclosure involves the construction of a permanent barrier to seal off the areas of the building containing ACM from those areas that are occupied. The ACM, which remains in place, must still be monitored, controlled, or replaced. As a result, enclosure is generally a high-cost method in the long term. Many of the costs of performing abatement remain. Because the construction of the barriers can cause the release of fibers, the same safety precautions as for removal (workplace enclosure, monitoring, decontamination) are normally required.

Finally, special maintenance and monitoring procedures provide an additional short-term solution. This approach minimizes short-term cost and may offer a reasonably low level of risk until the owner is willing or able to undertake a permanent solution. However, maintenance requires continuous upkeep

and inspection; therefore, extensive future costs will be incurred without eliminating liability from the existing asbestos. The ACM must be non-friable and in
good condition.[17] Maintenance and monitoring activities include thorough
cleaning procedures (including wet-wiping and use of specially filtered vacuums), repair of ceilings and walls, and establishing regular inspections, building
maintenance procedures, and worker safety procedures.

§ 6.3 Regulation of Asbestos as a
Hazardous Air Pollutant

Asbestos has been designated as a hazardous air pollutant (HAP) under CAA,
which also authorizes the EPA to establish federal emission standards in order
to limit release of HAPs.[18] These standards are called the National Emissions
Standards for Hazardous Air Pollutants (NESHAPS), which was also the name
of the program that regulated HAPs prior to the more comprehensive scheme
enacted in 1990. While the same standards have been maintained under the
1990 amendments, the EPA must review these standards by the year 2000.[19]
In addition, the EPA is currently considering modifying the NESHAPS for asbestos to require maximum achievable control technology (MACT) standards.
   The EPA applies these standards to a broad category of activities involving
ACMs, including:

1. Demolition and renovation of buildings
2. Waste disposal
3. Installing or removing insulating materials
4. Spraying or fabricating.[20]

Existing regulations establish procedural requirements for conducting these activities, as well as controlling disposal of asbestos-containing waste, and imposing prior notification requirements for all of these activities.
   While the regulation of asbestos is largely defined and regulated as a source
of air pollution (as under CAA), both RCRA and CERCLA, as well as their
state counterparts, also apply to asbestos remediation. Asbestos is a HAP under
CAA; therefore, it is automatically designated a hazardous substance under
CERCLA.[21] For a discussion of the limitations of liability for asbestos, see
§ 6.5. RCRA classifies asbestos as a nonhazardous solid waste. Therefore,

---

[17] Esposito at 29.

[18] 42 U.S.C. § 7412(b)(1) (Supp. III 1991).

[19] *Id.*

[20] 40 C.F.R. §§ 61.140–.157 (1991).

[21] 42 U.S.C. § 9601(14)(E) (Supp. III 1991).

although RCRA permitting and other regulations regarding the handling, storage, and transportation of hazardous waste do not apply to disposal of asbestos, the general provisions of subtitle D, governing siting and operational requirements for solid waste disposals, do apply.[22]

§ 6.4 —Notification Requirements

The purpose of notification requirements is to make the EPA or local regulatory agency aware of asbestos-related activities, to allow the agencies to prepare for inspection of worksites for compliance with established procedures. Although the EPA does not generally conduct on-site inspections of smaller projects, the EPA requires notice of such projects further in advance. In demolition projects involving at least 80 linear meters of asbestos-wrapped pipe, or 15 square meters of any other ACM (such as wallboards, insulation, or ceiling materials sprayed with a surface compound containing asbestos), the party undertaking the work (usually the contractor or subcontractor) must notify the EPA in writing at least 10 days prior to starting work.[23] For projects involving a smaller amount of ACM, at least 20 days' notice must be given.

These federal reporting requirements may be increased by air quality management districts (AQMDs). For example, the South Coast Air Quality Management District (SCAQMD) in Southern California, facing the task of major reduction of air pollutants, has implemented very strict reporting requirements. SCAQMD rules require written notification regarding any demolition work or renovation work involving 100 square feet or more of ACM, including residential renovation.[24] This notification includes proof of contractor licensure and OSHA registration, transportation and disposal plans, and a description of the project and workplace procedures.[25]

State and local authorities have increasingly enacted legislation requiring contractors, employers, or owners engaged in asbestos-related construction work to notify employees, the public, and public agencies of such work. Typical statutes include requirements to give notice to employees working in a building in which asbestos is known to be present[26] or undergoing renovation.[27] State and local health and safety ordinances may require notifying local fire or health services departments of asbestos demolition or renovation.[28]

---

[22] These regulations are found in 40 C.F.R. §§ 240–257 (1991).

[23] *Id.* § 61.145 (1991).

[24] SCAQMD R. 1403(d) (Feb. 1991).

[25] *Id.* R. 1403(d)(1)(A).

[26] *See, e.g.,* Cal. Health & Safety Code § 25,359.7(b)(2) (West 1992).

[27] *See, e.g., id.* § 25,916.

[28] *See, e.g.,* N.Y. Lab. Law §§ 875–883 (McKinney 1992); N.Y. Pub. Health Law §§ 4800–4808 (McKinney 1992).

§ 6.5   —Inspection Requirements

A renovation or demolition project may be subject to requirements to inspect for the presence of asbestos. For example, in Virginia, such inspection is required to obtain a permit for the renovation or demolition of any public or commercial building built prior to 1978.[29] The owner must verify that an asbestos inspection has been conducted, and that remedial action, if appropriate, will be taken according to NESHAP, OSHA, and state health and safety regulations.[30]

Recent legislation in California requires that owners of buildings containing asbestos, employers of workers that may be exposed, and contractors who engage in asbestos-related work must make a good faith investigation regarding the presence of asbestos prior to beginning construction work.[31] Since asbestos-related work is defined as an activity that might release asbestos fibers into the air, inspection may be required for maintenance or minor renovation work, as well as major renovation and demolition. A contractor who does any work on a building constructed before 1978 must first request information from the owner regarding the presence of asbestos.

The primary effect of this law in terms of remediation contracting is to shift from the owner to the contractor the risks of costs and delays attributable to a hidden asbestos problem. While the owner normally bears the costs of extra work and delays associated with unanticipated hidden conditions, the duty to investigate makes it unlikely that hidden asbestos could be characterized as unanticipated.[32]

To protect contractors who are obligated to inspect or investigate, a specific provision shifting the risk to the owner will be required. For example, the Contractors State License Board recommends a clause providing compensation for extra work, and an extension of time if asbestos conditions not disclosed in the project plans are encountered.[33]

Owners, on the other hand, may want to negotiate a provision requiring the contractor to provide all labor, equipment, and material required to remediate newly discovered asbestos. However, since the amount of money at risk may be very large relative to the size of the project, the contractor may well refuse, or increase fees substantially. Therefore, it may be favorable to both sides to perform a significant amount of investigation prior to negotiating the contract. A typical clause could read as follows:

Contractor has investigated the site and made all necessary inspections and tests to determine the nature and scope of the project. To the extent that Contractor

[29] Va. Code Ann. § 36-99.7 (Michie Supp. 1990).

[30] *Id.*

[31] Cal. Lab. Code § 6501.9 (West 1991).

[32] *Asbestos. Delay, Disruption and Extra Work,* Calif. Constr. L. Rep., July 1991, at 134.

[33] Contractors State License Board, Consumer Guide to Asbestos 11 (1990).

subsequently encounters asbestos on site (beyond that disclosed by owner or described in exhibit _____ to the contract), Contractor shall, at its own cost, provide all labor, equipment, material, transportation, and job safety programs needed to abate this asbestos.

§ 6.6 —Procedures for Emission Controls

Because of concerns regarding the health hazards of even the most minuscule exposure to airborne asbestos and ACM, the standards for conducting asbestos remediation work are stringent. There are two areas of regulatory control: regulations designed to provide worker health and safety, administered by OSHA and the National Institute for Occupational Safety and Health (NIOSH); and requirements regarding removal and remediation procedures and disposal, designed to control releases of asbestos fibers, and administered by the EPA. Occupational safety standards are discussed in § **6.8.**

As mentioned in § **6.3**, the EPA is considering adopting a MACT standard for NESHAPS for asbestos. NESHAPS apply wherever friable ACM, or nonfriable ACM that has a high probability of becoming crumbled, pulverized, or reduced to powder in the course of demolition or renovation, is present.[34] Once NESHAPS apply, contractors must comply with strict procedures for asbestos emission control.[35] These controls include wetting down all affected ACM, sealing of the area under renovation or demolition, and decontamination procedures to ensure a minimum of leakage to the outside. See § **6.2** for a detailed discussion of these procedures. NESHAPS also require that no visible emissions to the outside air occur during the collection, treatment, packaging, transporting, or disposal of ACMs.[36]

In addition to NESHAPS, RCRA solid waste regulations apply to the disposal of ACM, even though asbestos is designated as nonhazardous. Far more stringent constraints are imposed by state law, which typically regulates the disposal of asbestos as a hazardous waste.[37] For example, under the California Hazardous Waste Control Act (HWCA), waste must be double-bagged, labeled, transported by a licensed transporter within 90 days of generation, and disposed of only in an approved landfill.[38] These regulations apply to any party that generates, handles, stores, treats, or disposes of hazardous waste.[39]

Regional air quality management districts (RAQMDs) may also develop and enforce standards in addition to or stricter than those included in NESHAPS.

---

[34] 40 C.F.R. § 61.141 (1991).

[35] *Id.* § 61.145.

[36] *Id.* § 61.150(a).

[37] *See, e.g.,* Cal. Health & Safety Code §§ 25,100–25,249.100 (West 1992).

[38] *Id.*

[39] *Id.* § 25,110.1.

See § **6.4** regarding notification. Therefore, contractors should be careful to ascertain and comply with all federal, state, and local agencies and regulations when disposing of asbestos.

§ 6.7 —Licenses, Certification, and Permitting for Asbestos Remediation

Several states require that contractors and workers who perform asbestos remediation work must be specially trained and licensed.[40] Local AQMDs may offer training programs for asbestos abatement workers. At the state level, the certification process, including examination, is often administered by the State Contractors License Board.[41] In addition, a list of accreditation programs approved by the EPA are published periodically in the *Federal Register.* The EPA has also published a list of accreditation programs and training courses for the Asbestos Hazard Emergency Response Act.[42]

Many states also require contractors to be registered. In California, contractors conducting asbestos-related work involving more than 100 square feet of ACM must be registered with the Division of Occupational Safety and Health of the State Department of Industrial Relations.[43] While no permits are required under RCRA or CAA, permits may be required for asbestos abatement projects under state law.[44]

The vast expansion in opportunities for asbestos remediation work, and the premium price paid to licensed and trained workers, contractors, and subcontractors, offers significant incentives for general contractors to contract with unlicensed subcontractors or for subcontractors to employ untrained workers. This practice is not only in violation of state or local ordinances in most locales, but also may expose the owner and contractor to liability for tort damages. For a discussion of the potential grounds, see the negligence and strict liability sections in **Chapter 8**.

A contractor who was recently conducting a major renovation involving ACMs in a downtown Los Angeles building discovered that one of the subcontractors, in trying to speed up work on the project, had resorted to hiring cheaper, but more available, untrained workers. Because of the frequency of violation by this subcontractor, and the potential hazard, this action was perceived by both the EPA and local regulatory agencies as a serious violation. The result

---

[40] *See, e.g.,* Cal. Bus. & Prof. Code §§ 7058.5–.01 (West 1992); Va. Code Ann. §§ 54.1-500 to 54.1-517 (Michie Supp. 1990); Va. Asbestos Licensing Regulations, VR190-05-1, 7 Va. Regs. Reg. 712 (Dec. 3, 1990).

[41] *See, e.g.,* Cal. Bus. & Prof. Code § 7058.5 (West 1992).

[42] *See* 56 Fed. Reg. 43,064 (1991).

[43] Cal. Lab. Code § 6501.5 (West 1992). *See* Cal. Bus. & Prof. Code § 7058.5 (West 1992); Cal. Health & Safety Code §§ 25,915–25,925 (West 1992).

[44] *See, e.g.,* Cal. Lab. Code §§ 6500–6511 (West 1989); Asbestos Project Permits & Permit Fees Regulation, VR425-01-74, 6 Va. Regs. Reg. 3663 (Aug. 13, 1990).

was a suspension of work, with concomitant cost increases and delay. Moreover, the local District Attorney's office filed misdemeanor charges against representatives of the contractor and the owner. As of this writing, no personal injury actions have been brought, but they could also be forthcoming. To avoid similar violations, the owner or contractor should ensure that compliance with the licensure, training, and other relevant requirements is specified in the contract, and procedures for documenting such compliance are established.

§ 6.8 —Occupational Safety for Asbestos Remediation

The federal OSHA may delegate administration of its regulations to the states, provided they apply federal standards.[45] OSHA requirements require employers to monitor levels of asbestos in the work area, establish permissible limits of employee exposure to asbestos, establish requirements for containment areas, and specify types of safety clothing and equipment to be used by workers. These requirements apply to all employers conducting construction work involving asbestos, including alteration, repair, maintenance, renovation, and demolition activities.

The employer has a duty to monitor (measure by air sampling) for asbestos if the employer has reason to believe that asbestos is present at the worksite. If sampling reveals a level at or above 0.1 fiber per cubic centimeter,[46] the employer must institute measures that include employee information and training programs and periodic medical examinations.[47]

OSHA establishes a two-tiered regulatory scheme for asbestos. First, the agency has established a permissible exposure limit (PEL), which is the maximum amount of asbestos exposure to which employees may be subjected. Currently, the PEL is defined at 0.2 fiber per cubic centimeter per eight-hour period.[48] In projects involving only brief exposure to a minimal release of asbestos, employers may be allowed to apply the short-term exposure limit (STEL), which is one fiber per cubic centimeter averaged over a 30-minute sampling period. If the PEL is exceeded, or can reasonably be expected to be exceeded, employers must comply with stricter regulated-area requirements.[49]

Employers are also generally required to create a negative pressure enclosure prior to starting a project involving asbestos removal, demolition, or renovation.[50] OSHA does not generally require such enclosures for minimal exposure

---

[45] 29 U.S.C. § 667(b) (Supp. III 1991).

[46] This measure is taken as an eight-hour time-weighted average. 29 C.F.R. § 1926.58(b) (1991).

[47] *Id.* § 1926.58(b).

[48] *Id.* § 1926.58(c).

[49] *Id.*

[50] *Id.* § 1926.58(e)(6)(i).

activities such as pipe repair, valve replacement, roofing, or other general building maintenance.[51] These negative pressure enclosures can be extremely expensive to maintain. They require a ventilation system that draws fresh air into the work area and filters asbestos fibers from the outbound exhaust. The regulated area must be fully enclosed by a sealed plastic envelope with a three-stage entrance/exit chamber, which is under negative air pressure. Employers must also either maintain the asbestos exposure level to action level standards or equip all employees with approved supplied-air respirators,[52] and provide OSHA-regulated protective clothing, such as coveralls, gloves, and foot and head coverings.[53] See § **6.2** for further discussion of these procedures.

The regulated area must be monitored on a daily basis. If monitoring reveals that the PEL will be exceeded, the employer must institute a number of procedures to maintain the asbestos fiber level below the PEL.[54] For some renovation and demolition work, however, the engineering controls and work procedures that are physically and financially feasible cannot maintain the required levels of airborne asbestos. In such cases, the employer must institute the necessary controls to achieve the lowest level attainable and, in addition, provide respiratory protection for employees.[55]

§ 6.9 Liability under CERCLA

Although asbestos is designated as a hazardous substance under CERCLA,[56] the courts have struggled with the issue of liability for asbestos contamination in cost recovery actions under the Act. See **Chapter 4** for a general discussion of cost recovery. Early attempts to use CERCLA's strict liability provision to bring cost recovery actions against manufacturers as potentially responsible parties (PRPs) were denied on the grounds that CERCLA was not intended as a products liability statute.[57]

In *3550 Stevens Creek v. Barclays Bank,*[58] the court barred a private action under CERCLA § 107(a)(2)(B)[59] against a former owner who was responsible

---

[51] *Id.* § 1926.58(e)(6)(iv).

[52] 29 C.F.R. § 1926.58(f)(3), (4).

[53] *Id.* § 1926.58(i).

[54] *Id.* § 1926.58(g).

[55] *Id.* § 1926.58(g)(1)(ii).

[56] 42 U.S.C. § 9601(14)(E) (Supp. III 1991).

[57] *See, e.g.,* Corporation of Mercer Univ. v. National Gypsum Co., 24 Env't Rep. Cas. (BNA) 1953 (M.D. Ga. 1986).

[58] 915 F.2d 1355 (9th Cir. 1990).

[59] *Codified at* 42 U.S.C. § 9607(a)(2) (Supp. III 1991). This section makes a present or former owner of property liable for the disposal of a hazardous substance on the property at the time the party was the owner.

for the installation of asbestos products, for recovery of the cost of voluntarily removing that ACM. The court's reasoning was that a party could be held liable only for an "affirmative act of disposal."[60] In a similar vein, in *Anthony v. Blech*[61] a state agency, which was a tenant, brought a cost recovery action against the owner/landlord for costs of cleanup of asbestos released in a fire. The district court relied on *Stevens Creek* to deny the action, arguing that § 107(a)(1)(A), although not limited to disposal, does not apply to an asbestos product installed and in current use in a building, which is excluded from CERCLA regulation as a "consumer product in consumer use."[62]

A different, if not conflicting, rationale was utilized in *CP Holdings, Inc. v. Goldberg-Zoino & Associates, Inc.,*[63] in which the former owner of a building, who had failed to disclose that the building contained asbestos even though the owner knew it was to be demolished, was held liable under CERCLA. The court distinguished the case from *Stevens Creek* by noting that the cleanup action in *Stevens Creek* was voluntary, while the remediation in *CP Holdings* was conducted pursuant to a state order.

The only continuity to these holdings is that the government ultimately has more control than the private sector. This delineation of liability seems to arise from the realization that environmental remediation can create liability out of proportion to the assets or activities of the PRPs, so that some ability to limit recovery is needed. Commentators have suggested that the sharply circumscribed basis for recovery is the result of the hesitation of Congress to expand liability, given the magnitude of the asbestos problem and the trend toward favoring management over removal.[64] However, the issue of liability is not settled, which leaves any party handling asbestos with serious potential liability exposure.

UNDERGROUND STORAGE TANKS

§ 6.10   Introduction

The problems associated with removal of, or contamination from, underground storage tanks (USTs) seem to be part of virtually any remediation effort. In some projects, these tanks are the focus of the environmental cleanup. In other situations, they are merely part of a larger remediation effort. Often, the tanks are unexpectedly encountered during the construction of a conventional project.

---

[60] 3550 Stevens Creek v. Barclays Bank of Cal., 915 F.2d 1355, 1361.

[61] 760 F. Supp. 832 (C.D. Cal. 1991).

[62] CERCLA § 101(9), 42 U.S.C. § 9601(g) (Supp. III 1991).

[63] 769 F. Supp. 432 (D.N.H. 1991).

[64] Moskowitz, *Commentary,* 1 Cal. Env't L. Rep. 29, 30 (June 1991).

To prepare for such a possibility in the contracting phase, see **Chapter 3**. If the tanks are the focus of the cleanup effort, it is likely that they will receive a complete analysis and that a cleanup program will be given thorough consideration. If, however, the tanks are ancillary to the main thrust of the effort, or are discovered as part of the construction process, the method of handling them may receive little, if any, consideration. The treatment of such tanks is often further complicated by the lack of charts and accurate records. See **§ 6.14** concerning these problems.

In 1984, certain amendments to RCRA included a number of regulations aimed at USTs[65]. Although initial proposals were intended to put the UST program under the authority of CERCLA, so that federal funds would be used to address the problems and to assist in regulating them under TSCA, those proposals were eventually dropped and USTs are now regulated under RCRA. The UST program covers tanks containing petroleum products, as well as any wastes not listed as hazardous under RCRA. If a tank contains a RCRA subtitle C (hazardous) waste, it is still regulated under 40 C.F.R. §§ 264 and 265(j). This dichotomy is worthy of note. Although RCRA does not treat petroleum products as hazardous wastes (and arguably excludes them from coverage), for purposes of UST problems, petroleum products are regulated under RCRA, albeit not as hazardous waste. If hazardous wastes and petroleum products were combined in tanks, such wastes would probably be treated as hazardous, following the rationale of the *Mid Valley Bank* decision discussed in **Chapter 4**.

§ 6.11 —Coverage

UST regulations apply to all storage tanks that are 10 percent or more below ground.[66] Underground piping is included when computing this percentage. Small tanks (with a capacity of less than 1100 gallons) are exempt if they are located on a farm or residence, as opposed to a commercial or industry facility.[67] Petroleum pipelines are exempt to the extent that they are regulated under the Hazardous Liquid Pipeline Safety Act (HLPSA).[68]

The owner of a leaking UST is subject to strict and retroactive liability in essentially the same manner as under CERCLA. Under the provisions of 40 C.F.R. § 280, the regulations contain standards for installation, operation, maintenance, and removal of any regulated system. There are also standards for corrective action when leaks are detected, and for record keeping and monitoring. Finally, and perhaps most important, UST owners must establish adequate

---

[65] 42 U.S.C. §§ 6991–6991(i) (Supp. III 1991).

[66] 42 U.S.C. § 6991(1) (Supp. III 1991).

[67] *Id.*

[68] *Id.* § 6991(1)(D)(i).

insurance or guarantee their ability to take any necessary corrective action and to compensate any injured third parties. Although the requirement that new tanks be installed with certain leak prevention detection features has no immediate effect on remediation, tanks that were not so installed had to be upgraded or removed by December 22, 1988.[69]

§ 6.12 —Determination of the Contaminant in UST Closure

It is imperative to determine the exact substance (or combination of substances) stored in USTs, the substance's proximity to the local groundwater, and the precise location of the tanks, when attempting to remove these tanks and treat the contamination that may have occurred in the contiguous soils.

Many of the tanks contained fuel oil and lubricants. Familiarity with the migration and persistence properties of bulk hydrocarbons is therefore often crucial to a successful UST cleanup project. Bulk hydrocarbons (crude oil, refined petroleum, and petrochemicals such as trichloroethylene) may enter the soil and replace water as the primary solvent. The action of these bulk hydrocarbons in the soil, once they are released from the underground tank, is a reflection of whether they are floaters (having a density less than that of water) or sinkers (having a density greater than that of water). The action will also depend on the makeup and permeability of the surrounding soil, the impact of capillary forces, and other factors. Because these factors affect the migratory pattern of contaminants, they will ultimately determine the impact of the tank leakage on groundwater. Thus, this analysis of the likely migration pattern of the contaminant in the affected area will in turn tell the contractor what the scope of the project must be.

A carefully defined regulatory profile describes the mandatory steps for a UST closure:

1. The tanks must be emptied and cleaned.

2. A site assessment must be performed to determine if a leak has occurred. If that assessment reveals probable contamination, remedial action must begin.

3. Tanks removed must be filled with an inert select material and the site must be closed.

4. Owners must keep records of the closure for three years.[70]

---

[69] 40 C.F.R. § 280.21 (1991).

[70] For a thorough discussion of these issues, *see, e.g.,* R. Bernardino, *Recordkeeping Requirements for Underground Storage Tank Program,* 1 Cal. Envtl. L. & Reg. Rep., July 1991, at 124 [hereinafter Bernardino]; 40 C.F.R. § 280.45 (1991).

§ 6.13   —Preremoval Analysis

As discussed in § **6.12**, the owner and the contractor undertaking the actual removal of the tanks and the remediation of any contamination must be equipped with a thorough analysis of the tanks and the surrounding soil. Contaminant plumes must be mapped and characterized as accurately as possible, thus enabling the contractor to anticipate the size and scope of the problem at the outset, and arrange to have adequate machinery and manpower for the effort. Reflecting this initial analysis, the contractor should also prepare a comprehensive and systemic plan for removal of the tanks. If it is determined that the tanks contain any additional contaminants, those contaminants should be removed before the removal of the tank. The contractor should attempt to seal off any downstream areas from the potential migration of contaminants during the tank removal. A host of devices such as catch basins, slurry walls, and intermediate pump and treatment facilities are designed to ameliorate the consequences of excavation work involving already contaminated soil, including the movement of pollutants into groundwater.

Because tanks cannot be removed without a prior site assessment, the contractor should demand that the owner have the study performed and provide the resulting documentation. A contractor who undertakes removal of USTs without such an assessment could be liable as a generator and transporter of a regulated substance.

§ 6.14   —Problems Frequently
Encountered with USTs

Inaccurate or incomplete mapping of tanks and tank fields, along with missing, incomplete, or inaccurate pre-RCRA (and in some cases post-RCRA) tank leakage measurement statistics, often creates situations in which the composition and extent of the plume of contaminants, and the plume's projected impact on the site and groundwater, is totally unknown. The EPA identification notice form allows the answer unknown to be inserted on the form in the event prior information is unavailable[71]; however, that allowance is little comfort to the contractor who must remove the tank. The problem is often further compounded by the lack of charts or topographical layouts showing the tanks' location and depth.

The recordkeeping requirements of the 1984 RCRA amendments are monumental, and require release detection systems, retention of the detection system manufacturer's written representations for at least five years, and retention of all calibration records[72]; however, in practice, compliance with the requirements

---

[71] Bernardino at 124; 40 C.F.R. §§ 280.70–.74 (1991).

[72] 40 C.F.R. §§ 280.71, 280.74.

is often woefully inadequate. We were recently involved in the sale and subsequent development of a property that had a gas station on it, among other things. The buyer's due diligence investigation revealed that the records were internally inconsistent and would not reconcile with the data on volume of delivery and volume of sales. When excavation began, the contractor almost immediately encountered an unknown set of old tanks in a remote corner of the property. The gas station had evidently been originally sited there, and relocated later when a more modern station was installed. No one at that time had recorded the existence of this old set of tanks. This problem might have been avoided by a more diligent system of record keeping. Once again, the necessity of effective day-to-day project management is demonstrated. The most stringent and detailed regulations available are worthless in the absence of skilled and trained personnel to oversee compliance. Furthermore, although violations of such regulations may provide a basis for the agency to assess fines and penalties, there is no assumption of the information necessary for performing the task.

HAZARDOUS WASTE

§ 6.15   Confinement of Hazardous Wastes

The volatile relationship between the remediation contractor's obligations and the ever-fluctuating regulatory requirements is perhaps most obvious in the evolution of the regulations dealing with confinement and neutralization of hazardous waste. Prior to the passage of the Hazardous and Solid Waste Amendments (HSWA) of 1984,[73] the EPA regulations for waste disposal were calculated to be technologically neutral. However, land disposal quickly became the preferred method for disposing of hazardous waste because of the rather lenient regulatory climate and the low disposal costs.[74] Congress attempted to reform this predisposition toward land disposal in the provisions of HSWA, which establishes a policy encouraging waste minimization and alternative disposal and treatment methods. The amendments provide four directives:

1. Reduce the amount of hazardous waste generated
2. Minimize land disposal of hazardous waste
3. Require generators and TSDF operators to periodically certify that they have waste reduction programs in force
4. Implement a land disposal minimization policy.[75]

---

[73] 42 U.S.C. §§ 6901–6992k (Supp. III 1991).

[74] C.R. Fortuna & D.J. Lennett, Hazardous Waste Regulation: The New Era 181 (1987) [hereinafter The New Era].

[75] 42 U.S.C. § 6902.

In 1986, the EPA created rules to implement the land disposal prohibitions of HSWA. These amendments are extremely complicated, and a complete explication is beyond the scope of this work. Basically, however, the amendments prohibit land disposal of certain wastes unless they have been successfully treated to meet certain specified extraction levels.[76] (Certain limited exemptions are available, but they are irrelevant to this discussion.) Another method of qualifying a prohibited waste for land disposal is through a site-specific petition process involving a number of requirements, including the demonstration by the applicant of a reasonable degree of certainty that hazardous materials will not migrate from the land disposal units.[77]

Along with the land disposal restrictions, permitting standards were developed that applied to landfills, surface impoundments, and certain waste piles. Prior to 1982, those standards were based on a liquids management strategy, which was designed to prevent the migration of hazardous material into the groundwater. The standards as applied, however, proved to be inadequate. Only one liner was required for new landfills and surface impoundments. No leachate collection and monitoring system was required. Furthermore, liberal definition and interpretation of terms exacerbated certain problems by allowing substandard treatment.[78] HSWA responded by placing greater emphasis on management and monitoring of landfills.[79] As a result, certain minimum design standards (including double liners and leachate monitoring and collection systems) were mandated. In addition, retrofit of existing surface impoundments was required.[80]

As discussed in § **6.15**, the regulatory standards related to the treatment of hazardous waste are ambiguous and changing. Battles between the courts and environmental agencies have failed to clarify or settle these requirements. For example, a recent decision of the Court of Appeals for the District of Columbia invalidated the EPA's leachate monitoring rules (among other rules) because of a lack of proper notice and opportunity for public comment prior to the rules' promulgation.[81] The EPA responded by issuing interim rules. Even the classification of waste has been complicated by a recent EPA rule stating that a waste will not be considered hazardous merely because it contains a listed hazardous ingredient, but only if the administrator determines that the waste is capable of causing substantial harm if managed improperly.[82] The potential implications

---

[76] 40 C.F.R. §§ 268.1–.50.

[77] *Id.* § 268.6.

[78] The New Era at 237–38.

[79] *Id.* at 239–40.

[80] 40 C.F.R. § 268.4.

[81] Shell Oil Co. v. EPA, 950 F.2d 741 (D.C. Cir. 1991). Curiously, the court softened the impact of this ruling by suggesting the EPA reenact the rules on an interim basis under the good cause exception to the Administrative Procedure Act, 5 U.S.C. § 553(b)(3)(B), until such time as the procedural shortcoming could be obviated by publishing adequate notice and providing for public comment.

[82] 57 Fed. Reg. 12 (1992) (*discussed in* Chem. & Eng'g News, Jan. 13, 1992 at 13).

of these changing regulations, and their application and interpretation by courts, are profound for any remediation project.

An example of problems that can arise was demonstrated during our defense of a remediation contractor who had agreed to retrofit a surface impoundment with a liner, install a leachate collection and monitoring system, and provide a bentonite cap for the impoundment. The owner was faced with a deadline on the closure permit for the project, thus necessitating a design/build fast-track type of effort.

The problems began with erroneous laboratory reports showing acceptably low levels of hazardous substances, as a result of neutralization treatments of the contaminated soil. These misleading readings prompted the contractor to go forward with remediation plans and mix the treated material with fresh soil. Because the soil was, in fact, still contaminated, this mixing only increased the total volume of contaminated soil on the project.

Excavation also proved more difficult than was initially anticipated, because rock formations were discovered in the impoundment area. This discovery re-quired some added excavation and partial relocation of the site, which required further negotiations and clearances from local officials and further slowed the process. Once this excavation was complete, the liner proved to be inadequate because of the expanded size of the excavation, thereby creating further delay while an acceptable liner was obtained. Installation of the liner was again de-layed when the contractor discovered that the excavation was inadequate for the increased volume of fill material that had resulted from the mixing of fresh and contaminated soils.

Once this problem was corrected, it was determined that the leachate moni-toring system was insufficient to cover the expanded area and mixture of con-taminants. Additional devices had to be procured and installed, which in turn delayed installation of the bentonite cap. Finally, in an effort to complete the project within the permit period, the excavation contractor double- and triple-shifted the crews, which led to faulty workmanship (an insufficient number of lifts on the cap, an apparent absence of bentonite in certain lifts, and lifts of varying and unacceptable thickness). The contractor was ultimately termi-nated, the project completely uncovered, and the liner and cap retrofitted. The entire episode caused the contractor to suffer millions of dollars in losses from unpaid contract balances, cancelled errors and omissions (professional liability) insurance coverage, and direct payments to the owner.

In this example, a close check of the lab results and a delay in mixing the treated soil would have prevented the problem. Even more importantly, if the owner had employed the contractor before extreme time pressure was created by the threatened permit lapse, the need for a fast-track approach could have been avoided. Failing that, the owner and the contractor could have agreed to share the cost of obtaining a one-year permit extension. Had the owner been unwill-ing, the contractor would still have been better off paying for the extension. The cost would have been about $250,000, admittedly an onerous burden, but clearly preferable to the losses incurred as a result of attempting to adhere to an impossible schedule.

§ 6.16   Evaluation of Remedial Approach

A wide range of treatment and containment techniques are available, not all of which work well within legal constraints. There is a logical process for formulating a remediation program. The essential components of the process are:

1. Site evaluation and determination of the scope of response actions
2. Initial evaluation and screening of technologies
3. Detailed evaluation of technologies
4. Selection of remedy.[83]

The remedy is evaluated, selected, and approved during the remedial investigation and feasibility study (RI/FS) phase of the process. An integral part of this process is the risk assessment, described in **Chapter 4**. The risk assessment can best be broken down into two broad areas—exposure and evaluation.[84]

Human exposure is often determined by various complex chemical and physical factors. For example, dioxin has been shown to have low water solubility and high sorption on soils. Thus, the degree of human exposure is a function of dioxin movement and photochemical degradation on soil particles. The analysis can be complicated by the presence of oil or solvents, which tend to have increased concentrations near the surface.[85] Studies have shown that the presence of oil or water weakens the dioxin's bond with the soil,[86] thereby expanding the migratory plume.

Commentators have critically noted that the evaluation of substances as toxic or hazardous is based on nine fundamental assumptions, none of which are certain:

1. Experimental animal data showing adverse effects allow presumption of such adverse effects in humans, even where no human data is available.
2. Dose-response model results can be extrapolated outside observed experiments to create estimates of harmful dosage.

---

[83] R. Stanford & E. Young, *Summary of Legislation and Regulations and the EPA Superfund Program in* H.M. Freeman, Standard Handbook of Hazardous Waste Treatment and Disposal 1.38 (1988).

[84] J. Exner, *Solving Hazardous Waste Problems; Learning From Dioxins,* ACS Symposium Series at V (1987) [hereinafter Exner].

[85] G. Miller & R. Zepp, *Tetrachlorodibenzo-p-dioxin: Environmental Chemistry, in* Exner at 91.

[86] V. Houk, *Uncertainties in Dioxin Risk Assessment, in* Exner at 175 [hereinafter Houk]; R. Freeman et al., *Experiments on the Mobility of 2, 3, 7, 8-Tetrachlorodibenzo-p-dioxin at Times Beach, Missouri, in* Exner at 114.

3. Observed experimental results can be extrapolated across species.

4. There is no threshold for cancer, but thresholds may exist for other toxicological outcomes.

5. When dose rates are not constant, average dose rates give a reasonable measure of exposure.

6. In the absence of data, the effective target dose is proportionate to the administered dose.

7. Risks from multiple exposures to the same chemical are additive.

8. Lacking contrary data, 100 percent sorption across species is assumed.

9. Results from a specific route of exposure are potentially relevant to other routes of exposure.[87]

These types of uncertainties are major contributors to the difficulties encountered by the scientific community in making the exposure determinations.

Once the exposure is determined the analysis proceeds to evaluation of the risks associated with proposed remedies. Factors that bear on the evaluation include proximity to urban areas, amount of traffic generated, potential impact on groundwater, and potential air quality issues. Technologies such as bioremediation, while inexpensive, require long treatment times and large areas, must be sealed off from groundwater, and may affect air quality. If a source of drinking water is exposed, extreme care must be taken. Unfortunately, effective evaluation of proposed remediation methods can be frustrated by the changing political climate. The litigation between the EPA and Chemical Manufacturers Association (CMA) regarding whether PRPs should conduct their own risk assessments (see **Chapter 4**) is indicative of the lack of consistent approaches to effective treatment evaluation that results from bureaucratic infighting and concerns about conflicts. In that case, the EPA seemed to imply that PRP risk assessments would be biased, a contention vigorously contested by the CMA. On a national scale, the problems are often compounded by the imposition of a standardized approach to remediation, rather than an evaluation based on a site-specific analysis, the latter being clearly favored by technical experts.[88] The divergent approaches described above often lead to delays and increased costs. This result, has in turn caused pressure on government agencies to cut costs.[89]

Parties to the contract must be aware that there are basically two kinds of remediation technologies: control technologies and treatment technologies. Many of these technologies have been discussed in **Chapters 3** and **4**. The

---

[87] Houk at 176.

[88] *Cleanup Approaches Studied*, Engineering News-Rec., Sept. 23, 1991, at 9, 16.

[89] *See* Rubin, *Superfund under the Gun*, Engineering News-Rec., Dec. 16, 1991, at 9. The article not only deals with efforts to cut costs, but also discusses the phenomenon that nearly 20% of all Superfund sites are municipal landfills, which in turn has caused the EPA to publish new guidelines regarding municipalities as PRPs.

control technologies basically fall into four broad categories: groundwater control, surface water control, soil and waste control, and air control. These control technologies and the means for their implementation must be considered in the context of the chosen treatment technology and the long-term disposition of the contaminant.

Groundwater can be controlled with a variety of methods, such as slurry walls, grout curtains, sheet pile, cutoff walls, block displacement, pumping, and subsurface drains. Surface water control technologies include dikes, terraces, channels, chutes and downpipes, grading, surface seals, vegetation, and various coverings of viscuine or other materials. Soil and waste may best be controlled through excavation, drum handling, encapsulation, or dewatering.

The four major areas of treatment technology are biological, chemical, physical, and direct. Biological treatments include surface impoundments, rotating biological discs, trickling filters, and activated sludge. Chemical treatment includes neutralization, precipitation/fixation, reduction, wet air oxidation, chlorination, and ozonation. Physical treatments include reverse osmosis, carbon absorption, stripping, sedimentation, and filtration. Direct treatments include in-situ leachate/groundwater treatment, in-situ physical and chemical treatment, on-site physical and chemical treatment, in-situ vitrification, and incineration.[90]

Each of these approaches have myriad advantages and disadvantages that will require careful consideration. For example, chemical decontamination of soils containing dioxins creates major concerns about the toxicity of reagents or reaction products that may remain after treatment.[91]

Integral to the assessment program are various monitoring techniques, which may be required or prudent during three separate phases in the life of a remediation project:

1. Prior to treatment, to determine the actual or potential effects of contamination on humans, nonhuman species, and the environment

2. As a technology is being selected, to evaluate the impact of site-specific factors on the various treatments proposed in the design of a remedial action program

3. During and after treatment, to evaluate the need for health and safety procedures (see **Chapter 7**), and whether the levels of pollution are in compliance with permit, hazardous waste, closure, or other requirements.[92]

Accurate risk and site assessments typically depend on a vigorous and comprehensive preremediation monitoring system. The purpose of conducting

---

[90] T. Ehrenfeld & T. Bass, *Evaluation of Remedial Action at Hazardous Waste Disposal Sites*, Pollution Tech. Rev. No. 110 (1984) [hereinafter Ehrenfeld & Bass].

[91] R. Peterson et al., *Comparison of Laboratory and Field Test Data in the Chemical Decontamination of Dioxin-Contaminated Soils*, in Exner at 292.

[92] Ehrenfeld & Bass at 391.

monitoring is to provide sufficient information to accurately characterize the site itself, as well as the levels and patterns of site-related contamination.[93] This information should enable the parties to determine where, when, how, and what types of wastes are likely to be found at the site; the likely pathways of on- and off-site migration, and the probability and speed of contaminant migration. If a plume exists, data obtained by monitoring should allow estimation of how far the plume has traveled and if there are any other sources of contamination in the vicinity.

Sampling is an additional or alternative means of obtaining information. Sampling may be done near the property or political boundaries, randomly on a predetermined grid, and near distant residential sites.[94] There are many variations on these approaches, some offering greater efficiency and cost reduction. One variation, a product of esoteric and arcane geostatistical mapping techniques, is the variogram, which permits the estimation of contaminant concentrations on a site.[95]

Diligent monitoring, assessment, and preparation of a remediation action plan will enable the parties to develop an approach that is both effective, comprehensive, and meets the mandates of the National Contingency Plan (NCP), a requirement that is articulated in the federal and many state environmental protection laws.

OTHER REMEDIATION ISSUES

§ 6.17   Considerations in Projects Affecting Wetlands

Recent federal legislation has established stringent constraints on any activities that affect wetlands in the United States. Section 404 of CWA requires permits issued by the U.S. Army Corps of Engineers, and reviewed by the EPA, for discharge of dredged or fill materials into waters of the United States, including adjacent wetlands. The primary impact of wetlands regulation has been on land developers; however, environmental cleanups, ordinary construction, and projects related to industrial property can easily encounter situations in which wetlands permits would be required, or in which violations may inadvertently occur. Even where contractors are engaged in marsh building[96] or restoration, they have run afoul of wetlands regulations because of the nature of the activity (for

---

[93] *Id.* at 392.

[94] *Id.* at 394–95.

[95] R.C. Bryan & D.E. Splitstone, *Risk-Qualified Mapping of Polychlorinated Dibenzodioxin Contamination, in* Exner at 247.

[96] *Water Quality Effects Studied,* Engineering News-Rec., Feb. 10, 1992, at 12.

example, dredging and filling) or the potential for disturbing the delicate balance of marshes.

Three fundamental issues concern activities with the potential for affecting wetlands:

1. Definition of wetlands and delineation of areas covered by regulatory restrictions
2. Determination of what types of activities will be allowed in or adjacent to the wetlands
3. Evaluation of measures to restore, preserve, and avoid or mitigate any adverse effects on wetlands.

The issue of classifying wetlands has recently been hotly debated. Wetlands were not defined for purposes of land use regulation until 1989, when the federal government issued a manual, to be used by federal agencies as a basis for determining whether land qualifies for wetlands protection, which defined *wetlands* as:

1. Any depression where water accumulates for seven consecutive days during the growing season
2. Where certain water-loving plants are found
3. Where the soil is saturated enough with water that anaerobic bacterial activity can take place.[97]

The 1989 regulations prohibited any development of such land, or any activity that would affect such land, unless the party could show that there was no practical alternative to the action.[98]

In response to stiff opposition to this standard from developers and real estate interests, the current administration has proposed new regulations that have significantly narrowed the definition of wetlands, and relaxed the constraints on land development.[99] In the 1991 manual, *wetlands* are defined as land where standing water remains for 15 straight days and saturated soil remains for 21 days. The 1991 manual also provides a system that assesses the wildlife aspect of determining protected areas, based on ratings for certain types of vegetation.[100]

Critics immediately charged that the new wetlands policy, in particular the definition of wetlands, could accelerate the erosion of wetland areas, and result in declassification of up to 80 percent of land classified as wetlands under the

---

[97] EPA, Federal Manual for Identifying and Delineating Jurisdictional Wetlands (1991) [hereinafter Federal Manual]; 7 C.F.R. § 12.31 (1991).

[98] *Id.*

[99] Lemonick, *War Over the Wetlands,* Time, Aug. 26, 1991, at 53 [hereinafter Lemonick].

[100] Federal Manual at 1.

1989 manual.[101] The proposed changes also eliminate the no viable alternative standard used to obtain the exemption for an activity in a wetland area. Furthermore, there is a proposal to adopt a form of permit banking (similar to that described for air quality permits in **Chapter 5**) allowing landowners to earn credit by restoring lost wetlands, and exchange that credit for permission to destroy other wetland areas.[102]

If an owner or contractor is contemplating excavation, remediation, or construction on land that could even partially be defined as wetlands, an environmental consultant with wetlands expertise should be engaged. In a Phase I wetlands assessment, the consultant should gather background information regarding climate, precipitation, geology, and hydrology, and conduct a walk-through of the site (site reconnaissance). The consultant will then provide an opinion letter. If the consultant determines that the land involved is not a wetland, the opinion letter should provide specific bases for these findings.[103]

If the consultant determines that at least some of the land area is wetlands, further site evaluation should be performed to gather the following information:

1. Delineation of the wetland area, including a survey indicating wetland boundaries

2. Identification of endangered species and habitats

3. Evaluation of the potential impact of proposed activities on the wetlands and the wildlife they contain.

Because of their general and site-specific expertise, it can be beneficial to have the wetlands consultant serve as a coordinator for the permit application process, and as an intermediary with the Army Corps of Engineers, the EPA, and any state agencies involved. Under the 1989 regulations, and to a lesser degree under the proposed 1991 regulations, an application for a permit to develop, affect, or discharge into wetlands must give consideration to all alternatives. When evaluating alternatives, the cost of existing technology and its use for the site for purposes must be considered.[104]

The 1989 guidelines required a relatively strong demonstration of need to obtain a permit to use wetlands for projects that were not clearly water-dependent. Even under the 1991 regulations, wetlands that are particularly valuable are protected. If an activity is permitted, modification of the construction or remediation methods, or of the scope, processes, or techniques used, may be required to lessen the impact on wetlands. Finally, possible means of mitigating irreducible effects must also be considered.

---

[101] *Bush Manual Is Flawed, Tests Show,* Engineering News-Rec., Dec. 2, 1991, at 11.

[102] Lemonick at 53.

[103] Gutshal, *Treading Water on Wetland Construction,* Builder & Contractor, Aug. 1991, at 10–11 [hereinafter Gutshal].

[104] Gutshal at 11.

§ 6.18   Lead Paint, Sick Building Syndrome, and Nuclear Waste

An increased concern for energy-saving has led to the construction of well-sealed buildings. Sick building syndrome is a name given to the range of problems that can arise when toxic substances from building materials are released into the air and become trapped within these relatively airtight buildings. In addition, radon (a radioactive gas) can leak into buildings from beneath the foundations, to become trapped in the same manner. These problems have recently become a serious public concern, prompting the creation of a federal indoor air research program and a congressional mandate for the EPA and other federal agencies to investigate and develop regulations to address the issue.[105]

Owners, manufacturers, contractors, and architects all have potential exposure to considerable liability for damages due to sick building syndrome. One group of tenants, employees of the EPA, successfully sued the owner of the building, claiming that a negligent restoration had resulted in air pollutant levels that caused them to suffer poor health.[106] In *Pinkerton v. Georgia Pacific Corp.*, a single family was awarded $16.2 million in damages for exposure to formaldehyde that had leaked from particleboard.[107]

To the extent that hazards can be avoided or eliminated by proper design or construction, both contractors and architects may be liable for failing to adopt such practices. For example, a safe level of radon can be attained by proper sealing of the foundation and proper ventilation of the building.[108]

Regulations regarding indoor air quality are likely to become more extensive. Bills proposing regulations mandating notification, monitoring, and control of certain indoor air pollution levels in buildings have been introduced in both houses of Congress.[109]

Contamination from lead-containing materials, particularly lead paints, has also been of growing concern. It has been suggested that lead may be the asbestos of the 1990s.[110] Lead is a highly toxic substance. Manufacturers, employers, and other PRPs appear to have actively concealed knowledge regarding lead's toxic properties, and are now exposed to liability of massive proportions. In recognition of the high toxicity of lead, the EPA has begun an investigation into the most cost-effective method of reducing the considerable health hazards posed.[111]

---

[105] Long, *Senate Boosts Indoor Air Research Despite Administration Misgivings,* Chem. & Engineering News, Nov. 25, 1991, at 15.

[106] Bahura v. S.E.W. Investors, No. 90-CA10598 (D.C. Super. Ct., Oct. 26, 1990).

[107] No. Civ. 186-4651CC, 4 Tox. L. Rep. 1095 (Mo. Cir. Ct., Clayton City, Jan. 8, 1990).

[108] Christman, *Wetlands, Asbestos, Hazardous Waste, and the Sick Building Syndrome* 5 (presented at Construction Litigation Superconference, Nov. 15, 1991).

[109] *See, e.g.,* H.R. 1066, 102 Cong., 1st Sess. (1991); S. 455, 102 Cong., 1st Sess. (1991).

[110] Rice, *Lead Poisoning May Fuel Litigation,* L.A. Daily J., Nov. 4, 1991, at 1.

[111] *See* 56 Fed. Reg. 22,096 (May 13, 1991).

For the remediation contractor, this concern has led to a burgeoning business in lead paint removal services, estimated at $100 million in 1990.[112] At the same time, this combination of rapid expansion of the industry and serious health risks posed has led to a number of state and local licensing requirements related to lead. Owners must take steps to limit exposure to liability.

Projects involving remediation and disposal of nuclear waste should also expand dramatically in the 1990s. The Department of Energy (DOE), which has been facing a significant nuclear waste cleanup problem since the mid-1970s, has allocated $4.6 billion to the cleanup of nuclear waste in 1992.[113] Environmental management of weapons plants is expected to be contracted out to private maintenance and operations contractors.[114] There have been significant concerns regarding the insufficiency of the indemnity clauses, particularly with respect to long tail liability, that is, exposure liability lasting years after the project is completed. The industry is currently trying to pressure the DOE into fully indemnifying contractors, as has the Department of Defense in non-nuclear waste cleanup operations.[115]

A significant portion of the nuclear waste remediation efforts will go into the storage of nuclear waste until better waste treatment solutions are found. The DOE has, however, encountered significant opposition from both the public and the courts in locating nuclear waste storage sites. Public concern related to nuclear waste has increased dramatically, which is reflected in increased storage facility standards and subsequent significantly increased costs.[116] Total life-cycle storage costs are currently estimated at between $300 to $500 per cubic foot of waste for facilities that are designed to be absolutely safe for at least 500 years.[117]

To create and operate a nuclear waste site, the DOE must comply with both RCRA and permit requirements under any state regulators, prior to any hazardous waste disposal or testing.[118] Although the standards to be met for the disposal of nuclear waste under RCRA are uncertain, the EPA recently issued rules for radioactive waste disposal.[119]

---

[112] *Id.* at 1.

[113] Rubin et al., *After the Bomb, A War Against Waste,* Engineering News-Rec., Nov. 25, 1991, at 35.

[114] *Id.*

[115] *Id.* at 38.

[116] Setzer, *Public Phobia Hiking Low-Level Disposal Costs,* Engineering News-Rec., Dec. 2, 1991, at 10.

[117] *Id.*

[118] Setzer, *Court Blocks Testing of Nuclear Waste Site,* Chem. & Engineering News, Feb. 10, 1992, at 6.

[119] 57 Fed. Reg. 22,024 (codified at 40 C.F.R. pt. 268 (1992).)

CHAPTER 7

MANAGEMENT OF THE REMEDIATION*

ISSUES RELATED TO GOVERNMENT INSPECTIONS

§ 7.1   Avoiding Inspections by Government Agencies

Workplace inspections by government agencies can create a number of problems. They may disturb productivity at the jobsite, affect employee morale, and

---

*Barbara G. Mikalson of Crowell & Moring contributed to this chapter.

223

create unnecessary safety hazards for agency personnel who are not under strict control of project supervisors. Inspections may also attract unwanted publicity, particularly if agency inspectors expect to encounter or sample for contamination (in which case they commonly arrive in moon suits), or if uniformed officers accompany agency officials. Finally, a government agency has far more access to documents and information during an inspection than would be obtained by civil discovery procedures or even by subpoena. While the scope of information obtained can be limited by properly preparing and responding to an inspection (see §§ 7.2 and 7.3), the best way to limit exposure is to prevent unanticipated inspections from occurring.

Most environmental lawyers remind their clients that environmental agencies are not their friends. Stories abound of friendly, minor inspections that lead to extremely invasive searches or criminal investigations. The best strategy for an owner or contractor to adopt (as discussed in **Chapter 4**) is active communication with the agency. The EPA's own policies state that facilities with effective self-auditing systems, and which make genuine efforts to comply with regulations and to promptly correct problems or violations, have low priority in the Agency's inspection and enforcement efforts.[1] Government investigators are motivated to conduct searches only where they suspect that the company is a potential violator, that information is being concealed or falsified, and that the parties either would not respond in good faith to a subpoena or would attempt to destroy evidence. Moreover, since criminal liability generally requires that the individual or business entity has committed a knowing violation (see **Chapter 8**), the appearance of an attempt to conceal evidence of violation can increase the likelihood of a criminal investigation. Thus, it is necessary to cooperate with government requests for information, to clearly display a company policy of compliance with environmental regulations, and to assure the agency that the company intends to act in good faith in resolving any problems.[2]

§ 7.2   Preparing for Government Inspections

There are several measures a company can take to minimize the disruption and potential exposure resulting from the search. First, the parameters of potential site inspections may be negotiated with the government agency during the permitting process.[3] This approach offers two advantages: (1) If the agency views the company as cooperative and responsible, the intended scope of the inspection, and subsequent workplace disruption, may be reduced;

---

[1] EPA, Environmental Auditing Policy Statement (July 1986).

[2] J. Burns, *How to Respond to an Environmental Investigation* 7–8 (1991).

[3] T. Bois, *How to Survive an Administrative Environmental Investigation,* Orange County Law., June 1991, at 19.

(2) By having information regarding the scope and possibly the timing of the inspection, adequate preparation can minimize unintended exposure of confidential or privileged material, and workplace disruption. Procedures should be established for responding to an inspection (these procedures may be based on the checklist in § 7.3). A manager or supervisor who can work well with people should be designated as inspection coordinator, and be familiarized with those response procedures.

Special attention should be paid to safety problems that may arise during the inspection, and to the potential for inadvertent discovery of confidential information. Employees may be instructed in advance regarding particular safety precautions and the nature of their contact with inspectors. Documentation that is required to be available under permitting or other regulations should be separated from other documents. Documents with confidential information, especially those protected under attorney-client or attorney work-product privileges (such as communications with attorneys regarding environmental compliance), should also be segregated from other materials and, if possible, kept in an attorney's office. Some owners and contractors involved in remediation projects routinely have their legal counsel hire and communicate with environmental consultants who perform remedial investigations and feasibility studies, to protect the information obtained in the consultants' reports.

§ 7.3 Responding to a Demand for Inspection

There are four fundamental elements that are critical to a successful response to a government inspection:

_____ 1. Ascertain the type and specific scope of the inspection
_____ 2. Manage employee contact with inspectors
_____ 3. Monitor and record all conduct of the search and seizures
_____ 4. Obtain all possible information regarding the search and any evidence seized.

When first confronted with the demand for inspection, it is important to be cooperative, but *not give consent* to the search. Withholding consent preserves the right to object to the search and any use of evidence obtained, in the event that there are no valid grounds for the search. Ask to see the warrant and obtain a copy if possible. Read it carefully to determine whether it is an administrative warrant (which authorizes a search pursuant to statute) or a search warrant (based on a suspicion of criminal violation). If the inspectors have no warrant, there is no obligation to comply and a search should not be permitted.

An attorney should be contacted immediately and informed of the type of warrant, the agencies involved, and the scope of the warrant, including the areas to be searched and the types of evidence to be seized. If the inspection is pursuant to a search warrant, it may be important to have an attorney with some criminal law experience present, to prevent officers and employees from inadvertently waiving their rights or unnecessarily giving information or evidence to inspectors. If the search is to be extensive, or if criminal prosecution is suspected, it may be wise to send workers home.

The inspection coordinator should conduct a pre-inspection conference to determine:

1. The purpose and grounds for the search
2. Precisely which areas will be searched
3. Which specific documents and types of evidence, if any, are to be seized.

The coordinator should make a record of this information. The coordinator should also understand that, although company policy is to comply with the demands of the warrant, attempts to go beyond the scope of the warrant are unreasonable and will not be allowed. Finally, the coordinator should instruct the inspectors regarding the site safety rules, and stress that, as a matter of safety, all questions should be directed to the coordinator and that the inspectors should be accompanied by the coordinator or a designated employee at all times during the search.

The coordinator or other designated employees should monitor the progress of the inspection as closely as possible, identifying and recording all items of physical evidence seized, all information recorded, and any interviews with employees. If the inspectors take photographs or make tape recordings, the contents of each photograph or recording and the number of photographs or length of recording should be noted, and the inspector should be asked for copies of all materials. If samples are taken (for example, of soil, waste, or materials used), information should be recorded regarding the sampling method and the care and preservation of the samples.

It is important that neither the coordinator nor employees interfere with the search, which could lead to charges of obstruction. However, there is no need to facilitate the inspection by helping locate documents or other items listed in the search warrant.

Employees should be instructed not to discuss anything with inspectors unless an attorney or the inspection coordinator is present. In a criminal investigation, employees should also be advised of their rights and should be sent home, if so allowed by the agency officials.

Following any search, the firm is entitled to a receipt for all items seized, including such items as soil samples. It is a wise precaution to insist that the receipt contain a detailed list, which notes the specific identifications of documents (of which copies may be requested). Care should be taken to make sure that every item on the receipt matches or can be identified with records made of the search, to ensure that the evidence cannot be misconstrued and to substantiate possible challenges to the items seized.

Once the administrative search has been completed, the inspection coordinator should arrange a debriefing conference. Agency officials should be asked whether the inspection revealed any compliance problems and whether there will be a continuing civil or criminal investigation. During the debriefing, all information obtained by the inspectors should be verified for completeness and accuracy, and any disputes over existing conditions should be discussed at that time. The company should request a copy of the report, as well as copies of photographs or recordings made, and test results of any samples taken.

§ 7.4 Avoiding Exposure to Criminal Liability

A common but mistaken notion in business circles is that firms attempting to comply in good faith with environmental regulations are not subject to criminal liability. Reliance on such an assumption, and any consequential failure to prepare for and deal with such potential liability, can be a grave error. Criminal fines and penalties are no longer uncommon. An increased scope and enforcement of environmental regulations have led to soaring levels of criminal fines imposed in recent years. In 1983 and 1984, the average criminal fine imposed as a consequence of an EPA criminal investigation was $300,000.[4] By 1988, this figure had risen to $8 million.[5] There is every indication that the average will continue to climb. It is no longer only the firm dumping waste on the roadside at midnight that is vulnerable to prosecution. Even if a criminal prosecution is not pursued or successful, the expense and the negative impact on the company's reputation with clients, subcontractors, and the public, and on employee morale, can be devastating.

An individual or company facing a search or other investigation by an environmental agency must consider the implications for criminal liability. Primary areas of concern are:

1. A search pursuant to an administrative warrant, or investigation of a suspected civil violation, may reveal evidence that would prompt authorities to conduct a criminal investigation.

2. The broad investigatory powers given the prosecutor in a criminal investigation may lead to evidence upon which a civil action may be taken, even if the criminal charges are dropped or the defendant is found not guilty.

---

[4] According to EPA National Enforcement Investigation Center, Denver, Colo., *in* Owens & Mollenkamp, *Hazardous Waste Cleanup 1991: Civil Penalties and Criminal Enforcement,* app. A, presented to CLE International, Denver, Colo. (Feb. 1991).

[5] *Id.*

3. Company policies and actions can be structured to avoid liability for criminal actions.

The problem of evidence being uncovered that suggests a criminal violation has been addressed in § **7.3.**

Federal courts have held that information cannot be obtained for the purposes of criminal prosecution through the use of civil discovery devices.[6] However, the transfer of information from civil administrators to criminal prosecutors has been allowed when the agency acted in good faith, and had a legitimate purpose for the investigation.[7] Since the scope of civil discovery is very broad, and an investigation can proceed without probable cause of a criminal violation, the potential for obtained information to be used in a criminal proceeding is a serious concern in any inspection.

The key to avoiding this occurrence is awareness of whether a criminal investigation is pending. First, if the inspectors appear to demarcate a specific problematic area of the site, which they do not inspect, that area may be a target for a criminal investigation. The involvement of inspectors from federal agencies may also be a warning, because in many smaller states, state agencies handle routine inspection and civil investigations, and federal agencies are brought in to conduct criminal prosecutions.

Finally, the owner or contractor should ask the agency, as well as the individuals conducting the inspection, whether criminal charges are being considered, or if any of the information discovered is likely to lead to a criminal prosecution. If the government denies the existence of a criminal investigation, the court may dismiss an indictment or refuse to admit evidence obtained.[8] Furthermore, although notification is not legally required, EPA guidelines recommend that notice of potential criminal prosecution be given upon initiation of a criminal proceeding.[9]

If there is any likelihood of parallel proceedings, the company should move for a motion to stay the civil action. This action will not only allow the party to fight one battle at a time, but will avoid the potential for information used in one proceeding to apply to the other.

The most effective way for companies to shield themselves from criminal liability for violations of environmental regulations is to establish and enforce an effective environmental policy. The Department of Justice issued a set of guidelines in July 1991, which establishes the criteria the Department will use in deciding whether and how aggressively to prosecute a company for an

---

[6] United States v. Interstate Dress Carriers, Inc., 280 F.2d 52, 54 (2d Cir. 1960).

[7] SEC v. Dresser Indus., Inc., 628 F.2d 1368, 1387 (D.C. Cir.), *cert. denied,* 449 U.S. 993 (1980).

[8] *See, e.g.,* United States v. Rodman, 519 F.2d 1058 (1st Cir. 1975); SEC v. ESM Gov't Sec., Inc., 645 F.2d 310 (5th Cir. 1981).

[9] *Policy and Procedures on Parallel Proceedings at the EPA,* EPA Memorandum, Jan. 23, 1984, at 1–3.

environmental violation. In using prosecutorial discretion in favor of the company, the Department will consider whether the company:

1. Employs a systematic, intensive, and comprehensive auditing program to ensure environmental compliance

2. Has disclosed the matter under investigation in a voluntary, timely, and complete manner

3. Has fully cooperated with government investigators and prosecutors

4. Has taken prompt and complete action to remedy any environmental harm

5. Has taken disciplinary action regarding the employees who participated in the violation.[10]

Although the Department of Justice has not yet adopted sentencing guidelines, the new sentencing guidelines developed by the Sentencing Commission regarding criminal violations by organizations will likely be extended to environmental violations in the near future.[11] As with the prosecutorial guidelines, these sentencing guidelines recommend that sentences imposed upon companies (or any institution) may be mitigated if the company has an effective environmental compliance program. In order to qualify under the guidelines, the program should include the following characteristics:

_____ 1. Established company policy—The company must develop formal compliance standards and procedures that will be effective in reducing potential criminal violations by that company's employees and agents.

_____ 2. Education—The company must institute training programs or other effective means of communicating and explaining these compliance standards and procedures to employees.

_____ 3. Detection—Reasonable steps must be taken to ensure compliance by establishing effective systems of detection of violation and reporting of criminal conduct.

_____ 4. Enforcement—The company must take disciplinary action against individuals who commit violations or who fail to detect or report violations for which they are responsible.

_____ 5. Follow-through—The company must respond to a violation in an appropriate manner, including any necessary modifications of its environmental policies or enforcement mechanisms.

---

[10] Environmental Enforcement, U.S. Dep't of Justice, Factors in Decisions on Criminal Prosecutions for Environmental Violations in the Context of Significant Voluntary Compliance or Disclosure Efforts by the Violator (July 1, 1991).

[11] See Recent Developments in Criminal Enforcement: DOJ Policy and Sentencing Guidelines, in Environment, Health & Safety Law, 2–3 (Pillsbury, Madison & Sutro, Nov. 26, 1991) (briefing paper).

WORKER HEALTH AND SAFETY CONCERNS

§ 7.5   Occupational Safety and Health
Administration Regulations

The Occupational Safety and Health Administration (OSHA) has the responsibility to promulgate safety and health standards under the Occupational Safety and Health Act (referred to here as the OSH Act) of 1970[12] "to assure so far as possible every working man and woman in the nation safe and healthful working conditions."[13] OSHA is not only authorized to delegate the responsibility of promulgating and enforcing standards for worker health and safety;[14] it is also supposed to encourage states to develop, administer, and enforce their own programs.[15] While the state plans are required to be at least as effective as the federal OSHA requirements, many states, including California and New Jersey, have adopted more stringent regulations.

OSHA regulations and administrative activities affect the remediation process by placing constraints on feasible workplace processes, personnel training, licensing, and protective clothing and devices, and requiring (as in other aspects of hazardous substance handling) increased planning and precautions. Violations, particularly those involving serious injuries to workers, may make the firm liable for criminal as well as civil penalties, or damages in tort actions. Thus, regulation of worker health and safety will have an impact on cost, time, and exposure to liability.

OSHA, or the state agencies that administer occupational health and safety programs, has the responsibility to:

1.   Promulgate mandatory occupational safety and health standards for all employers affecting interstate commerce
2.   Establish rights and responsibilities of both employers and employees, including development of programs and requirements to reduce workplace hazards
3.   Inspect for and enforce standards.[16]

The development of occupational safety and health standards has also been given under the OSH Act to the National Institute for Occupational Safety and

---

[12] 29 U.S.C. §§ 651–678 (Supp. II 1990) (originally enacted as Pub. L. No. 91–596, § 2, 84 Stat. 1590 (1970)).

[13] *Id.* §§ 651(a), (b).

[14] *Id.* § 667.

[15] *Id.* § 651(b).

[16] *Id.*

Health (NIOSH), in the Department of Health and Human Services.[17] The research and development of standards is conducted by NIOSH, which submits recommended standards to OSHA for their adoption.

§ 7.6   —Promulgation and Review of OSHA Regulations

Since OSHA regulations directly affect the conduct of remediation, and therefore the costs and even feasibility of certain types of activities, it is important for remediation contractors and their associations to be aware of the rulemaking process. To promulgate, amend, or revoke a standard, OSHA must undertake the following procedures:

1. The proposed rule, amendment, or revocation must be published in the Federal Register.
2. During the 30 days following publication, any interested person may file a written objection with OSHA and request a public hearing.
3. Within 30 days, OSHA must publish a notice in the Federal Register responding to public comment.
4. OSHA must also arrange and give notice of a public hearing regarding the proposal, if requested.[18]
5. OSHA must then either issue a rule or determine not to do so within 60 days.[19]

An OSHA standard can also be challenged within 60 days of the date it is promulgated, by a petition to the federal court of appeals.[20] However, it is difficult to prevail in a challenge to an OSHA standard. The directive under which OSHA promulgates health and safety standards is ambiguous, and the agency's standards are stringent. Furthermore, factual determinations made by OSHA in the administrative record are conclusive in the course of judicial review, as long as the determinations are supported by substantial evidence in the record.[21]

Temporary standards may also be issued by OSHA in emergency cases. OSHA must first determine that employees are exposed to great danger from a hazardous or toxic substance, and that an emergency standard is necessary to protect employees.[22] Once the temporary standard has been published in the

---

[17] *Id.* § 671.

[18] 29 U.S.C. §§ 655(b)(2)–(3).

[19] *Id.* § 655(b)(4).

[20] *Id.* § 655(f).

[21] *Id.*

[22] *Id.* § 655(c)(1).

Federal Register, it is effective for six months, or until it is superseded by a new standard.[23]

§ 7.7 —Application for Variance

In situations in which an OSHA regulation establishes a requirement that appears to be unjustified because of the hardship on the employer and the existence of an alternative safety method, the employer can apply to OSHA for a variance from that standard. An application for a temporary variance must contain the following:

____ 1. A statement as to why the employer is unable to comply with the OSHA standard

____ 2. Proposed steps the employer will take to protect the employees from those hazards to which the standard is directed

____ 3. A statement explaining the steps the employer will take to come into compliance with the standard

____ 4. A certification that employees have been given notice of the application for a variance.[24]

A temporary variance is valid for up to one year after issuance, but a new temporary variance can be requested upon expiration of the first one.[25]

If the employer is requesting OSHA to issue a rule or order granting a permanent variance, the employees must be given an opportunity to participate in a hearing.[26] OSHA may grant the variance upon determination that the steps taken by the employer will provide the same level of health and safety as would be provided by the established standard.[27] It is not unlikely, however, that OSHA will continue to monitor and inspect following the issuance of an order for variance. Any such rule or order issued may be revoked or amended within the six-month period following its issuance.[28]

---

[23] *Id.* §§ 655(c)(2)–(3).

[24] 29 U.S.C. § 655(b)(6)(B).

[25] *Id.*

[26] *Id.* § 655(d).

[27] *Id.*

[28] *Id.*

§ 7.8   OSHA Regulations Related to Hazardous Substances

OSHA has a heightened responsibility to set standards for occupational contact with hazardous materials. The agency is directed by statute to set standards that "most adequately assures, to the extent feasible, on the basis of the best available evidence, that no employee will suffer material impairment of health or functional capacity, even if such employee has regular exposure to the hazard dealt with by such standards for the period of his working life." Two sets of OSHA standards relevant to remediation work are the hazard communication standard (HCS) (see § 7.9) and the permissible exposure limit (PELs). OSHA has also been directed to establish standards in terms of objective criteria and performance levels.[29] This requirement has led to an increased emphasis on monitoring both workplace health and safety elements and medical condition of workers, but has also led to frequent changes in requirements to achieve certain standards.

In addition to the general health and safety regulations, OSHA has issued regulations specifically pertaining to the procedures and protective equipment required for handling and storing hazardous materials,[30] and to standards for employee exposure to toxic and hazardous substances.[31] For a detailed example of the types of requirements that result from these regulations, see the discussion of asbestos in **Chapter 6**.

PELs establish the maximum permissible exposure levels for certain airborne contaminants over a specified period of time. For each contaminant, there are two types of PELs: (1) the time-weighted average (TWA), an average exposure to an airborne contaminant over time, which may not be exceeded during any eight-hour shift of a 40-hour workweek;[32] and (2) the short-term exposure limit (STEL), a 15-minute time-weighted exposure level, which may not be exceeded at any time during a workday.[33] In addition to these requirements, there are regulations regarding skin contact for certain toxic substances.

The impact of these standards on employers is three-fold:

1.   The workplace must be monitored for contamination levels to determine the means of compliance required.
2.   If PELs are not attained, work procedure or engineering controls must be implemented.

---

[29] 29 U.S.C. § 655(b)(5).

[30] 29 C.F.R. §§ 1910.21–1910.100, 1910.141–1910.149 (1991).

[31] *Id.* §§ 1910.1000–1910.1500.

[32] *Id.* § 1910.1000(a)(5)(i).

[33] *Id.* § 1910.1000(a)(5)(ii).

3. If PELs are still not fully attained, protective equipment, clothing, or other measures must be used.[34]

Work protection equipment or health and safety control measures must be approved by OSHA or by a competent industrial hygienist or other qualified persons.[35]

OSHA has promulgated additional regulations regarding certain hazardous substances. Twenty-seven chemicals or mixtures are specifically regulated, including asbestos, lead, benzene, and vinyl chloride. While OSHA still follows the general requirements regarding hazardous substances, the agency has dictated additional monitoring requirements, workplace procedures, protective equipment, and engineering control requirements for these specific substances. In addition, OSHA has promulgated specific regulations regarding the training of workers, notice to employees about hazardous substances and emergency procedures, and requirements regarding medical screenings or examinations.

§ 7.9   Hazard Communication Standard

OSHA has established a set of standards to inform employees of the risks of exposure to hazardous substances, by requiring all chemical manufacturers, importers, and employers using hazardous chemicals to comply with the HCS. Although the construction industry originally was temporarily exempted from the HCS requirements, in *Associated Builders & Contractors, Inc. v. Brock,*[36] the Court of Appeals for the Third Circuit ordered the standard, to be enforced against employers in the construction industry.

It is the responsibility of manufacturers and importers of hazardous chemical substances to assess the dangers and risk of exposure, and make such information available to distributors, and subsequently to users of these chemicals. It is the employer's responsibility to provide this information to any employee who may be exposed in the workplace.[37] Distributors must supply a material and safety data sheet (MSDS), including the physical and chemical characteristics of all hazardous ingredients, their specific health hazards and exposure symptoms, and OSHA PELs, if any.[38]

Employers must develop and implement a program to manage communication regarding hazardous substances.[39] This program should be developed in conjunction with a site safety plan. See § **7.10.** The program should (1) establish

---

[34] *Id.* § 1910.1000(e).

[35] *Id.*

[36] 862 F.2d 63, 69 (3d Cir. 1988); *see also* 54 Fed. Reg. 6886 (1989).

[37] 29 C.F.R. § 1910.1200(b)(1).

[38] *Id.* § 1910.1200(g)(2)(i).

[39] *Id.* § 1910.1200(e)(1).

and maintain a list of hazardous chemicals used in the workplace, and a file of MSDSs; and (2) establish protocol to inform employees of hazards, including warning labels, training information, and non-routine tasks. Since the employer is also responsible for communicating the hazards to *any* employees present, contractors should make sure that subcontractors and their employees are appropriately warned.

Employers must ensure that employees have access to the most recent MSDS available for any hazardous substance to which they may be exposed. Specifically, all containers of hazardous chemicals must be labeled with the identity of the chemical and any warning regarding physical or health hazards, for example: if the substance is flammable, corrosive, or explosive; if the substance is carcinogenic or otherwise toxic; the substance's boiling point, temperature at which it is flammable, or substances with which it may not be safely combined; and symptoms of overexposure, such as dizziness, skin irritation, or whether danger may exist without symptoms. Employers may use a variety of forms of communication. The information, however, must be easily accessible to employees. Labels should be written in English and any other appropriate languages. All labels should also be readily visible during the work shift.[40] While labels are not required where containers only hold hazardous substances temporarily, this exception should only apply when workers would obviously be aware of the substance and its temporary storage.

Specific training requirements have been established for workers who will be exposed to hazardous chemicals. This information must include:

1. Information regarding the health risks posed by hazardous chemicals present in the workplace
2. Means of detecting the presence or release of those hazardous chemicals
3. Proper work procedures, clothing, and use of equipment to protect workers from exposure to hazardous chemicals
4. The location of MSDSs in the workplace, and the means to interpret MSDSs, labels, and warnings.[41]

§ 7.10   Workplace Safety and Health Program

Heightened standards for worker safety are required under SARA for situations involving Superfund cleanups, routine operations at hazardous waste treatment, storage, or disposal facilities (TSDFs), hazardous waste cleanups or corrective actions, and emergency responses to the release of hazardous substances.[42] To

---

[40] *Id.* § 1910.1200(f)(9).

[41] *Id.* § 1910.1200(h)(1)(i)–(iii), (2)(i)–(iv).

[42] 54 Fed. Reg. 9294 (1989).

extend coverage to all state and local government employees exempted under OSHA, the EPA has issued the same regulations for state and local government employees engaged in cleanup, TSD operations, or emergency response activities.[43] These regulations establish a number of requirements, including the following:

1. Preparation of a written safety and health program.[44] A Sample Site Safety Plan is given in **Appendix E**.
2. Site assessment developed prior to entry by workers
3. Site control and monitoring requirements
4. Work training requirements for all workers involved in hazardous waste
5. Medical surveillance of workers exposed to hazardous waste
6. Engineering controls, work practices, clothing, and other personal protective equipment.[45]

A safety and health program may be incorporated with similar plans mandated by other programs, such as RCRA. In addition to general evaluations of overall safety and health implied by the existence of hazardous waste, the plan should pay particular attention to characteristics of the particular site. For example, for asbestos-related remediation work, the presence of water to wet down the asbestos may present a hazard if electrical equipment is being used. Special monitoring problems, including potential releases from containers or wind conditions, and different phases of the remedial operations and their safety and health implications should be addressed. The program should include procedures to ensure that workers are aware of safety requirements.

Worker training requirements vary according to whether cleanup activities, emergency response activities, or routine TSD operations are involved. Supervisors require additional training. Furthermore, all employees, including managers, are required to take annual refresher training courses. A routine site employee involved in a hazardous waste cleanup must be given 40 hours of initial training, 24 hours of training under supervision in the field, and an eight-hour refresher course each year. Supervisors and managers involved in cleanup operations must also have eight hours of hazardous waste management training.

Monitoring of airborne contaminants must be conducted prior to worker entry to the site. Accurate monitoring is necessary to select appropriate personnel protective equipment, assess the need for engineering controls and other work procedural requirements, and anticipate the need for specific medical surveillance.

---

[43] 40 C.F.R. § 311 (1991).

[44] Employers are required to develop and implement a written health and safety program for their employees involved in hazardous waste operations, pursuant to 29 C.F.R. § 1910.120(b) (1991). A list of requirements for each site or workplace program is found in 29 C.F.R. § 1910.120 app. C (compliance guidelines).

[45] 29 C.F.R. § 1910.120(b).

§ 7.11   —Medical Surveillance Program

Employers must establish a medical surveillance program for the following categories of employees:

1. Employees potentially exposed to hazardous substances or other designated health hazards in excess of the PELs for more than 30 days per year
2. Employees who wear respirators more than 30 days per year
3. Employees who have been exposed to unanticipated releases of hazardous waste without appropriate protective equipment, or who show signs or symptoms that may have resulted from exposure to hazardous substances
4. Employees who are members of hazardous materials teams.[46] (For a description of such teams, see **Chapter 1**.)

The employer must provide for physical examinations of the employees in each of the above categories, provided without cost to the employee and at a reasonable time and place. Such examinations must be given prior to employment, at termination, or prior to reassignment to a nonhazardous area, and must be repeated every two years or when the examining physician is of the opinion that a medical followup is necessary. The employer must also ensure that the examining physician is aware of the substances to which the employee was or may have been exposed, the estimated exposure level, and any information available from prior medical examinations or health records. The employer must obtain and maintain records of written statements from the examining physicians regarding any diagnosed medical conditions that could be related to the work environment.[47]

§ 7.12   —Work Practices and Procedures

One important function of the site safety and health plan (see **Appendix E**) is to establish procedures for handling hazardous waste and controlling contamination at the site. These procedures must include decontamination of equipment, clothing, and personnel. For special requirements related to asbestos work, see **Chapter 6**. If employees are required to shower, employers must provide facilities.[48] If contaminated clothing is cleaned outside the site, employers must ensure that information about potential hazards is provided to people involved in the laundering process.[49]

---

[46] Occupational Safety & Health Administration, U.S. Dep't of Labor, Pub. No. 3114, Hazardous Waste and Emergency Response 11 (1990) [hereinafter Hazardous Waste and Emergency Response]; for a description of such teams, *see* 29 C.F.R. § 1910.120(c)(3) (1991).

[47] *Id.* at 11–12.

[48] 29 C.F.R. 1910.141.

[49] *Id.*

Engineering controls and work practices have been established that are specific to the type of remediation task or the hazardous substances involved. It is beyond the scope of this book to provide the detailed standards and protocol that state and federal programs have developed for each particular remediation task. Contractors must obtain updated information regarding such requirements prior to preparing a site safety plan.[50]

The handling of drums or containers of hazardous substances has been of particular concern to OSHA. Protocols for these activities must include:

1. Drums must be properly labeled or sufficient information regarding contents obtained through inspection

2. The handling of drums containing hazardous materials must be kept to a minimum

3. Damaged drums must be handled with devices appropriate for the contained hazardous contaminants

4. If spills, leaks, or ruptures have occurred, employers must furnish workers with appropriate salvage drums or containers, an appropriate amount of absorbent material, and appropriate fire equipment or other protective equipment or devices

5. Employers must inform workers of the dangers of handling drums (as well as provide training for handling the contents)

6. Employers must adopt precautions for preventing contamination of protective or other equipment, and hazardous situations related to such equipment (such as keeping electrical equipment behind an explosion barrier).[51]

Emergency response procedures must also be developed. Special communication protocol, medical emergency procedures, procedures for establishing emergency exclusion zones, and procedures and routes of entry and exit must be incorporated into a site safety plan. At hazardous waste sites, the emergency response plan must contain the following:

_____ 1. Personnel roles and lines of authority

_____ 2. Procedures to identify hazards and prevent emergencies

_____ 3. Emergency medical procedures

_____ 4. Communication procedures, including emergency warning

---

[50] 29 C.F.R. §§ 1910.120(g)–(z); however, specific questions should be addressed to the particular state OSHA office, or federal OSHA if the state does not have occupational health and safety requirements. Because § 1910.120 deals only with "hazardous substances," questions regarding air pollutants and toxic substances should be answered by consulting specific codes and regulations.

[51] Hazardous Waste and Emergency Response at 15–16.

_____ 5.   Plans for evacuation: routes of egress and places of refuge
_____ 6.   Decontamination procedures for equipment and personnel
_____ 7.   Personal protective equipment, and the requirements for use.[52]

Any emergency or safety plan is only worthwhile to the extent that the individuals know how to follow it when the need arises. Remediation contractors or owners should establish that all workers on the site are actually knowledgeable regarding emergency and safety procedures.

CONFLICTS OF INTEREST

§ 7.13   Quality Assurance and Quality Control

In the environmental field, the conflict-of-interest issue has historically focused on the designer and contractor. When one entity performs both functions, many commentators believe that the situation presents conflict-of-interest problems. The issue also arises when the contractor assumes a continuing operations and maintenance (O&M) role.

The party contracting for environmental remediation services must give close attention and scrutiny to who is responsible for the quality assurance/ quality control (QA/QC) on the site, their relationship to the contractor, and issues such as contractor reliance upon third-party information[53] and potential O&M responsibility.

The phased evolution of any remediation plan offers a multitude of opportunities for potential conflict of interest problems to arise. The points in the process that are most likely to give rise to such conflicts are:

1.   Research and investigation/feasibility study (RI/FS) stage
2.   Remedial design/remedial action (RD/RA) stage
3.   Overall QA/QC (inspection of work as it is performed, and testing treated material)
4.   O&M.

---

[52] 29 C.F.R. 1910.120(q).

[53] For example, IT Corp., the cleanup contractor on the halted Motco Superfund site, has filed suit against the Motco Trust Group, claiming the parties responsible for the cleanup misrepresented the waste. IT Corp. walked off the job after contending that the cost of the cleanup would be greater than their $30 million fixed-cost contract. *Motco May Change Cleanup Plans,* Engineering News-Rec., Jan. 13, 1992, at 16.

§ 7.14   —Potential Conflicts of Interest

The first potential for conflict may arise from the decision as to whether the concerned government agency or the PRP will undertake the cleanup. While there is a tendency to assume that PRPs, motivated by cost-cutting, may devise and implement ineffective remediation plans, studies have shown that government-sponsored cleanups also create potential conflicts by opening the door to contractor abuse. Recent investigations have revealed that, notwithstanding a history of abuse by EPA-hired contractors, the EPA Inspector General's office has come under fire for conducting superficial investigations, not effectively pursuing potential fraud and abuse, and various other leadership failures.[54]

Concerns about potential conflicts at the RI/FS stage also arise when PRPs are involved in the process. Indeed, these concerns at the federal Superfund level have spawned substantial litigation and a series of contradictory rulings. Prior to June 1990, PRPs could perform their own risk assessment as part of their RI/FS study. However, this policy was changed by a controversial EPA directive barring such activities. Industry experts were troubled by this action, in part because EPA's own studies showed that the PRPs' risk assessments had been as environmentally protective as the EPA's assessments. A suit filed by the Chemical Manufacturers Association (CMA) has caused EPA to reexamine this directive. Industry executives have noted that the new policy has extended the average time to complete the risk assessment portion of the RI/FS from 33 months to 47.5 months. They also suggest that, since the directive surfaced for the first time at a congressional hearing, it was politically motivated and aimed at punishing the industry rather than at cleaning up sites.[55] Whether the motive was cosmetic or political, it is clear that the outcome generated only litigation and inefficiency, not a better cleanup.[56]

The RD/RA phase also presents opportunities for abuse. Most often these abuses involve the assessment of whether a failed remediation was caused by defective design or defective workmanship. Such internal conflicts are less likely when one entity is responsible for both elements of the remedial action, thus enhancing the one entity's exposure, but at the same time precluding the classic designer/contractor liability argument. Of course, if one entity is engaged for both designing and carrying out the remediation, the QA/QC may be

---

[54] Ichniowski & Bradford, *EPA's Inspector Generals and Contractors Need More Monitoring,* Engineering News-Rec., July 15, 1991, at 7.

[55] *EPA to Review Risk Analysis,* 69 Chem. & Engineering News, Dec. 23, 1991, at 15.

[56] In February 1992, in an attempt to address industry criticism resulting from its June 1990 announcement, the EPA asked for public comments on whether PRPs should be allowed to conduct risk assessments at Superfund sites. A report will be made on the EPA's evaluation, which should be in effect for approximately one year, after which time the public will again be invited to comment. *EPA Asks for Comments, Will Evaluate Policy on Who Conducts Risk Assessments,* Daily Report for Executives, Feb. 20, 1992, Section on Regulation, Economics and Law, DER No. 34, at A-17.

compromised. The best solution is to employ a separate QA/QC firm to monitor both design and construction, much as a construction manager does for an owner in many contemporary operations. Many government agencies are also concerned about monitoring PRP activities at all levels, and have enacted legislation to provide for such monitoring.[57]

Aside from design/construction and QA/QC issues, further potential for conflict exists if the remediation plan calls for post-closure O&M. Concerns about the selection of O&M contractors have generated serious comment at the federal level.[58] Greater efficiency may be possible if the remediation contractor also provides the O&M for the job; however, such an arrangement may permit the contractor to use its O&M function to hide or minimize improper design or construction.[59] A provision for client site inspection and testing could help minimize this risk, provided the client actually availed itself of such rights.

---

[57] *See, e.g.,* Cal. Health & Safety Code § 25,355.7.

[58] Ichniowski & Bradford, *DOE Plans to Tighten Outside Contractor Liability,* Engineering News-Rec., Feb. 11, 1991, at 7.

[59] The concern of the Department of Energy that traditional plant O&M contractors do not adequately understand the regulations has led Energy Secretary James D. Watkins to turn environmental management at the weapons plants over to an Environmental Restoration Management Contractor. This is an attempt to bring new players to the sites, control cleanups, and avoid the inbred O&M contractor network. D. Rubin et al., *After the Bomb, A War Against Waste,* Engineering News-Rec., Nov. 25, 1992, at 35–36.

PART III
LIABILITY ISSUES

CHAPTER 8

THEORIES FOR IMPOSING LIABILITY

STATUTORY LIABILITY AND COMPLIANCE

§ 8.1   Introduction

The numerous regulations concerning protection and cleanup of the environment have exposed remediation contractors to enormous potential liability. The following statement prepared by the Associated General Contractors of America for House of Representatives hearings addresses the need for concern:

> The uncertain and unpredictable status of the law as it may be applied to Superfund cleanup work operates as a strong disincentive for responsible contractors to enter the marketplace of Superfund cleanup . . . The unpredictable liabilities facing cleanup contractors are compounded and intertwined with the present insurance crisis in the environmental/pollution field.[1]

This statement demonstrates the importance of the contractor's awareness of potential liability, and the need to take measures to avoid or at least minimize exposure. This portion of the chapter will outline the major federal and state statutes that may impose liability on the remediation contractor and owner, will suggest means to avoid or minimize liability, and will give some insight into the future of such liability concerns.

§ 8.2   Comprehensive Environmental Response, Compensation, and Liability Act

In 1980, Congress passed CERCLA, reenacted and amended in 1986 as the Superfund Amendments and Reauthorization Act (SARA).[2] CERCLA provides a means for the federal government to respond to the threat of hazardous waste, and a basis for imposing costs and responsibility on those parties who created the threat.

Under CERCLA, Congress empowered the EPA to seek out contaminated or potentially contaminated sites that pose an imminent and substantial threat

---

[1] *Reauthorization of Superfund, Hearings Before the Subcomm. on Water Resources of the House Comm. on Public Works and Transportation,* 99th Cong., 1st Sess. 1706, 1711 (1985) (statement of Associated General Contractors of America).

[2] *Codified at* 42 U.S.C. §§ 9601–9675 (Supp. III 1991) (as amended).

to the public health or to the environment, and to choose one of two routes to remedy the situation. The EPA may take direct action and administer the cleanup work itself and then sue the responsible parties to recover the cost. Under this approach, the responsible parties are given a chance to assume responsibility for the development of the cleanup if the EPA determines that the parties' action will be prompt and proper. Alternatively, the EPA may issue orders or sue the responsible parties in a civil suit to force them to clean up the site themselves.[3] See **Chapter 1** for further discussion of CERCLA and the types of cleanup work performed, and **Chapter 4** for a discussion of cost recovery actions.

§ 8.3 —Liability of the Remediation Contractor and the Owner

To recover under CERCLA a plaintiff must show that a release has occurred or is threatened, that such release or threatened release is of a hazardous substance, and that the release is from a facility or vessel. Four categories of persons may be held liable for a cleanup under CERCLA:

1. The owner or operator of a facility or vessel from which the release emanates or is threatened
2. Any person who at the time of disposal of the contaminant owned or operated a facility where the substances were placed
3. Any person who arranged for the disposal or treatment of contaminants
4. Persons who accepted any hazardous substance for transport to sites selected by such person.[4]

The owner of a contaminated site obviously falls into the first category, and from this broad definition of liable parties, it is easy to envision situations where a remediation contractor may be a potentially responsible party (PRP).

Under the first two categories, a remediation contractor would be a PRP if the contractor disposed of, treated, or otherwise placed contaminants at a site owned or operated by the contractor. If the contractor temporarily stored contaminants in a container, such as a truck, which leaked, the contractor would be a PRP. A contractor would fall into the fourth category by picking a dump site and transporting wastes to that site.

The third category poses the greatest threat of liability to a remediation contractor, because it is the most difficult to avoid. The contractor can be held liable for any part whatsoever in arranging the disposal, treatment, or transport

---

[3] *Id.*

[4] 42 U.S.C. § 9607(a) (Supp. III 1991).

of contaminants at or to a facility, even if prior to those efforts the contractor had no connection with the substance. By arranging transportation from one site to another, the contractor can be considered a PRP for the cleanup at the second site if it subsequently requires remediation.

CERCLA does not define *arranged* in this context. Case law indicates that the party who makes the decision on how the hazardous substances are disposed of or treated is liable. The arranger does not determine the essential terms of the activity, but merely decides who will perform the activities to become liable. The question of liability depends on, "Who decided to place the waste into the hands of a particular facility that contains hazardous wastes?"[5] This test is based on the type of analysis utilized in the common law context, in the *Kenny* and *Russell-Stanley* cases discussed in §§ **8.20** and **8.26**.

§ 8.4 —Liability of Corporate Officers, Directors, and Shareholders

Under the common law, officers, directors, and shareholders are generally shielded from liability for acts of the corporation, unless a plaintiff shows that the formalities of the corporate form were not followed, that the corporation was undercapitalized, or that the corporation was merely the alter ego of these officers, directors, and shareholders. Since this essentially requires a showing of fraudulent use of the corporate form, the law offers a strong shield to liability.

Officers, directors, and shareholders of owner or contractor corporations, however, have faced increasing liability in the environmental context. Cost recovery suits under CERCLA, including both government and private-party actions, have circumvented common law protections in two ways. Disregarding the common law, directors, officers, and shareholders have been held to be responsible parties and thus directly liable for cleanup and abatement costs. In addition, the traditional arguments for piercing the corporate veil to impose individual liability have been adapted to create a new federal corporate veil doctrine for environmental cases, involving an even lower standard to pierce the veil.

The most important criteria for a finding of liability as an owner/operator are the party's ownership interest in the property or the facility, and actual control and participation in the management of the facility.[6] Directors and officers have been held liable as operators if they owned stock and actively participated in managing the business. Parent corporations that exercise significant

---

[5] United States v. A&F Materials Co., 582 F. Supp. 842, 845 (S.D. Ill. 1984); United States v. Kayser-Roth Corp., 910 F.2d 24, 26–27 (1st Cir. 1990), *cert. denied,* 111 S. Ct. 957 (1991).

[6] The term *facility* is broadly construed under CERCLA to include any kind of business or activity at which hazardous substances are generated or disposed. 42 U.S.C. § 9601(9) (Supp. III 1991).

management and control have also been found liable under CERCLA.[7] It is important to note that active participation in the violation, such as generation or disposal of waste, may not be required for a finding of liability. In *State of New York v. Shore Realty Corp.,*[8] a sole shareholder and president of a corporation was held personally liable for all cleanup costs, after failing to prevent continued dumping of hazardous waste, of which he was aware, on land the corporation had recently acquired.

The criteria for finding a party liable as a generator are virtually identical to those for liability as an owner/operator, except that the participation in management must be linked to the generation or treatment and disposal of hazardous substances. For example, a corporate officer and majority shareholder was found to be liable as a generator for hiring an unqualified third party to dispose of waste, who later dumped the waste illegally.[9] The court found that the defendant's failure to exercise his ability to affect the company's waste handling practices, and to arrange for proper disposal of hazardous substances, qualified him as a generator. At the same time, some level of active participation is required. The Fifth Circuit recently held, in *Riverside Market Development Corp. v. International Building Products, Inc.,*[10] that a majority shareholder who infrequently visited a plant to review financial records had no opportunity to personally participate in improper asbestos disposal, and was therefore not liable under CERCLA.

One court has attempted to summarize and clarify the criteria for finding corporate directors, officers, and shareholders liable. The *Kelly test,* as it is called, examines (1) the *power* of the individual or entity to affect the hazardous waste handling practices of the company, depending on the position held, the distribution of power in the corporation, and percentage of shares owned or controlled; and (2) the *responsibility* for the hazardous waste practices, determined by the authority or degree of participation in making or effectuating hazardous waste policies.[11]

A number of courts have indicated that a capacity to control may be sufficient to establish liability as an operator. Parent corporations have been held liable when officers were aware of the waste disposal practices of a subsidiary, and had the capacity to control those practices and prevent contamination.[12] In one case, the president of a parent company, who lived in a different state from the business that generated the hazardous waste, and had delegated operational authority to a vice-president, was held personally liable (under RCRA, rather than CERCLA, because the disposal site was not owned or operated by the

---

[7] Mobay Corp. v. Allied Signal, Inc., 761 F. Supp. 345 (D.N.J. 1991).

[8] 759 F.2d 1032 (2d Cir. 1985).

[9] United States v. Ward, 618 F. Supp. 884 (E.D.N.C. 1985).

[10] 931 F.2d 327 (5th Cir.), *cert. denied,* 112 S. Ct. 636 (1991).

[11] Kelly *ex rel.* Michigan NRC v. Arco Indus., 721 F. Supp. 873 (W.D. Mich. 1989).

[12] *See, e.g.,* Idaho v. Bunker Hill Co., 635 F. Supp. 665 (D. Idaho 1986).

corporation) based on his ultimate authority to control disposal of the company's waste.[13]

The capacity-to-control finding has the potential to erode nearly all protections of corporate structure, and cause liability in cost recovery actions to expand in an unprecedented fashion. There are indications, however, that courts are not prepared to extend liability to all parties with potential control over contamination. Additional threshold requirements, such as pervasive control by the parent company, or the use of a subsidiary as a mere instrumentality, have been imposed.[14]

In seeking the boundaries of CERCLA liability, some courts have rejected the line of reasoning in cases that have disregarded the common law doctrine and required plaintiffs to pierce the corporate veil by demonstrating facts that show the corporate entity was disregarded, in order to find officers, directors, and shareholders liable. This line of decisions has resulted in the creation of a new federal doctrine incorporating the policy goals of environmental cleanup into its determination of liability (the *corporate veil* doctrine). For example, the public interest in encouraging firms to undertake the cleanup of properties by limiting the extent of the companies' risk, justified maintaining the corporate shield for a company that had purchased a subsidiary with contaminated property.[15] The court in *John Boyd* stated that a corporate entity can be disregarded in consideration of public convenience, fairness, and equity, but that pervasive control of defendants over the environmental policy must be shown.[16]

Although the evolving role of the corporate veil doctrine in CERCLA actions is still undecided, it is very clear that the role is being influenced by two different policy views. On one hand, disregarding the corporate veil doctrine enables parties who undertake cleanups, whether they are private parties or the government, to have access to the personal assets of the shareholders and directors of closely held corporations, which are often undercapitalized relative to the wealth of their owners and the riskiness of their businesses. This approach would allow for recovery of more cleanup costs from the private sector, thus preserving the Superfund. Furthermore, there would be incentive for anyone in a position of control to prevent contamination.

The opposite view is that increased liability will discourage investment and decrease the willingness of firms to clean up contamination. For firms that handle any hazardous wastes, officers may demand liability insurance or increased salaries, the cost of which would be passed on to consumers, thereby decreasing international competitiveness.

---

[13] United States v. Northeastern Pharmaceutical & Chem. Co., 579 F. Supp. 823 (W.D. Mo. 1984), *aff'd in part, rev'd in part on other grounds,* 810 F.2d 726 (8th Cir. 1986).

[14] *See, e.g.,* John Boyd Co. v. Boston Gas Co., 775 F. Supp. 435, 442 (D. Mass. 1991).

[15] *In re* Acushnet River & New Bedford Harbor, 675 F. Supp. 22, 31 (D. Mass. 1987).

[16] John Boyd Co. v. Boston Gas Co., 775 F. Supp. 435, 442 (D. Mass. 1991).

§ 8.5 —Potential Plaintiffs

If the EPA chooses to clean up a contaminated site, the Agency may sue PRPs for the cleanup costs. To recover, the government must show that:

1. Costs it seeks to have reimbursed fall within the statutory definition of removal or remedial action.
2. Costs were incurred by the federal or state government.
3. Costs are not inconsistent with the National Contingency Plan (NCP).[17]

In addition, any person who conducts response action may recover necessary costs of response "incurred . . . consistent with the national contingency plan."[18] The case law has interpreted this provision to mean that private parties may sue PRPs to recover for their cleanup costs.[19] Private parties do not need any government approval to bring their suits, although the EPA has set forth other standards that private parties must follow to conduct response actions consistent with the NCP.[20] These and other aspects of cost recovery actions are discussed in § 8.6.

§ 8.6 —Available Remedies to Plaintiff's Exposure

If the government is the plaintiff in an action under CERCLA, PRPs are liable for "all costs of removal or remedial action incurred by the United States Government or a State not inconsistent with the national contingency plan."[21] Moreover, if the PRP fails to perform the response action ordered by the president of the United States, CERCLA allows punitive damages equal to three times the amount of all costs incurred. CERCLA, however, imposes some limitations on response actions, depending on the type of response.

A removal action is a short-term, immediate action to address a release or threatened release of a hazardous substance. Such action involves the actual removal of the hazardous materials and any related, necessary measures. Except in certain emergency situations, a removal action cannot continue after $2 million has been spent or 12 months have elapsed from the date of initial response.[22] Expenses that do not aid in the cleanup, such as worthless studies, arguably are not recoverable by the government.

---

[17] 42 U.S.C. § 9607 (Supp. III 1991).

[18] *Id.*

[19] Jones v. Inmont Corp., 584 F. Supp. 1425, 1428 (S.D. Ohio 1984).

[20] 40 C.F.R. 300.700 (1991).

[21] 42 U.S.C. § 9607(a)(4) (Supp. III 1991).

[22] *Id.* § 9604(c)(1).

A remedial action, on the other hand, is instituted when a removal action will not remedy a problem. Remedial action is a long-term cleanup plan lasting from one to three years, involving permanent cleanup of a site, as well as long-term monitoring of the site to ensure that any remaining contaminants do not pose a public threat. The EPA may recover any planning, legal, fiscal, economic, engineering, architectural, and other studies or investigations deemed necessary to enforce the provisions of CERCLA.[23] Unlike a removal action, Congress has not placed limits on the amounts recoverable as defined above, other than consistency with the NCP. Recoverability of attorneys' fees and other costs of litigation by the EPA, however, is not settled under the law.[24] Moreover, the case law is not clear as to whether the EPA must have incurred some costs before bringing an action.[25]

In private party suits under CERCLA, the courts are inconsistent regarding whether a private plaintiff may bring an action for expenditures made to investigate the problem, or whether a cause of action requires costs incurred for actual cleanup.[26] Once a cause of action arises, the plaintiff may recover "any . . . necessary costs of response."[27] These costs do not include, however, any damages for diminution of value of the property or consequential damages.

In addition to the limitations on recovery by the government and private plaintiffs for response actions, CERCLA establishes limits on the liability imposed on each PRP.[28] These limits, however, do not apply if:

1. The release or threatened release resulted from willful misconduct or willful negligence by the PRP.

2. The primary cause of the release was a known violation of safety standards or regulations.

3. The PRP did not reasonably cooperate with the EPA in its response activities.[29]

Liability is limited to $300 per gross ton or $5 million for vessels carrying hazardous substances as cargo or residue, and to $300 per gross ton or $500,000 for any other vessel.[30] For motor vehicles, aircraft, or rolling stock, the president

---

[23] *Id.* § 9604(b).

[24] Frost, *CERCLA for the Contractor, in* Hazardous Waste Disposal and Underground Construction Law 231–32 (R. Cushman & B. Ficken eds., John Wiley & Sons 1987).

[25] *Id.*

[26] Connolly, *Successor Landowner Suits for Recovery of Hazardous Waste Cleanup Costs: CERCLA Section 107(a)(4)*, 33 UCLA L. Rev. 1737, 1753–59.

[27] 42 U.S.C. § 9607(a).

[28] *Id.* § 9607(c).

[29] *Id.*

[30] *Id.*

may limit the liability to any amount between $5 million and $50 million.[31] For any other facility, liability is capped at the total response costs plus $50 million for damages.[32]

If several PRPs are involved, their liability is joint and several.[33] The courts will allow apportionment among the PRPs, and will allocate liability using equitable factors it considers appropriate.[34]

§ 8.7   —Defenses and Immunities

The defenses available to PRPs under CERCLA are limited. A defendant may avoid liability by proving that the release or threatened release of a contaminant, and any resulting harm, were caused solely by:

1. An act of God
2. An act of war
3. The act or omission of a third party, unrelated to the defendant by employment or contract, if the defendant can show that due care was exercised with respect to the hazardous waste, and precautions were taken against the foreseeable acts or omissions by the third party and the consequences that could foreseeably result from such acts or omissions
4. Any combination of the three defenses above.[35]

If none of these defenses can be proven, the defendant will be held strictly liable. The exercise of due care and the use of state-of-the-art technology to prevent contamination are irrelevant.[36]

Aside from the defenses defined under CERCLA, some additional defenses are available. The defendant may contend that the EPA did not comply with the conditions under CERCLA or the NCP. The defendant may also assert equitable defenses.[37]

CERCLA specifically addresses the potential liability of a remediation contractor, by providing that the contractor is not liable to any person, under CERCLA or any other federal law, for injuries, costs, damages, expenses, or other liability resulting from a release or threatened release of a contaminant, unless the release is caused by the contractor's negligence, gross negligence, or

---

[31] *Id.*

[32] *Id.*

[33] United States v. Chem-Dyne Corp., 572 F. Supp. 802 (S.D. Ohio 1983).

[34] 42 U.S.C. § 9613(f)(1).

[35] 42 U.S.C. § 9607(b) (Supp. III 1991).

[36] United States v. Argent, 21 Env't Rep. Cas. (BNA) 1356, 1356 (D.N.M. 1984).

[37] United States v. Conservation Chem. Co., 619 F. Supp. 162, 204 (D. Mo. 1985).

intentional conduct. See further discussion at § **8.21**.[38] This provision, however, does not make clear whether state law can impose liability on the remediation contractor,[39] and is not applicable to situations where the contractor is exposed to liability as an employer for workers' compensation.[40] Finally, the statute does not provide immunity for a consultant's negligence in arranging the treatment, transportation, or disposal of hazardous wastes.[41]

In addition to this provision, SARA allows the EPA to indemnify and hold harmless its remediation contractor against the contractor's own negligence (but not against gross negligence or intentional conduct), as long as the contractor can prove that diligent but unsuccessful efforts were made to obtain insurance.[42] The EPA has expressed its intention to limit the use of this power, in spite of vehement opposition by contractors.[43]

§ 8.8   —Means for the Remediation Contractor to Deal with Liability

A remediation contractor must consider the liability exposure in the project, and take steps to minimize that exposure. Many of these steps will involve shifting the liability to another party; therefore, negotiations will be necessary. The following are suggestions for the remediation contractor:

_____ 1.   Avoid classification as a PRP under CERCLA. See § **8.3**.

_____ 2.   Seek indemnification from the client.

_____ 3.   Buy insurance if possible.

_____ 4.   Obtain commercial alternatives to insurance. See **Chapter 9**.

_____ 5.   Accept remediation contracts only in one's area of expertise.

It may be possible to avoid classification as an owner/operator or transport facility. Limiting the range of activities in the project may avoid liability by limiting the scope of responsibility, but will also reduce the effective control the contractor has over the scheduling, efficiency, and quality (and thus potential contamination) of the project. Certain tasks (such as waste disposal and transportation) can be contracted out to reputable, licensed and permitted subcontractors. Other potential liability traps, such as being classified as a storage facility when waste disposal is delayed, or permit violations when unknown

---

[38] 42 U.S.C. § 9619(a)(1).

[39] 42 U.S.C. § 9619(a)(3).

[40] *Id.*

[41] *Id.* § 9607(d).

[42] *Id.* § 9619(c).

[43] 9 Haz. Waste Rep. 5 (Mar. 21, 1988).

contaminants are found on the site (see **Chapter 5**), may be dealt with through insurance or specific indemnity clauses in contracts. See **Chapter 9**. To a limited extent, liability may be shifted to the owner, by requiring the owner to clearly accept ownership of all transport equipment and contaminated materials (such as soil).

The remediation contractor may also be able to pass on to the owner the entire responsibility for arranging dealings with hazardous wastes, through provisions in the remediation contract. In this case, the contractor should assure that the owner actually takes responsibility and signs all appropriate documentation. Again, title to the contaminated material should remain with the client.

These ways of avoiding liability may not ultimately be possible in the real world of remediation. Courts have held that § 107(e)(1) of CERCLA[44] allows liable parties to contractually shift responsibility for their response costs among themselves;[45] however, liability can only be shifted for a price. If the contractor takes on such exposure, the cost of a cleanup will go up. If the contractor wants the owner to retain liability (as is often the case), the contractor will be pressed for cost concessions. Owners, who are aware of the high stakes and the fact that the contractors have more control over projects, are using such issues for leverage with liability issues.[46] As noted above (see **§ 8.7**), if the remediation contractor's client is the government, the EPA has the power to indemnify the contractor, but only if the contractor is unable to obtain insurance after diligent efforts.

Although indemnification is not as limited in a private contract, the value of an indemnity clause is limited to the extent of the client's ability to pay. The clause would be worth little if the client were to die, go bankrupt, or simply refuse to pay. The best solution to this problem is to have the client post a bond or provide some other type of insurance. In addition, as discussed in **§ 8.22** (in the context of consent as a defense to a response cost recovery action), any contract clause shifting liability must be carefully and precisely worded.

If a remediation contractor is able to obtain insurance, it is important to carefully review the policy to determine the extent and conditions of the coverage provided. See further discussion regarding insurance in **Chapters 3** and **9**.

Because of the limited availability of insurance, remediation contractors may need to consider alternatives. Examples include self-insurance and the formation of captives or risk-pooling arrangements. Self-insurance can be accomplished by creating an internal reserve of funds that would be available to pay losses. To fund this reserve, the remediation contractor must incorporate the amount of funds needed for the internal reserves into the price of each contract. Determination of the necessary amounts should be based on an assessment of potential

---

[44] 42 U.S.C. § 9607.

[45] *See, e.g.,* Purolator Prods. Corp. v. Allied Signal, Inc., 772 F. Supp. 124 (W.D.N.Y. 1991).

[46] Korman & Setzer, *Sticking It to the Other Guy,* Engineering News-Rec., May 20, 1991, at 38–39.

liability, perhaps through the implementation of an environmental risk management program.[47]

If the contracting firm is too small or financially vulnerable to self-insure by means of internally held reserves, the firm can form a captive insurance broker or a risk-pooling arrangement. A *captive insurance company* is a subsidiary formed by a parent company for the purpose of writing all or some of the parent's loss exposures. The captive can be owned by a single firm, or jointly by several remediation contractors. The primary difficulty faced by these captives is a lack of reinsurance support.[48]

Finally, the most practical way for a contractor to avoid liability is to comply with all pertinent environmental regulations. To ensure such compliance requires familiarity with, or knowledgeable advice about, each stage of the remediation process: contracting, site assessment, choice of remediation techniques, permitting, remedial work, and closure/monitoring. See **Chapters 3** and **4.** Remediation contractors should hesitate to enter into contracts for projects that are not within the firm's area of expertise. The potential for error and the resulting costs are both considerable in the remediation field.

§ 8.9　Resource Conservation and Recovery Act

RCRA was signed into law in October 1976 as an amendment to the Solid Waste Disposal Act of 1965. The Act addresses the "last remaining loophole in environmental law, that of unregulated land disposal of discarded materials and hazardous wastes."[49] See **Chapter 5** for a further review of hazardous waste regulations. RCRA is a cradle-to-grave tracking and regulatory system for hazardous wastes. The Act authorizes the EPA to enforce the Act and the regulations, and to recommend prosecution of owners and operators of waste disposal facilities that fail to meet the disposal standards.[50]

§ 8.10　—Liability of Owners and
Remediation Contractors

Parties involved in the handling, storage, transportation, and disposal of hazardous wastes are required to notify the EPA of their activities, to obtain an

---

[47] Miller & Murphy, *Insuring and Assessing Hazardous Waste Contractors, in* Hazardous Waste Disposal and Underground Construction Law 305–07 (R. Cushman & B. Ficken eds., John Wiley & Sons 1987).

[48] *Id.*

[49] H.R. Rep. No. 1491, 94th Cong., 2d Sess. 4 (1976), *reprinted in* 1976 U.S.C.C.A.N. 6238, 6241.

[50] 42 U.S.C. § 6912 (Supp. III 1991).

identification number from the EPA, and to maintain various records. For more detail about these procedures, see **Chapter 5**. Failure to comply with these notification and record-keeping requirements may result in liability. These same parties may also be sued if their activities involving hazardous wastes result in the endangerment of the public welfare.[51]

The owner of a site that contains hazardous wastes is obviously subject to RCRA's requirements. Depending on the scope of the remediation contract, the contractor who is involved with hazardous wastes may also be subject to liability under RCRA. Thus, the owner and the remediation contractor may be liable for failure to notify the EPA, failure to maintain adequate records regarding the wastes, or any endangerment resulting from activities involving hazardous wastes.

Several situations exist in which a remediation contractor would be potentially liable when hazardous wastes endanger the public health or the environment. First, liability would result if a remediation contractor transports hazardous wastes. Second, the remediation contractor may be liable when handling wastes to prepare them for shipment by another party. The third, and most ambiguous, situation is when the contractor is contributing to the handling, storage, treatment, or disposal of the wastes in some other more attenuated fashion. Because of RCRA's broad definition of the term *contributing*,[52] the remediation contractor may be liable in a number of circumstances.

The potential sources of liability are numerous and the remediation contractor's involvement with hazardous wastes on any level causes uncertainty regarding this liability. RCRA does not directly state whether negligence is necessary by the contributing person, or whether any conduct, including innocent conduct, resulting in endangerment will support liability. Congress has expressly noted that liability is without regard to fault.[53] The remediation contractor, however, is protected to some extent under SARA § 119.[54] See discussion at **§§ 8.6** and **8.8**.

Even this protection is limited, however. The National Constructors Association has issued a draft environmental restoration contractor liability statement (letter from National Constructors Association on file with author) regarding Department of Defense (DOD), Department of Energy (DOE), and Superfund site cleanup liabilities. The draft states:

1.   The DOD should provide an indemnity for strict liability arising under both federal and state laws. Current terms hold the contractor responsible regardless of fault.

---

[51] 42 U.S.C. §§ 6972(a)(1)(B), 6973 (Supp. III 1991).

[52] *See id.* § 6903.

[53] H.R. Conf. Rep. No. 1133, 98th Cong., 2d Sess. 119 (1984), *reprinted in* 1984 U.S.C.C.A.N. 5649, 5690.

[54] 42 U.S.C. § 9619.

2. Cleanup contractors should be liable for their negligence up to some level, above which the government would assume responsibility. The value for the upper level of contractor responsibility should be related to the size of the contract.

3. The DOD should provide contract language that establishes a time limit for the contractor's responsibility after government acceptance of the work. This limit would eliminate long tail claims that can occur long after the work has been performed. See **§ 8.20**.

4. The contract should be structured so that government claims concerning contractor negligence are initially administered through the contract vehicle rather than the courts.

5. Changes to liability terms should be implemented as a matter of DOD policy, and not on a case-by-case basis. Further liability issues should be established and made known well in advance of any procurement.

6. Innovative technologies will be needed to solve many of the DOD's environmental contamination problems. The uncertainties about the ultimate effects resulting from the application of innovative technologies result in additional risks. Adequate indemnifications are needed to encourage contractors to use innovative technologies.

§ 8.11   —Potential Plaintiffs

RCRA authorizes the administrator of the EPA to enforce RCRA and the regulations promulgated thereunder. There are several methods of performing these enforcement duties. First, after determining that the owner or the remediation contractor violated regulations under RCRA, the administrator may issue an order assessing a civil penalty for any past or current violation.[55] Moreover, criminal penalties can be imposed if the administrator finds that the remediation contractor knowingly transported, or caused to be transported, hazardous wastes, without a manifest or to a facility without a permit, or that either party knowingly altered, concealed, destroyed, or failed to file any of the required records.[56] Second, the administrator may commence a civil action in federal district court for relief, including a temporary or permanent injunction.[57] Third, the administrator may bring a civil suit on behalf of the federal government if an owner's or remediation contractor's past or present handling, storage, treatment, transportation, or disposal of hazardous waste presents an imminent and substantial danger to the public health or the environment.[58]

---

[55] 42 U.S.C. § 6928(a)(1) (Supp. III 1991).

[56] *Id.* § 6928(d).

[57] *Id.* § 6928(a)(1).

[58] *Id.* § 6973(a).

RCRA also permits private citizens to sue parties who allegedly violate the Act's regulations, or who contribute in any way to the handling, storage, treatment, transportation, or disposal of hazardous waste that may present an imminent and substantial danger to the public health or environment.[59] When the suit is presented, the court may enforce the regulation that was violated or restrain the dangerous involvement with the hazardous waste.[60]

Neither type of citizen suit is allowed, however, if the administrator has commenced and is diligently prosecuting an action.[61] Prosecution is considered diligent if an agency is engaging in activity from which it can accord substantially equivalent relief to that available to the EPA in the federal courts.[62] For example, if the administrator issued an order under RCRA for surface cleanup of a site, that order would not be considered diligent prosecution of a private action, if the action alleged that groundwater contamination at the site may present an imminent and substantial danger.[63] To give the government the opportunity to diligently prosecute, RCRA requires prospective private plaintiffs to notify the EPA administrator and the state where the alleged contamination occurred or may occur. RCRA also requires notification of any defendant before filing suit.[64]

§ 8.12   —Civil and Criminal Penalties under RCRA

The EPA may bring an administrative action seeking a temporary or permanent injunction and penalties of up to $25,000 per day *per violation.* In addition, a finding of violation may result in suspension or revocation of any related permit, not just the permit allegedly violated.[65]

Any person who knowingly commits a violation in regard to treating, storing, or disposing of a hazardous or medical waste without a permit is subject to EPA criminal proceedings.[66] A violator is subject to a maximum fine of $50,000 per day of violation and two to five years' imprisonment. These penalties increase with subsequent violations and convictions.[67] If the violator knowingly placed

---

[59] *Id.* § 6972(a)(1).

[60] *Id.* § 6972(a).

[61] 42 U.S.C. § 6472(b).

[62] Baughman v. Bradford Coal Co., 592 F.2d 215, 219 (3d Cir.), *cert. denied,* 441 U.S. 961 (1979) (case involving interpretation of a citizen suit proviso under the Clean Water Act).

[63] H.R. Conf. Rep. No. 1133, 98th Cong., 2d Sess. 118 (1984), *reprinted in* 1984 U.S.C.C.A.N. 5649, 5689; 42 U.S.C. § 6972(b)(2)(B)(i).

[64] 42 U.S.C. § 2672(b)(2)(A) (Supp. III 1991).

[65] 42 U.S.C. § 6928(c) (Supp. III 1991).

[66] *Id.* § 6928(d).

[67] *Id.*

another person in imminent danger of death or serious bodily injury, the violator is then subjected to a fine of up to $250,000 and imprisonment for up to 15 years.[68]

In addition, if the EPA finds violations of underground storage tank (UST) provisions (see **Chapter 6** for a discussion of USTs), the agency is authorized to impose civil penalties of up to $25,000 per day when the order is not satisfied.[69] Temporary or permanent injunctions may be ordered by the EPA in civil actions.

Under the RCRA hazardous waste manifest program, every transaction involving hazardous waste is accounted for by both the sending and receiving parties. Each party is required under RCRA to completely fill out and maintain manifests that track the waste from the time it leaves the generator until it reaches and is disposed of at a RCRA-licensed disposal facility.[70] This program allows the immediate detection of an unauthorized release or dumping, hastens the cleanup process, and helps the EPA determine who and what caused the release.

Private-citizen suits authorized by RCRA are injunctive in nature, empowering the court to order the defendant to cease a certain action or take affirmative steps to abate the contamination. RCRA does not authorize private suits for money damages.[71] Courts, however, may be flexible and provide injunctive relief that in effect resembles private damages. For example, the court may order the defendant to perform or finance studies to determine the scope of a problem.[72] Moreover, RCRA authorizes the court to award litigation costs, including attorneys' fees and expert witness fees, if appropriate.[73]

§ 8.13　Clean Water Act

The Clean Water Act (CWA) prohibits the discharge of pollutants into the waters of the United States unless a permit is obtained from the EPA, or authorization is given by a state.[74] Waters protected include rivers, streams, estuaries, the territorial seas, and most ponds, lakes, and wetlands.[75] The remediation contractor should therefore evaluate the potential for leakage of hazardous materials into any waterways. If such potential exists, a permit authorizing such disposal must be obtained. See **Chapter 5**.

---

[68] *Id.* § 6928(e).

[69] *Id.* §§ 6991(e), (d).

[70] 40 C.F.R. §§ 262.20–262.23 (1991).

[71] Walls v. Waste Resource Corp., 761 F.2d 311, 314 (6th Cir. 1985).

[72] United States v. Ottati & Goss, Inc., Civ. No. C80-225-L (D.N.H. Dec. 2, 1980).

[73] 42 U.S.C. § 6972(e).

[74] 33 U.S.C. §§ 1251–1387 (Supp. III 1991).

[75] *Id.*

As under CERCLA, provisions of CWA can apply even if the violator was not aware or negligent regarding the violation. Defenses available under CERCLA are also available against an action under CWA.[76]

Whenever any party violates any effluent limitation, permit, or pretreatment standard under CWA, the EPA may issue an administrative compliance order (ACO), requiring the facility to comply with its permit.[77] Furthermore, the ACO requires the violator to report to the agency the nature of the violation, and measures that will be taken to come into compliance with the permit.[78] If the violation persists, the EPA may have a basis for alleging a knowing or willful violation, which may result in criminal enforcement action.[79]

When state agencies have been delegated the authority to enforce CWA standards, the EPA has obligations to monitor state enforcement. If the EPA finds widespread permit violations due to lack of enforcement by the state, the Agency is required to notify the state. If the state does not comply with the ACO within 30 days, the EPA will assume state enforcement after giving public notice.[80]

In addition to ACOs, the EPA may commence a civil action requesting either a permanent or temporary injunction for any violation for which the EPA is authorized to issue an ACO.[81] In situations when the violation presents an "imminent and substantial endangerment" to the public health or welfare,[82] however, the EPA may "immediately restrain any person causing or contributing" to the endangering pollution.[83] Civil penalties may be assessed by an administrative order of the EPA for up to $25,000 per day, per violation, and per person found in violation of a permit (without limit).[84] The penalty is assessed according to the following criteria:

1. Seriousness of the violation
2. Economic benefit gained from the violation
3. Prior history of violations
4. Economic impact of the penalty on the violator.[85]

---

[76] 33 U.S.C. § 1319.
[77] *Id.* §§ 1319(a)(1)–(3).
[78] *Id.*
[79] *Id.* §§ 1319(c)(1), (2).
[80] *Id.* § 1319(a)(2).
[81] 33 U.S.C. § 1319(b).
[82] *Id.* § 1364(a).
[83] *Id.*
[84] *Id.* § 1319(d).
[85] *Id.*

The most significant penalties may be incurred for violations of any permit condition, pretreatment standard, or effluent limitation that is negligently or knowingly violated.[86] In addition, both negligent and knowing violations may result in a separate criminal action charge. Criminal penalties, including fines and imprisonment, depend upon the degree of the violation and the degree of involvement of the violator.[87] The possible penalties for negligent violations are fines between $2,500 and $25,000 per day, and up to one year's imprisonment. For knowing violations, the penalties are fines of between $5,000 and $50,000 per violation per day and up to three years' imprisonment. The most extreme criminal penalties are available for a party who either knew or should have known that the acts or omissions would place another person in imminent danger of death or serious bodily injury. In such a case, the violator is subject to fines of up to $250,000 per day and up to 15 years' imprisonment.[88]

In addition to civil and criminal actions and administrative compliance orders, the EPA may also respond to a permitting violation by imposing administrative penalties.[89] Divided into two classes depending upon the nature of the violation,[90] violators may incur fines of up to $25,000 per Class I violation, and up to $125,000 per Class II violation.[91] It is also important to remember that CWA is a strict liability statute. Although the burden of proving a violation rests with the EPA, intent is not a factor in determining the liability of the violator.

In addition to permit compliance, it is the duty of any party in charge of a vessel or facility to immediately report any unauthorized discharges to the EPA.[92] The owner of a vessel or facility from which an unauthorized discharge has been released is also liable for removal or cleanup costs of the discharge.[93]

Finally, CWA authorizes citizen suits, similar in scope to those authorized under RCRA. See § 8.10. An individual who has an interest in a violation, or who may be adversely affected by it, may sue the violator to enforce compliance with the regulations, as long as the EPA or the state is not diligently prosecuting a civil or criminal action for the violation.[94] As with citizen suits under RCRA, CWA does not authorize private actions for damages.

However, it is important to note that the present 1987 law is due for renewal because funding is running out in the programs authorized under it. What has

---

[86] Id. §§ 1319(c)(1), (2).

[87] Id.

[88] Id. § 1319(c)(3)(A).

[89] Id. § 1319(g)(1).

[90] Id. § 1319(g)(3).

[91] Id. § 1319(g)(2).

[92] Id. § 1321(b)(5); 40 C.F.R. § 300.125(c). This duty can be satisfied by calling 800-424-8802, or 202-426-2675 if calling from Washington, D.C.

[93] 33 U.S.C. § 1321(f)(1).

[94] Id. § 1365.

been suggested as a replacement is a massive rewrite of CWA that includes proposed changes in industrial use of toxic chemicals through process change or materials substitution, and directs the EPA and the states to charge fees to dischargers to help cover costs of developing new effluent limitations and standards.[95] The bill also applies the program of the 1990 Coastal Zone Management Act to the entire country, and increases funding for the program.[96] Additionally, the bill authorizes a "new $2 billion grants program to help those states with combined sewage systems to overhaul them."[97]

Since the suggestion of S. 1081, offered by Senators Baucus and Chafee, in May 1991 to reexamine CWA, redrafts of the bill unique to each of the two senators have surfaced.[98] The $33 billion Baucus redraft contains 16 new sections, including a water conservation section but not a wetlands protection provision.[99] The redraft strengthens water quality standards and introduces several new grants programs, including help for state nonpoint source pollution control and control of combined sewage overflows, and requires the EPA to develop a plan for using Superfund's toxic release inventory data.[100]

A consensus bill acceptable to Senator Chafee would include stripdown provisions for nonpoint source control, wetlands protection, control of combined sewage overflow, permit fees, and money in a state revolving fund to build and maintain sewage treatment facilities.[101] Important to any proposed change will be resolution of the wetlands issue. See **Chapter 6**.

§ 8.14   Clean Air Act

The Clean Air Act (CAA) provides the basic framework for federal and state air pollution control.[102] The Act seeks to control both mobile sources of air pollution, such as vehicles, and stationary sources, such as industrial smokestacks.[103]

In remediation contracting, liability under CAA is most likely to be incurred by the failure to acquire (or maintain required standards of) a permit required for certain equipment or treatment methods. Therefore, the remediation contractor must be sure to obtain all necessary permits (see **Chapter 5**) before work begins. In addition, pollution control equipment must be carefully maintained

---

[95] S. 1081, 102 Cong., 1st Sess. (1991); L. Ember, *Clean Water Act Is Sailing a Choppy Course to Renewal,* Chem. & Engineering News, Feb. 17, 1992, at 19 [hereinafter Ember].

[96] *Id.*

[97] *Id.*

[98] *Id.* at 20.

[99] *Id.* at 21.

[100] *Id.*

[101] Ember at 21.

[102] 42 U.S.C. §§ 7401–7671(g) (Supp. III 1991).

[103] *Id.*

and emissions must be monitored throughout the job, to ensure that the emission levels designated by the permits are not exceeded.

When the EPA determines that a person (defined comprehensively to include business entities) is in violation of any portion of a permit pursuant to CAA guidelines, the EPA is required to notify both the violator and the state.[104] If the violation continues for more than 30 days after EPA notification, the EPA may pursue civil action for injunctive relief and a civil penalty.[105] The EPA may also request criminal action against a person in violation of Title IV, V, VI, or VII of CAA.[106]

Civil actions pursuant to CAA for either violations or noncompliance with emissions limitations or standards[107] may request permanent or temporary injunctive relief, and civil penalties.[108] Upon a finding that the violator committed a knowing violation of CAA standards, the violator is subject to criminal penalties including imprisonment and fines.[109] A second conviction can result in doubling both the fine and the term of imprisonment.[110]

Citizen suits authorized by CAA are somewhat more powerful than those authorized under RCRA or CWA. Under CAA, citizens may file suit to compel the EPA to perform any non-discretionary duty, and may also sue violators for civil penalties in addition to injunctive relief. However, the fines are not recovered by plaintiffs, but are placed into a United States Treasury fund established to finance EPA compliance and enforcement actions.[111] Because of the government's interest in such suits, it has a limited right to intervene. Upon the filing of a citizen's suit, the EPA and United States Attorney General have 45 days to comment, join, or otherwise intervene before a consent judgment is awarded.[112]

In addition to filing civil and criminal actions for violations, the 1990 amendments to CAA authorize the EPA to seek limited administrative penalties.[113] Minor violations of CAA may also result in field citations, which may not exceed $5,000 per day for each day the violation continues.

---

[104] *Id.* § 7413(a)(1).

[105] *Id.*

[106] *Id.* § 7413(a)(3).

[107] Allyn & Pocalyko, *Liability for Environmental Problems under Federal Statutes, in* Environmental Dispute Handbook: Liability and Claims 88 (D. Carpenter et al. eds., John Wiley & Sons 1991) [hereinafter Environmental Dispute Handbook].

[108] 42 U.S.C. § 7413(b).

[109] *Id.* § 7413(c).

[110] *Id.*

[111] *Id.* §§ 7604(a), (g).

[112] *Id.* § 7604(c)(3).

[113] *Id.* § 7413(d)(1).

§ 8.15 State Statutes

The statutory liability exposure of owners and remediation contractors is not limited to the federal statutes. Most states have adopted some equivalent to the federal statutes. The following sections briefly discuss the state counterparts to the federal statutes discussed above, focusing on California and New Jersey, two of the states considered progressive in their environmental legislation. The majority of states have environmental liability and cleanup statutes modeled after CERCLA. Some have additional statutes similar to other federal, California, and New Jersey statutes. For further discussion of state statutes, see **Chapter 2**.

§ 8.16 —California

The Hazardous Waste Control Law (HWCL) is California's counterpart to RCRA.[114] Administered by the Department of Health Services (DHS), HWCL establishes cradle-to-grave regulation of hazardous wastes, including discretion to order cleanups for violations, and a permitting system.[115] HWCL follows the same criteria as RCRA in deciding who should pay for cleanups. HWCL's provisions regarding permitting requirements, however, should be reviewed because they are not identical to RCRA's requirements.[116]

In 1981, California adopted the state Superfund legislation (the Carpenter-Presley-Tanner Hazardous Substance Account Act).[117] The California Superfund was enacted to establish a response authority to releases or threatened releases of hazardous substances, and to compensate persons injured by such releases.[118] The DHS administers the program in cooperation with the EPA.[119] As under CERCLA, the DHS may react to a release or possible release threatening imminent or substantial danger either by ordering a PRP to take appropriate action, or by taking the necessary remedial actions itself and suing for reimbursement.[120]

Generally, the California Superfund follows CERCLA in many respects. It refers to CERCLA in determining the PRPs in a response action.[121] California also allows for indemnification of remediation contractors.[122] Some differences, however, do exist. A 1990 amendment to the California Superfund provides that solid waste transporters who unknowingly transport contaminants to a waste

---

[114] Cal. Health & Safety Code §§ 25,100–25,249.100 (1991).

[115] *Id.*

[116] *Id.*

[117] *Id.* §§ 25,300–25,395.

[118] *Id.* § 25,301 (1992).

[119] *Id.*

[120] Cal. Health & Safety Code §§ 25,180–25,196.

[121] *Id.* § 25,323.5(a).

[122] *Id.* §§ 25,364.6, 25,364.7.

facility are not automatically responsible for a cleanup, unless they act negligently.[123] Additionally, unlike CERCLA, the California program explicitly limits a PRP's liability to the costs attributable to that party's actions, if the party can quantify its liability by a preponderance of evidence.[124] Finally, California allows parties preliminarily allocated more than 50 percent of the responsibility in an approved cleanup plan to call for binding arbitration.[125]

Pursuant to federal mandate, California has adopted the California Porter-Cologne Water Quality Control Act to conserve, control, and protect the quality of the state waters.[126] The EPA has authorized California to administer many components of CWA, and in some instances has adopted further regulations that are more stringent than CWA.[127] The state Water Resources Control Board has overall responsibility for the development and implementation of water quality control, which includes implementation of all of the delegated federal CWA powers.[128]

The California Clean Air Act is the state counterpart to CAA.[129] The purpose of the Act is to establish an "intensive, coordinated state, regional and local effort to protect and enhance the ambient air quality of the state."[130] The structure of the California Clean Air Act is very similar to the federal program.

California has a number of other hazardous waste statutes that are relevant to remediation work. Some of these statutes include the Hazardous Waste Disposal Land Use Law,[131] the Safe Drinking Water and Toxic Enforcement Act (Proposition 65),[132] the Hazardous Substances Underground Storage Tank Law,[133] the California Aboveground Storage Tank Act,[134] the Toxic Pits Cleanup Act of 1984,[135] and the Oil Spill Prevention, Abatement and Removal Act.[136]

§ 8.17 —New Jersey

New Jersey has several statutes for regulation of hazardous wastes. Two such statutes are noteworthy here.

---

[123] *Id.* § 25,323.6.

[124] *Id.* § 25,363(a).

[125] *Id.* § 25,356.3.

[126] Cal. Water Code §§ 13,000–14,075 (1991).

[127] *Id.*

[128] *Id.*

[129] Cal. Health & Safety Code §§ 39,000–39,915.

[130] *Id.* § 39,001.

[131] *Id.* §§ 25,220–25,241.

[132] 22 Cal. Code Regs. tit. 22, §§ 12,301–12,306 (1991).

[133] Cal. Health & Safety Code §§ 25,280–25,299.7.

[134] *Id.* §§ 25,270–25,270.13.

[135] *Id.* §§ 25,208–25,208.21.

[136] Cal. Gov't Code §§ 8670–8670.70 (West 1992).

New Jersey's version of CERCLA, the Spill Compensation and Control Act, preceded CERCLA by three years and was the model for CERCLA.[137] In fact, the Act has a more comprehensive program than most other states for cleaning up sites. New Jersey also passed the Environmental Cleanup Responsibility Act (ECRA), which requires that industrial facilities be investigated, and if necessary cleaned up, before they are transferred or closed.[138] See further discussion at §§ 2.1 and 2.13.

As under CERCLA, response costs can be recovered under ECRA from a party who is "in any way responsible" for the contaminants.[139] This language is more narrowly defined than under CERCLA, however, especially as to how it relates to an innocent owner's liability. At least one court has held that ownership or control over the property when the release occurred is sufficient grounds for imposing liability.[140]

§ 8.18 The Future of Liability Exposure for Participants in Hazardous Waste Cleanups

In developing environmental regulations, there is on the one hand the desire to encourage the growth of qualified remediation contracting firms, and on the other hand, the need to identify parties responsible for the costs of environmental cleanup. While the country faces a dwindling number of remediation contractors, the number and cost of environmental cleanups is on the rise.

Because of the fear of tremendous liability exposure, qualified remediation contractors are choosing to leave the industry.[141] This trend is directly counter to the EPA goal of providing multiple and diverse options for contracting, to ultimately enhance competitiveness and efficiency. The contractors claim that they cannot assume risks of which they are unaware and cannot control. They profess that to stay in business, they need indemnification or immunity from liability, or at least a cap on their ultimate exposure.[142] At the same time, someone must pay the high cost of remediating the growing number of contaminated sites. Instead of using its powers granted under CERCLA to indemnify contractors, the EPA has attempted to identify a wide range of available PRPs to pay for environmental cleanups.

---

[137] N.J. Rev. Stat. §§ 58:10-23.11 to 23.11(z); Morris, *Hazardous Waste in New Jersey: An Overview,* 38 Rutgers L. Rev. 623, 628 (1986).

[138] N.J. Rev. Stat. § 13:1K-6 to 13:1K-32 (1991).

[139] *Id.; see also* Lansco v. Department of Envtl. Protection, 138 N.J. Super. 275, 350 A.2d 520 (1976), *cert. denied,* 73 N.J. 57, 372 A.2d 322 (1977).

[140] State of N.J. Dep't of Envtl. Protection v. Ventron Corp., 468 A.2d 150, 165 (N.J. 1983).

[141] *Contractors Urge Restrictions on Liability, Tell Armed Services Panel Pool Could Dry Up,* Envtl. Rep., May 3, 1991, at 15 [hereinafter Environmental Rep.].

[142] *Id.*

The drafting and amending of environmental laws will be made even more difficult by the appearance of new liability concerns for the parties to remediation contracts. Right-to-know legislation has required public notification of the presence of hazardous substances, which are often carcinogenic. In response to this greater public awareness, private citizens are suing owners, operators, and others in the waste disposal chain for *fear of cancer*.[143]

Generally, tort law has held that fear alone is not compensable. To sue for fear, a plaintiff brings a claim for emotional distress, and most courts have held that recovery is not allowed unless the fear has some type of physical manifestation. The courts' rationale has been that the physical component helps ensure that the distress is not feigned. This limitation is not applied vigorously in the environmental contamination field.

For example, the California Court of Appeals, in *Potter v. Firestone Tire & Rubber Co.*,[144] abandoned the requirement of physical manifestation. The court held that, "in circumstances . . . where (plaintiffs) have ingested carcinogens-it is not necessary for (plaintiffs) to establish a present physical injury in order to recover for their fear of cancer . . . a plaintiff need not establish that cancer is reasonably certain to occur in order to recover." The only limit the court noted was that the plaintiffs must establish that their distress is serious and objectively reasonable under the circumstances.

In *Potter,* the plaintiffs, after learning that their tap water contained a number of known carcinogens, sued Firestone, a depositor of wastes at a nearby landfill, which they established as the source of contaminants. The court found that, although the plaintiffs did not prove any physical injury from the water consumption, nor had they been diagnosed with a precancerous condition, the plaintiffs did have an increased vulnerability to cancer that was less than probable. The court also found it relevant that the defendant had violated its own written manual for disposition of such substances. The court affirmed a $1.32 million judgment for compensatory damages (of which $800,000 was for fear of cancer, and the remainder for psychiatric illness and disruption of lives), and $2.6 million in punitive damages.

This case is not the first to allow a plaintiff exposed to a toxic substance to recover for fear of cancer. Similar decisions have been reached in Florida, Tennessee, Massachusetts, and in the federal courts.[145] The *Potter* case, however, is unique in rejecting the need for physical manifestation for recovery.

---

[143] F. Baker, *California Courts Address "Cancerphobia" Claims,* 1 Cal. Envtl. Rep. No. 4 at 100 (June 1991).

[144] 225 Cal. App. 3d 213, 274 Cal. Rptr. 885 (1990), *opinion superseded,* 806 P.2d 308, 278 Cal. Rptr. 836 (1991).

[145] Hagerty v. L&L Marine Servs., Inc., 788 F.2d 315 (5th Cir.), *reh'g denied,* 797 F.2d 256 (5th Cir. 1986); Eagle-Picher Indus., Inc. v. Cos, 481 So. 2d 517 (Fla. Dist. Ct. App. 1985), *review denied,* 492 So. 2d 1331 (Fla. 1986); Laxton v. Orkin Exterminating Co., 639 S.W.2d 431 (Tenn. 1982); Anderson V. W.R. Grace & Co., 628 F. Supp. 1219 (D. Mass. 1986).

Potter and other similar cases create further liability for parties to a remediation contract or elsewhere in the waste disposal chain. Under *Potter,* the plaintiff need only prove exposure to a carcinogen to recover. Failure of the remediation contractor and client to comply with their own written operating procedures and protocols can be used as grounds for recovery by plaintiffs. Because of the tremendous potential for exposure of citizens to carcinogens, the size of the potential class of plaintiffs is only limited by the size of the population. This potential liability is another element to be considered in the decision to enter into any remediation contract. As grounds for recovery expand to include fear of cancer and disruption of lives, the difficulty of negotiating remediation contracts increases.

COMMON LAW LIABILITY

§ 8.19   Introduction

For the most part, none of the federal environmental statutes authorize recovery of damages for personal injury or property damage.[146] Thus, while these statutes do provide a basis for recovery of response costs (see **Chapter 4** and **§§ 8.6** through **8.8**), they do not permit an injured party to seek redress for economic or physical injury.

Instances of significant environmental contamination have inevitably created a host of common law actions predicated on the following theories:

1. Negligence
2. Nuisance
3. Trespass
4. Strict liability.

A number of commentators have written historical reviews of those theories as applied in the environmental context.[147] This chapter will instead focus on how those theories and recent case law are relevant, in the remediation contracting process, to the owner, the contractor, contiguous property owners, and where applicable, the lender. See **§§ 8.3** through **8.17** for a discussion of the statutory

---

[146] *See, e.g.,* Exxon Corp. v. Hunt, 475 U.S. 355 (1986); Kouletsis, *Contractor Liability to Third Parties, in* Hazardous Waste Disposal and Underground Construction Law 179 (R. Cushman & B. Ficken eds., John Wiley & Sons 1987) [hereinafter Cushman & Ficken].

[147] *See, e.g.,* Cushman & Ficken at 179; Moskowitz, Environmental Liability and Real Property Transactions 149–73 (1989) [hereinafter Moskowitz]; Huitt & Warin, *Liability for Environmental Problems Under Common Law, in* Environmental Dispute Handbook at 145–69.

liability of remediation contractors and owner/operators in hazardous waste cleanups.

It is advisable to begin by examining limitations on the availability of a cause of action. There are several limitations, falling into three broad categories:

1. Statutory limitations
2. Statutes of repose and limitation
3. Contractual and doctrinal limitations.

§ 8.20   —Statutory Limitations

In the federal field, perhaps the most well-known limitation on actions is found in the provisions of SARA § 119.[148] This section provides that:

> A person who is a response action contractor with respect to any release or threatened release of a hazardous substance or pollutant or contaminant from a vessel or facility shall not liable under this title or under any other federal law to any person for injuries, costs, damages, expenses, or other liability (including but not limited to claims for indemnification or contribution in claims by third parties for death, personal injury, illness or loss of or damage to property, or economic loss) which results from such release or threatened release.

The statute goes on to provide that this limitation of liability does not apply in the case of release "caused by the conduct of the response action contractor which is negligent, grossly negligent, or which constitutes intentional misconduct." See further discussion of statutory defenses in § 8.7.

Similar limitations may be found in various state statutes. California Civil Code § 2782.6, for example, provides that an agreement to indemnify a professional engineer or geologist for various environmentally related activities, including remediation services, is valid, notwithstanding the anti-indemnity provisions of the statute for services in the construction field. The indemnification is valid only for damages arising from or related to subterranean contamination, and is not applicable to the first $250,000 of liability. Also, as with CERCLA, the indemnification is inoperative to the extent that it attempts to indemnify the promisee for claims arising from the promisee's own gross negligence or willful misconduct.

These statutes are reflective of the legislative desire to encourage contractors to enter into remediation efforts to achieve the cleanup required by the various state and federal statutes. The statutes came as a response to testimony from various representatives in the remediation industry that they are reluctant to perform certain remediation actions on federal projects because of the potential

---

[148] 42 U.S.C. § 9619.

for no-fault liability.[149] However, while representatives of contractors groups have urged these and even greater incentives (such as the adoption of comparative fault negligence and the requirement of federal indemnification),[150] federal agencies are also under a great deal of pressure to provide for increased contractor accountability.[151]

It is reasonable to assume that the tension between the desire to enhance contractor accountability, and to induce contractors to be more willing to enter into certain types of remediation contracts, will cause these and similar statutory limitations on liability to undergo both legislative and judicial scrutiny and modification in the future. See § **8.18**. There is an increasing judicial penchant for disregarding traditional limitations. As the court in *Kenney v. Scientific, Inc.* stated:

> The Court will not be sidetracked into a dissertation upon these ancient remedies. The days of strait jacket pleadings are behind us. There is no need for us to be obsessed with labels, and to endeavor to torture old remedies to fit factual patterns not contemplated when those remedies were fashioned. A new body of law is developing and will undoubtedly continue to evolve in the troublesome field of law relating to hazardous waste.[152]

§ 8.21   —Statutes of Repose and Limitation

The pervasive nature of environmental contamination has given rise to significant litigation concerning whether claims predicated on nuisance, trespass, strict liability, or other theories are time-barred. This litigation has led to in-depth court pronouncements concerning the distinction between continuing and permanent nuisances or trespasses. Two California cases (that would be likely to have an influence in other jurisdictions) have extensively analyzed this issue.

In *Mangini v. Arojet-General Corp.,*[153] the Manginis, and other owners of 2,400 acres of land that had previously been leased by Arojet, sued Arojet for alleged contamination that occurred during the company's tenancy. The complaint alleged nine causes of action, among which were public and private nuisance, negligence per se, negligent trespass, and strict liability. A demurrer to the complaint was sustained without leave to amend.

The opinion dealt with a wide variety of issues, including the subtle and apparently merging concepts of nuisance and trespass; that is, whether nuisance

---

[149] Environmental Rep. at 15.

[150] Itchniowski & Bradford, *DOD Cleanup Liability Fears Raised,* Engineering News-Rec., May 6, 1991, at 7.

[151] *DOE To Spread the Risk on Weapons Plant Cleanups,* Engineering News-Rec., Feb. 8, 1990, at 11.

[152] 204 N.J. Super. 228, 497 A.2d 1310 (1985).

[153] 281 Cal. Rptr. 827 (Cal. Ct. App. 1991).

claims are limited to nuisances emanating from neighboring lands, and whether a party can commit trespass on land that is in that party's possession. The court also rejected a defense based on a very ambiguous lease term that implied the prior landlord's consent to the hazardous activities on the site (discussed in § 8.22). The nuances of the common law issues discussed in *Mangini* are discussed in §§ 8.7 and 8.8, dealing with the historical distinctions between actions predicated on nuisance and on trespass.

The case is important here because of its in-depth discussion of the distinction between a permanent and continuing nuisance. Noting that California Code of Civil Procedure § 338(b) states that a cause of action for trespass or nuisance begins to run when the permanent nuisance is created, and must be brought within three years, the court stated that the distinction between a permanent and a continuing nuisance is based on whether the nuisance may be discontinued or abated. If the nuisance is abatable, it is considered to be continuing.[154] The fact that the conduct occurred years prior to the present claim was held to be irrelevant, because the land may be subject to a continuing nuisance even though the alleged conduct occurred years earlier. The court reasoned that the continuing aspect refers to the ongoing damage created by the condition, and not to the time the acts that caused the offensive condition occurred. The distinction here was significant. The court found that the plaintiff's counts for negligence, negligence per se, and strict liability were time-barred by the applicable statutes of limitations, because plaintiffs could have learned of their injuries through the exercise of due diligence.

Because most contaminated sites remain long after the events that created the contamination, the court's finding that the continuing nature of the nuisance referred to the continuing damages, and not the acts causing the damages, is significant.

The reasoning of *Mangini* has been followed in *Arcade Water District v. United States*.[155] In this case, the water district had begun operating Well 31 in 1956. The federal government had been operating a laundry at a nearby military base since 1941. The water district produced tests showing that, from 1955 to 1979, the quality of the water from Well 31 had deteriorated because of contaminants generated by the laundry. This contamination occurred despite the closing of the laundry in 1973. Contaminants from the laundry were evidently still leaching into the well in 1991. The water district claim had been brought under the federal tort claims act (which has a two-year statute of limitations). When the administrative complaint was rejected, the water district filed its suit, which was dismissed by the district court.

The court of appeals reasoned that if the nuisance was permanent as defined by California law, it had arisen more than two years prior to the filing of the claim, and would therefore be time-barred. However, the court reversed the

---

[154] *Id.* at 840.

[155] 940 F.2d 1265 (9th Cir. 1991).

district court, holding that the nuisance was continuing. Relying on *Mangini,* the court noted that a continuing activity is not necessary to establish a continuing nuisance, and that it was immaterial that the laundry was no longer operating; what mattered was that the contaminants continued to leach into the well.[156]

Following this line of reasoning, if a remediation contractor fails to complete a job and contamination persists, the window of liability for the contractor could be extended. If the contract provides for subsequent operations and maintenance (O&M) or monitoring, or if the contractor uses a system or chemical additive that creates a hazardous residue, liability exposure may be further lengthened.

§ 8.22   —Contractual and Doctrinal Limitations

Defendants in common law actions may assert contractual defenses to avoid liability. One of the defenses relied on by Arojet, the defendant in the *Mangini* case (see § 8.21), was a clause in the lease that provided, in part:

> Lessors have acknowledged that they are aware that certain activities of lessee on the leased premises may be of a hazardous nature and that from time to time activities conducted on the premises may have an element of nuisance about them or resulting from them. In this connection, Lessors hereby covenant that they will acquiesce in any nuisance or hazard caused by Lessee on the premise.[157]

In rejecting the defendant's proffer of this clause as a defense based on consent, the court agreed that consent could be a valid defense, but not in this case because of inherent ambiguities and shortcomings in the language. The court first noted that the paragraph did not identify the nature of the hazardous activity of the contemplated nuisance, and pointed out the presence of other provisions in the lease that made it unclear whether the parties had contemplated and agreed to the volume of contamination. The court also noted that under provisions of the lease, the premises would be used for lawful purposes, the tenant would commit no waste of the property, and the property would, upon termination, be surrendered in as good as condition as it was received.

Taken as a whole, the court's analysis of this provision makes it clear that, for a consent clause such as this to survive as a defense to contamination in either a lease or remediation contract, the clause would have to be narrowly drawn both in terms of identification of the type of work to be done and in the volume of contaminant involved. Moreover, any inconsistent clauses elsewhere in the body of the document would have to be reconciled or eliminated. This

---

[156] *Id.* at 1268.

[157] Mangini v. Arojet-Gen. Corp., 281 Cal. Rptr. 827, 836 (Cal. Ct. App. 1991).

process, in itself, might sufficiently highlight such a clause so as to make it unpalatable and unattainable.

Another defense often asserted is the doctrine of caveat emptor. This doctrine is often given as a defense against claims by successors in interests against prior landowners. Although such action was successfully urged in *Philadelphia Electric Co. v. Hercules, Inc.*,[158] recent decisions have rejected or distinguished the holding in that case.[159] The case is discussed in greater detail in § 8.23.

§ 8.23 Theories of Liability

Commentators have identified five potential theories of liability that could be imposed on cleanup contractors:

1. Strict liability for abnormally dangerous activity
2. Negligence
3. Public nuisance
4. Private nuisance
5. Trespass.[160]

Most of the decisions reported over the past several years have demonstrated some judicial confusion as to the applicability of the nuisance and trespass causes of actions. Moreover, the peculiarities of state law affecting the ability of a claimant to seek recovery under these theories makes it virtually impossible to develop a cohesive and all-encompassing body of law that would be applicable in every circumstance. In general, it appears that, in the context of environmental contamination and remediation, the distinction between nuisance and trespass is becoming obscured, and the courts are showing an increased willingness to apply standards of strict liability to parties involved in contamination of a site.

§ 8.24 —Nuisance

Practically every environmental suit involving private parties contains some element of nuisance allegations.

Historically, nuisance causes of actions have been divided into private and public nuisances. A private nuisance affects an individual's right to use or enjoy

---

[158] 762 F.2d 303 (3d Cir.), *cert. denied,* 474 U.S. 980 (1985).

[159] *See, e.g.,* T & E Indus., Inc. v. Safety Light Co., 123 N.J. 371, 587 A.2d 1249 (1991); Russell-Stanley Corp. v. Plant Indus., Inc., 250 N.J. Super. 478, 595 A.2d 534 (1991).

[160] Cushman & Ficken at 179.

the land. A public nuisance affects public rights that are common to all. Several treatises and judicial pronouncements have articulated the distinction between the two types of nuisance.[161]

Further distinctions have been made on the basis of whether the nuisance is a permanent or continuing nuisance. The *Mangini* and *Arcade* cases discussed in § **8.21** deal with such distinctions in some detail. Customarily, the distinction between a permanent and continuing nuisance is only relevant for the purpose of determining whether the statute of limitations has barred the applicable claim.

Some commentators believe that the decision in *Philadelphia Electric Co.* (discussed in § **8.22**) also had an impact on the applicability of the nuisance theory.[162] In addition to applying the doctrine of caveat emptor to deny the plaintiff's right to pursue the litigation, the court also ruled that, in a situation such as existed in that case (where a nuisance undeniably existed), only neighboring property owners could assert that right.[163]

The court in *Philadelphia Electric Co.* relied on the ancient common law distinction between nuisance and trespass actions. That distinction has been lessened by other courts.

For example, in *T & E Industries, Inc. v. Safety Light Co.*, the court held that a property owner could assert a claim against a predecessor in title for strict liability for abnormally dangerous activities. The court rejected the defendant's contention that the holding in *Philadelphia Electric Co.*, by analogy, would prohibit such action.[164] Similarly, in *Mangini*, the court held that "[t]he California nuisance statutes have been construed according to their broad terms, to allow an owner of property to sue for damages caused by a nuisance created on the owner's property. Under California law, it is not necessary that a nuisance have its origin in neighboring property."[165] Thus, the court in *Mangini* also rejected the application of the *Philadelphia Electric Co.* decision.

§ 8.25   —Trespass

Commentators have noted the similarity of the trespass and nuisance torts, and the potential overlap.[166]

Recent opinions have tended to further obscure the distinction. For example, the *Mangini* court (see § **8.21**) noted that "California cases have also

---

[161] *See, e.g.,* Cushman & Ficken at 185, 189; United States v. Hooker Chem. & Plastics Corp., 722 F. Supp. 960 (W.D.N.Y. 1989).

[162] Moskowitz at 169, 172.

[163] Philadelphia Elec. Co. v. Hercules, 762 F.2d 303 (3d Cir. 1985), *cert. denied,* 474 U.S. 980 (1985).

[164] T & E Indus., Inc. v. Safety Light Co., 123 N.J. 371, 587 A.2d 1249 (1991).

[165] Mangini v. Arojet-Gen. Corp., 281 Cal. Rptr. 827, 833 (Cal. Ct. App. 1991).

[166] Moskowitz at 189.

recognized that invasions of plaintiff's property, otherwise amounting to a trespass, may also create a nuisance under the statutes."[167] Regarding the defendant's contention that "one cannot trespass upon land in his own possession," the court noted that the lease arguably did not give the defendant *unrestricted* use and possession of the land, and reasoned that a trespass could occur if the lessee, with a limited consent to enter, exceeded those limits.[168]

No owner of property would be likely to allow a tenant to enter with permission to contaminate the property; therefore, using the reasoning of the *Mangini* court, almost any use of property that led contamination could violate and exceed the original scope of the consent to enter. In the remediation context, it is easy to hypothesize an analogous situation, in which a contractor who is granted a right of entry for a specific limited purpose exceeds the scope of that consent, thereby creating exposure to a claim for damages.

§ 8.26   —Negligence

The remediation contractor who negligently performs a site cleanup obviously has substantial liability exposure. However, if the work is performed in a non-negligent fashion, consistent with the scope of the contract, the contractor may be able to resist the contribution claims under CERCLA, even though the contractor may otherwise have been a PRP under § 107(a)(4) as a transporter.[169] As one court put it, "[a] company which creates the Frankenstein monster of abnormally dangerous wastes should not expect to be relieved of accountability for the depredations of its creature merely because the company entrusts the monster's care to another, even an independent contractor."[170]

In this regard, commentators have noted that negligence describes conduct, whereas a nuisance is a condition resulting from that conduct.[171]

To establish a cause of action for negligence, the plaintiff ordinarily must prove the existence of four elements:

1. The duty owed to the plaintiff that required the defendant to conform to a certain standard of conduct and protect the plaintiff against unreasonable risks

2. The defendant's breach of this duty by failure to conform to the given standard of conduct

---

[167] Mangini v. Arojet-Gen. Corp., 281 Cal. Rptr. 827, 833 (Cal. Ct. App. 1991).

[168] *Id.* at 837.

[169] Danella-Southwest, Inc. v. Southwestern Bell Tel. Co., 775 F. Supp. 1227 (E.D. Mo. 1991).

[170] Kenney v. Scientific, Inc., 204 N.J. Super. 228, 232, 497 A.2d 1310 (1985).

[171] Cushman & Ficken at 183; Knoff v. American Crystal Sugar Co., 380 N.W.2d 313, 316 (N.D. 1986).

3. A reasonably close causal connection between the plaintiff's conduct and the defendant's injury

4. Loss or damage.[172]

As discussed in **Chapter 3**, a remediation contractor or consultant claiming special skills and expertise will be presumed to have an obligation to the plaintiff that is commensurate with the scope of the representations and the contract's contents. For this reason, examination of the adequacy of the contractor's performance must, of necessity, be considered in light of the obligations undertaken pursuant to the contract.

Conversely, the *Kenney* court (see **§ 8.20**) noted a significant difference in exposure between a generator of hazardous wastes and the party who hauls the waste away. In that context, the court felt that the generator had comparatively greater exposure. This same type of analysis has been employed in CERCLA cases. See **§ 8.25**.

These cases reflect the delicate balance of factors used to assess negligence, and demonstrate judicial articulation of the competing ideas of promoting contractor willingness to participate and compelling contractors to be responsible for competent performance. See also **§ 8.18**.

Finally, to the extent that owners participate in or supervise remediation work, the opinions in *Kenney* and *Russell-Stanley*[173] would, by analogy, impose greater liability on those owners. *Kenney* discussed the possibility of differing degrees of liability for the generator who selected the dump site and the hauler who may not have known of any problems. *Russell-Stanley* found landlord liability because the landlord conducted frequent inspections of the building. Thus, owners who supervise operations expose themselves to potential liability from a negligence suit, as well as a suit based on statutory law. Furthermore, these cases suggest that explicit participation in the project will generate liability, as well as informed passivity in the face of environmentally insensitive conduct.

§ 8.27 —Strict Liability

The doctrine of strict liability, which may be applied against a contractor, owner, or a lessee of property who dumps contaminants onto the site, has its genesis in *Rylands v. Fletcher*.[174] This case involved two neighbors in a mining area of England. One party built a reservoir that flooded his neighbor's

---

[172] W. Page Keeton et al., Prosser and Keeton on the Law of Torts § 30, at 164 (5th ed. 1984). For a discussion of how these commentators have viewed the application of these concepts in an environmental context, *see* Moskowitz at 163, 164 *and* Cushman & Ficken at 183, 185.

[173] Russell-Stanley Corp. v. Camden Properties, Inc., 250 N.J. Super. 478, 595 A.2d 534 (1991).

[174] 3 H.&C. 774, 159 Eng. Rep. 737 (1865), *rev'd*, L.R. 1 EX 265 (1866), *aff'd sub nom.* Rylands v. Fletcher, L.R. 3 H.L. 330 (1868).

mineshaft. The court held the first party strictly liable for the damage caused by the flooding. In the *Ventron* case[175] the court reviewed the genesis of the strict liability concept and concluded: "We believe that it is time to recognize especially that the law of liability is involved so that a land owner is strictly liable to others for harm caused by toxic wastes that are stored on his property and flow onto the property of others."[176] The pronouncements in this case have been carried forward into more recent decisions.[177]

The decision that best relates to strict liability and the concept of abnormally dangerous activity in the environmental contamination and remediation context (as articulated in the recent Restatement of Torts §§ 519 and 520 dealing with pollution from toxic waste) is the *Kenney* case discussed in **§ 8.20**. It is a good barometer of judicial attitudes toward comparative contractor and client exposure.

Given the judicial and statutory predisposition to affix liability on generators or PRPs, as opposed to contractors, it can be safely assumed that the doctrine of strict liability will be applied more often to a client than a contractor, unless there is some egregious conduct by the latter.

---

[175] State of N.J. Dep't of Envtl. Protection v. Ventron Corp., 94 N.J. 473, 468 A.2d 150 (1983). See **§ 8.17** for further discussion.

[176] 468 A.2d at 157.

[177] *See, e.g.,* Russell-Stanley Corp. v. Camden Props., Inc., 595 A.2d 534 (N.J. 1991).

CHAPTER 9

INSURANCE AND ALLOCATION OF LIABILITIES*

§ 9.1   Introduction

The ability to minimize risk by effectively allocating potential liability is important to the success of any contractor. However, a construction contractor may be able to allocate liability by means of numerous insurance and bonding options;

---

*Thomas P. Quinn, Jr., of Crowell & Moring contributed to this chapter.

the remediation contractor's choices are severely limited. This limitation on available means of risk allocation stems mainly from the insurance industry's reluctance to broadly insure against losses caused by pollution.[1] Unfortunately, the chief source of the insurance industry's concern, which is the uncertainty of the extent to which liability may be imposed under comprehensive state and federal statutory and regulatory schemes, is also the main reason the contractor needs effective insurance coverage.[2]

This chapter examines insurance and bonding, the most common means of allocating risk. With respect to insurance, we focus on generally available types of insurance and their application to losses caused by the discharge of hazardous waste, as well as to the cleanup of such waste. The unique position of the remediation contractor with respect to insurance cannot be overemphasized. For example, the remediation contractor must be aware of the terms and conditions of the comprehensive general liability (CGL) policy that may act to exclude coverage for future liability associated with the cleanup of hazardous substances.

COVERAGE UNDER COMPREHENSIVE GENERAL LIABILITY POLICY

§ 9.2 Scope of the Comprehensive General Liability Policy

The CGL policy was developed to effectively insure against a number of potential hazards under one policy.[3] Prior to the creation of CGL insurance, a party was required to purchase separate policies for each potential loss against which the party desired coverage. In many cases, therefore, the party would be required to purchase multiple policies to obtain the necessary coverage.[4]

The CGL policy was initially drafted to insure against both bodily injury and property damage arising from an accident.[5] As originally drafted, however, the policy was subject to varying interpretations of the term *accident,* leaving both insured parties and insurers uncertain about exactly what would be covered under the policy.[6] Insurers argued that the term *accident* meant fortuity in a broad

---

[1] Miller & Murphy, *Insuring and Assessing Hazardous Waste Contracts, in* Hazardous Waste Disposal and Underground Construction Law 294 (R. Cushman & B. Ficken eds., John Wiley & Sons 1987) [hereinafter Miller & Murphy].

[2] Miller & Murphy at 292.

[3] Barber & Robertson, *Insurers and Insurance Coverage Issues, in* II Environmental Dispute Handbook 6 (D. Carpenter et al. eds., John Wiley & Sons 1991) [hereinafter Barber & Robertson].

[4] *Id.*

[5] Barber & Robertson at 7.

[6] *Id.*

sense, excluding unexpected losses from an intended act.[7] Insured parties, however, claimed that an accident required only fortuity as to the loss, thereby embracing unexpected losses from intended events or acts.[8] The term *accident* was also subject to varying interpretations with respect to bodily injury caused by disease.[9] In certain instances, courts held that a disease that developed gradually was not an accident within the meaning of the policy, thereby excluding coverage.[10]

In an effort to alleviate these ambiguities, beginning in 1966, CGL insurance replaced *accident* with *occurrence,* which was defined as: "an accident, including continuous or repeated exposure to substantially the same general harmful conditions."[11] While the term *occurrence* was to be the subject to exhaustive interpretation, it nonetheless removed certain of the ambiguities in earlier policies, by embracing both the term *accident* as originally construed, and repeated or continuous exposure.

When CGL coverage was initially created, today's complex state and federal regulatory and statutory schemes aimed at the cleanup of hazardous waste were not in place. Therefore, insuring against losses from hazardous waste probably was not even contemplated by drafters of early CGL policies. Such early policies arguably would not have included coverage for many hazardous waste claims, which are often based on a discharge of pollutants over an undetermined period of time. However, when CGL policies were modified to base coverage on occurrences, instead of accidents, the expanded definition created the potential for unintended coverage of hazardous waste cleanup. In an effort to limit liability for such claims, insurers began including language in their CGL policies to exclude coverage for losses from the discharge of hazardous substances.[12]

§ 9.3   —Pollution Exclusions

In 1970, the Insurance Rating Board began including a clause in its CGL policy forms that was intended to exclude insurance coverage for pollution.[13] In its earliest form, this clause excluded coverage for losses caused by toxic materials

---

[7] *Id.*

[8] *Id.*

[9] *Id.*

[10] *Id. See, e.g.,* Taylor Dredging Co. v. Travelers Ins. Co., 90 F.2d 449 (2d Cir. 1937); American Casualty Co. v. Minnesota Farm Bureau Serv., 270 F.2d 686 (8th Cir. 1959); Golden v. Lerch Bros., 300 N.W. 207 (Minn. 1941).

[11] Insurance Services Office, Inc., Commercial General Liability Coverage Form CG00011188 (1988).

[12] L. Miller & M. Mallonee, Insurance Claims for Environmental Damages 93 (1989) [hereinafter Miller & Mallonee].

[13] Barber & Robertson at 10.

unless the release of the materials was sudden and accidental.[14] Until about 1986, all CGL policies contained a clause resembling that set forth above.[15] With the increase in regulation of hazardous waste came a corresponding increase in claims for losses arising from the discharge of such waste. The pollution exclusion, therefore, was the subject of much interpretation by the courts. Indeed, because of the nature of the CGL policy as an occurrence form, these interpretations continue.[16]

The interpretation is focused mainly on the meaning of a *sudden and accidental* discharge of pollutants.[17] Insured parties have endorsed a broad interpretation to include gradually occurring dispersal of hazardous waste. Others have suggested that the meaning is ambiguous and must be interpreted against the insurer.[18] Insurers and the majority of the courts, however, have endorsed a more narrow interpretation excluding coverage for such gradual discharge.[19] As noted in a recent California court decision, the term *sudden* suggests an abrupt event, as opposed to something that happens over an extended period of time.[20]

In this old form, the pollution exclusion arguably would not defeat coverage of a claim brought by a cleanup contractor, who was responsible not for the dispersal or discharge of pollutants, but instead for their removal. Certain other exclusions, however, may have the effect of excluding coverage for claims arising out of work performed by the remediation contractor.[21]

Beginning in 1985, a more comprehensive pollution exclusion replaced the less comprehensive exclusion above.[22] This clause, sometimes referred to as the absolute pollution exclusion, acts to exclude:

> (1) 'bodily injury' or 'property damage' arising out of the actual, alleged or threatened discharge, dispersal, release or escape of pollutants: (a) at or from a premises you own, rent or occupy; (b) at or from any site or location used by or for you or others for the handling, storage, disposal, processing

---

[14] *E.g.,* Insurance Services Office, Inc., Commercial General Liability Coverage Form L6394 (1973).

[15] Miller & Murphy at 297.

[16] Miller & Mallonee at 34. *See, e.g.,* City of Carter Lake v. Aetna Casualty & Sur. Co., 604 F.2d 1052, 1058–59 (8th Cir. 1979); American Mut. Liability Ins. Co. v. Neville Chem. Co., 680 F. Supp. 929 (W.D. Pa. 1987) (applying Pennsylvania law).

[17] Miller & Mallonee at 94.

[18] *Id.* at 99; *see, e.g.,* Waste Management of Carolinas, Inc. v. Peerless Ins. Co., 315 N.C. 688, 340 S.E.2d 374 (1986).

[19] Miller & Mallonee at 95; *see, e.g.,* Jackson Township Mun. Utils. Auth. v. Hartford Accident & Indem. Co., 186 N.J. Super. 156, 451 A.2d 990 (1982).

[20] Masonite Corp. v. Great Am. Surplus Lines Ins. Co., 224 Cal. App. 3d 912, 915–17, 274 Cal. Rptr. 206 (1990).

[21] *See §§* **9.4** and **9.5**.

[22] Miller & Murphy at 296; *see* Insurance Services Office, Inc., Commercial General Liability Coverage Form CG0002 (1985).

or treatment of wastes; (c) which are at any time transported, handled, stored, treated, disposed of, or processed as waste by or for you or any person or organization for whom you may be legally responsible; or (d) at or from any site or location on which you or any contractors or subcontractors working directly or indirectly on your behalf are performing operations:

* * *

(2) Any loss, cost, or expense arising out of any government direction or request that you test for, monitor, clean up, remove, contain, treat, detoxify or neutralize pollutants. Pollutants means any solid, gaseous or thermal irritant or contaminant, including smoke, vapor, soot, fumes, acids, alkalides, chemicals, and waste. Waste includes materials to be recycled, reconditioned or reclaimed.[23]

This more comprehensive exclusion does not include the previous exception for sudden and accidental pollution. This exclusion also specifically addresses work by cleanup contractors, eliminating the previously existing ambiguity in this regard. However, despite this ambiguity, additional policy provisions in the older forms may well have acted to exclude coverage for claims by the cleanup contractor.[24] These clauses are worth noting and continue to exist in standard CGL policies issued today.

§ 9.4 —Exclusions for Liabilities Assumed under Contract

All CGL policies contain a clause that excludes liabilities assumed by the insured under contract. These clauses exclude coverage for "'Bodily injury' or 'property damage' for which the insured is obligated to pay damages by reason of the assumption of liability in a contract or agreement."[25] Because most cleanup contractors perform services pursuant to an agreement, many claims against these contractors for which insurance payment is likely to be sought will be based, at least in part, on the contractual provisions for cleanup. These breach of contract claims are uniformly denied by insurance companies, based on the liabilities assumed under contract exclusion.

This clause may not, in and of itself, relieve the insurer of an obligation to defend the cleanup contractor in the event a lawsuit is brought against the contractor. The difference between the duty to defend and the obligation to indemnify is significant, and is discussed in greater detail in § 9.14. In the event the cleanup contractor's liability is based solely on a contractual obligation, this

---

[23] Insurance Services Office, Inc., Commercial General Liability Coverage Form CG0002 (1985).

[24] See §§ 9.4 and 9.5.

[25] Insurance Services Office, Inc., Commercial General Liability Coverage Form CG00011188 (1988).

exclusion alone, without consideration of the pollution exclusions contained within the policy, may be enough to defeat coverage.

§ 9.5 —Completed Operations Exclusion

Most CGL policies contain a clause excluding liability for claims arising from the completed operations of the insured. These clauses act to exclude property damage from work performed by the insured after the work has been completed.[26]

Claims against the cleanup contractor may often be made long after the work has been completed. In these cases, indemnity under the insurance policy may not be available; however, the insurance company may still retain an obligation to defend the cleanup contractor.[27]

Analogous exceptions occur in standard CGL policies in the construction industry, where the exclusion operates to deny coverage for defective construction. For example, in certain circumstances, resultant damage from defective construction may be covered. Thus, the cost to replace a leaking roof will not be covered, but damage to the premises will.[28] The same interpretation could be applied to the remediation field. That is, a remediation contractor may be named in a lawsuit that alleges property damage *in addition* to allegedly defective work. This property damage may fall within the coverage provisions of the CGL policy.

§ 9.6 —Meaning of *Property Damages* in the Hazardous Waste Context

The concept of *property damage,* as defined under the CGL policy, has been the subject of much judicial interpretation.[29] Principally at issue is the question of whether response costs are property damage under the policy. The courts are divided on this issue.

Three federal circuit courts, interpreting the issue under four separate state laws, have held that response costs are not covered damages under CGL policies.[30] In general, these courts hold that the meaning of *damages,* in the

---

[26] *E.g.,* Insurance Services Office, Inc., Commercial General Liability Coverage Form CG00011188 (1988).

[27] *See* § **9.14**.

[28] *See* Diamond Heights Homeowners Ass'n v. National Am. Ins. Co., 227 Cal. App. 3d 563, 277 Cal. Rptr. 906 (1991).

[29] For a discussion of the various interpretations of the term *property damage, see* Aetna Casualty & Sur. Co. v. Pintlar Corp., 948 F.2d 1507 (9th Cir. 1991).

[30] *See, e.g.,* A. Johnson & Co. v. Aetna Casualty & Sur. Co., 933 F.2d 66 (1st Cir. 1991); Continental Ins. Co. v. Northeastern Pharmaceutical & Chem. Co., 842 F.2d 977 (8th Cir.),

insurance context, does not include restitutory relief or injunctive relief, and therefore does not include CERCLA response costs.[31]

In contrast with these cases, four federal circuit courts and the California Supreme Court have held that response costs *are* covered as property damages under a CGL policy.[32]

Representative of these cases is *AIU Insurance Co. v. Superior Court (FMC Corp.),* decided by the California Supreme Court in November 1990.[33] Applying "ordinary principals of interpretation" to the insurance policies reviewed, the court noted that the policies at issue provided coverage for "damages," which the insured was "legally obligated" to pay "because of property damage."[34] The court easily concluded that such cleanup costs were an obligation of the insured.[35] The critical issue was whether these obligations were legal in nature. Broadly interpreting this term, the court concluded that these cleanup costs were, in fact, legal obligation.[36]

Next, the court addressed whether the cleanup costs were damages within the meaning of the policies. Rejecting the argument that response costs were not damages,[37] the court found the policy language to be ambiguous in this respect and construed the policy in favor of coverage. Finally, the court addressed the issue of property damage within the meaning of the policy.[38] The court concluded that contamination of the environment generally constitutes property damage, regardless of whether the property is owned by the government, the insured, or some third party.[39]

While these cases indicate a willingness by the courts to find coverage under CGL policies for certain environmental cleanup costs, none of the cases analyzed the effect of a pollution exclusion. Most of the cases reviewed policies issued in the 1960s, when pollution exclusions were not included in CGL policies. Whether courts would similarly conclude that coverage existed in a case where a pollution exclusion was contained within the policy, is unknown. However, given the general interpretation of pollution exclusions in favor of insurers,

---

cert. denied, 488 U.S. 281 (1988); Cincinnati Ins. Co. v. Milliken & Co., 657 F.2d 979 (4th Cir. 1988); Maryland Casualty Co. v. Armco, Inc., 822 F.2d 1348 (4th Cir. 1987), *cert. denied,* 484 U.S. 1008 (1988).

[31] *Id.*

[32] *See, e.g.,* Independent Petrochem. Corp. v. Aetna Casualty & Sur. Co., 944 F.2d 940 (D.C. Cir. 1991); New Castle County v. Hartford Accident & Indem. Co., 933 F.2d 1162 (3d Cir. 1991); Avondale Indus., Inc. v. Travelers Indem. Co., 887 F.2d 1200 (2d Cir. 1989); *cert. denied,* 110 S. Ct. 2588 (1990).

[33] 51 Cal. 3d 807, 799 P.2d 1253, 274 Cal. Rptr. 820 (1990).

[34] *Id.*

[35] *Id.*

[36] *Id.*

[37] *Id.*

[38] *Id.*

[39] 51 Cal. 3d 807, 799 P.2d 1253, 274 Cal. Rptr. 820 (1990).

and the broad scope of the absolute pollution exclusion contained in current CGL forms, the likelihood of a court finding such coverage for pollution claims is minimal.

§ 9.7   Occurrence versus Claims-Made Comprehensive General Liability Policies

Comprehensive general liability policies are generally occurrence forms. As such, the event that causes the loss must occur within the effective dates of the policy.[40] This requirement is significant with respect to hazardous waste claims, because damage caused by hazardous waste is often discovered long after the contamination first occurred. Without considering the exclusions discussed in §§ 9.3 through 9.6, this circumstance leaves insurance companies potentially exposed to liability claims long after a given policy has expired.[41]

In an effort to restrict coverage for these unforeseen claims, insurance companies have recently offered CGL policies on a claims-made basis.[42] Claims-made policies cover only losses that occur *and* for which claims were made during the policy period.[43] An optional extended reporting period, or tail, may be available to the insured for an additional premium, which would extend coverage to include those claims brought by the insured within that period.[44] However, with hazardous waste claims based on pollution discharge long after the initial occurrence, a claims-made policy, even with an extension, may not provide coverage.

In assessing coverage, therefore, the form of the policy offered by the insurance company, either claims-made or occurrence, must be considered. An occurrence form is more likely to provide broader coverage, extending to claims brought long after the expiration of the policy, so long as those claims are based on an occurrence that took place within the given policy period.

Notwithstanding the existence of certain case law suggesting the possibility of coverage for hazardous waste claims under CGL policies (see § 9.6), the insurance industry is tending to avoid such coverage. The most recent, broadly worded absolute pollution exclusion clearly indicates the insurance industry's stance on this issue. See § 9.3. Notwithstanding the trend away from coverage for hazardous waste claims under CGL policies, the need for insurance for such claims has never been greater. Therefore, the availability of alternative forms of insurance must be recognized by the environmental remediation contractor. See §§ 9.8 through 9.14.

---

[40] Miller & Murphy, § 12.5, at 295.

[41] *Id.* § 12.4, at 295.

[42] Miller & Mallonee at 50.

[43] *Id.*

[44] *Id.*

§ 9.8   Environmental Liability Insurance

As a result of the shift away from coverage for environmental claims in CGL forms, and the corresponding need for environmental insurance, a limited number of insurers began writing separate policies for environmental impairment liability (EIL).[45] By the early 1980s, a standard ISO pollution liability form was created to replace the coverage not available under CGL policies. Only two major insurance companies currently provide this EIL coverage.

Most EIL policies cover claims for third-party bodily injury or property damage resulting from the unexpected discharge of pollutants.[46] Most of these policies, however, are site-specific.[47] That is, the particular policy will only protect the insured from claims arising from pollution occurring at a specific location. In addition, these policies vary with respect to the level of coverage provided. Certain early forms covered only non-sudden pollution; that is, the type of pollution excluded under the early exclusionary clauses contained in CGL policies.[48] However, with the elimination of general liability coverage for sudden pollution, certain EIL policies are written to cover both sudden and non-sudden pollution.[49] The most significant characteristic of an EIL policy is that it is offered on a claims-made basis only. As such, coverage is only provided for losses for which claims are made during the policy period,[50] or an extended discovery period that may be available for an additional cost. The effect of the claims-made nature of the EIL policy is significant. The insurance industry recognizes the uncertainty of liability under the myriad state and federal laws relating to environmental pollution.[51] Under existing law, the potential exists for liability to be imposed for environmental pollution long after the pollution actually occurred. But liability for gradually occurring pollution, not discovered until years after the fact, is not included within the coverage of the EIL policy. From the remediation contractor's perspective, this restriction means that the contractor is without effective insurance coverage at a time when such coverage may be most needed. The claims-made nature of the EIL policy severely limits its utility, therefore, and may make the policy unsatisfactory for the remediation contractor.

EIL policies may also contain many of the same exclusions found in CGL policies. An EIL policy should be examined to determine whether the policy contains exclusions for obligations assumed under contract or completed operations. While insurers may generally include these exclusions in their EIL

---

[45] Barber & Robertson at 27.

[46] Miller & Murphy at 298.

[47] Miller & Mallonee at 76.

[48] *Id.*

[49] *Id.*

[50] *Id.*

[51] Miller & Murphy at 300.

policies, at least one insurer amends the policy with a special endorsement form to delete the contracts and completed operations exclusions.[52]

OTHER POLICIES PROVIDING ENVIRONMENTAL LIABILITY COVERAGE

§ 9.9 Automobile Liability Policies

The scope of the remediation contractor's work may include transporting hazardous waste, which may give rise to potential liability under CERCLA. The contractor should therefore consider the extent and scope of insurance coverage for the vehicles used in the transportation of hazardous waste.[53]

Automobile policies generally cover liability arising from the use, including loading and unloading, of vehicles. To the extent liability may be imposed upon a remediation contractor transporting hazardous materials, the scope of the automobile liability policy arguably should cover claims arising from this activity.

Unfortunately, no court has specifically held that automobile liability policies cover claims arising from the transportation of hazardous materials. However, one court's analysis suggests that coverage may exist under such policies.[54] At issue in *United States Fidelity & Guar. Co. v. Thomas Solvent Co.*[55] was the application of various liability insurance policies, including automobile policies, procured by a company engaged in the sale and distribution of industrial solvents.[56] In assessing whether the automobile insurance coverage applied, the court found that the possibility of coverage existed based on the allegation that the losses resulted from improper handling of toxic chemicals. It should be noted, however, that at issue in this case was not whether coverage existed, but rather whether the insurer had an obligation to defend its insured under the policy.[57] These issues are in fact distinct.[58]

A contractor engaged in the transportation of hazardous materials should carefully consider the terms of its automobile policy. Although the application of automobile insurance to hazardous waste claims has yet to be clearly defined by the courts, the possibility exists that such coverage may be provided under these policies.

---

[52] *Id.* at 298.

[53] Miller & Mallonee at 78.

[54] *Id.*

[55] 683 F. Supp. 1139 (W.D. Mich. 1988).

[56] *Id.*

[57] *Id.*

[58] For a discussion of the difference between the duty to defend and the duty to indemnify, see § 9.14.

§ 9.10 Property Policies

Property policies specific to the property on which the contamination is found may provide coverage for the cleanup of hazardous waste.[59] Specifically, if the property itself sustains physical damage resulting in loss as a result of contamination, this loss may be covered under the policy insuring the property.[60]

In addition, most property policies contain a debris removal provision. For example, the ISO form of a special multi-peril policy applying to property covers: "expense incurred in the removal of debris on the property covered which may be occasioned by loss by any of the perils insured against in this policy."[61] However, this provision should be reviewed carefully. Certain policies contain only coverage for debris *of* covered property and not debris *on* covered property.[62] Thus, damage caused by debris from a source outside the property would likely be excluded.

It should be noted that no reported case has applied debris removal provisions to environmental damage claims. However, given the general uncertainty of the application of insurance to environmental claims (with the exception of environmental EIL) that are limited in their scope, awareness of the existence of terms such as the debris removal term contained in the property policy may provide a basis for a claim for coverage.

§ 9.11 Umbrella Insurance Policies

Umbrella insurance is primarily meant to protect the insured from liability in excess of the coverage provided by primary liability policies.[63] However, certain umbrella policies may also provide coverage omitted from these primary policies. To the extent that the umbrella policy is worded to fill these gaps in the coverage provided under the primary policy, pollution coverage may be included.[64] While no case has specifically held that umbrella insurance applies to environmental claims, a basis may exist to assert the existence of coverage under these policies.

---

[59] Miller & Mallonee at 79.

[60] Environmental Issues in Real Estate and Construction Projects in California, A Strategic Guide for the 1990's 31 (June 20, 1991) (Cambridge Inst. seminar material).

[61] *Id.*

[62] *Id.*

[63] Miller & Mallonee at 81.

[64] *Id.*

§ 9.12   Directors' and Officers' Liability Insurance

The directors' and officers' liability policy is another potential source of insurance for environmental claims. These policies are intended to insure professionals who are directors and officers of hazardous waste contracting companies against liability arising from their failure to use due care and expected degree of skill. It should be noted that directors' and officers' policies, like CGL policies, contain an exclusion for claims arising from pollution.[65] However, certain older directors' and officers' liability policies did not contain this exclusion.[66] Thus, if a claim is brought based on pollution that occurred some time ago, the policy in effect at the time may in fact provide coverage for directors and officers, to the extent of claims brought against them individually.

§ 9.13   Professional Liability Insurance

Professional liability (or errors and omissions) insurance provides coverage for claims arising from the negligent acts or omissions of the insured. To the extent that an environmental claim arises from the negligent performance of the environmental contractor, coverage may be found under this policy.[67] However, there are limitations on coverage for environmental claims in the professional liability policies, similar to the limitations found in CGL policies.[68]

In 1985, professional liability insurers began including endorsements to their professional liability policies that excluded all claims arising from hazardous waste operations.[69] Current policies are likely to contain a similar exclusion; however, a pre-1985 policy may provide coverage, because these policies were written without the hazardous waste exclusion endorsement.

§ 9.14   Duty to Defend

An important and often misunderstood issue that arises in connection with the application of insurance is whether, under a particular policy, the insurer has a duty to defend the claim brought against the insured.[70] This issue involves an obligation under the insurance policy that is completely separate from the duty to indemnify. The obligation may, therefore, provide limited protection for an insured, at least with respect to the defense of any claim or lawsuit. In the

---

[65] Miller & Murphy at 301.

[66] *Id.*

[67] Zuckerman v. National Union Fire Ins. Co., 495 A.2d 395 (N.J. 1985).

[68] *Id.*

[69] *Id.*

[70] *See* Gray v. Zurich Ins. Co., 65 Cal. 2d 263, 419 P.2d 168, 54 Cal. Rptr. 104 (1966).

environmental context, the duty to defend has raised certain issues related to when the duty arises in connection with notification of a potential environmental claim.[71]

Generally, a liability insurance policy requires the insurer to provide the insured with a defense to a suit for damages. However, in the environmental context, an insured may receive notification of a claim as a potentially responsible party (PRP) prior to the initiation of any lawsuit. The question then arises whether the insurer's obligation to defend the insured begins with the PRP letter.[72] Insurers have generally taken the position that the duty to defend only arises once the insured becomes a defendant in a traditional lawsuit; courts have generally found that the more adversarial the agency action, the more likely it is that the duty to defend will arise.[73] Thus the insurer's obligation to defend does not depend on the initiation of a lawsuit against the insured.

Compared to the duty to indemnify (that is, provide coverage for the event causing the loss), the duty to defend is quite broad.[74] The duty arises when the potential for a covered claim exists, generally based either on facts as contained in a complaint against the insured, or facts about which the insurer is notified.[75] The insurer then has the obligation to defend all claims brought against the insured.[76]

This obligation is especially important in the context of environmental claims, and may provide the basis for defense under what may at first be considered inapplicable policies. For example, to the extent an action is brought against an insured that alleges damage caused by pollution as well as other causes, as long as any one of the other causes is covered under a given policy, the duty to defend all claims applies. Thus, general liability insurance may include a duty to defend pollution claims even if there is no duty to indemnify those claims. Similarly, as noted in § 9.9 with respect to automobile liability policies, an allegation that a claim arose from the use of a motor vehicle (including the transportation of hazardous material) would create an obligation to defend the claim under the automobile liability policy.

Although the duty to defend does not afford the complete protection that exists when both defense and indemnification obligations are acknowledged by the insurer, the obligation nevertheless provides the insured with coverage for what may be significant costs in defending the claim. As a practical matter, recognition of an obligation to defend under an insurance policy may also provide what

---

[71] Barber & Robertson at 27.

[72] Id.

[73] Id.; see, e.g., Fireman's Fund Ins. Cos. v. Ex-Cell-O Corp., 662 F. Supp. 71 (E.D. Mich. 1987).

[74] Gray v. Zurich Ins. Co., 65 Cal. 2d 263, 54 Cal. Rptr. 104 (1966).

[75] Id.

[76] Id.

amounts to indemnification of the claim, by making insurance monies available to achieve settlement of the claims against the insured.

With respect to settlement, the insurer normally has the obligation to accept all reasonable settlement offers.[77] To the extent an insurer refuses to participate in settlement, that insurer may ultimately be liable for judgment in excess of the policy limits if coverage is ultimately found to exist.[78] Therefore, prudence may often require the insurer to settle a claim early, even if coverage questions still exist, rather than incur significant defense fees and run the risk of responsibility for a judgment in excess of its policy limits.

These factors played a significant role in a recent case brought by a property owner against an environmental contractor whom we represented. The contractor was insured for property damage, including damage caused by pollution. The environmental contractor tendered the defense of the action to its EIL insurance carrier, who agreed to defend the claims, but reserved its rights[79] with respect to the issue of indemnity. While the case was in its early stages, the parties began settlement negotiations that led to a settlement proposal. The insurer, while initially balking at participation in settlement, agreed to pay the entire settlement amount after considering the potentially significant cost of litigation, and the risk in allowing the case to proceed to a judgment that could be in excess of its policy limits. The insured, therefore, ultimately had the benefit of both insurance and indemnity under the policy.

This situation, although fortunate for the particular insured party, is the exception rather than the rule. A more likely result, when the insurer has agreed to defend but not indemnify the insured, is a settlement negotiated between the insurer and the insured that requires both parties to contribute. However, even in this circumstance, the insured may obtain the benefit of indemnity under an insurance policy that, if tested, may not have been found to actually provide coverage.

---

[77] Crisci v. Security Ins. Co., 66 Cal. 2d 425, 426 P.2d 173, 58 Cal. Rptr. 13 (1967).

[78] Comunale v. Traders & General Ins. Co., 50 Cal. 2d 654, 328 P.2d 198 (1958).

[79] An insurance company, notwithstanding the existence of a duty to defend, may notify the insured that the company reserves its right to refuse to indemnify the insured against any judgment obtained by the injured party, to the extent that the claim is not covered under the policy. The effect of the reservation of rights is to permit the insurance company to meet its defense obligations, while at the same time preserve defenses with respect to a claim for coverage at a later date. See Kornblum et al., Bad Faith, in California Practice Guide § 8:164 (1990). Where the insurance company fails to assert a ground for denying coverage, it may risk waiving that ground. Miller v. Elite Ins. Co., 100 Cal. App. 3d 739, 161 Cal. Rptr. 322 (1980).

CHAPTER 10

ACCOUNTING AND FINANCIAL REPORTING IMPLICATIONS

John E. Altstadt*

§ 10.1 Accrual of a Loss Contingency

A company incurs costs to remove, contain, neutralize, or prevent existing or future environmental contamination. These costs can include removal of contamination, damage caused by leakage from underground tanks, acquisition of tangible property (such as air pollution control equipment), environmental studies, and fines levied under environmental laws. The methods used to account for these costs, and disclose them in financial statements, have a tremendous impact on such factors as a company's earnings, stock value, and banking relations. This chapter will address the accounting and reporting requirements as established by the Financial Accounting Standards Board (FASB) and, for companies whose stock is publicly traded, the Securities and Exchange Commission (SEC).

The critical and problematic nature of accounting and reporting methods arises because the existence and amount of remediation costs are largely

---

*John E. Altstadt is a senior manager in KPMG Peat Marwick's Litigations Services practice located in the firm's Orange County, California, office, where he provides services ranging from examination, review, and compilation of financial statements to consulting services in accounting, business acquisitions, and litigation. He is a CPA in California, a member of the American Institute of Certified Public Accountants, and a member of the California Society of Certified Public Accountants.

unknown, and therefore must be viewed as a contingency. A *contingency* is defined as an existing condition, situation, or set of circumstances from which gain or loss to an enterprise is uncertain, and dependent on one or more future events that may or may not occur. With a loss contingency, resolution of the uncertainty may confirm the loss or impairment of an asset, or the incurrence of a liability.[1]

Loss contingencies can include the potential costs of environmental matters and require only disclosure in the footnotes to the financial statements; a charge to earnings is not considered necessary. The disclosures include an estimate of the possible liability and the conditions that must be present before the contingency becomes a liability that must be accrued.

In general, a loss contingency is accrued by a charge to earnings, if both of the following conditions arc met: (1) Information available prior to the issuance of the financial statements indicates that it is probable that an asset has been impaired or a liability has been incurred (*probable* being defined in FASB 5 as a situation in which the future event or events are likely to occur); and (2) The amount of the loss can be reasonably estimated.[2]

As an illustration of this concept in an environmental dispute, assume that a company with a December 31 fiscal year-end learns of possible contamination in a building it owns. Although the contamination is first identified in December 1991, testing is required to determine the severity of the problem and whether cleanup procedures will be required. This testing is expected to take 30 to 60 days. As of December 31, 1991, it cannot be determined if it is probable that a liability has been incurred, as testing is not completed. Additionally, it is not possible to estimate the amount of any possible liability. Therefore, no accrual is required. If the potential liability is, however, considered reasonably possible, then disclosure of the contingency in the footnotes to the financial statements is still required. (*Reasonably possible* is defined in FASB 5 as a situation in which the chance of the future event or events occurring is more than remote but less than likely.)

Upon completion of the testing in February 1992, it is determined that serious contamination exists and cleanup efforts will commence immediately. It is also possible at this time to estimate the cost of the cleanup within a certain range. The two criteria described earlier have been met, and the liability must now be accrued on the company's books.

Special emphasis must be placed on the concept of a range of estimated amounts when determining the liability to be accrued. Some companies have inappropriately delayed the accrual of any environmental loss until sufficient information is available to determine the *best* estimate of the ultimate liability. Such a delay is prohibited under current accounting rules, which require a

[1] FASB Statement No. 5, para. 1 (Mar. 1975).

[2] *Id.*

company to accrue a loss contingency when "information available indicates that the estimated amount of loss is within a *range* of amounts."[3]

In our previous example, assume that the company estimates the amount of the liability for the contamination cleanup at between $750,000 and $1,500,000. No amount in that range appears at the time to be a better estimate than any other amount. Accounting rules require accrual of the $750,000 amount at December 31, 1992, disclosure of the nature of the contingency and the exposure to an additional amount of loss of up to $750,000, and possible disclosure of the amount of the accrual.

§ 10.2   Other Considerations in Determining Amount of Liability

In addition to the discussion in § 10.1, two other concepts are key in determining the amount of liability that a company must record in its financial statements. The first concept relates to joint and several liability. There are situations wherein more than one potentially responsible party (PRP) is associated with a contaminated site. For a discussion of PRP liability, see **Chapter 8**. In these cases, each of the PRPs may be contingently liable for the full amount of the cleanup costs and fines, because of the joint and several nature of liability under Superfund regulations. In evaluating the adequacy of the proposed accrual, care should be taken to consider the adequacy of the company's determination of its share of the aggregate costs, the ability of the other PRPs to pay their allocated portion, and the potential for additional costs to be absorbed by the company.

Using our previous example, assume instead that the company in question was a 50 percent owner of the contaminated building. Assume also that the company's 50 percent share of the cleanup costs is $750,000 to $1,500,000. In determining the amount of its accrual, the company must evaluate the ability of the other half-owner's ability to pay its share of the cleanup. If the other owner is in financial difficulty, and unable to pay its share, the amount of the accrual could actually be $1,500,000 to $3,000,000. Joint and several liability could require payment in full by the company. If that is the case, accounting rules would require accrual of $1,500,000 and disclosure of the potential additional amount of $1,500,000.

In determining the proper amount of the liability to accrue, care must be taken when attempting to discount the future payments and accrue only the present value. This treatment is proper only if the payments are fixed and determinable, and an appropriate discount rate can be identified.[4] In our previous example, assume that the company agrees to pay for the building cleanup over a

---

[3] FASB Interpretation No. 14, para. 2 (Sept. 1976).

[4] APB Opinion No. 21, para. 13 (Aug. 1971).

three-year period, with annual payments of $500,000. After identification of an appropriate discount rate, it would be possible to calculate the present value of the total amount to be paid over the three years. The face amount of the liability in the financial statements would be $1,500,000 reduced by the difference between the $1,500,000 and the calculated present value. This method has been abused by some companies, which calculate a present value even though future payments are not fixed and determinable. The amount to be paid for environmental costs can obviously be very difficult to determine, and can change drastically as the work progresses. The use of a discounted present value in this area should be scrutinized carefully.

§ 10.3   Capitalization of Costs to Treat Environmental Contamination

To this point, we have concentrated on the rules that govern the timing and amount of the liability that must be accrued and disclosed when environmental costs are incurred. A second, and even more important, issue is whether the costs incurred are to be capitalized as an asset of the company, or charged to the company's earnings in the current period. This decision could have an enormous negative effect on a company's earnings, thereby also adversely affecting its stock price, covenants on debt agreements, and the credit rating on its debt issues. The general accounting rule regarding capitalization of any cost is that the expenditure must provide future benefit to the entity before it may be capitalized as an asset. These capitalized costs are then amortized to expense over a prescribed period. Such classic expenditures are for property and equipment, inventories, and intangible assets such as patents and trademarks.[5]

The question has arisen in recent years as to whether environmental costs qualify for capitalization treatment. In 1990, the FASB's Emerging Issues Task Force (EITF) took up the issue and released its opinion in July of that year.[6] The EITF concluded that, in general, environmental contamination treatment costs should be charged to expense. These costs may be capitalized, if recoverable, but only if any of the following criteria are met:

1. The costs extend the life, increase the capacity, or improve the safety or efficiency of property owned by the Company.
2. The costs mitigate or prevent environmental contamination that has yet to occur and that otherwise may result from future operations or activities.
3. The costs are incurred in preparing, for sale, that property currently held for sale.

---

[5] For further information on capitalization of costs, *see* Statement of Financial Accounting Concepts Nos. 5, para. 85, and 6, paras. 171–182.
[6] EITF Issue No. 90-8, at 1–2 (July 1990).

To better explain the EITF's decision, the following examples are provided. These examples cover a broad range of major environmental expenditures.

Example 1. Tanker Oil Spill

Treatment A: Clean up waterway and beachfront.

Evaluation:

1. Costs to clean up the waterway and beachfront are not eligible for consideration under the first criterion because the oil company does not own the property.
2. The cleanup of the waterway and beachfront does not mitigate or prevent a future oil spill from future operations.
3. The waterway and beachfront are not owned assets; therefore, the third criterion does not apply.

Conclusion: Costs incurred for cleanup and restoration in connection with the oil spill should be charged to expense.

Treatment B: Reinforce tanker's hull to reduce risk of future spill.

Evaluation:

1. Reinforcing the hull improves the tanker's safety compared to when the tanker was originally constructed or acquired.
2. Reinforcing the hull lessens the risk that the tanker will experience a similar oil spill during future operations.

Conclusion: The costs incurred in connection with reinforcing the tanker's hull may be capitalized under either the first or second criterion.

Example 2. Rusty Chemical Storage Tank

Treatment A: Remove rust that developed during ownership.

Evaluation:

1. Removing the rust has mitigated the possibility of future leaks; however, removing the rust has not improved the tank compared with its condition when built or acquired.

Conclusion: Rust removal costs should be charged to expense unless the tank is currently held for sale and the costs were incurred to prepare the tank for sale.

Treatment B: Apply rust prevention chemicals.

Evaluation:

1. The application of rust prevention chemicals has improved the tank's condition compared with its condition when built or acquired.

2. Rust prevention chemicals mitigate the possibility that future rust will cause leaks.

Conclusion: The costs of applying the rust prevention chemicals may be capitalized under either the first or second criterion.

Example 3. Air Pollution Caused by Manufacturing Activities

Treatment A: Acquire and install pollution control equipment.

Evaluation:

1. The pollution control equipment improves the safety of the plant compared with its condition when built or acquired.

2. The pollution control equipment mitigates or prevents air pollution that has yet to occur but that may otherwise result from future operation of the plant.

Conclusion: Costs associated with acquisition and installation of the pollution control equipment may be capitalized under either the first or second criterion.

Treatment B: Pay fines for violations of the Clean Air Act.

Evaluation:

1. Payment of fines does not extend the plant's life, increase its capacity, or improve its efficiency or safety.

2. Payment of fines does not mitigate or prevent pollution that has yet to occur but that may otherwise result from future operations of the plant.

Conclusion: Fines paid in connection with violations of the Clean Air Act should be charged to expense. Even if the plant is currently held for sale, the fines should be charged to expense because the costs would not have been incurred to prepare the plant for sale.

Example 4. Lead Pipes in Office Building Contaminate Drinking Water

Treatment A: Remove lead pipes and replace with copper pipes.

Evaluation:

1. Removing lead pipes has improved the safety of the building's water system compared with its condition when the water system was built or acquired.

2. By removing the lead pipes, the building's owner eliminated an existing environmental problem and prevented any further contamination from *that* lead. However, by removing the existing pipes, the building's owner has not mitigated or prevented environmental problems yet to occur, if any, from future operation of the building.

Conclusion: Costs to remove the lead pipes and install copper pipes may be capitalized under the first criterion. The book value of the lead pipes should be charged to expense when removed.

Example 5. Soil Contamination from Solid Waste Disposal Facility

Treatment A: Refine soil on dump property.

Evaluation:

1. The life of a solid waste disposal facility is not extended by refining its soil. Further, the condition of the soil after refining will not be improved over its condition when the solid waste disposal facility was constructed or acquired. Removal of the toxic waste restores the soil to its original uncontaminated condition.

2. Removal of toxic waste from the soil addresses an existing environmental concern. It also prevents that waste from leaching in the future. However, removing the waste does not mitigate or prevent future operations from creating future toxic waste. The risk will continue regardless of how much of the existing soil is refined.

Conclusion: Soil refinement costs should be charged to expense unless the solid waste disposal facility is currently held for sale and the costs were incurred to prepare the site for sale.

Treatment B: Install liner.

Evaluation:

1. The liner does not extend the useful life or improve the efficiency or capacity of the solid waste disposal facility. However, the liner has improved the facility's safety compared to when the dump was constructed or acquired.

2. The liner addresses an existing and potential future problem. In this example, the solid waste disposal facility contains toxic waste from past operations and will likely generate toxic waste during future operations. The liner partly addresses the existing environmental problem by preventing future leaching of existing toxic waste into the soil. The liner also mitigates or prevents leaching of toxic waste that may result from dumping in future periods.

Conclusion: The liner may be capitalized under either the first or second criterion.

Example 6. Water Well Contamination Caused by Chemicals That Leaked into Wells Containing Water That Will Be Used in Future Beer Production

Treatment A: Neutralize water in wells.

Evaluation:

1.   The treatment does not extend the life of the wells, increase their capacity, or improve efficiency. The condition of the water is not safer after the treatment compared to when the wells were initially acquired.
2.   By neutralizing the water, the possibility of future contamination of the wells from future operations has not been mitigated or prevented.

Conclusion: Costs incurred to neutralize well water should be charged to expense unless the wells were held for sale and the costs were incurred to prepare the wells for sale.

Treatment B: Install water filters.

Evaluation:

1.   The water filters improve the safety of the wells compared with their uncontaminated state when built or acquired.
2.   The water filters address future problems that may result from future operations. Since the water filters are effective in filtering environmental contamination, they mitigate the effect of spilling new contaminants into the wells during future operations. In addition, the water filters represent an improvement compared with the wells' original condition without water filters.

Conclusion: The water filtering system may be capitalized under either the first or the second criterion.

Example 7. Underground Gasoline Storage Tanks Leak and Contaminate the Company's Property

Treatment A: Refine soil.

Evaluation:

1.   Soil refinement does not extend the useful life, increase the capacity, or improve the efficiency or safety of the land relative to its unpolluted state when acquired.
2.   By refining the contaminated soil, the oil company has addressed an existing problem. However, the company has not mitigated or prevented future leaks during future operations.

Conclusion: Soil refining costs should be charged to expense unless the property is currently held for sale and the costs were incurred to prepare the property for sale.

Treatment B: Encase tanks so as to prevent future leaks from contaminating surrounding soil.

Evaluation:

1. In some cases, encasement may increase the life of the tanks because of their increased resistance to corrosion and leaking. In other situations, the treatment may not increase the life of the tanks. However, the encasement has improved the tanks' safety compared with their condition when built or acquired.

2. Encasement has mitigated or prevented future leakage and soil contamination that might otherwise result from future operations.

Conclusion: The cost of encasement may be capitalized under either the first or the second criterion.

Example 8. Air in Office Building
Contaminated with Asbestos Fibers

Treatment A: Remove asbestos.

Evaluation:

1. Removal of the asbestos improves the building's safety over its original condition since the environmental contamination (asbestos) existed when the building was constructed or acquired.

2. By removing the asbestos, the building's owner has eliminated an existing environmental problem and has prevented any further contamination from *that* asbestos. However, by removing the existing asbestos, the building's owner has not mitigated or prevented new environmental problems, if any, that might result from future operation of the building.

Conclusion: Asbestos removal costs may be capitalized as a betterment under the first criterion.

§ 10.4 Disclosure of Current Expenses in the Statement of Operations

Once the amount of the liability has been quantified, and it is determined that the costs incurred are a current expense, rather than capitalizable, it must be further determined how to present the expense in the company's financial statements. Many companies have attempted to argue that environmental costs should be treated as extraordinary items, and therefore *not* included in the determination of earnings from regular operations. This consideration is extremely important, as extraordinary items are presented in a separate section of the operating statement and are typically excluded by analysts when evaluating the financial performance of an entity.

The criteria for considering an event or transaction as an extraordinary item are: (1) unusual nature—the underlying event or transaction is highly unusual and is clearly unrelated to, or only incidentally related to, the ordinary and typical activities of the enterprise, taking into account the environment in which the enterprise operates—and (2) infrequency of occurrence—the underlying event or transaction would not reasonably be expected to recur in the foreseeable future, taking into account the environment in which the enterprise operates.[7]

Companies that argue for extraordinary item treatment claim that environmental costs are both unusual and infrequent. However, a detailed review of the rules in APB Opinion No. 30 will show that most environmental costs do not qualify for extraordinary treatment, and therefore should be charged to earnings from regular operations.

The specific characteristics of the enterprise, such as type and scope of operations, lines of business, and operating policies, shall be considered in determining the enterprise's ordinary and typical activities. The environment in which an enterprise operates is a primary consideration in determining whether an underlying event or transaction is unusual and significantly different from the ordinary and typical activities of the enterprise. The environment of an enterprise includes such factors as the characteristics of the industry in which it operates, the geographical location of its operations, and the nature and extent of government regulation.

When one considers the definition of the environment in which a company operates, it is already apparent that most environmental costs will be considered a part of regular operations. The operations of many industries, such as public utilities or petroleum refining operations, inherently create hazardous waste that must be disposed of. Certain geographical areas are prone to environmental hazards. Any business that operates in an area that has long been a center of manufacturing will likely face contamination at its facility at some point. In addition, businesses that have built on sites formerly used as military facilities will often encounter significant contamination in the ground around their buildings. For many businesses, environmental regulations are an everyday part of operations. When analyzed in this manner, it is difficult for these companies to argue that the incurrence of costs to correct environmental problems is outside of their normal business operations.

An event or transaction of a type not reasonably expected to reoccur in the foreseeable future is considered to occur infrequently. The past occurrence of an event or transaction for a particular enterprise provides evidence to assess the

---

[7] APB Opinion No. 30, para. 20 (June 1973).

probability of recurrence of that type of event or transaction in the foreseeable future. An event or transaction of a type that occurs frequently in the environment in which the enterprise operates cannot, by definition, be considered as extraordinary, regardless of its financial effect.[8]

Again, this definition makes it difficult for many companies to claim that their environmental costs should be classified as extraordinary. A manufacturer with a plant that needs a new pollution control facility may very well have other plants with similar needs. A company that operates a chain of automobile dealerships may have several facilities with leaking underground storage tanks. A company that owns several old office buildings may have a significant problem with lead pipes causing contamination of the drinking water supply. It is very difficult for these companies to argue that their environmental costs are infrequent, especially considering the increasing scope and complexity of regulations. Therefore, caution should be taken in agreeing to extraordinary treatment for environmental costs.

§ 10.5   SEC Reporting Requirements

The previous sections in this chapter addressed the accounting and reporting rules that govern all entities, regardless of their ownership. Since 1933, companies whose stock or debt is publicly traded have been held to a higher standard of financial reporting than companies whose stock is held by a few private entities.[9] This reporting requirement includes more thorough disclosures in the annual financial statements, as well as supplementary discussion about the financial matters of the company as provided by management. This supplemental requirement, known as management's discussion and analysis (MD&A), is provided in a separate section of the annual report and must be reviewed by the company's outside auditors for consistency with the financial statements on which the auditors have issued their opinion.

The SEC adopted its first requirement for an MD&A in 1968, and instituted the current framework in 1980. That framework arose from the SEC's concerns that the earlier MD&A requirements had developed into a mechanical practice of commenting on percentage variations. The 1980 requirements changed the focus from a summary of earnings to the financial statements as a whole. The following factors must be discussed:

1. Liquidity
2. Capital resources
3. Results of operations

---

[8] *Id.* para. 22.

[9] Securities Act of 1933, 15 U.S.C. § 77a-77bbb (1992), and the Securities Exchange Act of 1934, 15 U.S.C. §§ 77A–77II (1992).

4. The future impact of known trends, demands, commitments, events, or uncertainties that may affect operations.[10]

The change was intended to allow the investor to look at the company through the eyes of management.[11]

While these general requirements were being formulated by the SEC, more specific requirements related to environmental matters were also being considered. As far back as 1971, the SEC was aware that requirements imposed by environment statutes could have a material economic impact on those companies that were subject to the statutes. Accordingly, the Commission issued a release informing registrants that the SEC's existing rules required disclosure of material environmental information, including the existence and nature of pending environmental litigation and instances in which compliance with environmental laws "may necessitate significant capital outlays, may materially affect the earning power of the business, or cause material changes in registrant's business done."[12]

In 1973, after monitoring the disclosures elicited by this general release, the SEC adopted environmental disclosure rules requiring all companies to disclose specific items of information related to environmental matters, in addition to the disclosures required by the rules that were explained in the 1971 release. More specifically, the new rules require disclosure of the material effects[13] that compliance with federal, state, and local provisions, which have been enacted or adopted regulating the discharge of materials into the environment, or otherwise relating to the protection of the environment, may have

---

[10] Guides for Preparation and Filing of Registration Statements, Securities Act Release No. 4936, pt. 1, [1968 Transfer Binder] Fed. Sec. L. Rep. (CCH) ¶ 77,636 (Dec. 9, 1968).

[11] Amendments to Annual Report Form, Related Forms, Rules, Regulations and Guides; Integration of Securities Acts Disclosure Systems, Securities Act Release No. 6231, [1980 Transfer Binder] Fed. Sec. L. Rep. (CCH) ¶ 72,301 (Sept. 2, 1980).

[12] Disclosures Pertaining to Matters Involving the Environment and Civil Rights, Securities Act Release No. 5170, pt. 1, [1971 Transfer Binder] Fed. Sec. L. Rep. (CCH) ¶ 78,150 (July 1971).

[13] Materiality is a pervasive concept that relates to qualitative characteristics, especially relevance and reliability. Materiality and relevance are both defined in terms of what influences or makes a difference to a decision maker, but the two terms can be distinguished. A decision not to disclose certain information may be made, for example, because investors have no need for that kind of information (it is not relevant) or because the amounts involved are too small to make a difference (they are not material). Magnitude by itself, without regard to the nature of the item and the circumstances under which the judgment has to be made, will not generally be a sufficient basis for a materiality judgment. The FASB's present position is that no general standards of materiality can be formulated to take into account all the considerations that enter into an experienced human judgment. Specific materiality criteria may be given by the FASB in the future, as appropriate. *See* Statement of Financial Accounting Concepts No. 2, at 3 and paras. 123–132 (May 1980).

upon the capital expenditures, earnings, and competitive position of the registrant and its subsidiaries.[14]

These rules also require disclosure of any administrative or judicial proceeding known to be contemplated by government authorities and arising under federal, state, or local provisions that have been enacted or adopted regulating the discharge of materials into the environment, or otherwise relating to the protection of the environment, or any other material pending administrative or judicial proceeding. Any proceeding brought by a government authority is deemed material.[15]

In the same release, the SEC also admonished registrants that its existing rule requiring disclosure of pending proceedings contemplated by government authorities included a requirement to disclose notices of violation, in the nature of cease and desist orders, issued by the EPA.

To assist registrants in complying with these specific environmental disclosure rules and applying its general disclosure requirements to environmental matters, the SEC addressed three significant interpretive questions:

1. When must a corporation disclose, in addition to its planned environmental expenditures for the next two fiscal years, the total costs of compliance with environmental statutes?

2. What disclosures must be made concerning administrative proceedings involving environmental matters that are contemplated by government authorities, and what is an administrative proceeding that must be disclosed?

3. When is a corporation required to disclose its policies concerning, or approach toward, compliance with environmental laws?[16]

The Commission's releases in 1971 and 1973 required that registrants indicate the material effects that compliance with environmental protection requirements would have on capital expenditures and earnings. Many registrants, in response to these releases, disclosed only prior actual and presently authorized capital expenditures. However, where a registrant expected that additional material capital expenditures would have to be authorized to achieve compliance for the periods beyond that for which information was given, and

---

[14] Notice of Adoption of Amendments to Registration and Report Forms to Require Disclosure with Respect to Compliance with Environmental Requirements and Other Matters, Securities Act Release No. 5386, pt. 1, [1973 Transfer Binder] Fed. Sec. L. Rep. (CCH) ¶ 79,342 (Apr. 1973).

[15] Notice of Commission Conclusions and Final Action on the Rulemaking Proposals Amended in Securities Act Release No. 5627 (Oct. 14, 1975) (relating to Environmental Disclosure), Securities Act Release No. 5704, para. 15, [1976 Transfer Binder] Fed. Sec. L. Rep. (CCH) ¶ 80,495 (May 6, 1976).

[16] SEC Interpretative Release No. 33-6130, pt. B, para. 2, [1979 Transfer Binder] Fed. Sec. L. Rep. (CCH) ¶ 23,507B (Sept. 27, 1979).

had in fact developed or received estimates with respect thereto, such estimates were generally required to be disclosed.

These principles were not changed in 1976, when the SEC prescribed disclosure of estimated capital expenditures for minimum periods to achieve more uniform minimum disclosures.[17] Thus, if the registrant has estimates suggesting that, after the two-year period, there will remain material capital expenditures sufficient to comply with such requirements, or material penalties or fines for noncompliance are likely to be imposed, disclosure of such additional known or estimated costs, penalties, or fines may be necessary to prevent the mandatory disclosure from being misleading. Furthermore, if the registrant reasonably expects that these costs for any future year will be materially higher than the costs disclosed for the mandatory two-year period, the registrant may, if it has not already done so, be obligated to develop estimates with respect to such costs. It may also be necessary for the registrant to specify the source of its estimates, the assumptions and methods used in reaching the estimates, and the extent of uncertainty whether projected future costs may occur.

The SEC's environmental rules, adopted in 1973, require, among other things, disclosure of administrative proceedings pending or contemplated by governmental authorities, and the relief sought in such proceedings. The definition of an administrative proceeding for the purposes of this rule has never been construed narrowly by the SEC. As stated by the Commission in explaining that this rule required disclosure of notices of violation issued by the EPA:

> By requiring a description of all (governmental) litigation regardless of whether the amount of money involved is itself material, the Commission believes it has given recognition to both the importance of the national environmental policy and to the far-reaching effects, both financial and environmental, of violations of environmental laws. Further, the fact that legal action, both pending and known to be contemplated, must be disclosed serves to foreshadow potentially serious environmental problems facing registrants.[18]

The Commission thus interprets its rule to require disclosure of administrative proceedings that are initiated by the registrant, as well as those initiated by the government. The obligation to disclose is in force whenever a government authority is a party to any administrative proceeding. For example, requests for an adjudicatory hearing to contest the provisions of a national pollutant discharge elimination system (NPDES) permit constitute an administrative proceeding that must be disclosed, whether an adjudicatory hearing is held or will actually be held.

---

[17] Notice of Commission Conclusions and Final Action on the Rulemaking Proposals Amended in Securities Act Release No. 5627 (Oct. 14, 1975) relating to Environmental Disclosure, Securities Act Release No. 5704, para. 11, [1976 Transfer Binder] Fed. Sec. L. Rep. (CCH) ¶ 80,495 (May 1976).

[18] *Id.* para. 25.

Similarly, the Commission interprets its rule as requiring disclosure of all administrative orders relating to environmental matters, whether or not those orders literally follow a proceeding. An administrative order may be entered without a proceeding, if a corporation directly consents to the entry of an order or the order is the product of negotiation between the parties. In this regard, the consequences of an administrative consent order, just as those of a judicial consent order, may be as significant as the consequences of a fully litigated proceeding. The Commission does not base its disclosure requirements on the technical issue of whether a registrant chooses to contest the entry of an order.

An additional matter related to disclosure of pending proceedings is the obligation to disclose the relief sought by the government. The Commission does not consider that mere disclosure of the government's intention to compel new pollution control efforts constitutes adequate disclosure of relief sought. Instead, the Commission's regulations require that an estimate of the level of expenditures needed to install the pollution control equipment sought by the government authority be provided, if such expenditures are likely to be material.

In its environmental proceedings, the Commission declined to impose an across-the-board requirement that all companies disclose their general environmental policy, because such a requirement "would result in subjective disclosures largely incapable of verification."[19] Notwithstanding the lack of a general rule that environmental policy be disclosed, two circumstances may create disclosure obligations in this area.

First, if a company voluntarily makes disclosures concerning its environmental policy, such disclosures must be accurate, and the company must make any additional disclosures necessary to ensure that the voluntary disclosures are not misleading.

Second, if a company has a policy or approach toward compliance with environmental regulations that is reasonably likely to result in substantial fines, penalties, or other significant effects on the company, the registrant may have to disclose the likelihood and magnitude of such fines, penalties, and other material effects, to prevent making misleading required disclosures with respect to descriptions of the company's business, financial statements, capital expenditures for environmental compliance, or legal proceedings.[20]

---

[19] Notice of Commission Conclusions and Rulemaking Proposals in the Public Proceeding Announced in Securities Act Release No. 5569 (Feb. 11, 1975), Securities Act Release No. 5627, [1975 Transfer Binder] Fed. Sec. L. Rep. (CCH) ¶ 80,310 (Oct. 14, 1975) (regarding (1) further disclosure, if any, of environmental matters in registration statements; (2) disclosure in such documents of other socially significant matters; and (3) investors' interest in and use of such information).

[20] S.E.C. Interpretative Release No. 34-16224, pt. B.3., paras. 2–3, [1979 Transfer Binder] Fed. Sec. L. Rep. (CCH) ¶ 23,507B (Sept. 27, 1979).

§ 10.6 —Formulating a Corporate Response to SEC Requirements

Although the benefits of the SEC's environmental regulations are open to question in terms of providing investor information and encouraging desirable corporate behavior, the pitfalls created for corporate management and counsel are quite real. Public corporations that are significantly affected by environmental regulation must bear in mind the SEC's disclosure requirements in the areas of material effects of environmental regulation, environmental litigation, and corporate environmental policy, as discussed in § 10.5. Although the broad outlines of the mandated disclosures are clear for each field, application is often difficult and perilous.

As with other aspects of compliance with environmental regulations, the obligations imposed by the SEC's environmental disclosure rules pose difficult challenges to corporate management and counsel that will often be compounded by the rules' ambiguity and impracticality. The rules may not prudently be ignored. That approach risks intensive SEC scrutiny and painful remedial steps that may coincide with pressure from environmental regulatory agencies.

Despite differing circumstances for each firm, any effective response must start with a tough-minded review of the company's reporting and planning mechanisms. Key managers and staff personnel at lower levels in the organization must understand the need to identify and highlight potentially reportable environmental developments, and have available reliable procedures to do so. The company should be equipped to develop required estimates and supporting data, perhaps by arrangements with accounting or consulting firms. In capital budgeting and other environmental planning, procedures should incorporate consideration of possible disclosure obligations.

More fundamentally, firms should develop a coherent, defensible analysis of how the SEC environmental disclosure rules should be applied to their particular operations and problems. An intelligent position on disclosure issues, developed in advance of specific applications but refined through experience, is preferable to after-the-fact rationalizations. A firm with a thoughtful and consistent approach, supported by strong information-generating systems and procedures, is most likely to avoid the pitfalls created by the SEC environmental disclosure requirements.

A disclosure duty exists where a trend, demand, commitment, event, or uncertainty is both presently known to management and reasonably likely to have material effects on the registrant's financial condition or results of operation.[21] Registrants preparing their MD&A disclosure should determine and carefully review the trends, demands, commitments, events, or uncertainties that are known to management.

---

[21] Financial Reporting Release No. 36, pt. B, para. 1 (May 1989).

In preparing the MD&A disclosure, registrants should focus on each of the specific categories of known data. For example, one specific category requires a description of the registrant's material commitments for capital expenditures as of the end of the latest fiscal period. However, even where no legal commitments, contractual or otherwise, have been made, disclosure is required if material planned capital expenditures result from a known demand, as where the expenditures are necessary to a continuation of the registrant's current growth trend.[22] Similarly, if the same registrant decides not to incur such expenditures, a known certainty would exist regarding continuation of the current growth trend. If the adverse effect on the registrant from discontinuation of the growth trend is reasonably likely to be material, disclosure is required. Disclosure of planned material expenditures is also required, for example, when such expenditures are necessary to support a new, publicly announced product or line of business.[23] Often, a matter that had a material impact on past operating results also involves prospective effects, which should be discussed.

Events that have already occurred or are anticipated often give rise to known uncertainties. For example, a registrant may know that a material government contract is about to expire. The registrant may be uncertain whether the contract will be renewed, but nevertheless would be able to assess facts relating to whether it will be renewed. The registrant may know that a competitor has found a way to provide the same service or product at a price less than that charged by the registrant, or may have been advised by the government that the contract may not be renewed. The registrant also would have factual information relevant to the financial impact on the registrant of nonrenewal. In situations such as these, a registrant would have identified a known uncertainty reasonably likely to have material future effects on the registrant's financial conditions or results of operations, and disclosure would be required.[24]

The SEC views MD&A as a focal point in the disclosure system of the securities acts. The SEC has enhanced and expanded it through recent releases.[25] Although the SEC appropriately concluded that no new regulations are required, MD&A drafters must read and understand the SEC's latest interpretive guidance and not simply rely on the initial regulations. The interpretive guidance does provide significant information to assist management in drafting a meaningful MD&A.

---

[22] *Id.* para. 5.

[23] *Id.*

[24] *Id.* para. 4.

[25] Financial Reporting Release No. 36, Management's Discussion and Analysis of Financial Condition and Results of Operations; Certain Investment Company Disclosure, Securities Act Release No. 6835, Exchange Act Release No. 26,831, Investment Company Act Release No. 16,961, [1989] Fed. Sec. L. Rep. (CCH) ¶ 72,436 (May 18, 1989).

APPENDIXES

PHASE I ENVIRONMENTAL SURVEY CHECKLIST[1]

I. SITE DESCRIPTION/INVESTIGATION

Street Address, City, County, and State

Assessor's Parcel Number

Name of Owner

Acreage/Area/Square Footage

Shape of Plat

Property Access, Fences, Roads, Trails, Driveways, Etc.

Easements (for example, Electrical, Railroad)

Buildings

1. Size—Square Footage
2. Construction—Possible Asbestos-Containing Materials
3. Age/Condition
4. Past and Present Occupants/Operations
5. Signs
6. Hazardous Materials Storage
    a. Container Type
    b. Proper Labeling
    c. Size of Container
    d. Contents
    e. Compliance with Storage Holding Time Constraints
    f. Posted Permits
    g. Location of Property in Question (PIQ)
    h. Spillage, Leaks, etc.

---

[1] Many such lists are becoming available on computerized data services. For specific information, contact individual state agencies.

7. Floor Drains, Sumps, Clarifier
   a. Capacity
   b. Construction
   c. Former Uses
   d. Current Uses
   e. Location on PIQ
   f. Permits
8. PCB Fluorescent Lights
9. Transformers with PCBs
10. Underground Storage Tanks/Above-Ground Storage Tanks
    a. Age
    b. Tank Construction
    c. Capacity
    d. Overfill Protection
    e. Monitoring System
    f. Location on PIQ
11. Wastewater Disposal Practices
12. Hazardous Waste Disposal Practices
13. Air Emissions/Permits

Vacant Land

1. Size/Shape
2. Roads/Trails/Fences
3. Easements
4. Terrain/Vegetation
5. Structures, Wells, Drums, Tanks, Etc.
   a. Size/Type of Container
   b. Labels
   c. Contents
   d. Volume of Material
   e. Spillage, Leaks, Etc.
   f. Location on PIQ
6. Burial Mounds, Landfills, Pits, Ponds
7. Stained Soil
8. Transformers with PCBs

Adjacent Properties—Buildings

1. Address
2. Occupant/Usage
3. Drums, Tanks, Stained Soil, Etc.

Adjacent Properties—Vacant Land

1. Terrain/Vegetation
2. Other Features of Interest

Site Vicinity

1. One-Mile Radius Investigation of Published Lists

II. HISTORICAL INFORMATION

General History of the Land

1. Land Grant/Early Land Uses
2. Post-War Development

Site History

1. 50-Year Chain-of-Time
2. Development History on the PIQ—Former Uses/Occupants
3. Historical Aerial Photographs Review

III. REGIONAL BACKGROUND INFORMATION

Regional Physiographic

1. Mountain Ranges
2. Watersheds
3. PIQ Elevation
4. Fault/Flood Zones
5. Nearby City/Community/County Lines
6. Nearby Oil Fields

Soil

1. Soil Type
2. Soil Derivation
3. Soil Profile
4. Depth to Bedrock
5. Permeability
6. Runoff/Erosion

Groundwater

1. Well Number
2. Distance and Direction of Well from PIQ
3. Well Use (Domestic, Industrial, Monitoring)
4. Date of Latest Measurement
5. Depth to First Water
6. Water Quality
7. Groundwater Gradient

IV. AGENCY RECORDS

City

1. Building Department/Building Permits
2. Fire Department/Fire Prevention
3. Planning Department
4. Water District
5. Chamber of Commerce
6. Public Library
7. Historical Society

County

1. Environmental Health Department
2. Agricultural Commissioner's Office
3. Assessor's Office
4. Public Works Department
5. Flood Control and Water Conservation District

State

1. Regional Water Quality Control Board
2. Air Quality Management District
3. State Water Resources Control Board
4. Department of Oil and Gas
5. Department of Health Services

Federal

1. EPA

V. PUBLISHED LISTS

[Information regarding past and present environmental sites, prepared by government agencies, should be checked. The following is a list of such data sources compiled for a project in California.]

1. ASPIS—Abandoned Site Program Information System, Facility Profile Reports (State of California Department of Health Services)
2. BEP—Expenditure Plan for the Hazardous Substance Cleanup Bond Act of 1984 (State of California Department of Health Services, Toxic Substances Control Division)
3. CERCLIS—Superfund Program Site/Event Listing, List 8 (U.S. Environmental Protection Agency)
4. CORTESE—Hazardous Waste and Substances SITES-LIST (State of California Office of Planning and Research, Office of Permit Assistance)

5. LUFT—Report on Releases of Hazardous Substances from Underground Storage Tanks (State Water Resources Control Board)

6. RCRA (HWIS)—List of Hazardous Waste Generators, Transporters and Treatment, Storage, and Disposal Facilities (State of California Department of Health Services)

7. SWAT—Solid Waste Assessment Test Program, Ranked List of Solid Waste Disposal Sites (State Water Resources Control Board)

8. SWIS—Active and Inactive Sanitary Landfills and Disposal Facilities (State of California Waste Management Board)

SAMPLE PROPOSAL FOR PHASE I SITE ASSESSMENT

Re: Proposal to Perform a Limited Phase I Investigation of Property Located in [_____]

[Date]

Dear [_____]

[_____] is pleased to submit this proposal to perform a limited Phase I Site Investigation of the property located at [_____]. We have prepared this scope of work and cost estimate to perform a limited Phase I investigation in response to your [_____] request. We understand that you are the [owner/lessee/other] of the property.

[Define the site. Describe the client's relationship to the site.]

We understand that the site is currently used for [_____] and in the past has been a [_____]. We further understand that it is your intention to [develop] the property and that your firm is the [_____] of the property.

[Any representation as to current and prior site usage should be spelled out.]

I. Purpose

This limited Phase I investigation will be conducted to determine the history of the property, its ownership, and the purposes for which it has been used. From that investigation, we will attempt to pinpoint the probable contamination that may have resulted from those operations. Detailed characterization of those contaminants, and measuring the plume and profile of the contamination on the property, would have to be done as part of a Phase II investigation. It is not the purpose of this investigation to make such determination. This investigation will determine what additional on-site testing must be done to gain a more comprehensive and detailed grasp of the situation.

[Discuss the scope of the inquiry. If litigation is contemplated, the expected issues and scope of such litigation should be stated. Disclaim any of the typical Phase II work (such as drilling, soil samples, hydrological studies, and lab work).]

II. Scope

[The client should review the following steps carefully to determine if they suit the purpose. They may be too rigorous, or too superficial, depending upon the financial status and needs. There is a dichotomy here between the desire to conduct a sufficiently thorough analysis (for example, to qualify as an innocent landowner) and the fear that such rigorous scrutiny may reveal potential problems that would necessitate extra expenditures for a Phase II analysis and a costly remediation. It is generally better to understand the scope of the problem than to be expedient.]

Our investigation will begin with the review and research of public records to determine any known releases of hazardous materials in the vicinity of the property. We will endeavor to determine the past and present surrounding land usage, and where possible, interview knowledgeable parties about past practices in the area and on the site of your property.

We will research geologic water and vegetation features to determine the hydrological profile and likely soil situation for the area.

We will review available regulatory agency waste incident databases, such as state and federal Superfund reports, underground storage tank action lists, EPA CERCLA listings, and the AB 3750 Hazardous Waste and Substances Site list.

We will attempt to obtain and review those aerial photographs that are available.

We will conduct a review of the preliminary title policy on the site to determine previous ownership and operations, and where possible, check the business records of those companies and individuals. We will also check those entities with the [_____] Secretary of State. Finally, we will check the local court records to determine if there has been any litigation that is likely to have involved any prior owners of the property.

We will check with the county recorder to determine what, if any, disputes or liens have been recorded on the property.

We will also conduct a similar title search of the contiguous property, as well as a search of the business and court records to determine possible contribution of the owners of these properties to contamination.

Once this investigation is completed, we will formulate a detailed proposal for further investigative on-site and laboratory testing.

[Evaluation of contiguous properties is always desirable if there is a strong likelihood of migrating contamination, or if the property is in a highly industrialized zone. One of the most common features of unsuccessful remediations has been failure to adequately assess the potential impact of contamination arising off-site.]

The results of our efforts and any information provided to us will be kept confidential, except to the extent that revelation is required by law. In that case, we would provide you with notice and delay production as long as possible.

[Confidentiality is important, even at this early phase.]

We are not party to any agreement that would prevent us from performing services hereunder, nor are we involved in any project that would adversely affect our performance hereunder.

[Conflict of interest provision should be present.]

SAMPLE PROPOSAL FOR PHASE II SITE ASSESSMENT

Re: Proposal to Perform a Limited Phase II Investigation of Property Located in [_____]

[Date]

Dear [_____]:

[_____] is pleased to submit this proposal to perform a Limited Phase II Site Investigation of the property located at [_____]. We have prepared this scope of work and cost estimate to perform a limited Phase II Investigation of property located in [_____] and described as _____ in response to your request. We understand that you are the [owner/lessee/other] of the property.

[The site should be specified with particulars. It is also advisable to state the client's relationship to the property (owner, lessee, other).]

I. The Site

It is our understanding that your client wishes to investigate the site in anticipation of [_____]. The site is currently used for storage of steel beams and scrap metal. For the purposes of this proposal, we have made certain assumptions that are spelled out in the remaining sections and we list as assumptions.

[This portion of the proposal succinctly states the purpose of the assessment (for example, preliminary to redevelopment, or in anticipation of litigation) and the current usage of the site. If there have been representations regarding past usage, such representations should be included. The assumptions set forth later in the proposal should be referenced.]

II. Purpose

This Site Investigation will be undertaken to determine whether there has been a release of [_____] on the property or onto the soils that could constitute a significant contamination problem. Soil Sampling and analytical testing will be performed to identify the presence of [_____], and whether the extent is limited or the plume extends to adjacent properties as well.

[This section specifies the focus of the investigation (such as a specific contaminant). If a broader, full-spectrum analysis is contemplated, that should be stated.]

Site soils have been redistributed to provide level areas on which to lay the steel products stored on the site, and to provide a level area on the north side of the land. [_____] has been informed by [_____] that some fill was placed on the property approximately [_____] years ago from an off-site ditch, which had been used for agricultural drainage. It is not known whether any other agricultural chemical may be involved.

[This section is a site-specific description of the suspected source of contamination, as well as a description of the physical layout. This description is necessary because the scope of work description is tied to the physical layout.]

A preliminary Phase I Site Assessment, which is not included in this proposal and would cost approximately an additional [$_____], could be performed prior to this site investigation to determine if additional testing is advisable. At this time, a Phase I Investigation has not been requested.

[This section could be adjusted to report the outcome of the preliminary Phase I Site Assessment, if one was performed. In this case, the owner was concerned about only a specific contaminant that probably resulted from a specific spill. In a typical situation, a Phase I Site Assessment would be standard. In this case, the consultant merely pointed out what its typical Phase I Study would entail, thereby alerting the owner to other possible issues.]

III. Commencement

[_____] is a leading environmental services firm with more than [_____] technical and support personnel that provides comprehensive and fully integrated services to private industry. We specialize in solving and preventing a broad range of complex environmental problems, particularly in the areas of hazardous materials and toxic pollutants, through sound, cost-effective strategies. Our [_____] office is sufficiently staffed to conduct a site investigation upon written authorization to proceed.

[The importance of this paragraph is that it clearly requires a notice to proceed before the Site Assessment will begin.]

IV. Scope of Work

[This scope of work is critical. Presumably, it will be geared to be compatible with the owner's needs, the probable source of contamination, and any Phase I data obtained.]

To complete the Site Investigation, [_____] will perform the following:

A. Borings by Hollow-stem Auger Drill Rig

[_____] will obtain soil samples for laboratory analyses by drilling four borings to a depth of approximately 25 feet, and six borings to approximately five feet, on the [_____] site in areas where it is believed that fill soils and native soils exist.

Three of the four deeper borings will be placed on the level elevated area above the embankment on the north end of the property adjacent to the freeway. The fourth boring will be placed along the access to the north elevated level ground that is east of the steel storage area. Each boring will be advanced to a depth at which undisturbed native soil is reached and a sample will be obtained (bottom depth anticipated to be no deeper than 25 feet).

[These three borings are located in relation to a fixed point ("the north end of the property adjacent to the freeway"). The fourth boring is sited in relation to a mobile landmark (the steel storage area), which could become a problem later if the steel were moved.]

The six shallower borings will be placed at selected locations on the level lower area of the site, at points accessible between the stored steel beams. Soils in this area are elevated a few feet higher than those of the property to the west, indicating native or off-site fill was used to create the present grade elevation. It is anticipated that native undisturbed soil may be reached in most of this area at a depth of approximately five feet.

All borings will be backfilled with a bentonite cement grout, and cuttings will be contained on-site in DOT-approved drums pending the results of the soil analyses. Proper disposal of the drums and cuttings will be the responsibility of the client.

[This use of hazardous material could be changed. However, in this case the consultant is disowning any responsibility for transport or disposal of any portion of the potentially hazardous material.]

B. Soil Sampling

Three soil samples will be collected from each of the six shallower borings; one sample from just below the ground surface, one sample from a depth of approximately 18 inches, and one from the bottom of the boring.

The four 25-foot borings will be drilled and sampled at five-foot intervals, commencing at the ground surface, to a depth of approximately 25 feet or to the interface between the fill soil and native soil. Samples not analyzed are collected for accurate logging purposes.

This task will be performed by an [_____] geologist assisted by an [_____] field technician. We anticipate that the drilling and sampling can be completed during two days of field work.

It is assumed that site soils can be augered by a hollow-stem auger drill rig. Should alternate equipment be required to advance the borings due to unforseen site conditions, the cost of such additional equipment is not included in this proposal.

[This statement allows for changed conditions to call for a contract price increase. However, it does not say why they have assumed the hollow-stem auger will work. Such assumption should be spelled out in the Assumptions section following.]

Soil samples will be obtained using a split-spoon or California sampler lined with brass sample rings. A log of each boring will be maintained and soils will be classified therein using the Unified Soil Classification System. It is not anticipated that groundwater will be encountered.

Based on an anticipated maximum depth of 25 feet for four of the borings, and five feet for six of the borings, a total of 30 soil samples will be collected from these borings (not including two QA/QC samples). All samples will be submitted to the laboratory, but only selected samples will be analyzed initially to avoid an excessive number of analyses if no [_____] or related compounds are found in significant levels in the first group of analyses. Three samples from each of the four 25-foot borings and two from each of the six 5-foot borings, plus the QA/QC samples, will be analyzed initially (24 samples plus the two QA/QC samples).

[It might be advisable to spell out, in the Assumptions section, why the 25-foot depth was selected.]

From the six shallow borings, the surface and 18-inch depth sample will be analyzed initially (12 samples). The bottom sample from each of these six borings will be held pending the results of the upper two. If no [_____] or related compound is present in the upper two samples at or above regulatory action levels, no further analyses will be performed on the bottom sample. Samples will be analyzed within seven days, so that, should the bottom sample require analysis, the holding time of seven days will not be exceeded.

[This protocol assumes a certain level of penetration based on the nature of the suspected contaminant. Obviously, it would have to be modified to agree with the nature of the investigation, the suspected contaminant, and the soil characteristics.]

From each of the four deeper borings, the surface sample, one sample at five feet from two borings, one sample at ten feet from two of the borings, and one from the bottom of each boring will be analyzed (12 samples).

C. Laboratory Analyses for [_____]

Laboratory analyses of all soil samples for the presence of the [_____] will be performed by an independent [state] Certified Laboratory for analysis by EPA Test Method 8080, which is used for detection of Organochlorine Pesticide and Polychlorinated Biphenols (PCBs). The practical quantitation level for 4,4'-DDT in soil by this analytical method is 50 ppb (parts per billion).

[The text will vary, depending on the genesis of the assessment and the purpose of the investigation.]

D. Quality Assurance/Quality Control

Quality Assurance/Quality Control (QA/QC) procedures will include the following:

[_____] Chain of Custody Forms shall be maintained for the holding and transport of samples collected for analyses.

The field investigation will be performed under the direction of a [state, if appropriate] Registered Geologist.

A trip blank of deionized water will be submitted for analyses by EPA Test Method 8080 on each day soil samples are submitted to the laboratory (estimated two samples maximum).

An independent [state] Certified Hazardous Waste Testing Laboratory will perform the soil analyses.

All [_____] field personnel have been trained in accordance with OSHA 29 CFR 1910.120 to perform hazardous waste investigations in a safe and informed manner.

[No provision is made for splits or for confidentiality. If litigation or government action were contemplated, they would have to be provided for.]

E. Report

A written report of the data collected during the field investigations, and interpretation of the subsequent analytical results, will be prepared with our recommendations following the completion of our field investigation and receipt of the final laboratory results.

[The report should go to the owner's attorney.]

F. Project Cost

[_____]'s Site Investigation will be performed on a time and materials basis in accordance with our standard commercial terms, which are attached and made a part of this proposal. The estimated project cost is [$_____]. This cost is based on the following assumptions: 1. [_____] project personnel will have full access to the facility; 2. our requests for information regarding past and present site activities, materials contained therein, and modifications to site topography past and present will be responded to in a candid and timely manner.

[Some of the other assumptions addressed above should be detailed here.]

The estimated costs for this project are as follows:

LABOR [$_____]
SUBCONTRACTS:
DRILLING [$_____]
LABORATORY ANALYSES [$_____]
OTHER DIRECT COSTS [$_____]
Total Estimated Cost [$_____]

G. List of Assumptions

1. All field activities are conducted in a safe and timely manner
2. [_____] and its subcontractors are provided unencumbered access to the site and boring locations.
3. [_____] will make an attempt to identify subsurface structures, utilities, and conduits prior to drilling. [_____] will not be held responsible for damage or liability resulting from any unidentified subsurface structures encountered during drilling activities.
4. Drilling will be accomplished using a hollow-stem auger drill rig. [Here, conditions should be stated under which alternative equipment will be used.]
5. All soil cuttings will be stored on-site. It will be the client's responsibility to dispose of this material in an appropriate manner pending the results of laboratory analysis.
6. Samples will be analyzed using a normal laboratory reporting time of 10 working days with verbal results prior to the seven-day initial holding time, to allow timely analyses of the remaining samples if required.
7. Four borings will be drilled to a depth of 25 feet and six borings will be drilled to a depth of five feet.
8. No groundwater samples will be collected and analyzed within the scope of the work.
9. At least 26, but no more than 32, soil samples from the borings will be collected and analyzed with the scope of the work.
10. One revision of the final report will be provided within the cost of this project. Cost for additional revisions will be charged on a time and materials basis.
11. No resurfacing of investigated areas is included within the scope of work.
12. No special vapor emission controls will be required during excavation and sampling.
13. The work is expected to be performed under Level D health and safety conditions; if the work is upgraded to Level C or higher, all pricing will be renegotiated.
14. [_____] will not be responsible for obtaining access or permission to drill at off-site locations.

[Site-specific assumptions should be added here.]

H. Project Schedule

This schedule depends on timely responses from the contract analytical laboratory, drilling contractor, state and county agencies, and from [_____] and [_____], should any additional information be required.

[_____] is prepared to proceed with scheduling of this site investigation upon receipt of written authorization. Barring unforeseen difficulties, [_____]'s written report will be submitted within two weeks of the receipt of the laboratory results of the soil analyses. This proposal is valid for 90 days.

[_____] appreciates the opportunity to provide environmental services to [_____] and [_____]. If you accept this proposal and authorize [_____] to proceed with this assessment, please sign below and return a copy to us. If there are any questions regarding the commercial terms, it is assumed that both parties will act in good faith to come to a mutual agreement on the contract terms. However, should such questions arise and until we do reach an agreement, the enclosed commercial terms will apply.

[If this letter were part of a litigation defense or resistance to government attack, the letter should reflect that the attorney-client and work product privileges attach to the document.]

I. Limitations of Use

This proposal or bid document (document) was prepared by [_____] solely for your *internal* use in evaluating [_____]'s business proposal and deciding whether or not to contract with [_____] to perform the services described in this document. [_____] considers the pricing and other business considerations set forth in this document to be the proprietary and confidential business information of [_____]. This document and the information contained herein shall not be used for any purpose other than as specifically stated above and shall not be disclosed to any other party without [_____]'s written consent.

The results of our efforts and any information provided to us will be kept confidential, except to the extent that revelation is required by law. In that case, we would provide you with notice and delay production as long as possible.

[Confidentiality is important, even at this early phase.]

We are not party to any agreement that would prevent us from performing services hereunder, nor are we involved in any projects that would adversely affect our performance hereunder.

[Conflict of interest provisions should be present.]

APPENDIX D

SAMPLE REMEDIATION CONTRACT

The sample remediation contract that follows is designed primarily to suggest to the reader various contractual issues that should be covered in any such agreement. Commentary follows suggested clauses, to help the reader understand how the suggested clauses might best be modified for a particular situation on the project. There are points of contention between contractors and owners, and often between designers and contractors, about these issues. Our intention is not to resolve those disputes here, but rather to suggest certain basic concepts that must be addressed if the remediation contract is to be a fully integrated document that will enable the parties to achieve successful remediation of the contaminated property.

A recent and fairly succinct remediation contract checklist covered the following 13 items:

_____ 1. Scope of work (detailed description)
_____ 2. Date of commencement and requirement for diligent prosecution of the work
_____ 3. General high-quality performance standard
_____ 4. Consultant's obligation to comply with all applicable laws
_____ 5. Prohibition against liens
_____ 6. Compensation, invoicing, and payment procedures, including budget forecasts and provisions for offsets and retainage, if any
_____ 7. Requirement for confidentiality and prohibition against publicity
_____ 8. Conflict of interest prohibitions
_____ 9. Specification of consultant's, counsel's, and client's principal representatives
_____ 10. Insurance, risk of loss, and indemnification provisions
_____ 11. Suspension or termination of work provisions, for convenience or cause, including default and excused nonperformance provisions
_____ 12. Subcontracting and assignment limitations
_____ 13. General provisions concerning notices, taxes, amendments, and governing law.[1]

---

[1] 2 Liability in Commercial Transactions Reporter No. 1, at 4 (Nov. 1991).

Unfortunately this list is obviously oriented toward protection of the owner, and is more concerned with collateral liability issues than with contracting issues. The prohibition against liens set forth in item 5 is not a neutral provision, and will ostensibly help the owner. However, before arguing about waiving lien rights in a contract, the contractor should consider that a lien is only as valuable as the property involved. One must question, therefore, whether a lien on a toxic waste site has any value worth discussing. The question of lien rights is largely a function of the nature of the project and the relationship of the parties. It is clear, however, that the contract should address the issue in some fashion.[2]

The proposed list also fails to address other fundamental issues. Items 7 and 8, while clearly appropriate, concern issues that are peripheral to the remediation. At the same time, the list fails to mention hidden conditions, change orders, and dispute resolution. With these caveats in mind, the following contract checklist is suggested:

_____ 1. Contract cost
_____ 2. Contract time
_____ 3. Assumptions
_____ 4. Contract object:
    _____ a. What type of site?
    _____ b. Where is the site?
    _____ c. When must the project be completed?
    _____ d. How will remediation be performed?
    _____ e. Why is action necessary (e.g., government order)?
_____ 5. Scope/Level
    _____ a. Project
    _____ b. Work
    _____ c. Remediation
_____ 6. Payment terms
_____ 7. Permits/Compliance with laws
_____ 8. Liens/Bonds
_____ 9. Hidden conditions
_____ 10. Change orders
_____ 11. Limitation of liability
    _____ a. Contract limits
    _____ b. Indemnity
    _____ c. Insurance

---

[2] The parties will also want to address the possible availability of other statutory remedies for recovery, such as the recently enacted general contractor's stop notice rights in California. *See* Cal. Civ. Code § 3159. For a thorough discussion of how lien and stop notice rights are evolving in California, *see* R. Erickson & F. Albert, *Recovery for Extra Work,* L.A. Law., Jan. 1991, at 22.

____ 12. Conflict of interest
____ 13. Confidentiality
____ 14. Subcontracting/Assignment
____ 15. I.D. representatives
____ 16. Suspension/Termination
____ 17. Damage limitations/Liquidated damages
____ 18. Dispute resolution
____ 19. Governing law
____ 20. Notices.

The following sample contract uses addenda to establish job-specific criteria: scope of work (including government approvals), contract documents, contract price, a summary of client-supplied information, and a health and safety plan. Some of these addenda would have to be developed on a project-by-project basis. If desired, a standard set of general conditions could be developed. Care must be taken, of course, to ensure the conditions' compatibility with the base contract. For certain public projects, a prevailing wage clause may be necessary. Some of the terms of this sample contract are reflective of typical construction clauses. Other terms have been taken from various contract dispute files, and some are based on the author's experience in remediation contracting.

CONTRACT FOR REMEDIATION

ARTICLE 1: DEFINITIONS AND GENERAL PROVISIONS
  1.1 The Project
  1.2 The Proposal
  1.3 Scope of Work
  1.4 Scope/Level of Remediation
  1.5 Contract Documents
  1.6 Definitions

ARTICLE 2: SITE ENTRY AND INVESTIGATION, SITE INFORMATION, AND PERMITS
  2.1 Rite of Entry
  2.2 Project Site Information Supplied by Client
  2.3 Lien Information
  2.4 Financial Assurances by Owner
  2.5 Surveys
  2.6 Permits
  2.7 Client Information and Services
  2.8 Drawings
  2.9 Title to Found Materials

ARTICLE 3: CONTRACTOR DUTIES AND OBLIGATIONS
  3.1 Site Investigation
  3.2 Nature of the Work

CONTRACT FOR REMEDIATION

The parties to this Agreement are:

Contractor

Client

[The organization of this contract assumes strictly a bilateral agreement between Owner (Client) and Contractor.

In situations wherein the remediation Contractor did not perform initial assessments or design the remediation, the Client or Contractor may wish to make the entity who performed such services a party to the Agreement. The Contractor should at least know what the Agreement(s) between the Owner and the other consultant(s) provide. The Contractor may want a recital that attempts to grant the Contractor third-party beneficiary status in those agreements.

The term *Client* is used in lieu of Owner because in some cases the party contracting for the work may be a lessee or secured party. The Contractor should be certain to confirm the Client's status, as it may be relevant to a number of collateral issues such as lien rights, availability of insurance, and so forth.]

ARTICLE 1. DEFINITIONS AND GENERAL PROVISIONS

[This section can be as complex and lengthy as required by the sophistication and ingenuity of the parties, and the need for complex and detailed definition.]

1.1 The Project

[This can be as simple or as complex as the situation requires. At a minimum, it should provide the physical location of the project, describe the surrounding properties, and outline the broad goals of the undertaking. See **Chapter 3** in the text. If any work is to be carried out by others, that provision should be indicated both here and in contract § 1.3.]

1.2 The Proposal
Contractor has submitted a proposal dated _____. Client has relied on that proposal in selecting the Contractor. The proposal was arrived at following:
1.2.1 Site visits on _____.
1.2.2 Test well reports described in the proposal.
1.2.3 Discussions with Client's representatives.
1.2.4 Assurances that [for example, no toxic wastes, PCBs, asbestos] are present.

[Many remediation contracts are entered into following Client acceptance of a proposal. The proposal is the basis upon which the Contractor is selected, and often provides the basic cost estimates. For that reason, the contract should reflect the proposal, spell out assumptions that were made, identify any factors that have changed since the proposal was created, reflect a detailed Phase I and II study (where performed), numerous trips to the site, a detailed field investigation, and bench and field tests. If some of these were not performed, then those limitations should be spelled out. Such information is a departure from standard construction industry practice, where reference to prior documents is not favored.]

1.3 Scope of Work
Contractor has developed a scope of work for the project identified above and in accordance with the provisions described in the proposal identified above. This scope of work is set forth in Addendum I attached to this Agreement, and considered part of the contract documents. Addendum I is based on information provided by Client or Client's agent. If hazardous waste, pollution sources, nuisance or chemical or industrial waste disposal problems, other than those described in Addendum I, are discovered after the date of the commencement of work, or if Client desires additional services from Contractor, a revised Scope of Work shall be prepared, with corresponding changes in fees payable by Client to Contractor by written change order mutually agreed to by Client and Contractor. Where charges are not to exceed a specified sum, Contractor shall notify Client before such limit is exceeded and shall not continue to provide service beyond such limit unless Client authorizes in writing an increase in the amount of the limitation. If a

not to exceed limitation is broken down into budgets for specific tasks, the task budget may be exceeded without Client authorization as long as the total limitation is not exceeded.

[The key assumption of this section is that the Contractor has based the proposal and scope of work on information provided by the Owner or the Owner's agent. The scope of work may even have been designed by the Owner's agent. If so, this paragraph would require substantial modification to reflect that fact. If, on the other hand, the Contractor designed the remediation effort, the third sentence would be deleted and the contract modified to reflect the expanded liability of the Contractor under this design-build arrangement.

The discussion of changes anticipates Article 7 and may be deleted. The detailed discussion of not to exceed limitations and task budgets is useful when a project has numerous sites or phases. This particular contract would permit any one task to exceed budget, so long as the entire project does not. It assumes that excess costs can be recovered through subsequent savings on other phases or sites.]

The government approvals for completion are set forth in Addendum I. Contractor shall obtain such approvals.

[This requirement relates to § 1.6.3, which provides that substantial completion is partly achieved when these approvals are acquired, and § 1.6.2, which provides that substantial completion is the determining factor in achieving completion for purposes of contract time. The clause is reflective of the fact that government approval is usually the goal of the effort. If completion is to be measured against another standard, that fact should be stated.]

1.4 Scope/Level of Remediation

In preparing its proposal, Contractor has responded to Client's request to establish a scope of work and a scope of remediation designed to treat the soil [and groundwater] on the project located at _____. The contaminants are to be treated and disposed of in accordance with the scope of work to achieve:

_____

_____

_____

Contractor [and Owner's consultant] have developed a remediation/treatment/work plan to carry out the scope of work and attain the project goal.

[In this section, the Client and Contractor should precisely define the goals of the project. The paragraph should address such issues as the acceptable level of remediation, for example: "reduction of pH to 11," "extraction of TCEs to attain a level of nondetectability (as currently defined)." The relationship of this project to contiguous properties should also be discussed. Any post-completion or post-closure monitoring that is necessary should be referenced here and detailed in Addendum I, with detailed payment provisions. If the Client warrants that there has not been, and will not be, migration of contaminants to or from the site, that warranty should be included.]

1.5 Contract Documents

[In this section, all written materials that form the contract should be identified and incorporated. Any documents relied upon by the Owner or Contractor in formulating the project, the proposal, the scope of work, and the scope/level of remediation, should be specified. If the work is to be performed pursuant to a consent decree or government directive, the terms of the decree or directive should be incorporated and should supersede any conflicting contract terms.]

The contract documents consist of all documents set forth in Addendum II and specified in subparagraph 1.5 to this Agreement and are incorporated herein, as well as all change orders, modifications, and amendments arising after the date of the agreement.

The contract documents are a complete list of tasks, methods, and techniques needed to achieve project completion. Anything required of one is required of all.

The following rules apply:

1.5.1 The contract documents are intended to be integrated.

1.5.2 The contract documents include this Agreement, the general and special conditions, drawings, specific time, addenda, and the remediation/treatment/work plan.

[If the Contractor designs the remediation plan, this subsection may need to be deleted. Also, if the Client provides the design from a third party, the Client will want to insure that a correlative obligation from the designer to the Client is present in that contract.]

1.5.3 Client shall be responsible for the adequacy of design and the sufficiency of drawings and specifications.

1.5.4 In the event of an inconsistency between drawings and specifications, the specifications govern.

1.5.5 In the event of a conflict between the proposal and the contract, the terms of the contract shall govern.

1.6 Definitions

1.6.1 The contract price is the total compensation to be paid to Contractor in accordance with Addendum III.

[This definition, using the Addendum to describe the price, allows for flexibility in the contract. The terms of Addendum III may provide for a lump sum or fixed-price contract, a cost contract based on time and materials, a guaranteed maximum price contract with a fee and with or without a savings clause, or some combination thereof. The Addendum may provide line item estimates or budgets for sub-sites or phases, and may provide for alternatives to allow greater contractor flexibility.]

1.6.2 The contract term shall be the number of days specified in the contract to achieve substantial completion. If an early or late completion date are provided for, then the float (the period of time between early start and last day to start, and early and late completion dates) shall belong to the Contractor for purposes of computing time used and remaining.

[The days should be consecutive and should be specified without regard to holidays and weekends. The discussion of the float is designed to avoid a long-standing dispute over who owns it for purposes of delay computation.]

1.6.3 Substantial completion shall be the point at which the scope/level of remediation of subsection 1.4 has been achieved and all requisite government approval has been obtained.

[Addendum I should provide a detailed list of all required government approvals. Since most remediation efforts are intended to achieve government approval, that is the most logical point to establish substantial completion. This sample contract ties substantial completion to both a level/scope of remediation and government approval. Certain projects may require a different definition. The point is to assure that substantial completion is measured against some objective standard that the Contractor has within its means to attain.]

ARTICLE 2. SITE ENTRY AND INVESTIGATION, SITE INFORMATION, AND PERMITS

2.1 Right of Entry

Client grants to Contractor and warrants (if the project site is not owned by Client) that permission has been granted for a right of entry from time to time, by Contractor, its employees, agents, and subcontractors, upon the project site for the purpose of providing the scope of work set forth in Addendum I attached to this Agreement and considered part of this Agreement.

[The issues of right of entry and site information pose thorny questions for the Client at the contract level, the proposal level, and the Phase I and II audit levels. Often the Client is unsure of the full scope of the contamination, and thus has exposure. Is it wise to permit entry and document copying before a contractual obligation is defined and exists? At the very least, the Client would want a strongly worded confidentiality agreement before permitting pre-contract entry.]

2.2 Project Site Information Supplied by Client

Client has made available to Contractor all relevant information in its possession regarding existing and proposed environmental, geologic, and geotechnical conditions of the site and surrounding area. Client has provided to Contractor, in writing, all criteria, design and construction standards, and all other information relating to Client's requirements for the project. The information includes, but is not limited to, plot plans, topographic surveys, hydrographic data, and previous soil data, including borings, field or laboratory tests, and written reports. This information is listed in Addendum IV attached hereto and incorporated by this reference.

[This section does not obligate the Client to have actually performed any tests, borings, studies, or the like. It only requires that, to the extent that such items and information exist, they have been provided by the Client. It may be advisable to create a detailed list of surveys, data, and other information that has been provided.]

Prior to the commencement of services, and continuing thereafter, Client shall notify Contractor of any known potential health or safety hazard existing on or near the project site where services are being or will be performed by Contractor or its subcontractors, with particular reference to hazardous substances or conditions. If hazardous substances or conditions that were not disclosed to Contractor prior to signing this Agreement are discovered by Contractor during the performance of the scope of work (Addendum I) or during the performance of a change order, then upon notification of such discovery, Client and Contractor shall seek to determine the equitable adjustment (if any) to be made to the Agreement or change order.

[This agreement to make adjustment for discovery of hidden conditions again anticipates Article 7.]

Client will promptly transmit to Contractor new information or plan changes that require a change order. Client shall indicate to Contractor the property lines, and Client is responsible for the accuracy of markers. Client shall locate for Contractor all underground utilities and installations, and shall assume responsibility for the accuracy of all such locations. In the prosecution of its work, Contractor will take reasonable precautions to avoid damage or injury to subterranean structures or utilities that Client has in advance brought to Contractor's attention. Client agrees to defend and hold Contractor harmless from any damage, either direct or consequential, to subterranean structures or utilities not called to Contractor's attention in advance.

Client recognizes that environmental, geologic, and geotechnical conditions can vary from those encountered at the times and locations where data are obtained by Contractor, and that the limitation on available data results in a degree of uncertainty with respect to interpretation of these conditions, despite the use of due professional care.

[This subsection imposes many design and organizational obligations on the Client and may be modified for situations in which the Contractor undertakes this work.]

2.3 Lien Information

Client shall provide Contractor with information required to enable Contractor to enforce mechanic's lien rights. Such information shall include which entity has legal title to the property on which the project is located, and Client's interest therein when the contract was entered into. Within five days of any change, information of such change in title will also be provided.

[This provision is designed to enable the Contractor to obtain necessary information to enforce lien rights. Statutory notices must be given to property owners. Subcontractors should be familiar with the preliminary notice requirements for protecting lien and stop notice rights.[3] If the lien right is valueless, it may be deleted. The Client may want the Contractor to waive its lien/stop notice rights. A preferable compromise might be to provide for eight hours of mediation prior to recording of liens.]

2.4 Financial Assurances by Owner

Client shall provide Contractor, prior to execution of the Agreement, with reasonable evidence that financial arrangements have been made to fulfill Client's obligations under the Contract. In the event of a late payment or a failure to pay, Contractor may demand further assurances thereafter.

[This new provision permits the Contractor to verify that the Client is financially able to perform. This provision is analogous to the law of sales, where a party has the right to demand adequate assurance of due performance. In the law of sales, however, the right exists in California only if the demanding party has "reasonable grounds for insecurity."[4] The clause is found in the AIA 201 agreement and has seen increased use in our current troubled economic climate.]

2.5 Surveys

Client shall furnish surveys describing physical characteristics, legal limitations, and utility locations for the site of the project, and a legal description of the site.

2.6 Permits

Except for permits and fees that are the responsibility of Contractor under Addendum I of the contract documents, Client shall secure and pay for necessary approvals, easements, assessments, and charges required for construction, use, or occupancy of permanent structures, or for permanent changes to existing facilities.

[This section clarifies that a permit is the Client's responsibility unless specifically indicated as the Contractor's responsibility.]

2.7 Client Information and Services

Information or services under Client's control shall be furnished by Client with reasonable promptness, to avoid delay in orderly progress of the work.

---

[3] *See, e.g.,* Cal. Civ. Code §§ 3097, 3114.

[4] Cal. Com. Code § 2609.

2.8 Drawings

Unless otherwise provided in the contract documents, Contractor will be furnished, free of charge, such copies of drawings and project manuals as are reasonably necessary for execution of work.

2.9 Title to Found Materials

The title to water, soil, rock, gravel, sand, minerals, timber, or any other materials developed or obtained in the excavation or other operation of Contractor or subcontractors, and the right to use or dispose of said materials, is reserved to Client. Neither Contractor nor subcontractors have, nor shall they make, any claim of right, title, or interest therein.

[This section is for the Client's benefit. A reciprocal clause dealing with ownership of on-site materials, that would protect the Contractor, would read: "Title to, ownership of, and legal responsibility and liability for any and all preexisting contamination shall at all times remain with Client. 'Pre-existing contamination' is any hazardous or toxic substance present at the site(s) that was not brought onto such site(s) by Contractor." Depending on the scope of the Contractor's work, this clause could obligate the Client to indemnify and defend the Contractor for claims made involving pre-existing contamination. The clause could also obligate the Client to arrange for prior transportation, storage, and delivery to any off-site treatment facility.]

ARTICLE 3. CONTRACTOR DUTIES AND OBLIGATIONS

[The following list of contractor obligations is designed to complement the scope of work provisions. The list is largely typical of standard boilerplate contracts. It may be modified without risk of doing substantial damage to the rest of the contract terms.]

3.1 Site Investigation

Client has disclosed to Contractor, prior to the receipt of bids, all information of which Client is aware regarding surface and subsurface conditions in the vicinity of the work, including topographical maps, reports of exploratory tests, written opinions of technical advisers, and other information that might assist Contractor in properly evaluating the extent and character of the work that might be required. Such information is the best information available to Client from its employees, agents, and consultants, through the exercise of reasonable diligence.

3.2 Nature of the Work

Contractor has satisfied itself as to the nature and location of the work, equipment and facilities needed prior to and during prosecution of the work, the general and local conditions, and other matters that can reasonably be expected to affect the work under this Contract.

3.3 Review of Contract Documents and Field Conditions by Contractor

3.3.1 Contractor shall review all information and contract documents furnished by Client, and shall at once report any potential problems to Client or its authorized representative. Contractor has not undertaken any obligation to design the remediation/treatment/work plan, and shall not be liable to Client for damage resulting from errors, inconsistencies, or omissions therein, unless Contractor recognized such error, inconsistency, or omission and knowingly failed to report it to Client. If Contractor utilizes any remediation technique that it knows to be inadequate, Contractor shall be liable for such action and shall reimburse Client for the amount necessary to correct the work.

[This subsection requires the Contractor to continually monitor the feasibility of the project goals, and their compatibility with design documents. It does not charge the Contractor with design responsibility. If the Contractor has performed assessments or devised the remediation plan/treatment, the terms should be modified accordingly.]

3.3.2 Contractor shall perform its own evaluation to verify field conditions, and evaluate those conditions and other information known to Contractor against the proposed treatment/remediation/work plan, prior to commencing activities. If Contractor concludes that an aspect of the plan is defective, Contractor shall promptly inform Client of that conclusion.
3.3.3 Contractor shall perform the work in accordance with the Contract Documents, specifically the treatment/remediation/work plan.

[Section 2.2 requires the Client to furnish surveys describing physical characteristics, legal limitations, and utility locations. This subsection obligates the Contractor to verify field conditions and compare them to the treatment/remediation/work plan before starting the work.]

3.3.4 Contractor shall be responsible to Client for acts and omissions of Contractor's employees, subcontractors and their agents and employees, and other persons performing portions of the work under a contract with the Contractor.

3.4 Labor and Materials

3.4.1 Contractor shall provide and pay for labor, materials, equipment, tools, construction equipment and machinery, water, heat, utilities, transportation, project safety costs, and other facilities and services necessary for proper execution and completion of the treatment/remediation/work plan.
3.4.2 Contractor shall maintain good order on the project site, and shall be responsible for all project safety costs associated with Contractor's scope of work.

[This language enlarges typical construction contract language by adding project safety costs which can be astronomical in some remediation contexts.]

3.4.3 Contractor shall supervise and direct the work. If any aspect of the treatment or remediation plan is outside of Contractor's scope of work the Client shall be so notified in writing. Contractor shall be solely responsible for all portions of the work under the Contract, unless Contract Documents or Client's representatives give other specific instructions concerning these matters.

3.4.4 Contractor shall at all times conduct operations in such a manner as to avoid the risk of bodily harm to persons and damage to the property. Contractor shall design and implement the health and safety program set forth in Addendum V.

[The health and safety program should meet certain minimum standards, but must also be site-specific to deal with atypical problems. If a health and safety plan is incorporated into the contract, then it must be carefully correlated with § 6.1.]

3.5 Warranty

Contractor warrants the materials and equipment furnished under the contract for a period of _____ years. The work will be free from defects not normally found in such materials and equipment. Contractor's warranty excludes damage or defect caused by abuse, improper or insufficient maintenance, improper operation, and normal wear and tear under normal use, and is inoperative if third parties complete any portion of the work.

3.6 Taxes

Contractor shall pay all taxes for the work or portions thereof performed by Contractor.

3.7 Permits, Fees, and Notices

3.7.1 Unless otherwise provided in Addendum I, Contractor shall not be required to secure or pay for permits and governmental fees, licenses, and inspections necessary for proper execution and completion of the work.

3.7.2 Contractor shall comply with and give notices required by laws, ordinances, rules, regulations, and lawful orders of public authorities bearing on performance of the work.

3.7.3 It is not Contractor's responsibility to ascertain that the remediation/treatment techniques are in accordance with applicable laws. However, if Contractor observes that portions of the contract documents do not comply, Contractor shall promptly notify Client in writing, and necessary changes shall be accomplished by appropriate modification. Contractor shall be liable for work knowingly performed in violation of law.

[This is an evolving area in remediation contracting. It touches on areas of expertise, conflict of interest, and common sense. For an expanded discussion see **Chapter 3** of the text.

Subsection 3.7.3 assumes that the Contractor did not design the work plan, closure plan, or other remediation effort. If the Contractor performed such work, this subsection would be inappropriate.]

3.8 Prosecution of the Work

3.8.1 By [within two weeks of signing the contract], Contractor shall prepare and submit to Client an estimated progress schedule indicating the starting and completion dates for the various stages of the work, and the sequence of construction. Thereafter, Contractor shall submit, when reasonably requested by Client, updates of the schedule reflecting any changes in such dates or sequence.

[The time period may be adjusted; the important task is to establish a planned construction sequence.]

3.8.2 Contractor shall perform the work with the goal of achieving substantial completion within the contract term.

3.9 Conflicts

Contractor warrants that it is not a party to any other existing or previous agreement that would prevent it from entering into this Agreement, or that would adversely affect its ability to perform under this Agreement.

[Designed to obviate conflicts, this subsection has serious implications. Since it is couched in terms of a warranty by the Contractor, its violation could yield an immediate claim of breach with possibility of termination.]

ARTICLE 4. SUBCONTRACTORS/ASSIGNMENT/SEPARATE CONTRACTS

4.1 Assignment

Neither party to the contract shall assign the contract in whole or part, including an assignment by Contractor of any monies due or to become due, without the written consent of the other party. This section shall not apply to the subcontracting by Contractor of any portion of the work.

4.2 Subcontract Definitions

4.2.1 Subcontractors may be utilized by Contractor to perform a portion of the work. The term *subcontractor* means an entity having a direct contractual relationship with Contractor.
4.2.2 A *sub-subcontractor* is an entity having a direct or indirect contract with a subcontractor of Contractor.

[These definitions may be deleted in the interest of shortening the contract.]

4.3 Subcontracts and Separate Contracts

4.3.1 Contractor shall inform Client in writing of the names of persons or entities (including those who are to furnish materials or equipment fabricated to a special design) proposed for each principal portion of the work. If Client objects to any subcontractor, such objection must be given in writing within a reasonable time, specifying the basis for the objection.

[Omitted from these subcontracting provisions are terms calling for subcontractors to be bound to the Contractor in the same manner that the Contractor is bound to the Client. While such an arrangement protects the Client, it would be redundant here, as any competent contractor would have such incorporation language in the subcontract as a protection. The best protection for the Client would be to see the contractor/subcontractor agreement.

Also omitted are requirements for contingent assignment of subcontracts to the Client in the event of termination by the Client. Instead, subparagraph 4.3.5 defines the subcontractor/client relationship.]

4.3.2 Contractor shall not contract with a person or entity reasonably objected to by Client.

[If the work is to be performed pursuant to a consent decree or government edict, the scope of persons who may object might have to be enlarged.]

4.3.3 If Client or a government agency having jurisdiction over the project has reasonable objection to a person or entity proposed by Contractor, Contractor shall propose another entity. Client shall have the right to make objection, provided such objection is reasonable. Contractor shall have the right to request a change in contract amount, to the extent there is a cost increase caused by the change.

[In CERCLA Superfund cleanups, the fact that the new model consent decree allows the government to reject a proposed contractor has some relevance.]

4.3.4 Client shall have the right to make reasonable objections to any proposed subcontractor change.
4.3.5 No contractual relationship shall be created between any subcontractor or sub-subcontractor and Client.

4.4 Client's Right to Perform Construction and Award Separate Contracts

[This section protects the Client's ability to contract out parts of the project to entities other than the General Contractor. While customary for construction forms, it could be omitted without damaging the essence of this agreement.]

4.4.1 Client reserves the right to perform portions of the remediation/treatment itself, and to award separate contracts for other operations on the site. Contractor may make claims for added costs and extra time arising from the acts of other Client-hired contractors and consultants.
4.4.2 Each entity executing a separate agreement with Client for work on the site shall be known as a Separate Contractor.
4.4.3 Client must coordinate its activities and those of each Separate Contractor with the work of the Contractor signed to this Agreement. All separate contractors shall review their construction schedules from time to time and when directed, and make any revisions necessary to maintain orderly progress of all work on the site. The original schedules shall be used by Contractor, Separate Contractors, and Client until subsequently revised. Separate Contractors and Client must be notified in writing of any revisions prior to acting thereon. Client shall insure that its work and that of each Separate Contractor is performed so as not to delay, disrupt, or hamper Contractor's performance and execution of work.

4.4.4 To the extent that Contractor's prosecution of its work is dependent upon the performance of work by any other contractor or by Client, Contractor shall promptly inform Client in writing of any effect on the progress of its work arising from improper or untimely execution of work by Separate Contractors, consultants, or Client's own actions.

ARTICLE 5. DIFFERING SITE CONDITIONS

5.1 Definitions

A differing site condition includes, but is not limited to:

5.1.1 The presence of subsurface or latent physical conditions that differ materially from those indicated by the contract documents, revealed by Client, or which differ materially from those conditions customarily encountered in the area of the project or in performing the work described herein.

5.1.2 The absence of some property, element, physical characteristic, or other attribute relied upon by Contractor in preparing the proposal and the scope of work.

5.1.3 The presence of any hazardous materials not previously identified on the project site.

[Subsections 5.1.2 and 5.1.3 are based on the author's experiences in litigating changed conditions issues in remediation contracting disputes.]

5.2 Client Investigation

Client shall promptly investigate the conditions and, if it finds that such conditions do so materially differ and cause an increase or decrease in the cost of, or the time required for, performance of this contract, an equitable adjustment in the contract price and time shall be made.

5.3 Hazardous Material

[This section reflects the concept that a remediation contractor only contracts to deal with specific items identified in the scope sections. If other, previously unidentified contaminants are found, they should be treated as a differing site condition just as in any other type of construction contract. Obviously, if the contractor undertook the open-ended task of remediating all contamination, then this clause would be improper. The definition of hazardous material may also be too limiting.]

The discovery of hazardous material, not specifically identified in the contract documents as additional hazardous material with respect to its location and quantity, shall be deemed to be a differing site condition pursuant to this article. Hazardous material is defined as PCBs, asbestos, or any other material, removal of which is governed by the doctrine of strict liability under federal or state law. If such additional hazardous material is discovered:

5.3.1 Contractor shall immediately notify Client of such discovery, stop that portion of the work affected by such additional hazardous material, and sufficiently protect the work to prevent exposure of persons to such material.

5.3.2 Contractor shall have no obligation to perform any corrective or remedial work that would require handling of or exposure to this additional hazardous material. However, if Contractor agrees to perform such work:

a. Client agrees to indemnify, hold harmless, and defend Contractor from and against any claim, action, or legal proceeding brought against Contractor, seeking to make Contractor strictly liable for the performance of such work.

b. Client shall provide specific instruction to Contractor with respect to the handling, protection, removal, and disposal of such material.

c. An equitable adjustment in the contract price and time shall be made for such work.

ARTICLE 6. CONSTRUCTION PROCEDURES AND PAYMENT

6.1 Health and Safety

Unless expressly provided in the scope of services, or Addendum IV (and then only to the extent expressly defined), Contractor shall not specify construction procedures aimed at, manage or supervise construction, or implement or be responsible for health and safety procedures (other than for its own operational requirements and conduct or for the work); shall not be responsible for the acts or omissions of other contractors or other parties on the project; and shall not have control or charge of and shall not be responsible for construction means, methods, techniques, sequences, or procedures, or for safety precautions and programs. In the event Contractor, by change order or Addenda I and II, expressly assumes health and safety responsibility for certain concerns (such as toxic concerns), the acceptance of such responsibility shall not be deemed an acceptance of responsibility for other health and safety requirements. Contractor's testing or inspection of portions of the work of other parties on a project shall not relieve such other parties from their responsibility for performing their work in accordance with applicable plans, specifications, and safety requirements, and shall not make Contractor responsible for the correct performance of the work.

[See § 3.4.4. This is a thorny issue, which has its genesis in the sulfides case discussed in **Chapter 3** of the text. In a major project, it is not uncommon to find that the Client has a separate contract for health and safety on the project site with a specialty firm, particularly when the project is multi-sited or multi-phased. At the very least, inclusion of this language will highlight the issue.]

6.2 Samples

Contractor will retain all soil, rock, water, and other samples obtained from the project site, as it deems necessary for the project, but no longer than 120 days after the issuance of any document that includes the data obtained from those samples, unless other arrangements are mutually agreed upon in writing. Further storage or transfer of samples will be made at Client's expense following written request of Contractor.

[The Client may wish to provide for sequestration and preservation of these samples for a longer period. The Client should probably provide for a person(s) to be made responsible for this preservation.]

6.3 Payment Conditions

Contractor will submit invoices to Client by progress billing methods and a final invoice upon authorized completion of work. The frequency of the progress billing and the mechanics thereof shall be set forth in Addendum III as part of the payment conditions. *Substantial completion* shall be as defined in subparagraph 1.6.3. All Client deposits submitted to Contractor at the beginning of a project will be credited against Client's final invoice for the project. Payments are due 10 working days after *receipt* of invoice, and considered past due on the 11th working day after receipt of invoice. Client agrees to pay a finance charge at the rate of 1½ percent per month on past due accounts, as well as reasonable attorneys' fees, court costs, and other related expenses that may be incurred by Contractor in collecting past due invoices.

[The payment terms reflect recent California case law.[5] It may be objectionable to the Client or inappropriate in other states.]

In addition to the above, if payment of Contractor invoices is not maintained on a current basis, Contractor may, by written notice to Client, suspend further performance and withhold any and all data from Client until such invoice payment is restored to a current basis.

ARTICLE 7. CHANGES

7.1 Notice

The work shall be subject to change by additions, deletions, or revisions by Client. Contractor will be notified of such changes by receipt of additional or revised drawings, specifications, exhibits, or written orders.

[This language reflects certain AGC/AIA concepts, with additions by the author. It has the advantage of years of application in the construction industry. The cumbersome *inter vivos* arbitration clauses found in the 1987 AIA documents have been avoided.]

7.2 Equitable Adjustment

Whenever an equitable adjustment in the contract price or time is provided for under the contract documents, or if Client has notified Contractor of a change, Contractor shall submit to Client within a reasonable time a detailed estimate with supporting calculations and pricing, along with any adjustments in the schedule reflecting any changes in the contract price and time. Pricing shall be in accordance with the pricing structure of this contract; however, to the extent that such pricing is inapplicable, the cost of the change or the amount of the adjustment shall be determined on the basis of cost to Contractor (except in the case of Contractor-owned equipment rates) plus reasonable amounts for overhead and profit.

---

[5] Southwest Concrete Prods. v. Gosh Constr. Corp., 51 Cal. 3d 701, 798 P.2d 1247 (1990).

7.3 Procedure

Contractor shall not perform changes in the work in accordance with paragraphs 7.1 and 7.2 until Client has approved in writing the changes in the contract price and time, except as set forth in paragraph 7.4 below. Upon receiving such written approval from Client, Contractor shall diligently perform the change in strict accordance with this contract.

7.4 Authorization

Notwithstanding paragraph 7.3, Client may expressly authorize Contractor in writing to perform the change prior to approval of price and schedule adjustments by Client. Contractor shall not suspend performance of this contract during the review and negotiation of any change, except as may be directed by Client, as long as the change is a reasonably foreseeable alteration of the work originally contemplated by the contract documents. In the event Client and Contractor are unable to reach agreement on changes in the contract price and time, the matter shall be resolved in accordance with Article 8.

ARTICLE 8. CLAIMS

8.1 Notice

Subject to the provisions of Article 7, Contractor shall provide Client with written notice, within a reasonable time after the occurrence of any event that Contractor believes may instigate a claim for an equitable adjustment in the contract price or time. Within a reasonable time after such an event, Contractor shall supply Client with a statement supporting such claim, which statement shall include a detailed estimate of the change in the contract price and time. If requested by Client in writing, Contractor shall provide reasonable documentation to substantiate its claim. Contractor agrees to continue performance of the work during the time any claim is pending, as long as the work requested is a reasonably foreseeable addition to the work originally contemplated in the contract documents, and Client expeditiously moves to resolve pricing of the claim. If no satisfactory resolution is achieved within 30 days, Contractor shall have the right to suspend work. Client shall not be bound to any adjustments in the contract price or time unless expressly agreed to by Client in writing. No claim shall be allowed if asserted after final payment under this contract.

[The parties might prefer to set a specific time (for example, 20 days) for written notice and supporting statement. Under this clause, the Contractor need continue working for only 30 days pending resolution of the claim.]

8.2 Time

Claims by either party for added time and damages due to injury or damage to person or property, or for delay, interference, suspension, or interruption of work, or for any other damage, shall be made in writing to the other party within 20 days of the occurrence of such event or the first observance of such cause for damage.

ARTICLE 9. OWNERSHIP, USE, AND MAINTENANCE OF DOCUMENTS

All original boring logs, field data, laboratory test data, portions of samples, calculations, estimates, and other documents prepared by Contractor as instruments of service shall remain the property of Contractor. Contractor retains the right of ownership with respect to any patentable or copyrightable concepts arising from its services.

Client agrees that all reports and other work furnished to Client or its agents that are not paid for will be returned upon demand and will not be used by Client for any purpose whatsoever. Reuse of any materials described above by Client on extensions of this project or on any other project without Contractor's written authorization shall be at Client's risk, and Client agrees to indemnify and hold harmless Contractor from all claims, damages, and expenses, including attorneys' fees, arising out of such unauthorized reuse. Any such verification or adaptation will entitle Contractor to further compensation at rates to be agreed upon by Client and Contractor. Contractor shall maintain for Client all such materials in kind or on microfilm, except for samples, for no less than three years after completion of its services. Client shall specify in advance, in writing, and be charged for all arrangements for special or extended-period maintenance of such materials by Contractor.

[For further protection of the parties, use of the documents may be limited, for example:

"Materials produced hereunder shall not be utilized in connection with any prospectuses, proxy solicitations, loan documents, purchase/sale transactions, or any other publications, correspondence, or communication that might effect any investment decisions."]

ARTICLE 10. CONFIDENTIALITY

[This clause, or something similar, is virtually indispensable.]

10.1 Confidential Information

Confidential information means all technical, economic, financial, marketing, or other information that has not been published or is not otherwise available to members of the public, and includes, without limitation, trade secrets, proprietary information, customer lists, scientific, technical, and business studies, analyses, processes, methods, procedures, and policies. Contractor agrees that the information it receives, and the documentation that has been provided to it, will not be revealed to third parties. In the event that either party discloses confidential information to the other party in connection with this Agreement (excluding Contractor's work product delivered to Client or others hereunder), the party receiving such confidential information agrees to hold as confidential and to not disclose to third parties the confidential information for a period of 10 years from the date of disclosure. These restrictions shall not apply to information that:

a.   the parties had in their possession prior to disclosure
b.   becomes public knowledge through no fault of the receiving party
c.   the receiving party lawfully acquires from a party not under obligation of confidentiality to the other party
d.   is independently developed by the receiving party.

Contractor's obligation of confidentiality shall not apply to disclosures compelled by law, an order of Court, or a subpoena, in which event Contractor shall immediately inform Client of the circumstances requiring said disclosure and shall avoid disclosing to the maximum extent available under law.

10.2 Confidentiality Agreements

Contractor, upon Client's request, shall have employees, agents, and subcontractors sign reasonable and customary confidentiality agreements furnished by Client.

10.3 Use of Client Name

Client agrees that Contractor may use and publish Client's name and a general description of the services provided to Client by Contractor, in describing Contractor's experience and qualifications to other clients or potential clients.

ARTICLE 11. PROFESSIONAL RESPONSIBILITY

Contractor represents that its services shall be performed, within the limits prescribed by Client, in a manner consistent with the level of care and skill ordinarily exercised by other members of the profession currently practicing under similar circumstances. No other representations to Client, express or implied, and no warranty or guarantee is included or intended in this Agreement, or in any report, opinion, document, or otherwise. Contractor shall not be responsible for the interpretation by others of the information developed by Contractor.

ARTICLE 12. COMPLIANCE WITH LAW

Contractor and Client will use reasonable care to comply with applicable laws in effect at the time the services are performed hereunder, which to the best of their knowledge, information, and belief, apply to their respective obligations under this Agreement.

Any provisions of this Agreement held in violation of any law or ordinance shall be deemed stricken, and all remaining provisions shall continue valid and binding upon the parties. Contractor and Client shall attempt in good faith to replace any invalid or unenforceable provisions of this Agreement with provisions that are valid and enforceable and that come as close as possible to expressing the intention of the original provisions.

Client shall pay for any reasonable charges on written change orders from Contractor for services, modifications, or additions to facilities or equipment required on the part of Contractor to comply with laws or regulations that become effective after the execution of this Agreement, and any change order to this Agreement.

ARTICLE 13. LIMITATIONS OF LIABILITY

The liability of Contractor, its agents, employees, and subcontractors, for Client's claims of loss, injury, death, or damage, including, without limitation, Client's claims of contribution and indemnification with respect to third-party claims, shall not exceed in the aggregate under this Agreement, unless specifically provided in the scope of service or a change order:

1. The total sum of $1,000,000 for claims or liability arising out of:
   a. any environmental pollution or contamination, including, without limitation, any actual or threatened release of toxic, irritant, pollutant, or waste gases, liquids, or solid materials;
   b. professional negligence, including errors, omissions or other professional acts, and including unintentional breach of contract;
2. The total sum of $1,000,000 for injury, loss, or damage caused by negligence, or other causes for which Contractor has any legal liability, other than as described in categories 1.a and 1.b above.

In no event shall either Contractor or Client be liable for consequential damages, including, without limitation, loss of use or loss of profits, incurred by one another or their subsidiaries or successors, regardless of whether such claim is based on alleged breach of contract, willful misconduct, or negligent act or omission, whether professional or nonprofessional, of either the parties or their employees, agents, or subcontractors.

The limit of $1,000,000 for purposes of subparts 1.a and 1.b above may be increased upon receipt of Client's written request, prior to entering this Agreement, and agreement of Client to pay an additional percentage fee for any increase in the limit.

[This limitation is designed to blend into the insurance provisions of Article 15. The limitation can be expressed in a number of ways. It may be limited to the contract value, a deductible may be provided, or a copayment may be required after a certain threshold is achieved.]

ARTICLE 14. INDEMNIFICATION

[This rather tortured language could be avoided in a state such as California, where under certain circumstances, the remediation contractor may be totally indemnified for performance of remediation services.[6]]

Client acknowledges that Contractor has played no part in the creation of any hazardous waste, pollution sources, nuisance, or chemical or industrial disposal problem, if any, which may exist, and that Contractor has been retained for the sole purpose of assisting Client in assessing any problem that may exist and in formulating a mitigation program, if such is within the scope of service that Contractor has assumed. The responsibility for making any disclosures or reports to any third party and for taking of corrective, remedial, or mitigative action shall be solely that of Client.

Subject to the last paragraph of this section, and only to the extent consistent with the provisions of Section 13 hereof, if any claim is brought against either Contractor or Client by any third party, relating in whole or in part to the

---

[6] *See* Cal. Civ. Code § 2782.6.

negligence or willful misconduct of Contractor or Client, each party shall indemnify the other against any loss or judgment, to the extent that such loss or judgment is caused by that party's negligence or willful misconduct, on a comparative negligence basis. For these purposes, *negligence* shall be deemed to include both negligent acts and omissions, or willful misconduct, and the negligence of a party shall be deemed to include the respective negligence of its officers, directors, employees, agents, contractors, subcontractors, or representatives.

Contractor shall not be responsible for any liability, damage, loss, cost, or expense, real or alleged, arising from Contractor's performance, whether sole negligence or not, relating to shoring or non-shoring of excavations. Client shall retain outside geotechnical counsel to determine the requirement or non-requirement of shoring.

[This provision may be removed where the contractor takes on this responsibility under its scope of work or as a health and safety issue.]

If any claim is brought against Contractor by any third party relating to services under this Agreement, unless it is proven that Contractor was guilty of negligence or willful misconduct in connection with its services, Client shall indemnify Contractor for all claims, liabilities, loss, legal fees, consulting fees, and other costs of defense reasonably incurred by Contractor. Pending a determination as to negligence or willful misconduct of Contractor, Contractor's legal fees, consulting fees, and other defense costs in the third-party action shall be paid as incurred—50 percent by Contractor and 50 percent by Client.

In addition to the foregoing, and to the fullest extent permitted by law, Client shall indemnify and hold harmless Contractor, its agents, employees, and subcontractors, for all liability arising from the risks described in Article 11 of this Agreement in excess of the limits of liability set forth therein.

ARTICLE 15. INSURANCE AND BONDS

15.1 Insurance

Contractor and Client agree to maintain statutory workers' compensation, commercial general liability (CGL), and automobile liability insurance coverage in the sum of not less than $1,000,000 per occurrence ($1,000,000 aggregate). Contractor further agrees to maintain professional liability and pollution liability insurance in the sum of not less than $1,000,000 annual aggregate, all of which is on a claims-made basis, as long as it is reasonably available under standard policies at rates comparable to those currently in effect.

15.2 Surety Bonds

Client shall have the right, prior to the execution of the contract, to require Contractor to furnish bonds executed by one or more financially responsible sureties, and in such form as Client may reasonably prescribe, covering the faithful performance of the contract and payment of all obligations under the contract. If such bonds are required prior to the receipt of bids, the premium shall be paid by Contractor; if bonds are required subsequent to such receipt, the premium shall be paid by Client.

[Surety bonds are a good idea when a small contractor is undertaking a large job. Practically speaking, the bonding may not be available. See **Chapter 3** of the text.]

ARTICLE 16. DELAYS

In the event that Contractor's work performance is interrupted by factors outside of its control (including a suspension of work pursuant to Article 17), Contractor shall be equitably compensated for the additional labor, equipment, and other delay costs (in accordance with Contractor's current schedule of fees) associated with maintaining its work force and equipment during the interruption, or at the option of Client, for such similar charges that are incurred by Contractor for demobilization and subsequent remobilization. In no event shall Contractor be required to maintain a field force on standby status in the field for a period in excess of three calendar days.

Except for the foregoing provision, neither party shall hold the other responsible for damages or delays in performance caused by force majeure, acts of God, or other events beyond the control of the other party, and that could not have been reasonably foreseen or prevented. For this purpose, such acts or events shall include unusual weather affecting performance of services, floods, epidemics, war, riots, strikes, lockouts or other industrial disturbances, protest demonstrations, unanticipated site conditions, and inability, with reasonable diligence, to supply personnel, equipment, or material to the project. Should such acts or events occur, both parties shall use their best efforts to overcome the difficulties and to resume as soon as reasonably possible the normal pursuit of the services under the applicable change order. Delays within the scope of this section that cumulatively exceed 30 days shall, at the option of either party, make the applicable change order subject to termination for convenience or to renegotiation.

[Article 17 gives the Client a right to suspend upon 10 days' notice. This provision merely provides that Client must pay for suspension.]

ARTICLE 17. SUSPENSION OF WORK

Client may, at any time, with 10 days' written notice, suspend further performance by Contractor. The notice shall specify the date, cause, and anticipated duration of the suspension. If payments of invoices by Client are not made when due, Contractor may, upon 10 days' written notice, suspend further performance until such payment is restored to a current basis. Suspension for any reason exceeding 30 days shall, at the option of Contractor, permit Contractor to terminate. All suspensions shall extend the time schedule for performance on a day-for-day basis unless Contractor claims added time for inefficiency, demobilization, or similar issues. Contractor shall be paid for services performed, charges made prior to the suspension date, and any damages arising as a result of the suspension.

ARTICLE 18. TERMINATION

18.1 Insolvency/Failure to Pay Subcontractors

Should Client become insolvent or commit a material breach or default under the contract, including, but not limited to, failure to pay timely undisputed sums due to

Contractor, and fail to act in good faith to remedy the same within 10 days after notice from Contractor, Contractor may terminate this contract. Contractor shall be entitled to all damages incurred as a result of such termination.

[Before implementing this option, the Client should obtain a current statement of costs to avoid post-termination disputes.]

18.2 Failure to Man the Job

Should Contractor refuse or neglect to supply a sufficient number of properly skilled workers, tools, or material within Contractor's control, or should Contractor commit a substantial breach of this contract and fail to act in good faith to remedy such breach within 10 days after written demand by Client, Client may terminate this contract. Upon any such termination, Contractor shall be compensated for all costs incurred for that portion of the work already performed. Contractor shall be liable for any costs incurred by Client in completing the contract in excess of the difference between the contract price and the amount paid to Contractor to the date of termination.

18.3 For Convenience

Client reserves the right to terminate the work at its convenience, upon notice in writing to the Contractor. In such event, Contractor shall be paid its actual costs for that portion of the work performed to the date of termination, and for all costs of termination, including demobilization and any termination charges by vendors and subcontractors, plus 15 percent of all such costs for overhead and profit. If, for any reason, Client elects to resume the work within six months of the actual date of cessation of work, using another contractor, Contractor shall be entitled to payment of its profits for performance of all of the work.

[A troublesome clause often found in government contracts. Viewed by clients as a panacea for a job gone bad, invocation of its terms often creates further problems. Before implementing the clause, the Client should obtain a current statement of costs to avoid post-termination disputes.]

ARTICLE 19. EXTENSIONS OF TIME

19.1 Reasons

The contract time shall be extended as necessary to compensate for delay in the progress of the work resulting from changes in the work, suspension of the work in whole or in part by Client, any other act or omission by Client or its employees, agents, or representatives contrary to the provisions of the contract, or by another contractor employed by Client, or any other cause that could not have been reasonably foreseen or is beyond the control of Contractor, its subcontractors or suppliers, and is not the result of their sole fault or sole negligence, including, but not restricted to, acts of any government authority, public enemy, fire, unusual delay in transportation, abnormal weather conditions, or labor disputes.

19.2 Notice

Contractor shall give notice to Client of any delay within a reasonable time after the occurrence or commencement of a cause of delay. Failure to give notice of any delay within a reasonable time shall constitute a waiver by Contractor of any claim for extension of the contract time resulting from that cause of delay. Contractor's notice shall include an estimate of the probable effect of the cause of delay on progress of the work.

[The parties might prefer a set period of time for notice (for example, 20 days).]

ARTICLE 20. INSOLVENCY

If an order for relief is entered against Client, or Client makes an assignment for the benefit of creditors, or becomes insolvent, or is not generally paying its debts as they mature, or if Contractor deems itself insecure because it has a good faith belief that the prospect of payment or performance by Client is impaired, or if the work by Contractor is suspended, abandoned, or terminated by Client for any reason other than a substantial breach by Contractor (in which event the normal legal consequences shall apply), or if Client fails to pay Contractor promptly (in any event no later than 10 days after an invoice is tendered), Contractor shall have the right to terminate the Agreement for cause pursuant to Article 17 above. Contractor shall be paid the reasonable value of all work theretofore performed, together with termination expenses, as stated in Article 17 above. In determining reasonable value under this Article, the contract price shall be deemed reasonable.

ARTICLE 21. DISPUTE RESOLUTION

All disputes, claims, and demands not resolved by the parties shall be subject to arbitration in accordance with the commercial arbitration rules of the American Arbitration Association. Discovery will be permitted in accordance with the laws of the state where the dispute arose. The arbitration shall take place in the county where the project is located.

[This is a generic arbitration clause. It provides for discovery. The site selected is the location of the project, because the arbitrators may often have to rule on the validity of liens filed on the project. The clause should be tailored to meet the specific state law requirements. The parties may choose to delete the clause altogether.]

ARTICLE 22. SUCCESSORS

This Agreement shall inure to the benefit of, and shall be binding upon, the successors, assigns, heirs, administrators, executors, and legal representatives of the respective parties hereto. This Agreement shall not create any rights or benefits to parties other than Client and Contractor.

ARTICLE 23. ADDRESSES FOR NOTICES

Whenever under the terms of or in connection with this Agreement it is necessary, appropriate, or desirable for Client or Contractor to give notice to one another, such notice may be given by registered or certified mail, with first-class postage prepaid, addressed to Client or Contractor, as the case may be, at the respective addresses as given at the end of this document. Either Client or Contractor may at any time designate a new or different address to which notices are sent, which notice of a new or different address shall be given as provided herein. Any notice shall be effective as of the time the same is personally delivered, or if notice is sent by mail, as of a date two business days after the same is properly deposited in the United States mail.

ARTICLE 24. INTEGRATED AGREEMENT

This Agreement constitutes a final and complete repository of the Agreement between Contractor and Client. It supersedes all prior or contemporaneous communications, or agreements, whether oral or written, relating to the subject matter of this Agreement. Modifications (change orders) of this Agreement shall not be binding unless made in writing and signed by an authorized representative of each party.

ARTICLE 25. INTERPRETATION

It is expressly understood and agreed that this Agreement is not to be construed either for or against either Client or Contractor, that technical words, phrases, and provisions are to be given their technical and legal significance and effect, and that this Agreement is to be construed fairly, reasonably, and impartially as between Client and Contractor.

ARTICLE 26. ARTICLE HEADINGS

Article headings are not a part of this Agreement, are contained herein for convenience only, and shall not be considered in connection with the construction or interpretation of this Agreement.

ARTICLE 27. TIME BAR TO LEGAL ACTION

All legal actions by either party against the other for breach of this Agreement, or any addendum or change order, or for the failure to perform in accordance with the applicable standard of care, however determined, that is essentially based on such breach or failure, shall be barred two years from the time that claimant knew or should have known of its claim, but, in any event, not later than four years from the substantial completion of Contractor's services.

[These contractual statutes of limitation reflect California law, but probably would be inoperative for latent defect clauses, which in California are only subject to a 10-year statute of repose,[7] which itself is inapplicable to personal injury actions. It may be that such a time bar would be struck down as a violation of public policy.]

ARTICLE 28. NOTICES, SIGNATURES, AND AUTHORIZED REPRESENTATIVES

Each of the individuals signing this Agreement warrants that he or she possesses authority to bind the party for which he or she purports to act. The following

---

[7] Cal. Civ. Proc. Code § 337.15.

signatories for the signing of this Agreement are the authorized representatives of Client and Contractor for the execution of this Agreement and its Addendum I, Scope of Services. Each change order shall set forth the name and address of the respective authorized representatives of the parties for the administration of that change order. Any information or notices required or permitted under this Agreement or any change order shall be deemed to have been sufficiently given if delivered either personally or by mail to the undersigned representative or any other authorized representative identified in the applicable change order.

ARTICLE 29. AUDIT

Client may audit and inspect Contractor's records and accounts for a period of 12 months following the completion of the work described in this Agreement. The audit shall cover only direct reimbursable costs. Contractor shall not have to provide data regarding any costs covered by the fee, fixed rates, or costs that are expressed as percentages of others.

[The audit is for the Client's protection. The limitation or scope of the audit is for the Contractor's protection.]

IN WITNESS WHEREOF, the parties have caused this Agreement to be executed by their duly authorized representatives, as follows:

Client   Contractor

_____   _____
Signature   Signature

_____   _____
Typed Name   Typed Name

_____   _____
Title   Title

_____   _____
Date of Signature   Date of Signature

APPENDIX E

SAMPLE SITE SAFETY PLAN[1]

I.   SITE DESCRIPTION

II.   PROJECT OBJECTIVES SCOPE

III.   ON-SITE ORGANIZATION AND COORDINATION

IV.   GOVERNMENT AGENCIES: PERMITS AND CONTACT PERSONS

V.   HAZARDOUS SUBSTANCES/CHEMICAL

VI.   PERSONAL PROTECTIVE EQUIPMENT AND CLOTHING

VII. DECONTAMINATION PROCEDURES

EMERGENCY PROCEDURES

I.   ON-SITE EMERGENCY PERSONNEL

II.   COMMUNICATION PROCEDURES

III.   EMERGENCY MEDICAL CARE

IV.   EMERGENCY PROCEDURES

I. SITE DESCRIPTION

Address: [Include description of site boundaries.]

Geological/Topological Conditions: [Note wetlands, ground conditions, type of soil/rocks; note whether survey map exists, if appropriate.] _____

_____

_____

Weather Conditions That Could Pose Risks: [Is site in a flood plain; is there stormwater runoff?] _____

_____

_____

Hazards: [Are there underground tanks or utilities, building hazards, hazardous substances/chemicals, waste storage?] _____

_____

_____

---

[1] This Sample Site Safety Plan is meant to be used as a guide for Site Safety Plans in remediation projects. Different projects and different locales present different requirements regarding the contents of such a plan. This sample plan is not all-inclusive of current regulations, federal or state, and should not be used without adaptation for the particular project's requirements.

Surrounding Population: [List sensitive populations, such as hospitals, schools, farms.] _____

_____

_____

Location of Charts, Maps & Surveys: _____

_____

_____

Additional Information: _____

_____

_____

II.   PROJECT OBJECTIVES SCOPE [Describe phases of the remediation project, including tasks to be accomplished; for example, identify contaminated soil, monitor conditions.]

Phase 1: RI/FS.

Tasks: _____

_____

_____

Phase 2: Excavation

Tasks: _____

_____

_____

III. ON-SITE ORGANIZATION AND COORDINATION

Site Safety Officer: _____
   Responsibilities: _____
Project Team Leader/Manager: _____
   Responsibilities: _____
Scientific Advisor: _____
   Responsibilities: _____
Emergency Response Leader: _____
   Responsibilities: _____
Public Information Officer: _____
   Responsibilities: _____
Security Officer: _____
   Responsibilities: _____

Recordkeeper: _____

   Responsibilities: _____

Financial Officer: _____

   Responsibilities: _____

[**Comment.** To ensure the program is effective, it is important that *specific* personnel be designated and trained to carry out well-defined functions in the safety program. In smaller projects, one person may carry out more than one job function. A backup person for each role should also be trained and informed. To guard against civil and criminal liability, cross-checking functions to detect errors or intentional violations should be formally built into this personnel organization.]

IV. GOVERNMENT AGENCIES: PERMITS AND CONTACT PERSONS

   Federal Agency: [EPA, OSHA] _____

      Address: _____ Contact: _____

      Phone: _____ Title: _____
      Authority [to approve permit/variance/aspect of compliance]: _____

      Permit [mobile service, treatment facility, stormwater]: _____

      Application Number: _____

      Application Date: _____

      Obtained: _____

      Expiration Date: _____

   State Agency: _____

V. HAZARDOUS SUBSTANCES/CHEMICALS

Substance	*Characteristics*	*Precautions*
_____	_____	_____
_____	_____	_____

[**Comment.** Material safety data sheets for chemical or other substance(s) giving characteristics, medical hazards, and emergency information regarding medical treatment should be obtained from distributors and distilled into the plan. Emergency measures are given in Section II of the Emergency Procedures part of this plan.]

VI. PERSONAL PROTECTIVE EQUIPMENT AND CLOTHING

Based on evaluation of potential hazards, the following equipment for personal protection has been designated for the applicable work areas or tasks:

Location	Job Function	Equipment
Exclusion Zone [Refers to sealed-off area, exceeding acceptable levels of contamination.] Contamination Zone	_____ _____ _____ _____ _____ _____ _____	[such as respirators] _____ _____ _____ _____ _____
Reduction Zone [Means contamination levels are kept below a certain level.]	_____ _____ _____ _____	_____ _____ _____ _____

The following protective clothing materials are required for the listed substances:

Substance	Clothing Type
[Include chemical name, for example, asbestos, DBS, tyrolene.]	[These can range from ordinary cotton overalls to special materials such as Viton.]
_____	_____

VII. DECONTAMINATION PROCEDURES

Personnel and equipment leaving the exclusion zone (or defined area of site) shall be thoroughly decontaminated. The decontamination protocol below shall be used with the following site areas/tasks or as directed by [safety officer].

_____

_____

_____

Decontamination equipment required: _____

_____

_____

Decontamination process required: _____

_____

_____

_____

[Normally detergent and water] will be used as the decontamination solution.

Disposal of decontamination products: _____

_____

_____

Off-site information required: [Note instructions that must be given for any equipment/clothing to be cleaned off-site.] _____

_____

_____

[**Comment.** Decontamination procedures may well vary by task or area.]

EMERGENCY PROCEDURES

I. ON-SITE EMERGENCY PERSONNEL

In case of emergency, the teams designated below will perform the following tasks:

Project Team Leader ____[name]____ _____[function]_____

_____

_____

Work Party #1 _____ _____

_____

_____

Work Party #2 _____ _____

_____

_____

Rescue Team _____ _____

_____

_____

Decontamination Team _____ _____

_____

_____

II. COMMUNICATION PROCEDURES

Radio:

Personnel in the exclusion zone should remain in constant radio communication or within sight of the project team leader. Any failure of radio communication requires an evaluation of whether personnel should leave the exclusion zone.

Signals:

[such as horn blast, or siren] is the emergency signal to indicate that an emergency has occurred. All personnel, except members of an Emergency Team, should leave the [exclusion zone or site]. The following standard hand signals will be used in case of failure of radio communications:

1. *Hand gripping throat:* Problem breathing.
2. *Hands on top of head:* Need assistance.

3. *Thumbs up:* OK, I am all right, I understand.
4. *Thumbs down:* No, negative.

III. EMERGENCY MEDICAL CARE
Qualified Emergency Medical Personnel On-site:

_____

_____

Emergency Medical Facility:
   Name: _____
   Address: _____
   Phone: _____

Local Ambulance Service: _____
   Phone: _____
   Response time is _____ minutes.

First-aid equipment is available on-site at the following locations:
   First-aid kit   _____
   Emergency eye wash   _____
   Emergency shower   _____
   (Other)   _____

Emergency medical information for on-site hazardous substances present:

Substance	*Exposure Symptoms*	*First-aid Instruction*
_____	_____	_____
_____	_____	_____
_____	_____	_____

Emergency Phone Numbers:

Police _____

Fire _____

NRC _____

Public Health Advisor _____

IV. EMERGENCY PROCEDURES
Emergency Response:
Hazardous Releases/Spills:

Substance	*Procedure*	*Special Precautions*
_____	_____	_____
_____	_____	_____

Fire/Explosion:

Area   *Procedure*

_____   _____

_____   _____

Equipment Failure:

Type   *Procedure*

[for example, ventilation   [for example, shutdown of equipment, utility

system, mobile incinerator,   lines, or outlets, or use of alternative equipment

vapor extraction   such as respirators]

procedure]   _____

[**Comment.**   Emergency procedure information is clearly very project-specific. Site hazards, the surrounding population, and site-geology must be considered. Complex emergency response procedures must be developed for projects involving mixtures of hazardous substances. Employees must, of course, be able to understand and follow these procedures. A simple approach is to establish two or three classes of responses that apply to groups of situations.]

Personnel Protection Equipment Failure:

Monitoring:

The following environmental monitoring instruments shall be used in [areas] or on [personnel] at the [specified intervals] or if the following conditions occur:

Monitoring Instruments   *Area*   *Times*

_____   _____   _____

_____   _____   _____

[Daily] records of monitoring results should be signed by _____, and maintained for [time period].

Notification:

The following is a list of agencies that must be notified if a release, spill, or other event occurs:

Event	*Reporting Threshold*	*Agency*	*Phone #*	*Form/Info*	*Time*
	[quantity, elements at risk]			[oral/written/ fax, level of detail]	

EPA FIT AND REM OFFICES

I. FIT Contract: Zone I (EPA Regions I–IV)

A. Zone Program Management Office

NUS Corporation
1300 North 17th Street
Suite 1320
Arlington, VA 22209
Subcontract Manager: Norman
    Howard

B. FIT Regional Offices

1. Region I
   NUS Corporation
   19 Crosby Drive
   Bedford, MA 01730
   (617) 275-2970
   Manager: Robert Juback

2. Region II
   NUS Corporation
   1090 King George's Post Road
   Suite 1103
   Edison, NJ 08837
   (201) 225-6160
   Manager: Ronald Naman

3. Region III
   NUS Corporation
   999 West Valley Road
   Wayne, PA 19087
   (215) 687-9510
   Manager: Garth Glenn

4. Region IV
   NUS Corporation
   1927 Lakeside Parkway
   Suite 614
   Tucker, GA 30084
   (404) 938-7710
   Manager: Phil Blackwell

II. FIT Contract: Zone II (EPA Regions V–X)

A. Zone Program Management Office

Ecology & Environment, Inc.
    (E&E)
1700 North Moore Street
Arlington, VA 22209
(703) 522-6065
Zone Program Manager: Henry
    Van Cleave
Subcontract Manager: Lewis A.
    Welzel

B. **FIT Regional Offices**

1. Region V
   Ecology & Environment, Inc. (E&E)
   111 West Jackson Boulevard
   Chicago, IL 60604
   (312) 663-9415
   Manager: Jerome Oskvarek

2. Region VI
   Ecology & Environment, Inc.
     (E&E)
   1509 Main Street
   Suite 1400
   Dallas, TX 75201
   (214) 742-4521
   Manager: K. Malone

3. Region VII
   Ecology & Environment, Inc.
     (E&E)
   6405 Metcalf Street
   Cloverleaf Building, #3
   Suite 404
   Overland Park, KS 66202
   (913) 432-9961
   Manager: Phillip C. Dula

4. Region VIII
   Ecology & Environment, Inc.
     (E&E)
   1776 South Jackson Street
   Suite 200
   Denver, CO 80210
   (303) 757-4948
   Manager: John A. Duwaldt

5. Region IX
   Ecology & Environment, Inc.
     (E&E)
   160 Spear Street
   San Francisco, CA 94105
   (415) 777-2811
   Manager: Patricia Cook

6. Region X
   Ecology & Environment, Inc.
     (E&E)
   101 Yesler Way
   6th Floor
   Seattle, WA 98104
   (206) 624-9537
   Manager: Andy Hafferty

ERCS CONTRACTORS

Zone Program Management Offices

Zone 1:
O.H. Materials Company
P.O. Box 551
Findlay, OH 45839
Contact: Robert Panning
(419) 423-3526

Zone 2:
O.H. Materials Company
P.O. Box 551
Findlay, OH 45839
Contact: Marsha Robinson
(419) 423-3526

Zone 3:
PEI Associates, Inc.
11499 Chester Road
Cincinnati, OH 45246
Contact: Doug Wehner
(513) 782-4700

Zone 4:
Riedel Environmental Services
4611 North Channel Avenue
Portland, OR 97217
Contact: Dick Heymann
(800) 334-0004

Regional ERCS Contractors

A. Region II

1. S&D Environmental Services,
   Inc.
   2 Gourmet Lane
   Edison, NJ 08837
   Contact: Edward McCracken
   (201) 549-8778

2. Haztech, Inc.
   5240 Panola Industrial
      Boulevard
   Decatur, GA 30035
   Contact: Bob Carton
   (404) 593-3803

B. Region III

1. Guardian Environmental
      Services, Inc.
   1230 Porter Road
   Bear, DE 19701
   Contact: Joseph Cunane
   (302) 834-1000

2. Environmental Health, Research
      & Testing Inc.
   2414 Regency Road
   Lexington, KY 40503
   Contact: Paul Sabharwal
   (606) 276-1436

3. Environmental Technology, Inc.
   P.O. Box 1236
   Richmond, VA 23209
   Contact: Richard Guilford
   (804) 358-5400

C. Region IV

1. Ensite, Inc.
   5119 South Royal Atlanta
      Drive
   Tucker, GA 30084
   Contact: Chris Leggett
   (404) 934-1180

2. Haztech, Inc.
   5240 Panola Industrial
      Boulevard
   Decatur, GA 30035
   Contact: Tim Morrow
   (404) 981-9332

3. O.H. Materials, Inc.
   1000 Holcomb Woods Parkway
   Suite 112
   Roswell, GA 30076
   Contact: Mark Rigatti
   (404) 641-1066

D. Region V

1. MAECORP
   17450 South Holsted Street
   Homewood, IL 60430
   Contact: Chris Rice
   (312) 957-7600

ARCS CONTRACTORS

Region I

1. Arthur D. Little, Inc.
   Acorn Park
   Cambridge, MA 02140-2390
   Contact: Ms. Renee Wong
   (617) 864-5770

2. NUS Corporation
   187 Ballard Vale Street
   Wilmington, MA 01887
   Contact: Thomas J. Parkes
   (508) 658-7889

3. Roy F. Weston, Inc.
   1 Van de Graff Drive
   Burlington, MA 01803
   Contact: Rick Keller
   (617) 229-2050

4. Ebasco Services, Inc.
   211 Congress Street
   Boston, MA 02110
   Contact: Luis Seijdo
   (617) 451-1201

5. TRC Companies, Inc.
   213 Burlington Road
   Bedford, MA 01730
   Contact: John Blake
   (617) 275-9000

6. CDM Federal Programs
   Corporation
   98 North Washington Street
   Suite 200
   Boston, MA 02114
   Contact: Mr. Fred Babin
   (617) 742-2659

7. Metcalf and Eddy, Inc.
   10 Harvard Mill Square
   Wakefield, MA 01880
   Contact: William J. Farino
   (617) 246-5200

Region II

1. Ebasco Services, Inc.
   160 Chubb Avenue
   Lyndhurst, NJ 07071
   Contact: Mr. D. Sachdev
   (201) 460-6434

2. ICF Technology, Inc.
   379 Thornall Street
   5th Floor
   Edison, NJ 08837-0001
   Contact: William Colvin
   (201) 603-3755
   John Bachmann
   (212) 264-2702

3. CDM Federal Programs
   Corporation
   40 Rector Street
   New York, NY 10006
   Contact: Charles W. Robinson
   (212) 693-0370

4. TAMS
   655 Third Avenue
   New York, NY 10067
   Contact: Brian Styler
   (212) 867-1777

5. Roy F. Weston, Inc.
   355 Main Street
   Armonk, NY 10504
   Contact: Thomas Stevenson
   (913) 273-9840

6. Malcolm Pirnie, Inc.
   2 Corporate Park Drive
   Box 751
   White Plains, NY 10602
   Contact: Ralph Sarnelli
   (914) 694-2100

Region III

1. Black & Veatch, Inc.
   Public Ledger Building
   Suite 272
   Philadelphia, PA 19106
   Contact: David Wright
   (215) 627-1443

2. CH2M Hill, Mid-Atlantic
   Office
   P.O. Box 4400
   Reston, VA 22090
   Contact: Bob Dagostaro
   (703) 471-1441

3. Ecology & Environment, Inc.
   1528 Walnut Street
   Suite 1603
   Philadelphia, PA 19102
   Contact: Mr. Joseph Pearson
   (215) 875-7370

4. NUS Corporation
   One Devon Square
   Suite 222
   724 West Lancaster Avenue
   Wayne, PA 19087
   Headquarters:
   910 Clopper Road
   Gaithersburg, MD 20878
   Contact: Robert E. Stecik, Jr.
   (215) 971-0900

5. Tetra Technologies, Inc.
   P.O. Box 675
   Newark, DE 19711
   Headquarters:
   630 North Rosemead Boulevard
   Pasadena, CA 91107-2190
   Contact: Dr. Carl Su
   (302) 738-7551

Region IV

1. CDM Federal Programs
   Corporation
   2100 River Edge Parkway
   Suite 400
   Atlanta, GA 30328

   Contact: Richard C. Johnson
   (404) 952-8643
   Abe Dunning
   (404) 952-7393

2. Bechtel Environmental, Inc.
   P.O. Box 350
   800 Oak Ridge Turnpike
   Oak Ridge, TN 37830
   Contact: G. Phillip Crotwell
   (615) 482-0440

3. Ebasco Services Incorporated
   145 Technology Park
   Norcross, GA 30092-2979
   Contact: David Knapp
   (404) 662-2378

4. CH2M Hill, SE
   229 Peachtree Street, NE
   Suite 300
   Atlanta, GA 30303
   Contact: David Ellison
   (404) 523-0300

5. Black & Veatch, Inc.
   Suite 212
   Perimeter Center West
   Atlanta, GA 30338
   Contact: Kendall M. Jacob
   (404) 392-9227

6. Roy F. Weston, Inc.
   6021 Live Oak Parkway
   Norcross, GA 30093
   Contact: Michael Foulke
   (404) 448-0644

Region V

1. Black and Veatch Architects
     and Engineers
   230 West Monroe, Suite 2250
   Chicago, IL 60606
   Contact: William Bruce
   (312) 346-3775

2. CH2M Hill, Inc.
   310 West Wisconsin Avenue
   P.O. Box 2090
   Milwaukee, WI 53201
   Contact: John T. Fleissner
   (414) 272-2426

3. Donohue and Associates
   111 North Canal Street
   Chicago, IL 60606
   Contact: Roman Gau
   (312) 902-7100

4. Ecology & Environment, Inc.
     (E&E)
   111 West Jackson Boulevard
   Chicago, IL 60604
   Contact: Ben Horenziak
   (312) 663-9415

5. PRC Corporation
   233 North Michigan Avenue
   Suite 1621
   Chicago, IL 60601
   Contact: Majid Chaudhry
   (312) 856-8700

6. Roy F. Weston
   3 Hawthorne Parkway
   Suite 400
   Vernon Hills, IL 60001
   Contact: John W. Thorsen
   (708) 918-4000

7. WW Engineering and Science
   5555 Glenwood Hill Parkway
   P.O. Box 874
   Grand Rapids, MI 49588-0874
   Contact: Robert Phillips
   (616) 940-4263

Regions VI, VII, and VIII

1. Jacobs Engineering Group, Inc.
   251 South Lake Avenue
   Pasadena, CA 91101-3603
   Contact: Steve Houser
   (913) 492-9218

2. CH2M Hill Central, Inc.
   6060 South Willow Drive
   Englewood, CO 80111
   Contact: James Schwing
   (303) 771-0900

3. Fluor Daniel, Inc.
   12790 Merit Drive
   Suite 200
   Dallas, TX 75251
   Contact: Mark DeLorimer
   (214) 450-4100

4. Roy F. Weston, Inc.
   5599 San Felipe
   Suite 700
   Houston, TX 77056
   Contact: Calvin Spencer
   (714) 621-1620

5. CDM Federal Programs
   Corporation
   7 Pine Ridge Plaza
   8215 Melrose Drive
   Suite 100
   Lenexa, KS 66214
   Contact: Michael Malloy
   (913) 492-8181

6. Sverdrup Corporation
   801 North Eleventh Street
   St. Louis, MO 63101
   Contact: Arl Altman
   (314) 436-7600

7. Morrison Knudsen
   1120 Lincoln Street
   Suite 1200
   Denver, CO 80203
   Contact: Ed Baker
   (303) 831-8200

8. URS Consultants, Inc.
   5251 DTC Parkway
   Suite 800
   Englewood, CO 80111
   Contact: John Coats
   (303) 796-9700

Regions IX and X

1. Ecology & Environment, Inc.
   (E&E)
   101 Yesler Way
   Suite 600
   Seattle, WA 98104
   Contact: Ronald Karpowitz
   (206) 624-9537

2. CH2M Hill
   6425 Christie Avenue
   Suite 500
   Emeryville, CA 94608
   Contact: Stephen Hahn
   (415) 652-2426

3. Roy F. Weston, Inc.
   201 Elliot Avenue West
   Suite 500
   Seattle, WA 98119
   Contact: Frank Monahan
   (206) 286-6000

4. URS Consultants, Inc.
   2710 Gateway Oaks Drive
   Suite 250
   Sacramento, CA 95934
   Contact: Gary Jandgian
   (916) 929-2346

5. Bechtel Environmental, Inc.
   P.O. Box 3965
   50 Beale Street
   San Francisco, CA 94110
   Contact: Dr. Robert Hughes
   (415) 768-2797

6. ICF Technology, Inc.
   160 Spear Street
   Suite 1380
   San Francisco, CA 94105-1535
   Contact: Earle Krivanic
   (415) 957-0110

STATE HAZARDOUS WASTE MANAGEMENT OFFICIALS

ALABAMA
Daniel E. Cooper, Chief
Special Projects
Alabama Department of Environmental Management
1751 Congressman W.L. Dickinson Drive
Montgomery, AL 36130
(205) 271-7730

ALASKA
David Ditraglia, Program Manager
Waste & Superfund Programs
Division of Environmental Quality
Alaska Department of Environmental Conservation
P.O. Box O
Juneau, AK 99811-1800
(907) 465-2666

ARIZONA
Daniel Marsin, Manager
Waste Compliance Unit
Arizona Department of Environmental Quality
2005 North Central Avenue, Room 400
Phoenix, AZ 85004
(602) 257-2215

ARKANSAS
Doice Hughes
Superfund Section
Hazardous Waste Division
Department of Pollution Control & Ecology
8001 National Drive
P.O. Box 9583
Little Rock, AR 72209
(501) 562-7444

CALIFORNIA
Stan Phillips, Chief
Site Mitigation Section
Toxic Substances Control Division
Department of Health Services
400 P Street
P.O. Box 942732
Sacramento, CA 94234-7320
(916) 324-1789

COLORADO
Daniel Scheppers, Director
Superfund Unit
Hazardous Materials & Waste Management
Department of Health
4210 East 11th Avenue
Denver, CO 80220
(303) 331-4830

CONNECTICUT
Donald Burton
Spills and Emergency Cleanups
Hazardous Materials Management Unit
Department of Environmental Protection
1765 Capital Avenue
Hartford, CT 06106
(203) 566-4633

DELAWARE
Gerald Molchan, Manager
Air & Waste Management
Natural Resources & Environmental Control Department
89 Kings Highway
P.O. Box 1401
Dover, DE 19903
(302) 736-3672

DISTRICT OF COLUMBIA
Angelo Tompros, Chief
Pesticides & Hazardous Waste Management
Department of Consumer & Regulatory Affairs
5010 Overlook Avenue, S.W., Room 114
Washington, D.C. 20032
(202) 783-3194

FLORIDA
John Ruddell, Chief
Bureau of Operations
Department of Environmental Regulation
2600 Blair Stone Road
Tallahassee, FL 32399-2400
(904) 488-0190

GEORGIA
Randall Williams, Program Manager
Site Investigations Program
Land Protection Branch
Industrial & Hazardous Waste Management Program
Department of Natural Resources
205 Butler Street, S.E., Room 1154
Atlanta, GA 30334
(404) 656-7404

HAWAII
Bruce Anderson, Ph.D., Deputy Director
Environmental Health
Environmental Protection & Health Services Division
Department of Health
P.O. Box 3378
Honolulu, HI 96801
(808) 548-4139

IDAHO
John Moeller, Manager
Policy & Standards Section
Hazardous Materials Bureau
Division of Environment
Department of Health & Welfare
450 West State Street
Boise, ID 83720
(208) 334-5879

ILLINOIS
Bharat Mathur, Deputy Manager
Land Pollution Control Division
Illinois Environmental Protection Agency
2200 Churchill Road
P.O. Box 19276
Springfield, IL 62794-9276
(217) 782-6760

INDIANA
Glenn Pratt, Assistant Commissioner
Office of Environmental Response
Department of Environmental Management
5500 West Bradbury Avenue
Indianapolis, IN 46241
(317) 243-5177

IOWA
Morris Preston
Superfund Unit
Air Quality & Solid Waste Bureau
Department of Water, Air & Waste Management
Henry A. Wallace Building
900 East Grand Avenue
Des Moines, IA 50319-0034
(515) 281-4968

KANSAS
Larry Knoche, Chief
Remedial Section
Bureau of Waste Management
Department of Health & Environment
Forbes Field
Topeka, KS 66620
(913) 296-1675

KENTUCKY
Doyle Mills, Supervisor
Unconstructed Sites Section
Division of Waste Management
Department of Environmental Protection
18 Reilly Road
Frankfort, KY 40601
(502) 564-6716

LOUISIANA
William Deville, Administrator
Office of Solid & Hazardous Waste
Inactive & Abandoned Sites Division
Department of Environmental Quality
P.O. Box 44066
Baton Rouge, LA 70804
(504) 342-8925

MAINE
David Sait, Director
Division of Response Services
Bureau of Oil & Hazardous Materials Control
Department of Environmental Protection
State House Station 17
Augusta, ME 04333
(207) 289-2651

MARYLAND
Frank Henderson, Chief
Waste Management Administration
Support Services Division
Department of the Environment
201 West Preston Street
Baltimore, MD 21201
(301) 225-6953

MASSACHUSETTS
James Colman, Director
Office of Incident Response
Division of Hazardous Waste
Department of Environmental Quality Engineering
One Winter Street, 5th Floor
Boston, MA 02108
(617) 292-5648

MICHIGAN
William Bradford, Chief
Superfund Section
Environmental Response Division
Department of Natural Resources
P.O. Box 30028
Knapps Center
Lansing, MI 48909
(517) 335-3393

Claudia Kerbawy, Chief
Site Management Unit
Superfund Section
Environmental Response Division
Department of Natural Resources
P.O. Box 30028
Knapps Center
Lansing, MI 48909
(517) 373-8448

MINNESOTA
Gary Pulford, Chief
Site Response Section
Groundwater & Solid Waste Division
Minnesota Pollution Control Agency
520 Lafayette Road N.
St. Paul, MN 55155
(612) 296-7290

MISSISSIPPI
Caleb Dana, Coordinator
Uncontrolled Sites Section
Bureau of Pollution Control
Hazardous Waste Division
Mississippi Department of Natural Resources
P.O. Box 10385
Jackson, MS 39209
(601) 961-5062

MISSOURI
Keith Schardein, Chief
Superfund Section
Waste Management Program
Department of Natural Resources
P.O. Box 176
205 Jefferson Street
Jefferson City, MO 65102
(314) 751-3176

MONTANA
Victor Anderson
Superfund Program
Solid & Hazardous Waste Bureau
Department of Health & Environmental Sciences
Cogswell Building, Room 201B
Helena, MT 59620
(406) 444-2821

NEBRASKA
Richard Schlenker
Hazardous Waste/Superfund Section
Land Quality Division
Department of Environmental Control
P.O. Box 94877
State House Section
301 Centennial Mall S.
Lincoln, NE 68509-4877
(402) 471-4217

NEVADA
Verne Rosse, Director
Waste Management Section
Division of Environmental Protection
201 South Fall Street, Room 221
Carson City, NV 89710
(702) 885-4670

NEW HAMPSHIRE
Carl Baxter, Administrator
Superfund Site Management Bureau
Waste Management Division
Department of Environmental Services
6 Hazen Drive
Concord, NH 03301-6509
(603) 271-2906

NEW JERSEY
Anthony Farro, Director
Division of Hazardous Site Mitigation
Department of Environmental Protection
401 East State Street, CN-028
Trenton, NJ 08625
(609) 984-2902

NEW MEXICO
Raymond Sisneros, Program Manager
Special Waste Bureau
Environmental Improvement Division
2nd Floor, Room N2250
Harold Reynolds Building
1190 St. Francis Drive
Santa Fe, NM 87503
(505) 827-2775

Peter Maggorie, Chief
Superfund
Hazardous Waste Department
Environmental Improvement Division
2nd Floor, Room N2154
Harold Reynolds Building
1190 St. Francis Drive
Santa Fe, NM 87503
(505) 827-2775

NEW YORK
Michael O'Toole, Director (Acting)
Hazardous Waste Remediation Division
Department of Environmental Conservation
50 Wolf Road
Albany, NY 12233
(518) 457-5861

NORTH CAROLINA
Lee Crosby, Supervisor
CERCLA Program Unit
Solid & Hazardous Waste Management Branch
Department of Human Resources
P.O. Box 2091
Raleigh, NC 27602
(919) 733-2178

NORTH DAKOTA
David Cameron, Environmental Scientist
Superfund Program
Waste Management & Special Studies Division
Department of Health
1200 Missouri Avenue, Room 302
P.O. Box 5520
Bismarck, ND 58502-5520
(701) 224-2366

OHIO
David Strayer, Manager
Corrective Actions Section
Solid & Hazardous Waste Division
Ohio EPA
1800 Watermark Drive
P.O. Box 1049
Columbus, OH 43266-1049
(614) 644-2055

OKLAHOMA
R. Fenton Rood, Director
Waste Management Service
Solid Waste Division
Department of Health
P.O. Box 53551
1000 N.E. 10th Street
Oklahoma City, OK 73152
(405) 271-7159

OREGON
Michael Downs, Administrator
Environmental Cleanup Division
Department of Environmental Quality
811 S.W. Sixth Avenue
Portland, OR 97204
(503) 229-5356

PENNSYLVANIA
Donald Becker, Chief
Remedial Response Section
Bureau of Solid Waste Management
Pennsylvania Department of Environmental Resources
P.O. Box 2063
Fulton Bank Building
Harrisburg, PA 17120
(717) 783-7816

PUERTO RICO
Juan Merced Mateo, Director
Emergency Response & Removal Area
Air Quality Program
Environmental Quality Board
Environmental Emergency Commission
P.O. Box 11488
Santurce, PR 00910
(809) 722-0077

RHODE ISLAND
Alicia Good
Superfund Program
Solid Waste Management Program
Department of Environmental Management
204 Cannon Building
75 Davis Street
Providence, RI 02908
(401) 277-2797

SOUTH CAROLINA
Lynn Martin, Director
Site Engineering & Screening Division
Bureau of Solid & Hazardous Waste Management
Department of Health & Environmental Control
2600 Bull Street
Columbia, SC 29201
(803) 734-5200

SOUTH DAKOTA
Joel C. Smith, Administrator
Office of Air Quality & Solid Waste
Department of Water & Natural Resources
Foss Building, Room 217
523 East Capitol
Pierre, SD 57501
(605) 733-3153

TENNESSEE
James Ault, Director
Division of Superfund
Division of Solid Waste Management
Customs House
701 Broadway, 4th Floor
Nashville, TN 37219-5403
(615) 741-6287

TEXAS
Jack Kramer, Chief
Contract Remedial Activities Section
Hazardous & Solid Waste Division
Texas Water Commission
P.O. Box 13087
Capitol Station
1700 N. Congress
Austin, TX 78711
(512) 463-7785

UTAH
Brent Bradford, Executive Director
Bureau of Solid & Hazardous Waste
288 North 1460 West
P.O. Box 16690
Salt Lake City, UT 84116-0690
(801) 538-6170

Kent Gray, Manager
CERCLA Section
Environmental Health Division
Bureau of Solid & Hazardous Waste
288 North 1460 West
P.O. Box 16690
Salt Lake City, UT 84116-0690
(801) 538-6170

VERMONT
Thomas Moye, Coordinator
Superfund Program
Waste Management Division
Department of Environmental Conservation
Agency of Natural Resources
West Building
103 South Main Street
Waterbury, VT 05676
(802) 244-8702

VIRGINIA
K.C. Das, Director
Administration & Special Programs
Department of Waste Management
James Monroe Building
101 North 14th Street, 11th Floor
Richmond, VA 23219
(804) 225-2667

WASHINGTON
Jerry Jewett
Hazardous Waste Cleanup Program
Office of Land Programs
Department of Ecology
Mail Stop PV-11
Olympia, WA 98504-8711
(206) 438-3039

WEST VIRGINIA
Pamela Hayes, Unit Leader
Site Investigation & Response Section
Waste Management Division
West Virginia Department of Natural Resources
160 Greenbrier Street
Charleston, WV 25311
(304) 348-2745

WISCONSIN
Mark Giesfeldt
Environmental Response Unit
Bureau of Solid Hazardous Waste Management
Department of Natural Resources
101 South Webster Street
Madison, WI 53707
(608) 267-7562

WYOMING
David Finely, Program Manager
Solid Waste Management Program
Department of Environmental Quality
Herschler Building
122 West 25th Street
Cheyenne, WY 82002
(307) 777-7752

WASTE EXCHANGES AND INFORMATION SERVICES

It is important to note that the life span of many hazardous and nonhazardous waste information exchanges is very short, and some listed exchanges may no longer be in existence by the time of publication. Updated information will be provided, where appropriate, in supplements to this book.

CALIFORNIA

California Waste Exchange (CWE)
Department of Health Services
Toxic Substances Control Division
Alternative Technology Section
714/744 P Street
P.O. Box 942732
Sacramento, CA 94234-7320
(916) 324-1366 (Robert McCormick)

CWE is strictly an information clearinghouse that produces a bimonthly newsletter/catalog of information for all types of waste exchange.

California for Research and Design (CFRI)
2928 Poplar Street
Oakland, CA 94608
(510) 893-8257

CFRI is primarily a waste warehouse that acquires and stores waste until the waste is purchased, and does not participate as an information exchange service for waste trade.

San Francisco Waste Exchange
2524 Benvenue #435
Berkeley, CA 94704
(510) 548-6659 (Portia Sinnot)

FLORIDA

Southern Waste Information Exchange (SWIX)
Florida State University
P.O. Box 960
Tallahassee, FL 32302
(904) 644-5516 (Eugene B. Jones)
(800) 441-7949

SWIX is strictly an information clearinghouse that produces a bimonthly newsletter/catalog of information for all types of waste exchange.

IDAHO

Idaho Waste Exchange
Idaho Department of Environmental Quality
Hazardous Materials Bureau
450 West State Street
Boise, ID 83720
(208) 334-0502 (Vicki Jewell)
(208) 334-5879

The Idaho Waste Exchange is a state regulatory agency for waste exchange and disposal. Although it is not a true waste exchange (it doesn't produce a catalog or facilitate another means of exchange), it will direct inquiries to the proper agencies.

ILLINOIS

Industrial Material Exchange Service (IMES)
P.O. Box 19276
2200 Churchill Road, #24
Springfield, IL 62794-0276
(217) 782-0450 (Diane Shockey)
Fax: (217) 524-4193

INDIANA

Indiana Waste Exchange
Purdue University
School of Civil Engineering
West Lafayette, IN 47907
(317) 494-5041 (Dr. Lynn Corsonam)
(317) 494-5063

The Indiana Waste Exchange is strictly an information clearinghouse, and does not limit its use to hazardous waste. Eighty-five percent of its subscribers are within Indiana, and are either in business or industry. The exchange also produces a bimonthly catalog.

MICHIGAN

Great Lakes Waste Exchange
400 Ann Street, N.W.
Suite 201-A
Grand Rapids, MI 49504-2054
(616) 363-3262 (Jeffrey Dauphin)

The Great Lakes Waste Exchange is strictly an information exchange that produces a bimonthly catalog for hazardous and nonhazardous waste exchange.

MONTANA

Montana Industrial Waste Exchange
Montana Chamber of Commerce
P.O. Box 1730
Helena, MT 59624
(406) 442-2405 (Sharon Miller)

The Montana Industrial Waste Exchange is strictly an information exchange that produces a bimonthly catalog.

NEW JERSEY

Industrial Waste Information Exchange
New Jersey Chamber of Commerce
5 Commerce Street
Newark, NJ 07102
(201) 623-7070 (William E. Payne)

Industrial Waste Technologies
8 Lister Avenue
Newark, NJ 07105
(201) 344-5020 (Carol Cooper)

Industrial Waste Technologies is a disposal consultant center, as opposed to an information exchange. It does not facilitate exchanges between parties.

NEW YORK

Northeast Industrial Waste Exchange (NIWE)
90 Presidential Plaza
Suite 122
Syracuse, NY 13210
(315) 422-6572 (Carrie Maughs-Pugh)
Fax: (315) 442-9051

NIWE is strictly an information clearinghouse that produces a catalog four times per year.

NORTH CAROLINA

Southeast Waste Exchange (SEWE)
Urban Institute
Department of Civil Engineering
University of North Carolina
Charlotte, NC 28223
(704) 547-4289 (Maxie May)

SEWE is an information clearinghouse that deals in all kinds of waste. Additionally, it treats each exchange on a case-by-case basis, is engaged in furthering education to industry on waste exchanges, sponsors workshops, and will research for an inquiry if their catalog is not sufficient for the client's needs. SEWE has been in existence for 14 years.

OHIO

Wastelink Division of TENCON, Inc.
140 Wooster Pike
Milford, OH 45150
(513) 248-0012 (Mary E. Malotke)
Fax: (513) 248-1094

Wastelink is strictly an information clearinghouse that produces a catalog bimonthly.

TEXAS

Resource Exchange Network for Eliminating Waste (RENEW)
Texas Water Commission
P.O. Box 13087
Austin, TX 78711-3087
(512) 463-7773 (Hope Castillo)

RENEW is an information clearinghouse that will list confidentially, and services mostly Texas clients. It produces a bimonthly catalog, but sends out an information update between catalogs. RENEW primarily deals in either hazardous or solid industrial waste.

WASHINGTON

Industrial Material Exchange (IMEX)
Seattle—King County Environmental Health
172 20th Avenue
Seattle, WA 98122
(206) 296-4633 (Bill Laurence)
Fax: (206) 296-0188

IMEX is strictly an information clearinghouse that deals in chemical, solid waste, and metals, and produces a bimonthly catalog.

Pacific Materials Exchange (PME)
S. 3707 Godfrey Boulevard
Spokane, WA 99204
(509) 623-4244 (Annett Dubois)

PME is strictly an information exchange that deals in all solid and hazardous waste, and produces a bimonthly catalog. Currently, PME is assisting development on a national on-line computer network through which all the exchange catalogs will be accessible.

Canadian Waste Exchanges

Alberta Waste Materials Exchange
Alberta Research Council
P.O. Box 8330
Postal Station F
Edmonton, AB, Canada T6H 5X2
(403) 450-5408 (William C. Kay)

British Columbia Waste Exchange
2150 Maple Street
Vancouver, BC, Canada V6J 3T3
(604) 731-7222 (Lynn Deegan)

Manitoba Waste Exchange
c/o Biomass Energy Institute, Inc.
1329 Niakwa Road
Winnipeg, MB, Canada R2J 3T4
(204) 257-3891 (James Ferguson)

Canadian Waste Materials Exchange (CWME)
ORTECH International
Sheridan Park Research Community
2395 Speakman Drive
Mississauga, ON, Canada L5K 1B3
(416) 822-4111 ext. 265 (Bob Laughlin)

Ontario Waste Exchange
ORTECH International
Sheridan Park Research Community
2395 Speakman Drive
Mississauga, ON, Canada L5K 1B3
(416) 822-4111 ext. 512 (Linda Varangu)

Peel Regional Waste Exchange
Regional Municipality of Peel
10 Peel Center Drive
Brampton, ON, Canada L6T 4B9
(419) 791-9400 (Glen Milbury)

Canadian Chemical Exchange
P.O. Box 1135
Ste-Adele, PQ, Canada J0R 1L0
(514) 229-6511 (Phillipe LaRoche)

   This is a for-profit waste information exchange.

Other Waste Exchanges

Union Chemical Laboratories
Industrial Technology Research Institute
321, Kuang Fu Road, Sec. 2
Hsinchu, Taiwan (Republic of China) 30042
(Ai-Lun Huang, Assoc. Researcher)

EPA Waste Minimization Information Sources

U.S. Environmental Protection Agency, *Report to Congress: Waste Minimization,*
Vol. I and II, EPA/530-SW-86-033 and -034. (Washington, D.C.: U.S. EPA,
1986).

U.S. Environmental Protection Agency, *Waste Minimization—Issues and Op-*
tions, Vols. I and III, EPA/530-SW-86-041 and -043. (Washington, D.C.: U.S.
EPA, 1986).

TABLE OF CASES

INDEX

416 **INDEX**